D1520651

The Withered Vine

THE WITHERED VINE

Logistics and the Communist Insurgency in Greece, 1945–1949

CHARLES R. SHRADER

PRAEGER

Westport, Connecticut
London

Library of Congress Cataloging-in-Publication Data

Shrader, Charles R.
    The withered vine : logistics and the communist insurgency in
Greece, 1945–1949 / Charles R. Shrader.
        p. cm.
    Includes bibliographical references and index.
    ISBN 0–275–96544–9 (alk. paper)
    1. Greece—History—Civil War, 1944–1949. 2. World War,
1939–1945—Underground movements—Logistics—Greece. 3. Communists—
Greece—Influence. I. Title.
    DF849.52.S54   1999
    949.507'4—dc21   99–25859

British Library Cataloguing in Publication Data is available.

Library of Congress Catalog Card Number: 99–25859
ISBN: 0–275–96544–9

First published in 1999

Praeger Publishers, 88 Post Road West, Westport, CT 06881
An imprint of Greenwood Publishing Group, Inc.
www.praeger.com

Printed in the United States of America

The paper used in this book complies with the
Permanent Paper Standard issued by the National
Information Standards Organization (Z39.48–1984).

10 9 8 7 6 5 4 3 2 1

Copyright Acknowledgment

The author and publisher gratefully acknowledge permission for the use of the following material:

From *INTERNATIONAL INTERVENTION IN THE GREEK CIVIL WAR*, by Amikam Nachmani. Copyright © 1990 by Amikam Nachmani. Reproduced with permission of GREENWOOD PUB-LISHING GROUP, INC., Westport, CT.

In Memory of Sterling S. Hart, 1943–1995

Contents

Illustrations

FIGURES

A photo essay follows page 105.

Note on Translation, Acronyms, and Measurements

An extended discussion of any military organization necessarily involves frequent repetition of terms, abbreviations, and acronyms, particularly those relating to unit types and designations. The problem is compounded when the discussion involves more than one military establishment, each of which is organized on a different pattern. Additional complexity is added by the necessity to translate from one language to another. The welter of lengthy designations and repeated acronyms can be confusing as well as distracting. The following procedures have been adopted in this volume to simplify the process of identifying political entities and military organizations.

Upon first mention in each chapter, Greek political and military organizations, both government and rebel, are identified in full by an English translation of the original Greek designation followed immediately in parentheses by the transliterated Greek designation and corresponding abbreviation. For subsequent references within the same chapter, either the full designation or the acronym may be used, usually the latter. Divisions of both the Greek national army (GNA) and the Greek Democratic Army (GDA) were normally identified by Roman numerals (e.g., I Division). However, in this study Arabic numerals are used (e.g., GNA 1st Division; GDA 7th Division). It should be noted that the corps of the GNA were identified by letters (e.g., "C" Corps) and that the units of the GDA were often identified by the name of their leader or the region in which they operated (e.g., Velissaris Brigade [GDA 18th Infantry Brigade]). The most frequently used acronyms and their English equivalents include:

EAM	National Liberation Movement
ELAS	National People's Liberation Army
GDA	Greek Democratic Army
GNA	Greek National Army

GNF	Greek national forces
JUSMAPG	Joint U.S. Military Advisory and Planning Group–Greece
KKE	Greek Communist Party
NOF	Slavo-Macedonian Liberation Front

The transliteration of Greek and Cyrillic characters is based on standard practice. Greek and other regional place names and the names of individuals have been rendered in the simplest or most familiar manner, and in most cases the orthography follows that most commonly seen in contemporary English-language maps and documents. For example, the Greek city of Thessaloniki is given as Salonika, and the name of the General Secretary of the KKE is given as Nikos Zachariades.

It is assumed that most readers are familiar with the metric measurements for weight, distance, and area but that they may be less certain about other metric measurements. Thus, most measurements are given in the metric system except for temperature, where the Fahrenheit system is used, and volume, in which case liters and cubic meters have been converted into gallons or barrels. Unless otherwise noted, the term "ton" refers to the metric ton of 2,204.62 pounds. It may be useful to recall the following equivalencies:

1 meter (m.) = 39.37 inches	1 metric ton (ton or tonne) = 2,204.62 lbs.
1 kilometer (km) = .6214 miles	1 short ton (ST) = 2,000 lbs. (907.2 kg)
1 square meter (m²) = 1.196 square yards	1 liter (l.) = .2641 U.S. gallons
1 hectare = 2.471 acres	1 cubic meter (m³) = 201.987 U.S. gallons
1 kilogram (kg) = 2.2046 lbs.	1 barrel (bbl.) = 42 U.S. gallons

Other terms, abbreviations, and acronyms are included in the glossary. Conventional military map symbols appear in Appendix C.

Preface

After fifty years, the causes, course, and outcome of the Greek civil war of 1945–1949 remain clouded by ideological and nationalist cant, Cold War mythology, and the lack of definitive information on even the most basic details. The assumption remains strongly entrenched that the attempt of the Greek Communist Party (KKE) and its allies to overthrow a weak and unstable constitutional monarchy—still reeling from the awful effects of thirty years of war, foreign occupation, internal political strife, economic devastation, and social upheaval—was directed and supported from Moscow as part of a coordinated Soviet plot to topple democratic nations unhinged by the Second World War. Many of the pertinent questions remain unanswered—or even unasked—and no aspect of the Greek civil war is less well understood than the logistical arrangements of the Communist rebels. How were the rebel forces organized? What were their logistical requirements? What were the sources of logistical support for the rebel forces? What types and quantities of matériel and other support were provided? How was that support organized and delivered? What impact did the logistical situation of the rebels have on the ultimate outcome of the rebellion?

Those questions are addressed in this study through an examination of the logistical requirements, organization, methods, and operations of the Greek Democratic Army (GDA) during the so-called "Third Round" of the Greek civil war, from February 1945 to August 1949. Although due attention is given to such logistical functions as the determination of supply requirements, the acquisition, storage, issue, maintenance, and disposal of equipment and supplies, and the provision of medical services, this study focuses primarily on the support provided to the Greek Communist guerrillas by the Soviet Union and its satellites, in particular Albania, Bulgaria, and Yugoslavia. The focus is essentially organizational and to a certain extent political and diplomatic. Thus, internal bureaucratic issues, Greek and international political developments, and the movement of men and matériel across the borders of Greece receive detailed consideration, while some aspects of operational logistics, such as the details of logistical support for specific guerrilla operations, receive less attention.

This study is based primarily on such declassified, translated records of the Greek national government, the Communist Party of Greece, the Greek Democratic Army, and other participants as have been reported or reproduced by contemporary Western military and civilian observers and intelligence agencies, particularly the U.S. military attachés in Athens; the Joint U.S. Military Advisory and Planning Group–Greece; and the office of the Deputy Chief of Staff, G-2, Intelligence, Headquarters, Department of the Army. Secondary works in the common Western languages (other than Greek) by Greek and other Western scholars have also been used. For the most part, access to such GDA and other Communist documentation as may have survived remains difficult, if not impossible, and access to the Greek national archives is similarly restricted, in large part due to their lack of organization. The somewhat one-sided nature of the sources thus requires that the results must be used with some caution.

The story of the logistical support of the Communist insurgents in Greece is interesting and significant in the broader context of post–World War II nationalist insurgencies. In the first place, the Communist insurgents in Greece shared with their counterparts in Indochina and Algeria a dependence on logistical support supplied by friendly neighboring states. Although able to generate significant resources internally, the Viet Minh in Indochina depended heavily on the arms, other supplies, and havens provided by the People's Republic of China. The Algerian rebels, unable to gather any substantial matériel resources within Algeria, were almost entirely dependent on the generosity of their Arab backers and on purchases abroad, funneled through two friendly neighboring states, Morocco and Tunisia. The Greek rebels, unable to find or produce significant military resources internally, had to rely almost entirely on the logistical support by Albania, Bulgaria, and Yugoslavia.

The Greek Communist revolt also provides an interesting case study of the impact of ideology on such military matters as strategy, tactics, organization, and logistics. In this respect, too, the Greek insurgency shares certain key decision points with the post–World War II nationalist revolts in Indochina and Algeria. Chief among those critical decisions is the selection of the optimum point at which a guerrilla war should transition to a conventional war in order to bring about the decisive defeat of the entrenched opponent. In all three cases, the decision to switch to conventional organization and tactics was ill timed or otherwise counterproductive. The Viet Minh were able to avoid serious consequences and go on to final victory only by quickly reverting to guerrilla warfare until they were in a better position to oppose the French by conventional means. In Algeria, the nationalist rebels created conventional forces but kept the bulk of them outside the borders of Algeria, except for the "Battle of the Barrages," in which they were decisively defeated. In any event, the conventional forces of the Algerian rebels played no important role in their ultimate success, which was achieved by political means despite significant military setbacks. Only in the case of the Greek revolt did a faulty assessment of when to proceed to conventional operations have a decisive, negative result, and what translated the fateful decision into disaster was not so much the resulting organization, strategy, or tactics as the insupportable logistical burdens that the decision imposed.

The study of the Greek civil war of 1945–1949 thus provides important insights to the problem of externally supported nationalist insurgencies so prevalent since the end of World War II. The following examination of the Greek case seeks to answer the key questions regarding only one particular aspect of the problem—logistics. Although no brief study focused on a single factor can bring full enlightenment on such a complex subject as the causes, course, and outcomes of insurgency, I hope that this study may contribute in some small way to a better understanding of the basic details and to the dissipation of cant, myth, and ignorance.

The late Sterling Hart played a prominent role in the initiation of this study and helped in many ways to improve it. Its faults are mine, but Sterling made them fewer. I am grateful also to the staff of the U.S. Army Military History Institute at Carlisle Barracks, Pennsylvania, particularly Mr. John Slonaker, Mr. Dennis Vetock, and Mrs. Louise Arnold-Friend, who were most helpful in pointing out and locating interesting and pertinent materials. My wife Carole was, as always, patient and supportive. She merits a medal, or at least a certificate of endurance.

Chronology: Greece, 1939–1949

1939

April 7	Italians occupy Albania

1940

October 28	Italians invade Greece (OXI Day)

1941

January 29	Death of Gen. Ioannis Metaxas
April 6	Germans invade Greece
9	Fall of Salonika
10	Fall of Thracian ports
21	British decide to evacuate Greece
23	Armistice between the Greek forces and the Germans signed by Gen. George Tsolakoglou
27	Athens falls to the Germans
30	Greek puppet government under Gen. Tsolakoglou established
May 20	German airborne invasion of Crete
June 1	Allied evacuation of Crete
September 27	EAM founded

1942

April 10	Formation of ELAS
October	Col. Eddie Myers and British SOE team arrives in Greece; British Military Mission established
November 25	Destruction of the Gorgopotamos Bridge
December	Constantine Logothetopoulos replaces Gen. George Tsolakoglou as prime minister of Greek collaborationist government

1943

April	Ioannis Rallis replaces Constantine Logothetopoulos as prime minister of Greek collaborationist government
June 24	Destruction of Asopos Bridge
June–July	Operation ANIMALS; support of Allied invasion of Sicily
July 26	Creation of Joint GHQ of EAM/ELAS, EDES, and EKKA
August 9	Cairo conference of guerrilla leaders; National Bands Agreement
September 8	Italy surrenders to Allies; Italian occupation army in Greece begins to surrender to Germans and to Greek resistance groups
October 12	Beginning of "First Round"

1944

February 12	ELAS, EDES, and BMM meet at Plaka Bridge in Epirus to resolve differences
29	Plaka Bridge agreement among guerrilla groups signed; end of "First Round"
March 10	PEEA created
31	Revolt of Greek forces in the Middle East begins
April 23	Revolt of Greek forces in the Middle East suppressed
May 17–20	Lebanon Conference; charter signed creating Government of National Unity under George Papandreou
July	Allied Military Mission established
28	Arrival of Soviet mission to guerrillas under Colonel Popov
August	EAM agrees to join government-in-exile Operation NOAH'S ARK to support liberation of Greece
September	Greek government-in-exile moved to Italy
26	Caserta Agreement signed

October	ELAS drives Gotchev's SNOF bands into Yugoslavia
9	Churchill-Stalin "percentage deal"
12	Germans evacuate Athens
17	British and Greek government return to Greece
November 27–28	"Second Round" begins
December	ELAS defeats EDES in Epirus
2	EAM ministers resign
3	Bloody EAM-KKE demonstration in Athens
31	Archbishop Damaskinos named regent

1945

January 11	Plastiras becomes prime minister
February 4–11	Yalta Conference
12	Varkiza Agreement signed; end of "Second Round" First phase of "Third Round" begins
May	Nikos Zachariades returns to Greece and reassumes leadership of KKE
June 16	Aris Velouchiotis murdered
25–27	Twelfth Plenum of KKE Central Committee
October	Seventh KKE Party Congress
December 15	Petrich Meeting of KKE/GDA with Yugoslavians and Bulgarians

1946

February 12	Second Plenum of Central Committee of the KKE; second phase of the "Third Round" begins
March 30–31	Communist guerrilla attack on Litochoron
31	Greek general election
July	Markos Vafiades goes to mountains to organize Communist military forces
September 1	Plebiscite approves return of King George II to Greece
24	Rebels attack Naoussa, first significant attack on a larger town
27	King George II returns to Greece
October 28	Formation of GDA announced

November 30	Greek government brings situation before the UN Security Council
December 3	Greek prime minister Tsaldaris petitions UN Secretary-General Trygve Lie to consider Greek situation
19	UN Security Council creates UN Commission of Investigation Concerning Greek Frontier Incidents

1947

January 2	Fall of Tsaldaris government; Maximos forms government
February	KKE decides to form a conventional military force; third phase of the "Third Round" begins
24	British government notifies U.S. government that its aid to Greece would be discontinued on 31 March 1941
March 3	Greek government formally requests U.S. economic, technical, administrative aid
12	President Truman's speech initiates "Truman Doctrine"
April 1	Death of King George II
5–30	Operation EAGLE to clear Agrafos and Tzoumerka
9	Operation TERMINUS to clear Roumeli south to north
14	USAAGG established
20	Suspicious death of Siantos, wartime leader of KKE
22	Accession of King Paul
May 1–31	Operation HAWK to clear Khasia and Antikhasia
7–15	Operation STORK to clear Ossa and Pelion
22	PL 75 signed by President Truman
24	First USAAGG personnel arrive in Greece
June 2–30	Operation SWAN to clear Mount Olympus area
27	UN Commission of Investigation Concerning Greek Frontier Incidents renders its report to the UN Security Council
June–July	Operation GROW to clear Smolikas and Grammos (26 June–22 July)
August	Greek government decides to use army to suppress "bandits" Bled Conference of KKE/GDA with Albanians, Yugoslavians, and Bulgarians

1949

January 11–15	GDA again attacks Naousa
21	Gen. Alexander Papagos reassumes command of GNA
27	Provisional Democratic Government issues peace proposal
30–31	Fifth Plenum of KKE Central Committee; Markos Vafiades denounced and ousted; begin final phase of the "Third Round"
19 Jan.–9 Feb.	Battle of Karpenision
February 4	Ouster of Markos Vafiades announced
12–15	Battle of Florina
April 5	Reshuffling of Provisional Democratic Government announced
31	Operation ends
April–June	GDA mop-up in the Peloponnesus, Samos, and Kefallinia
25 April–31 July	Operation ROCKET in south-central Greece
May 5–12	Operation ARIS to clear Angistron-Kraskhori region
July 4–8	Operation AJAX to clear Kaimaktsalan region
10	Tito closes Yugoslavian border with Greece
August 5–10	First phase of Operation TORCH in the Grammos
10–16	Second phase of Operation TORCH in the Vitsi
19–23	Final GDA offensive in the Beles Mountains
24–31	Final phase of Operation TORCH in the Grammos
26	Enver Hoxha announces disarmament and detention of Greek rebels entering Albania
October 1	USSR rejoins UNSCOB and initiates peace proposals
9	Sixth Plenum of the KKE Central Committee
16	Radio Free Greece announces the end of the Communist insurrection in Greece; end of the "Third Round"

1

Setting the Stage

Greece's harsh physical environment and turbulent political history were two of the most important factors that led to the Greek civil war of 1945–1949 and shaped its nature and course. Rugged terrain, limited natural resources, and difficult communications fostered the isolation and self-reliance reflected in the long tradition of armed resistance to central authority, resistance that molded the Greek character. The same physical conditions profoundly influenced the strategy, tactics, and logistical organization of the Communist rebels and dictated the nature of their military operations between 1945 and 1949. Political, economic, and social instability, another characteristic of modern Greek society, also contributed to the rise of the Communist insurgency and determined the paths the rebellion would take. More than a century of political strife, economic failure, and social disruption, not only in Greece but throughout the Balkans, set the stage for an all-out civil war. The curtain rose with the Axis invasion and occupation of Greece in 1940–1941, which prompted armed resistance to the occupying powers. The subsequent internal struggle for dominance among the various resistance groups led directly to the civil war of 1945–1949.

THE PHYSICAL ENVIRONMENT

Occupying the southeastern extremity of the Balkan peninsula, bounded on the west by the Ionian Sea, on the south by the Mediterranean Sea, and on the east by the Aegean Sea, Greece lies at the strategically important crossing of communication routes connecting Europe, the Middle East, and Africa.[1] In 1945, the Greek national domain extended from 34° to 41° 45' north latitude and from 19° to 28° east longitude and included mainland Greece, the Peloponnesian peninsula, and a large number of islands and associated territorial waters. The greatest north-south distance of the mainland area was about 630 miles, while the greatest east-west distance was approximately 490 miles. The total area of

Greece in 1945 was approximately 50,147 square miles, of which the mainland area and Peloponnesus constituted approximately 41,328 square miles, and the islands—including the largest, Crete—comprised about 8,819 square miles (see Map 1).

The varied topography of Greece is characterized by high, rugged mountain ranges, isolated valleys and plains, a limited number of usable waterways, an extensive coastline with numerous inlets and deep gulfs backed by narrow coastal plains, and some 1,425 islands, most of which are uninhabitable. No place in Greece is more than fifty miles from the sea. In 1945, the coastal areas were well populated, particularly the two major cities of Athens and Salonika (Thessaloniki), but the mountainous interior and most of the islands were sparsely settled and had many wild, uninhabited areas. The Greek-speaking population, augmented by refugees from the Greek areas of Asia Minor in the 1920s, was intermixed in the border areas with Slavic, Turkish, and other minorities.

Traditionally poor and underdeveloped, Greece was devastated by the Second World War, and postwar agricultural and industrial production was substantially below even the modest prewar levels. Agriculture, primarily the production of grain, tobacco, and olives, was limited to the narrow coastal plains and mountain valleys. Natural resources were similarly scarce and largely undeveloped. The level of industrialization was low, and internal commerce was limited by the poor land transportation network. The mountainous terrain of the interior inhibited the development of roads and railroad lines and so confined the bulk of internal commerce to coastal shipping.

In 1945, Greece shared land borders with Turkey, Bulgaria, Yugoslavia, and Albania as well as a water border with Italy. Greece's border with European Turkey was about 150 kilometers long and was marked for most of its length by the Evros (Maritza) River. The borders with Bulgaria, Yugoslavia, and Albania extended for some 1,030 kilometers (about 640 miles) and were of signal importance during the civil war of 1945–1949. Greece's boundaries with her northern neighbors, established as a result of treaties following the Balkan Wars of 1912–1913, World War I, and the Greco-Turkish War of 1921–1922, followed neither geographical nor ethnic boundaries and thus had long been disputed.[2] In particular, Greece and Albania had contested mutual claims in the region of northern Epirus (northwestern Greece and southern Albania). Both Yugoslavia and Bulgaria had laid claim to portions of Macedonia, and although a large part of the historical region of Macedonia is today an independent state, many of the issues that animated controversy in 1945 remain unresolved.

The northern border mountains are breached in several places by strategically important passes. Access to northern Greece from Albania is facilitated by the mountainous Mourgana salient and the plain southwest of the Prespa Lakes, through which passes the natural route linking Macedonia and Epirus. Two easy invasion routes extend into Greece from Yugoslavia: the Monastir Gap on the border north of Florina and the Vardar Gap deeper into Yugoslavia, through which flows the Vardar River to Salonika. The Rhodope mountains in Bulgaria dominate northeastern Greece, and the valleys of the Strymon (Struma), Nestos (Mesta), and Evros (Maritza) Rivers provide routes into northern Greece from Bulgaria.

The length, rugged terrain, and inaccessibility of Greece's borders with her northern neighbors posed a distinct disadvantage to government forces under all conditions. The very length of the border—some seven hundred miles—made it impossible to garrison or patrol regularly the traditional invasion routes into Greece from her northern neighbors.[3] With only eight divisions available during the period 1945–1949, had the Greek Army chosen to deploy its divisions along the frontiers, each division would have had a zone of operations nearly a hundred miles wide.[4] Moreover, the rugged terrain and lack of transportation facilities in the border areas made it nearly impossible for motorized forces to operate, and very difficult even for trained mountain troops. From a strategic standpoint, the northeastern frontier of Greece with Bulgaria was also a problem, due to its lack of depth. At one point in eastern Macedonia, the border was less than thirty kilometers from the Aegean Sea at Porto Lago. The one road and one rail line providing lateral communications through Grecian Thrace was thus extremely vulnerable.

Most of the operations of the Greek civil war of 1945–1949 took place in the remote and desolate mountains of Epirus, Thessaly, and the northern border areas. The rugged mountains of mainland Greece constitute a significant barrier to movement in any direction, and they channelize movement through the few usable passes connecting the mountain valleys. The lack of roads, particularly in the Pindus Mountains, restrict almost all movement to foot or mule. As a consequence, military units cannot easily operate in those areas, and the inhabitants of the region traditionally have been able to resist control by the central government. In the Greek civil war, the primitive state of the lines of communications in the area—the lack of roads, bridges, and all-weather mountain passes—further complicated logistical movements for both sides. The long and vulnerable lines of communications from the remote and nearly inaccessible northern borders and the guerrilla base areas in the mountains made government operations difficult but also hampered the supply of rebel forces elsewhere in Greece, the more so because the Greek national forces controlled the sea, the traditional means of communicating along the coasts of mainland Greece and among the islands of the Mediterranean and Aegean.

Two areas in the mountainous northern border region were of special importance during the civil war of 1945–1949: the Grammos and Vitsi base areas.[5] Fortified as rebel strongholds, they were the scenes of the heaviest fighting and the most decisive battles of the civil war. The Grammos base area took the shape of a trapezoid, with three sides of a hundred kilometers each and a fourth side of only fifty kilometers, along the Albania border. Bounded on the south by the Pindus range and on the north by the mountains of Albania, the Grammos was completely isolated from the rest of Greece and so formed an ideal location for a guerrilla base. Consisting of a series of steep, rocky ridges ranging in

Map 1
Greece, 1946

Legend:
- ★ Capital
- International boundary
- Selected road
- ┼┼┼ Railroad
- *VITSI* Region

Scale:
0 — 25 — 50 Kilometers
0 — 25 — 50 Miles

ALBANIA

YUGOSLAVIA

BULGARIA

TURKEY

Tirana

Skopje

Sofia

Veles

Argyrocastro

Lake Ohrid

Lake Prespa

Lake Little Prespa

Koritsa (Korcë)

Vrondero

Mikrolimni

Monastir Gap

Florina

Bitolj (Monastir)

Skra

Mt. Kaimaktsalan

KAIMAKTSALAN

VERNON

Mt. Vitsi

VITSI

Nestorion

Slimnitza

Mt. Grammos

GRAMMOS

MOURGANA

Metsovon Pass

Grevena

Kozani

Siatista

Servia

Metsovon

Jannina

EPIRUS

KHASIA

PIERIA-OLYMPUS MTNS.

Mt. Olympus

Katerine

Litochoron

Elasson

Kalabaka

Trikala

Larissa

Kastoria

Edessa

Amyntaion

Naousa

Veria

Plati

BELES MTNS.

BELES

Strumica

Petrich

Strum

Lake Doiran

Doira

Kilkis

Goumenitsa

Salonika

Gulf of Thermai

Chalcidice Peninsula

Mt. Athos Peninsula

Sithonia Peninsula

Kassandra Peninsula

Gulf of Kassand

Singitic Gulf

Strymonic Gulf

Ierissos

Stavros

Siderocastro

Lefkona

Nevrok

BOZ DAG

Drama

Kavala

Thásos

Samothrace

Imbros

Lemnos

Tenedos

Dardanelles Strait

Xanthe

Komotini

Alexandroupolis

EVROS

Evros

Nestos

Mesta

Struma

Vardar

Cma

Aliakmon

Mt. Ossa

Mt. Pindus

VERMION

VERMIOM

OMTNS.

Vardar Gap

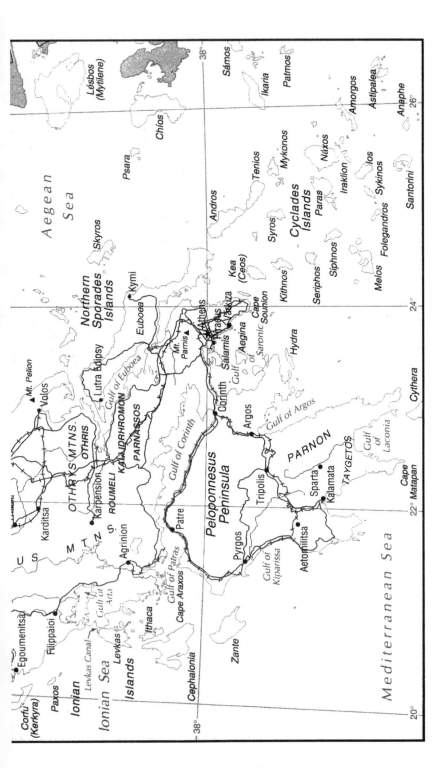

height from 1,500 to 2,500 meters and covered with dense forests, the area was wild, with many narrow valleys and small torrential streams. There were no roads, even dirt ones, on Greek territory in the Grammos, but an old road ran on the Albanian side along the entire length of the border. This road, repaired and widened by the Italians during World War II, was one of the main routes by which the Greek guerrillas received supplies from Albania. The village of Aetomilitsa, at an altitude of 1,400 meters, was for a time the seat of the Provisional Government and the rebel Supreme Military Council. Northeast of the Grammos, the Vitsi base area was a mountainous expanse of some 375 square miles bounded on the north by Yugoslavia and on the west by Albania. The Vitsi base area was composed of two mountain massifs in the form of an inverted V, with the Livadhopotamos River flowing southward between them to join the Aliakmon River. A secondary road paralleled the Aliakmon River from Kastoria north to join the main road running west from Florina into Albania. The Florina road was the main guerrilla supply route from Albania into the Vitsi. Safe from government attack from either the north or west, the Vitsi area was somewhat more approachable from the south and east, although the terrain there was difficult.

The rugged topography and lengthy border partially neutralized the advantages in armament and mobility of the government forces and thus favored the Communist guerrillas. However, extremely cold temperatures and heavy snowfall over the mountains of central Greece and on its northern borders limited military operations severely and posed significant dangers to Communist guerrilla and government soldier alike. The winters in the mountains are cold and wet, there is little shelter available, and the concealment normally provided by the deciduous forests is lacking. The perpetual snow cover and necessity for campfires made the guerrilla bands easier to locate and track. In winter, the guerrillas were also obliged to increase the amount of food and other supplies carried over the border from Albania, Yugoslavia, and Bulgaria, but conditions in the passes seriously limited transport. The more heavily motorized government forces were also subject to the adverse affects of weather on personnel and routes of communications. Frostbite and other cold injuries were common even among the relatively well-equipped Greek National Army forces. However, the government forces controlled the more populated areas and thus were able to find adequate troop billets. Control of the major roads and railroads and the possession of an aerial resupply capability also put the government in a much better position to resupply its forces, even during the winter. However, the effects of winter snows and ice in the passes and mountain roads, torrential rains and mud in springtime, and dusty conditions during the summer were distinct disadvantages for the more highly mechanized government forces. Ice made motorized transport particularly dangerous in northern Greece throughout January and February, and frost on the north-facing slopes of the mountains made even the mule trails dangerous from late November through the end of February.

Sunny skies and excellent visibility prevail throughout Greece during most of the year, facilitating aerial observation and tactical air operations. Visibility under five miles is usually considered "poor," and until the 1950s the lack of industry, automobiles, and home heating with carbon fuels made for remarkable clarity of the atmosphere even in urban areas, with the exception of the Athens-Piraeus zone. Heavy fog is almost unknown, but morning ground mists are common in the mountains and on the islands, and in summer dust and heat combine to create haze that limits visibility somewhat, particularly in northern Greece. The entire country is also quite windy throughout most of the year. The prevailing winds are continental and thus increase visibility, by dissipating clouds.

The devastation of Greek agriculture and industry during the years of war and occupation from 1941 to 1944 adversely affected both sides in the civil war of 1945–1949. The government was unable to generate adequate revenue either to provide the relief and reconstruction activities needed to dampen civil unrest or to increase the size and improve the capabilities of the military forces needed to put down the Communist insurgency. On the other hand, the chronic poverty and inaccessibility in the remote mountain areas, coupled with the devastation and economic disruption of the World War II years, made the local provision of food, clothing, and fuel for the guerrillas all but impossible. Only minimal levels of food and other supplies were available for either donation or confiscation, and the low level of Greek industrial production in the postwar years provided little opportunity for sub-rosa purchases on the open market.

The Greek insurgents were largely unaffected by the parlous state of Greek transportation facilities in the post–World War II period. Except for a limited amount of motor transport in areas they controlled, some furtive coastal shipping, and infrequent use of remote and unimproved airfields in guerrilla territory, the guerrillas relied on animal transport. Perhaps their most pressing transport problem was how to obtain and sustain the mules necessary to move supplies in the mountain fastness. The lack of all-weather roads and trails in the mountain stronghold areas did indeed limit guerrilla movements, but the effects on the motorized Greek National Army were more apparent. Control of the limited number of mountain passes and all-weather roads in the mountains was thus very important to both sides. The towns guarding the mountain passes—for example, Metsovon, on the road from Kalabaka to Ioannina, and Karpenision, on the road from Lamia to Agrinion—were thus of special strategic importance.[6] The transportation infrastructure and government efforts to reconstruct it were frequent targets of insurgent attacks, and the proximity of key terrain and transportation features, such as passes, roads, railroads, bridges, and viaducts to the rugged mountain guerrilla strongholds, made it possible for the guerrillas to come down from their mountain strongholds, stage hit-and-run attacks, and return to their base in a single night.[7]

Although at first glance Greece appears favorable as a theater of guerrilla operations, the rugged terrain, often harsh climate, difficulties of land communication, chronic poverty of the interior districts, and other factors made large-scale military operations throughout most of Greece as difficult for lightly armed insurgents as for more heavily equipped government forces. Similarly, the poor state of the Greek economy and the limited land transportation network imposed burdens on both sides. Despite support from friendly regimes in the neighboring countries, the Communist guerrillas had few resources with which to overcome the effects of the physical environment. On the whole, however, the Greek government forces, backed by Great Britain, the United States, and the United Nations, were better able to overcome the disadvantages of terrain, climate, economy, and limited transportation systems.

A CENTURY OF POLITICAL TURMOIL

The people of Greece have a long tradition of independence and self-reliance, manifested in chronic mountain banditry and armed resistance to the central government. That is especially the case when the government in Athens is seen to be under the domination of elements, foreign or domestic, and to be little concerned with the needs of a desperately poor but immensely proud people. Modern Greece was born out of that tradition of resistance to central authority. Aided by the Western European powers, the Greeks achieved independence from the Ottoman Turks in the early nineteenth century by a classic guerrilla war. However, the new nation was impoverished by a lack of natural resources, people, and capital. Fragmented geographically, politically, economically, and socially, Greece remained a conservative, agrarian, and underdeveloped society well into the twentieth century. Greece gained substantial territory and population as a result of the Balkan Wars of 1912–1913 and the First World War, and it rid itself of an unwanted Turkish minority in the exchange of populations following the unsuccessful Greco-Turkish War of 1921–1922. Nevertheless, in the years between the world wars, Greece—cursed by a great gap between the "haves" and "have-nots" and by a plethora of small, disparate political parties— failed to create a stable political, economic, and social order. The focal point of political instability was a profound conflict between Greeks who favored a constitutional monarchy and those who favored a republican form of government. In the 1920s and 1930s, the adherents of both philosophies frequently fought among themselves and botched their opportunities to resolve the question once and for all. Political, economic, and social instability grew as Greece experimented with monarchy, republic, and dictatorship.

The Origins of Modern Greece

From the end of the classical period, the Greeks found themselves under the heel of a succession of foreign conquerors—Romans, Slavs, Venetians, Crusaders, and, after the fall of Constantinople to Mohammed the Conqueror in 1453, the Ottoman Turks. Opposition to the foreign masters seethed just below the surface and periodically took the form of banditry or local revolt. It was not, however, until the revival of Greek culture and economic life in the early nine-teenth century that the effort to restore Greek independence began in earnest.[8] Spurred by an insurrection in Moldavia against the Turks in the spring of 1821 led by Alexander Ypsilanti, a Greek officer in the Russian army, the Greeks rose in the Morea (Peloponnesus) and the islands. On 13 January 1822, Greek independence and a liberal parliamentary government were declared at Epidau-rus. The Turks had some success in repressing the rebellion; however, Russia and the Western European powers, imbued with the spirit of Philhellenism but acting mainly in their own interests, supported the Greeks. In the London Pro-tocol of 22 March 1829, the Turks were forced to agree that Greece south of a line drawn from Arta to Volos, as well as Euboea and the islands of the Cyc-lades, would be an independent state under its own prince while remaining a tributary of Turkey. The modern Greek state was born, but it would have a turbulent childhood and adolescence.

For most of the nineteenth and early twentieth centuries, Greece was a pawn in the struggles of Turkey, Russia, and the Western European powers for ter-ritory and influence in the Balkans and eastern Mediterranean. However, being embroiled in the quarrels of others added substantially to the Greek territory and population. In June 1864, Britain ceded the Ionian islands to Greece, and in July 1881 Greece obtained from Turkey those portions of Epirus and Thessaly promised by the Congress of Berlin in 1878. Crete, encouraged by the Greeks in its revolt against the Turks, was finally united with Greece in December 1913. As a result of the treaties ending the First and Second Balkan Wars (1912–1913), Greece obtained the remainder of Epirus and Thessaly, most of Mace-donia (including the regions around Salonika and Kavalla), and Lemnos, Lesbos, Chios, Samothrace, and other, smaller, islands in the Aegean Sea.[9] In the Treaty of Sèvres (10 August 1920), having entered the First World War on the Entente side in June 1917, the Greeks obtained Smyrna in Asia Minor, western Thrace, the islands of the Dodecanese (except Rhodes), and the islands of Imbros and Tenedos.[10] However, the Greek territories in Asia Minor were subsequently lost in the unsuccessful Greco-Turkish War of 1921–1922. Thus, by 1923 the mod-ern borders of Greece were established, although disputes with Albania over northern Epirus and with Yugoslavia and Bulgaria over areas of Macedonia and western Thrace continued.

Territorial acquisitions were accompanied by proportionate increases in pop-ulation, the most notable of which was the influx of some 1,250,000 Greeks from Asia Minor following settlement of the 1921–1922 war by the Treaty of Lausanne (24 July 1923). The exchange of minority populations after 1918 reduced the size and influence of ethnic minorities on Greek territory, but several substantial groups intent on being "redeemed" by their racial brothers and thus inimical to Greek authority remained in northern Epirus, Macedonia, and Gre-cian Thrace.

Territorial expansion and population growth did little to improve the state of Greece's underdeveloped economy. Difficult terrain and the lack of natural resources, as well as political instability that inhibited investment in agriculture, industry, and infrastructure, kept Greece a poor and backward nation throughout the nineteenth century and into the twentieth. Unable to earn a living at home, many Greeks emigrated abroad, thus depriving their native land of manpower and expertise. Exports were limited primarily to agriculture products and raw materials, and Greece was obliged to import the bulk of the fuels and manufactured goods it required. Traditionally a maritime people, the Greeks did develop a significant merchant marine, and the opening of the Corinth Canal in August 1893 did much to facilitate communications between the western and eastern seaboards and to improve foreign trade. The transfer of Greek-speaking artisans and farmers to Greece from Asia Minor in the 1920s also significantly enhanced the Greek economy. Many of the refugees from Asia Minor settled in northern Greece, where they established one of Greece's major export industries, the growing and processing of tobacco.

Internal Political Conflict

For the first hundred years after independence was achieved, Greek foreign policy was dominated by the idea of *megale*, the "redemption of enslaved compatriots," and by the machinations of the great powers with respect to Turkey, the Dardanelles, and the eastern Mediterranean.[11] Internally, however, Greek political life was from the beginning preoccupied by the conflict over monarchy versus republicanism, a conflict that was often decided temporarily by the intervention of the Greek military forces. The Greek independence movement began with the declaration of the Hellenic Republic in 1822, but the new state was soon transformed into a monarchy by the imposition by the great powers in March 1832 of a Bavarian prince, Otho, as king. The unpopular reign of Otho I was characterized by a centralized bureaucratic government ill suited to the proud and independent Greeks, and the period was marked by internal dissent, continued banditry, and a poor economy. Forced to agree to the establishment of a bicameral parliament in 1843, Otho was finally deposed by a military revolt in February 1862; he left the country on 23 October 1862. A new King of the Hellenes was chosen from the Danish house of Schleswig-Holstein-Sonderburg-Glücksburg. George I ascended to the throne in 1863, and a new democratic constitution was drawn up and put into effect in November 1864. In January 1910, the Military League, an association of Greek military officers, forced a revision of the constitution, and on 18 October of that year the leader of the Liberal Party (*Phileleftheron Komma*), Eleutherios Venizelos, began his first term as prime minister and instituted a program of military and financial reform.

(A native of Crete, Venizelos was to be one of the central figures in Greek politics for over three decades. He served as prime minister several times and was by turns a revolutionary, a moderate monarchist, a liberal republican, and a maker of coups. During the First World War, Venizelos alternated as prime minister with politicians less favorable to the allies and more attuned to the wishes of the king. In 1916, he led a revolt in Crete and established at Salonika a Provisional Revolutionary Government, which soon fell. Venizelos died in exile in Paris in March 1936, but his influence lived on long after his death; his son Sophocles Venizelos was a prominent politician in the 1940s and early 1950s.)

King George I was assassinated on 18 March 1913, and his son Constantine ascended the throne. Exhausted by the Balkan Wars, Greece, along with Bulgaria and Romania, declared its neutrality at the beginning of World War I. However, the question of whether or not Greece should enter the conflict created a crisis that pitted King Constantine against Venizelos. Seeking to enlist the aid of both Bulgaria and Greece, the allies offered Smyrna (in Turkish Asia Minor) to Greece in return for cession of the Kavalla region in Macedonia to Bulgaria. King Constantine and his supporters opposed the offer, but Venizelos and his adherents generally favored cooperation with the allies. On 6 September 1915, the Bulgarians entered the war on the side of the Central Powers, and the following month British and French troops landed at Salonika to pursue a campaign against the Germans, Turks, and Bulgarians in Macedonia and Thrace. Finally, on 23 November 1916, Venizelos engineered a Greek declaration of war on Germany and Bulgaria, and on 27 June 1917 the Greeks entered the war on the allied side.

In 1917, King Constantine was compelled to withdraw, and his son Alexander was installed in his place. Alexander died on 25 October 1920, as the result of a monkey bite, and King Constantine returned, contrary to the wishes of the Entente powers. Defeated at the polls in November 1920, Venizelos resigned, but he returned to power in August 1922 on the heels of the Greek defeat by the Turks in Asia Minor. King Constantine was forced to abdicate, and another of his sons became king, as George II. George II was largely the puppet of the Greek military, and upon the electoral victory of the Venizelists in December 1923, he withdrew from political life without abdicating formally. On 13 April 1924, a plebiscite declared overwhelmingly for the establishment of a republic, which was duly proclaimed on 1 May 1924, with Venizelos' erstwhile political ally, Adm. Paul Kondouriotis, as president. The Kondouriotis government subsequently fell to a coup directed by Gen. Theodore Pangalos on 25 June 1925. Pangalos, nominally prime minister, voided the republican constitution of September 1925 and ruled as dictator from 3 January 1926. He in turn was overthrown by a coup mounted by Gen. George Kondylis in August 1926, and a new republican constitution was established in September of that year. The Kondylis coup was aided by Gen. Napoleon Zervas and his semiautonomous Republican Guard.[12] The Republican Guard was suppressed in September 1926, but Zervas survived to play an important role in the Greek resistance and subsequent civil war.

On 31 May 1928, Venizelos returned once more as premier, only to resign again on 31 October 1932, allowing the moderate royalists under Panayiotis Tsaldaris to form a government. A republican coup led by Gen. Nicholas Plastiras failed in March 1933, and in March 1935 a Venezelist uprising was put down by forces under General Kondylis. On 10 October 1935 Kondylis mounted his own coup, successfully ousted the Tsaldaris government, and induced the parliament to vote for the recall of King George II. A well-managed plebiscite followed, and George II returned to the throne on 24 November 1935. Both General Plastiras, who was forced into exile in Paris and sentenced to death in absentia, and Panayiotis Tsaldaris would play important roles in post–World War II Greek politics.

On 13 April 1936, Gen. Ioannis Metaxas, a former Army Chief of Staff and now the leader of the proroyalist Popular Party (*Laikon Komma*), became prime minister. Metaxas convinced King George II of the imminence of a Communist takeover and of the consequent necessity for dissolving the parliament, thereby converting his premiership into a dictatorship on 4 August 1936. Parliament was dissolved and martial law decreed; backed by the army, Metaxas instituted a regime of rigid repression, complete with suspension of political activity and an active secret police. Both liberal republicans and Communists were suppressed, republican officers of the armed forces were dismissed, and censorship and imprisonment without trial were imposed.[13] On the other hand, Metaxas, who was named premier for life in July 1938, brought a certain degree of efficiency and stability to Greek government, in much the same way that Benito Mussolini "made the trains run on time" in Italy. Metaxas also sought to dispel popular opposition by a vigorous program of public works and progressive economic and social legislation; however, it did little to lessen hostility among the independent-minded Greeks.[14]

The staggering succession of monarchy, republic, coup, and dictatorship that Greece endured during the interwar years created a sense of disgust with politics in general and particularly with (among progressives and republicans, at least) the fascist leanings of the Greek monarchy and its supporters. Among the myriad of political parties—over sixty different parties participated in one election during the interwar years—none proved able to rule long enough, either alone or in coalition, to accomplish anything of substance. Constant political instability prevented concentration on the development of the Greek economy and the resolution of long-standing social problems. As a result, Greece entered the 1940s nearly as poor, underdeveloped, and unstable as it had been before World War I.

Development of the Greek Communist Party

Among the many small parties contributing to the instability of Greek political life in the period between the two world wars was the Greek Communist Party. The Socialist Labor Party of Greece had been founded at Piraeus in September 1918 by a few Greek intellectuals and students inspired by the Bolshevik revolution in Russia. In 1924, the name of the party was changed to the Communist

Party of Greece (*Kommounistikon Komma Ellados*; KKE), and the KKE was admitted to the Comintern.[15] Inasmuch as Greece lacked a true urban proletariat, the KKE lacked a natural constituency, and it found little electoral success through most of the 1920s. It made efforts to attract disenchanted soldiers of the Greek army defeated by the Turks in Asia Minor, and it gained some strength among the Greek refugees from Asia Minor, who formed the growing industrial labor force in northern Greece. In true Marxist-Leninist fashion, the KKE sought to base its power on the urban working classes (which did not really exist in Greece at the time) and disdained the support of the peasants. Consequently, the KKE attracted almost no support outside the urban areas.[16] Despite its narrow base, the KKE was successful in infiltrating the growing Greek labor movement, and many Communists were elected to important posts within the General Labor Confederation, a combined trade union conference.[17]

Almost from the moment of its foundation, the KKE was divided into two competing wings. On one side were the so-called *KUTVists* and *hadjis*, who whole-heartedly accepted the leadership of the Communist Party of the Soviet Union and sought to follow the Moscow (Comintern) party line meticulously, even at the expense of Greek national interests and those of the KKE itself.[18] On the other side were those Greek Communists who placed national interests above those of the international Communist movement and opposed the direction of Greek affairs by Moscow. The key issue that divided the two wings of the KKE was the issue of the autonomy—or rather the cession to Bulgaria—of Macedonia and western Thrace. The Comintern supported Bulgarian claims in the region, and the submissive internationalist wing of the KKE blindly followed the party line, despite the fact that few Greeks of any political affiliation were willing to give up even an inch of the sacred national territory. Support for a Bulgarian-led Communist federation in the Balkans and the "independence" of Macedonia and Thrace was, for obvious reasons, soft-pedaled by the KKE from 1921 to 1935, at which time the matter was temporarily dropped, in an all-out effort to secure success at the polls.[19] Nevertheless, the issue festered inside the party and inhibited the achievement of its program, which in any case still called, in theory, for a stable, prosperous, and equitable order in Greek society.

The reluctance of many Greek Communists to submit entirely to party discipline and to decisions made in Moscow led to direct intervention by the Comintern in 1931. Anatole Lunacharsky, a former commissar of education in the Soviet Union, was sent to Athens in September of that year to sort out the situation.[20] As a result, George Siantos, the nationalist General Secretary of the KKE, was replaced by Nikos Zachariades, who was installed to push the Comintern program and instill party discipline.[21]

Nikos (Nicholas) Zachariades was one of the most prominent of the *KUTVists* and *hadjis*. Born in 1902 in Asia Minor and raised in Skoplje and Adrianople, he became a sailor. He jumped ship in the Black Sea in 1921 or 1922 to study in Moscow. Sent to Greece by the Comintern in 1923, he became a leader in the Communist youth movement and a full member of the KKE in 1926. He went to Moscow again in 1929, returning in 1931 to become Secretary of the KKE. In 1935, he was named head of the Balkan Communist Bureau.

The KKE played only a minor role in the Greek political struggles in the 1930s. Lacking a genuine political base, the party was unpopular and failed to achieve any substantial decree of electoral success.[22] Following the policies of the Comintern, in the mid-1930s the KKE adopted the "Popular Front" strategy of temporary and expedient cooperation with other "progressive" political parties in opposition to the growing strength of reactionary monarchism and incipient fascism. Participation in the Popular Front and, as noted, the temporary discarding of the detested policy of Macedonian independence brought the KKE to the modest heights of its pre–World War II power. The KKE won fifteen seats in the parliamentary elections of 1936, giving it the balance of power between the Popular Party and the Liberals.

It was the key position of the Communists in the National Assembly and the threat of strikes by the now-Communist-controlled Greek Federation of Labor that provided an excuse for the Popular Party leader, Gen. Ioannis Metaxas, as described above, to convince King George II in August 1936 to dissolve the parliament, declare martial law, and permit the assumption by Metaxas of dictatorial powers. Metaxas subsequently suppressed the KKE ruthlessly and imprisoned many of its leaders, including Zachariades. The members of the KKE who evaded Metaxas' net went underground and waited for better days. When the Germans occupied Greece in 1941, they found Zachariades in prison. They promptly bundled him off to Dachau, where he remained until he was rescued by the Allies and returned to Greece in May 1945. He thus played no role whatsoever in the wartime resistance movement, but, strangely enough, he would be able to regain his position as General Secretary of the KKE almost immediately upon his return. Largely unaware of all that had transpired in Greece and in the KKE since 1941, he would proceed to reimpose slavish adherence to the Moscow party line and the dictates of his master, Joseph Stalin.

THE INVASION AND OCCUPATION OF GREECE, 1940–1941

Preoccupied by its own internal problems, Greece adopted a policy of neutrality upon the outbreak of the Second World War in September 1939. Traditionally friendly with Great Britain and cognizant of the strength of the British Mediterranean Fleet, the Greeks were nonetheless apprehensive about the demonstrated military power of Germany. However, Greek relations with the Axis powers deteriorated rapidly after Italy declared war on Britain in 1940. Italian aggression against Greek shipping in the Mediterranean and the occupation of Albania were followed on 28 October by an Italian ultimatum demanding unimpeded passage of Italian forces through Greek territory. The Italian demand was emphatically rejected by General Metaxas with a famously terse reply— *OXI*! (No!)—which captured perfectly the spirit of the proud and mettlesome

Greeks. Rejection of the Italian demarche was followed the same day by a full-scale invasion of Greece from Albania by well-prepared Italian forces, some eight divisions and over 150 aircraft.[23] The main Italian thrust was south toward Ioannina and the Metsovon Pass, which controlled the only good road in the region. A secondary Italian offensive, directed against the town of Florina and thence Salonika and the Aegean coast, was led by armored forces supported by infantry and aircraft; it was opposed only by Greek infantry.

The Italians expected an easy victory. Indeed, it appears that Mussolini's primary motive in invading Greece was to demonstrate to his German ally that Italy too could successfully practice the art of *Blitzkrieg*. However, Mussolini's expectations were dashed when his troops made contact with the small but determined and well-led Greek forces. The Greek divisions under Gen. Alexander Papagos, outmanned but well trained and fighting on ground they knew, stopped the Italian offensive within five days. Despite severe logistical problems, they counterattacked successfully, pushing the Italians well back into Albania. The Greek counteroffensive, begun on 14 November, stalled in late December, principally due to the onset of winter weather and the problems of resupplying their advancing forces. They had penetrated some thirty miles into Albania, seized the main Italian bases at Argyrokastron, Koritsa, and Pogradia, and inflicted over 100,000 casualties on the original invaders. The stunned Italians reinforced, and in the spring of 1941 they attempted to renew their attack, under the direct supervision of Il Duce himself. Heavily outnumbered, outgunned, and outsupplied, the Greeks nevertheless managed to contain the Italian attack, and the Italians were forced to reluctantly call upon their German allies for assistance.

Bulgaria joined the Axis on 1 March 1941, and on 6 April heavily mechanized German forces invaded Yugoslavia and Greece through Bulgarian territory, in part to rescue their hapless Italian allies but more to secure their own lines of communications through the Balkans for the support of their forces in North Africa, and to protect their southern flank for the coming invasion of Russia. The Germans employed three armored and two infantry divisions in a three-pronged attack. One column went directly into Yugoslavia, took Belgrade the same day (6 April), and proceeded south to take Bitolj and the Monastir Gap, thereby positioning itself to cut off the advanced Greek forces in Albania; Yugoslavia capitulated on 17 April. The center column descended the Struma Valley and then divided, one group crossing the Rupel Pass into Greece and the other proceeding along the Strumitsa Valley toward Doiran; both groups converged on Salonika. The third German column penetrated Thrace and moved to take Kavalla.

Faithful to their agreements with the Greeks, the British rushed a 58,000-man expeditionary force, composed in large part of Australians and New Zealanders, to reinforce the defenses in northern Greece, but the Greeks, triumphant against the Italians, were no match for the Germans. With some 400 aircraft based in Bulgaria the Germans quickly gained air superiority and proceeded to pound the

Anglo-Greek forces, installations, and shipping at their leisure. On the ground, the German columns rolled steadily forward and took Salonika on 9 April, thereby isolating the Greek troops bypassed in eastern Macedonia and Thrace, who surrendered the following day. Greek morale collapsed, and while the desperate British Expeditionary Force attempted to stall the German advance near Mount Olympus in mid-April, panzers swept west to meet the column proceeding from the Monastir Gap and cut off the Greek forces in Albania, forcing their surrender on 20 April. On 21 April, the Greek government told its British allies that further resistance was futile; King George II and the more important government officials fled.[24]

The British withdrew to the south, fighting a doomed delaying action on successive positions in order to buy time for the evacuation of some 42,000 British troops and a large number of Greeks by sea from ports in Attica and the Peloponnesus. On 23 April Gen. George Tsolakoglou signed an armistice with the Germans and Italians, and on 27 April the Germans entered Athens and set up a puppet government. German-controlled collaborationist governments subsequently ruled in Athens from 30 April 1941 to October 1944. General Tsolakoglou, the first collaborationist prime minister (April 1941–December 1942), was followed by Constantine Logothetopoulos (December 1942–April 1943) and Ioannis Rallis (April 1943–October 1944).

The British and Greek forces withdrawn from the mainland and the Peloponnesus attempted to establish a defense in Crete. On 20 May 1941, in their only major airborne action of the war, German paratroops and glider forces invaded Crete, which they succeeded in capturing only with the greatest difficulty, nearly meeting disaster themselves. On 1 June, the decision was made to evacuate the British and Greek defenders by sea to North Africa.

Allied casualties during the period from April to June 1941 were heavy, and the Greek navy and merchant marine suffered particularly heavy losses during the evacuation of Greek and British troops from the mainland, the Peloponnesus, and Crete. The surviving Greek naval forces and merchant vessels made their way to Alexandria and were incorporated into the Allied forces for the remainder of the war. The escaped Greek ground and air forces formed two provisional army brigades and three air squadrons (two fighter squadrons and one bomber squadron). Based in Egypt, they were supplied by the British and participated in the subsequent campaigns in North Africa and Italy as well as in air operations throughout the Mediterranean.

The Axis Occupation of Greece

Once the conquest was complete and its southern flank and line of communication to North Africa secured, Germany withdrew its frontline troops and replaced them with garrison troops of lower quality. Greece was divided among the Germans, Italians, and Bulgarians for the purpose of occupation. The senior partner, Germany, retained control of key positions, including such transportation facilities as airfields, ports, railroads, and critical highways.[25] It also occupied the frontier with Turkey; the Athens-Piraeus region; Crete and the islands of Lemnos, Lesbos, and Chios in the Aegean; and most of Macedonia between the Axios River in the east and the Aliakmon River in the west. The Bulgarians occupied the remainder of Macedonia east of the Axios and Grecian Thrace, except for the German zone along the Evros River. Obviously intending to annex the occupied areas permanently, the Bulgarians replaced Greek administrators with their own and resettled a large number of ethnic Bulgars in the area.[26] The Italians occupied the largest part of Greece, but their control in many areas was undercut by German control of key facilities. The Italians had every intention of permanently annexing the Ionian islands, but their zone of occupation collapsed with the Italian surrender to the Allies in September 1943, and the Germans assumed full control of those areas formerly occupied by the Italians.

All things considered, the occupation was not particularly repressive, except in the Bulgarian zone. The Italian administration was lackadaisical, and the Germans were usually content to secure the key points and the lines of communications, without attempting to scour the remote mountain regions for the Greek resistance fighters. The Germans preferred to rely on the Greek puppet government to handle routine problems, and to keep all elements of the Greek population in line by promoting traditional hatreds and divisions.[27] However, retaliation for resistance attacks on German soldiers was swift and terrible, and Greek Jews were rounded up and transported to the extermination camps, albeit with little assistance from the Greeks. Internal movement and public communications were strictly controlled, and there was also the usual economic exploitation and involuntary draft of labor for the German war industry. Greek commerce, intellectual life, and education were severely curtailed, and chronic poverty and food shortages produced famine conditions throughout most of Greece in the winter of 1941–1942. The situation improved somewhat in 1942, in part because German construction needs produced some jobs.

The Axis occupation of Greece exacerbated the divisions in Greek society, and two very different Greek polities emerged, each of which was rife with factions. One was the Greece of occupation, puppet government, repression, starvation, and resistance movements in the mountains, with high aspirations for the postwar period. The other comprised the Greece monarchy in exile, itself divided between factions in London and in Egypt, and the Greek forces fighting on the Allied side, dependent upon the Allies for their maintenance. As always, the key issue that divided the two manifestations of Greece was the question of the monarchy. In general, the Greeks who accompanied King George II into exile were pro-monarchy, and those who remained in Greece under occupation were anti-monarchy. Of course, shades of opinion existed in both groups, but the central issue of monarchy versus republic animated the development of the wartime Greek resistance movement and the civil war that followed.[28]

NOTES

1. The physical and social geography of Greece is described in Allison Butler Herrick and others, *Area Handbook for Greece*, DA Pam 550-87 (Washington: USGPO, June 1970) [cited hereafter as *Area Handbook*]; Great Britain, Royal Navy, Naval Intelligence Division, *Greece*, 3 volumes, B.R. 516: Geographical Handbook Series ([London]: Naval Intelligence Division, Royal Navy, 1944); Stephen Merrill, *The Communist Attack on Greece*, Special Report No. 15, 21st Regular Course, U.S. Strategic Intelligence School (Washington: U.S. Strategic Intelligence School, 28 July 1952); and Hugh H. Gardner, *Guerrilla and Counterguerrilla Warfare in Greece, 1941–1945 (Draft)* (Washington: Office of the Chief of Military History, Department of the Army, 1962).

2. The 1945 boundary with Albania (190 kilometers) was established by the Protocol of Florence in 1913, but neither country accepted the Protocol as final. The boundaries with Yugoslavia (200 kilometers) and Bulgaria (400 kilometers) were set by the results of the Balkan Wars of 1912–1913, and by the Treaty of Neuilly in 1919 following the First World War. Certain Aegean islands were ceded by Turkey to Greece in 1913, and the Treaty of Lausanne in 1923 set the Turkish-Greek border. The Dodecanese Islands off Turkey's southwestern coast were ceded to Greece by Italy in 1947. See *Area Handbook*, 20.

3. Christopher Montague Woodhouse, *The Struggle for Greece, 1941–1949* (London: Hart-Davis, MacGibbon, 1976), 190.

4. J. C. Murray, "The Anti-Bandit War [Part IV]," *Marine Corps Gazette* 38, no. 4 (April 1954), 53.

5. The Grammos base area is described in Evangelos Averoff-Tossizza, *By Fire and Axe: The Communist Party and the Civil War in Greece, 1944–1949* (New Rochelle, NY: Caratzas Brothers, 1978), 180. The Vitsi base area is described in Theodossios Papathanasiades, "The Bandits' Last Stand in Greece," *Military Review* 30, no. 11 (February 1951), 23.

6. Edward R. Wainhouse, "Guerrilla War in Greece, 1946–49: A Case Study," *Military Review* 37, no. 3 (June 1957), 18.

7. E. E. Zacharakis, "Lessons Learned from the Anti-Guerrilla War in Greece (1946–1949)," *Revue Militaire Générale* 7 (July 1960), 181.

8. The course of modern Greek history is succinctly summarized in William L. Langer, ed., *An Encyclopedia of World History*, 5th edition revised and updated (Boston: Houghton Mifflin, 1972), from which the following account of Greek history from 1821 to 1941 is in part derived. Edgar O'Ballance, *The Greek Civil War, 1944–1949* (New York: Praeger, 1966), 19–31, also provides an excellent summary of the political events of the interwar period.

9. The First Balkan War began on 17 October 1912. It involved Bulgaria, Serbia, and Greece against Turkey, and it was ended by the Treaty of London on 30 May 1913. The Second Balkan War (29 June–30 July 1913) involved Bulgaria against Serbia, Greece, Romania, and Turkey and was settled by the Treaty of Bucharest on 10 August 1913.

10. The Dodecanese Islands, including Rhodes, were finally turned over to Greece by Italy in March 1947.

11. *Area Handbook*, 23 and 31.

12. O'Ballance, 28.

13. The dismissal of republican officers by the Metaxas regime created fissures in the Greek officer corps that carried over into the World War II resistance, the civil war of 1945–1949, and beyond (see O'Ballance, 31).

14. For example, although generally unaffected by Metaxas' strict regime, the peasants were much opposed to a law he passed limiting the number of goats that a peasant might own, despite the fact that the law was intended to improve animal husbandry and preserve Greece's thoroughly depleted and eroded soil (see O'Ballance, 29).

15. William Hardy McNeill, *The Greek Dilemma: War and Aftermath* (Philadelphia: J. B. Lippincott, 1947), 31; O'Ballance, 29. The Third Communist International (Comintern) was established in 1919 to ensure Soviet control of the international communist movement. It was dissolved in 1943 in an effort to placate the Soviet Union's wartime allies.

16. O'Ballance, 29–30.

17. Ibid., 30.

18. Averoff-Tossizza, 17. The nickname of *KUTVist* was given to members of the KKE who had been trained in Moscow at the institute for foreigners, the initials of which were KUTV. The *hadjis* were members of the KKE who had made the "pilgrimage" (in Arabic, *Hadj*) to Moscow to learn and admire "Socialism" in its purest manifestation— the Communist Party of the Soviet Union. Both terms were generally derisory.

19. Ibid.

20. Ibid., 16–17.

21. McNeill, 68–69; O'Ballance, 30. Born in 1890 of a poor family in Thessaly, Siantos became a tobacco worker and served as a technical sergeant in the Greek Army, 1911–1920. He became General Secretary of the Central Committee of the KKE in 1925 and later played a prominent role in the World War II resistance movement.

22. Merrill, 12.

23. The Axis invasion of Greece is outlined in O'Ballance, 37–42, and Gardner, 7–9.

24. General Metaxas, the Greek prime minister, died on 29 January 1941. His successor, Alexander Koryzis, committed suicide on 20 April. Koryzis' successor, Emmanuel Tsouderis, followed King George II into exile, first on Crete and then in Cairo. Eventually the Greek government in exile took up residence under British protection in London.

25. The territorial division of Greece during the occupation is outlined in Naval Intelligence Division, *Greece*, I, 233–34. Despite the allocation of zones to their Italian and Bulgarian allies, the Germans retained supreme power throughout Greece, except of course in areas controlled by the Greek resistance forces. The Germans were particularly concerned with the lines of communications, because about 80 percent of the support for the Afrika Korps passed through Greece (see *Area Handbook*, 39–40).

26. Naval Intelligence Division, *Greece*, I, 233–34. The Bulgarians annexed some 16,682 square kilometers of Greek territory in eastern Macedonia and western Thrace, and nearly 100,000 Greeks were expelled from the Bulgarian zone of occupation. See Stephen G. Xydis, *The Economy and Finances of Greece under Occupation* (New York: Greek Government Office of Information, n.d.) 13.

27. Naval Intelligence Division, *Greece*, I, 235; O'Ballance, 47. Even the Greek pup-

pet government was divided into factions, one mainly pro-Italian, the other mainly pro-German, and both hating the Bulgarians.

28. Amikam Nachmani, *International Intervention in the Greek Civil War: The United Nations Special Committee on the Balkans, 1947–1952* (Westport, CT: Praeger, 1990), 12.

2

The Greek Resistance Movement, 1941–1945

The quick defeat by the Axis powers in the spring of 1941 stunned the Greeks, and resistance to the occupying powers was slow to develop as Greeks of all classes and political persuasions concentrated on mere survival. Opposition to the Metaxas regime had melted with the Italian invasion of Greece in October 1940, but the absent King George II and his adherents were blamed for having abandoned their country in its moment of crisis in April 1941.[1] The right-wing collaborationist Greek government was thoroughly discredited, and the traditional leading parties were in disarray or unwilling to mobilize against the Axis occupation forces. Greek political and military leaders of all political persuasions displayed "a woeful dilatoriness" when it came to protecting national interests.[2] Moreover, large segments of the Greek population—particularly the peasants, in their remote villages—were largely indifferent to the Axis occupation and were unwilling to oppose it actively.[3]

The first glimmerings of active resistance to the Axis occupation began in the urban areas in the summer of 1941; they were undertaken by individuals or small groups, often children. These isolated incidents took the form of minor acts of sabotage, such as putting sand in gas tanks or slashing the tires of Axis vehicles. Gangs of Greek youths spread anti-Axis propaganda and stole food, clothing, and gasoline from Axis depots, and Greeks in contact with the British intelligence services began to gather information and establish escape lines for Greek and British soldiers left behind in the evacuation or shot down over Greece.[4] As Greeks began to regain their composure, there began to be discussion among serious citizens about organizing more active, coordinated resistance measures, including the formation of armed guerrilla groups in the mountains. Such covert discussion inevitably included the question of the form that Greek government should assume after liberation from the Axis yoke.

By the winter of 1941–1942, conditions were ripe for the development of a full-scale armed resistance movement based in the forbidding Greek mountains.

Certain preconditions for a successful guerrilla movement were in place: suitable terrain for secluded camps, a tradition of armed resistance, motivation, the emergence of effective leadership, growing civilian support, the possibility of outside assistance, and a reasonable chance of success.[5]

Of particular importance was the romantic image of the mountain bandits, or *kleftes*—free men who did as they pleased—which was a central part of the Greek self-perception. The war for independence in the early nineteenth century had been fought largely by independent bands of guerrillas—*andartes*—led by their chieftains, or *kapetanioi*. At the end of the war of independence, many of the bands continued to operate in the mountains, either in opposition to King Otho I and his army of Bavarian mercenaries or simply as bandits. Such bandit groups remained a serious problem for the central government until 1910.

In 1942, remnants of guerrilla bands first formed in the nineteenth century continued to exist and were the nuclei around which former members of the defeated armed forces and other adventuresome Greeks coalesced.[6] The *andarte* tradition, and the romantic image of the free Greek armed with rifle and crossed bandoleers that it evoked, had great appeal to young men with few prospects and embued with a hatred of their foreign masters.[7]

The formation of guerrilla resistance groups in the mountains, which began to accelerate in the spring and summer of 1942, was generally spontaneous and without direct connection to the underground groups already operating in the towns. Initially, political affiliation was relatively unimportant, and there was little or no coordination among the various groups. Only somewhat later did the political organizations based in the urban areas seek to reinforce and support the bands and to assume control of the various guerrilla groups for their own ends.[8]

FORMATION OF THE NATIONAL LIBERATION FRONT (EAM)

Two events signaled the beginning of active, armed opposition to the Italian, German, and Bulgarian occupiers. In September 1942 the Greek Fascist Party (EEE) Club in downtown Athens was blown up by the Patriotic Group of Fighting Youth (PEAN), a right-wing Greek resistance organization.[9] In November of the same year, the Gorgopotamos railroad viaduct was destroyed by a small group of British and Greek saboteurs.[10] By the time of the latter event, what would be the strongest and best-organized of the Greek resistance groups was already in existence.

In the first days of the occupation, the Greek Communist Party (KKE), under the leadership of its General Secretary, Nikos Zachariades, adopted a policy of tolerance with respect to the Axis powers, in accordance with the spirit of the German-Soviet Non-Aggression Pact.[11] However, the German occupation authorities soon cracked down on the Communists, and Zachariades and other party leaders were deported to concentration camps or imprisoned in Greece.

George Siantos was named acting General Secretary of the KKE in the absence of Zachariades, and the German invasion of Russia at the end of June 1941 ended the KKE's policy of cooperation. Siantos reformed the KKE and immediately set about to bring the various resistance groups under control of the party.

On 27 September 1941, the KKE established the National Liberation Front (*Ethnikon Apeleftherotikon Metopon*; EAM) and invited all Greeks opposed to the Axis occupation to be members. Adopting a program of national independence, democratic liberties, and resistance to the Axis powers, the EAM was nominally a "popular front" organization composed of a coalition of the KKE and five other left-wing parties and governed by a Central Committee in Athens.[12] However, there was little doubt from the beginning that the EAM was firmly controlled by the Communists, although initially the secretive and generally unpopular KKE was successful in concealing the fact that the EAM was a Communist front organization, despite the fact that many members of the KKE Central Committee also served on the Central Committee of EAM.[13] Eventually, the EAM incorporated 90 percent of the World War II Greek resistance movement, boasted a total membership of over 1,500,000 (including 50,000 armed guerrillas) drawn from all sectors of Greek society, and controlled much of rural Greece.[14]

THE NATIONAL PEOPLE'S LIBERATION ARMY (ELAS)

On 10 April 1942, the EAM announced the formation of its military wing, the National People's Liberation Army (*Ethnikos Laïkos Apeleftherotikos Stratos*; ELAS). The first EAM guerrilla band had been formed in Roumeli, near Mount Olympus, in January 1942, under the leadership of Aris Velouchiotis, an announced Communist.[15] There were perhaps a dozen Communist-led guerrilla groups in the mountains of Roumeli, Thessaly, and Macedonia at the time ELAS was formed, and the number was quickly expanded by the absorption, often involuntary, of many smaller, autonomous bands and by the recruitment, both voluntary and involuntary, of young men from the mountain villages.[16] ELAS took over most of the weaker bands by persuasion or outright threat of annihilation. Generally, the rank and file of ELAS was composed of non-Communist guerrillas; the motives for young men to join the guerrillas were a mixture of patriotism, hate, fear, the desire for adventure, and in many cases, simply the desire to escape the poverty and drudgery of peasant life.[17] The fighting strength of ELAS grew to about 5,000 guerrillas in the spring of 1943, and by October 1944 it totaled nearly 50,000, having more than doubled since the spring of that year.[18] The main strength of ELAS was in Macedonia, Thessaly, and Roumeli; it made only minor inroads in Epirus, the Peloponnesus, and Crete, where rival groups dominated.

At the time ELAS was formed, EAM also created a number of other formations, including the National People's Liberation Navy (*Ethnikon Laïkon Ape-*

leftherotikon Nautíkon; ELAN), which operated small boats along the coasts and between the islands. The strength of ELAN eventually rose to over 1,200 men and 100 small armed boats, organized in seven squadrons and three or four independent flotillas of up to six boats each.[19] From July 1944, ELAN was directed by ELAS General Headquarters (GHQ), but each squadron came under the direct command of the ELAS division in whose territory it operated. Much less visible, but altogether more sinister, were the Units for the Protection of the People's Struggle (*Omades Prostasias Laïkou Agonos*; OPLA), a secret security force designed to neutralize opponents of the KKE-EAM both within and outside the movement.[20] Among other activities, OPLA controlled the National Civil Guard (*Ethniki Politophylaki*; EP), which was organized to maintain public order and control anti-EAM elements in areas over which EAM-ELAS exercised dominion. The EAM also sponsored labor and women's groups as well as the United Panhellenic Youth Organization (*Eniaia Panellinios Organosis Neolaias*; EPON).

Organization

Aris Velouchiotis was the first commander of ELAS, but as the size of ELAS increased the EAM Central Committee sought a more experienced military figure to take command. Colonel Napoleon Zervas, the leader of a rival guerrilla group, was approached but could not be enticed to join ELAS.[21] In March 1943, ELAS attacked one of its smaller rivals, the Liberation Struggle Command (*Arkhigeion Apeleftherikon Agonos*; AAA), and captured its field commander, Colonel Stephanos Saraphis, a former regular army officer.[22] After several days of poor treatment, expecting to be shot at any moment, Saraphis became convinced that ELAS offered the best chance for doing damage to the Axis occupiers, and he agreed to accept command of ELAS.[23]

Immediately upon assuming command of ELAS, Saraphis set about reforming its haphazardly organized and commanded bands. ELAS adopted the tripartite command structure commonly found in other Communist-led guerrilla armies. Command responsibilities were shared among a military commander (often a former officer or noncommissioned officer of the Greek Army with some formal military training), a *kapetanios* (commonly the leader who had first formed the unit and who was trusted by the guerrillas), and a political officer (always a dedicated Communist).[24] The military commander—usually assigned by EAM-ELAS headquarters and often unfamiliar with the unit or the area of operations—planned, organized, and directed military operations. The *kapetanios* was responsible for propaganda, morale, recruitment, administration, and supply, and he acted as the second in command. The political officer, or commissar, insured that the EAM/KKE party line was followed by all concerned. This troika command system extended down to company level. With the formation of ELAS General Headquarters in March 1943, Saraphis assumed the post of military commander, Aris Velouchiotis that of *kapetanios*, and Andreas Tzimas that of

Table 2.1
Redesignation of ELAS Commands, September 1943

Former Designation	New Designation	Strength
Macedonia General Command	9th Western Macedonia Division	4,500
Thessaly General Command	1st Thessaly Division	8,000
Roumeli General Command	13th Central Greece Division	3,000
Epirus General Command	8th Epirus Division	2,000
Peloponnesus General Command	3rd Peloponnesus Division	2,500
Attica General Command	Attica Brigade	< 800

Sources: O'Ballance, *The Greek Civil War, 1944–1949*, 65; Gardner, *Guerrilla and Counterguerrilla Warfare in Greece, 1941–1945 (Draft)*, 131.

political commissar.[25] Later, the three-man command committees were reduced to two-man committees; the political officer was eliminated and his duties assumed by the *kapetanios*.

Saraphis imposed formal organization, a rank structure and promotion regulations, saluting, systematic training, tactics based on careful study, a formal supply system, and other changes intended to improve the control and fighting ability of ELAS.[26] The pattern was, of course, the prewar Greek regular army, with which Saraphis was most familiar. The new ELAS General Headquarters acted as a general staff, and six subordinate headquarters—the General Commands—were created, in Macedonia, Thessaly, Roumeli, Epirus, Peloponnesus, and Attica (Athens). All of the General Commands came under the direction of ELAS GHQ, except for those in the Peloponnesus and Attica, which were controlled directly by the ELAS Central Command in Athens.[27] ELAS headquarters, like those of the other armed resistance groups, were small and sparse, often housed in only a tent, small building, or cave. The number of staff personnel and the amounts of signal and other equipment were low, and few records were kept.[28] The idea, of course, was to keep the headquarters highly mobile, and in late 1943 ELAS GHQ could be moved with only ten trucks.

The basic field unit of ELAS was the "band" of thirty to a hundred men, which operated in much the same way as a company. In September 1943, all ELAS units were redesignated as regular military units. The General Commands became "divisions," the bands were regrouped into battalions, and the battalions into regiments. The new structure is shown in Table 2.1. In reality, the bands seldom operated as part of a larger force, and for the most part they were restricted to garrisoning villages and guarding passes. In fact, ELAS henceforth conducted few offensive operations on any scale; on one hand, small raids were considered "beneath the dignity" of a "battalion," "regiment," or "division," and on the other the watchfulness of German and Bulgarian commanders all but precluded the hope for success of large-scale operations.[29]

The new "divisions" were composed of varying numbers of regiments and battalions, including cavalry units. Each division included engineer, signal, supply, and medical units, as well as a training school for junior leaders and an attached unit for logistical and other tasks. At GHQ, Saraphis created a heavy weapons battalion incorporating mountain artillery pieces, mortars, and machine guns, and the divisions did so as well, insofar as their resources permitted. Despite their official designations, the ELAS units at each level were seriously understrength and in no way represented the military force usually associated with conventional units of division, regiment, or battalion size. Consequently, the ELAS divisions had only a limited ability to operate outside their designated geographical area.

Subsequently, three additional divisions were formed in Macedonia (the 6th, 10th, and 11th Macedonian Divisions), the Attica Brigade became the 2nd Attica Division, and a newly formed 16th Thessaly Division was reduced to a regiment and incorporated into the 13th Central Greece Division. In the spring of 1944, a further reorganization was carried out in order to strengthen command and control over the elements subordinate to ELAS GHQ. Greater autonomy was given to the various regional commands, and the northern divisions were grouped under a corps headquarters known as the Macedonian Group of Divisions. A few weeks later, similar corps headquarters were set up in Thessaly and Attica.

Saraphis also organized an ELAS Reserve to administer the large numbers of unarmed ELAS guerrillas who could not be maintained on full service. Formed into Home Guard–type units, the men remained in their home villages, usually receiving some training but unarmed and without uniforms, until they were needed as replacements or reinforcements for specific operations. The ELAS Reserve units were commanded by graduates of the ELAS GHQ training school for reserve officers, and they eventually reached a collective strength of perhaps 30,000.

The ELAS guerrilla army also included a sizable proportion of women, some of whom were organized for demonstration purposes into combat units. However, most of the female members of ELAS performed administrative or logistical duties or were assigned to the political and educational branches. Few took part in actual combat operations.

Training and Discipline

Under Saraphis' direction, an attempt was made to ensure that all ELAS recruits received at least some formal training based on prewar Greek Army regulations, but the training was limited by lack of time, equipment (particularly ammunition), and facilities.[30] Primary emphasis was placed on the use of weapons, demolitions, security, and basic guerrilla tactics. Training standards tended to vary with the interest and ability of the local commander. Some bands were well trained; others had only a rudimentary understanding of weapons and tactics.

Disciplinary standards were strict but also tended to be applied somewhat haphazardly, according to the whim of the local command. In September 1943, the system of military justice at unit level was changed from the earlier one of public confession, reprimand, and summary execution to an established system of courts-martial.[31] Traitors and anti-Communist agitators could expect little mercy, and even minor military offenses (for example, sleeping on guard duty or failing to execute orders) were punished with severity. In general, Communist indoctrination was accomplished discreetly in order to camouflage the degree to which ELAS was the creature of the KKE.[32] Individuals marked for promotion and positions of increased responsibility received special political instruction, apart from the ordinary soldiers.

Despite the best efforts of Saraphis and his subordinates, the military effectiveness of ELAS did not increase in proportion to its growth in size and formal organization, primarily because of overemphasis on political matters, the appointment of politically "safe" but inept commanders, and chronic low morale.[33] Indeed, as the structure of ELAS evolved in the direction of a conventional force, its military effectiveness actually declined.[34] As one military historian has noted:

The pride of a professional soldier [i.e., Saraphis] in seeing a well-organized army develop from a motley collection of untrained, unco-ordinated bands is understandable. ELAS, however, was better organized on paper than on the ground and as it gained in conventional organization, it lost its effectiveness for the only type of fighting it was equipped to do. It was deficient in many things necessary to a conventional force: communications, transport, heavy weapons, training, and individual discipline. Conventional in command structure only, it ceased to be a guerrilla movement without achieving the efficiency of a well-integrated military force.[35]

Supply

The logistical arrangements of ELAS are of particular interest in that, like its formal organizational structure, they were subsequently replicated in the Communist-led Greek Democratic Army that fought the civil war of 1945–1949. Even in the best periods, ELAS was beset with logistical shortages. Food and forage were scarce in the mountains, and military goods could only be acquired from the enemy or in small quantities from the British. Consequently, ammunition, signal equipment, food, and forage were often in short supply. Forage was a special problem. The 1st Thessaly Division's cavalry regiment had some 1,600 horses, the other divisions had smaller numbers, and all ELAS units depended on mules for transport.[36] Like the Confederate Army in the American Civil War, the Greek guerrillas were usually forced to disband their cavalry units during the winter; they parceled the horses out among friendly peasants in the plains.

The lack of arms was a major factor in limiting recruitment for the various guerrilla bands, including ELAS, since the guerrilla leaders were generally reluctant to recruit and maintain men for whom they could not provide arms. The first ELAS guerrilla groups were equipped with arms and other equipment hidden by the disbanded Greek Army in 1941 and subsequently "found" by EAM-ELAS.[37] Additional matériel was acquired by theft or capture from the Axis occupying forces, or was supplied by the British. Enemy bodies were routinely stripped of weapons, ammunition, and other equipment. Most of the guerrillas were armed with Greek or Italian rifles, but a variety of old hunting weapons and antique firearms were also used. ELAS had virtually no heavy weapons until the surrender of the Italian army of occupation in Greece on 8 September 1943; subsequently, a number of mountain guns, mortars, and machine guns fell into the hands of the guerrillas.[38] Shortages of ammunition were a continuing matter of concern, often limiting active operations as well as training. Italian rifle cartridges fit the Mannlicher rifles with which the prewar Greek Army had been equipped, and theft or capture of ammunition from Italian stocks was a major source for ELAS.[39]

ELAS received a major windfall of arms and equipment from Italian units in October 1943. With the fall of Mussolini, the surrender of Italy, and the subsequent declaration of "cobelligerence" with the Allies by the new Italian government in September 1943, the Italian forces in Greece either surrendered to the Germans or attempted to reach an agreement with the Greek guerrilla Joint GHQ (composed of ELAS, the British and EDES and EKKA, about which more below). The Italians who chose to surrender to the Germans frequently sold their weapons to the guerrillas before turning themselves in.[40] Two of the more important Italian formations, the Pinerolo Division and the Aosta Cavalry Brigade, managed to arrange to keep their arms and fight as units against the Germans. However, on 15 October, ELAS elements succeeded in isolating and disarming both units near Larissa, thereby acquiring a large quantity of weapons, ammunition, vehicles, and other equipment.[41] The Pinerolo Division was said to have had reserve stocks sufficient to reoutfit itself completely, and the equipment obtained from it (including some 12,000 small arms, twenty mountain guns, mortars, and machine guns) allowed ELAS to form another brigade, the 5th Attica-Euboea, and another division, the 16th Thessaly, which was used in the ELAS attack on the rival EDES.[42]

Except for arms and ammunition, the ELAS guerrillas lived for the most part off the land. Many of the ELAS bands survived early on by stealing and by "sponging on relatives in nearby villages."[43] The guerrilla diet was simple—bread, cheese, fruit, olives, and an occasional sheep or goat—and food was obtained by donation, purchase, or requisition in the mountain villages. However, the poverty of the villages limited their ability to support more than a small band, thus requiring a wide dispersion of ELAS units. Funds for the purchase of food and other supplies were provided by the British and by "taxes" imposed by EAM-ELAS. The ELAS guerrillas wore Greek Army, or even Axis, uniforms, whenever they were available, with a forage cap bearing the Greek national emblem and the initials "ELAS." Otherwise, ordinary civilian clothing sufficed. Medical supplies were a particular problem—a problem usually solved by ambushing Axis medical convoys, with complete disregard for the sanctity of the Red Cross.[44]

As ELAS grew in size and adopted a more conventional organization, the primitive ELAS supply system often broke down, particularly when units were called upon to operate outside their home territories. ELAS thus created a formal supply organization, ETA (*Epimeletis tou Andarte*), which was responsible for meeting overall ELAS logistical needs. ETA, essentially the tax-collection agency of EAM-ELAS, administered a progressive system of taxation in kind based on ability to pay. The schedule of "contributions" was established so as to leave the "taxpayer" with a certain minimum subsistence, but excess production was taxed on a sharply rising scale. The system of regular taxation was augmented by full-scale confiscation in the case of anti-EAM villages or failure to cooperate. About 20 percent of the amounts collected were reserved for support of local EAM activities, and the balance was delivered to ELAS depots for the use of its guerrillas and active auxiliaries.[45]

At unit level, responsibility for supply rested principally with the *kapetanios*, and much of the actual logistical work was performed by special youth detachments or local villagers. Formed in the summer of 1943, the EAM youth organization, EPON, played an important role in the logistical support of ELAS.[46] Given some basic military training, the young men and women of EPON were attached in small groups to the various ELAS units and performed such essential housekeeping tasks as office work, cooking, the distribution of supplies, and acting as messengers and guides.[47] The peasants of the villages in ELAS-controlled areas were also extremely important to the ELAS logistical effort. They provided shelter, medical care for wounded guerrillas, transportation services, and other types of labor and services required by the fighting elements of ELAS. The support efforts of the Greek villagers were coordinated by the village mayor, or *Ipefthiros*, who often, together with the village priest, was the primary link between ELAS and the local population.[48] Additional labor was provided by the 15,000 Axis prisoners of war held by ELAS in camps in the Pindus mountains.[49] Unable to care properly for the prisoners or to get the Allies to take responsibility for them, ELAS frequently loaned them out to work for peasants, who fed and sheltered them.

As to the nature and quantity of support provided by the Soviet Union to the Communist-led guerrillas in Greece and the consequent degree of control exercised by Stalin and the Communist Party of the Soviet Union over the KKE, EAM, and ELAS, the answer is quite simple—none. Apparently, there was no contact whatsoever between the Soviet Union and the KKE Central Committee in Athens or the EAM-ELAS forces in the mountains from 1941 until 28 July 1943, when eight Soviet officers, led by Colonel Gregori Popov, appeared at EAM-ELAS GHQ, and two others parachuted in to ELAS forces in Macedonia.[50] The Soviet officers subsequently acted as observers rather than as advisors to the ELAS forces with which they resided.[51] Nor did the Soviet Union provide any arms or other supplies to the Greek guerrillas; that service was left to the western Allies.[52] Having dissolved the Comintern in May 1943 in an effort to placate his allies, Stalin scrupulously avoided any intervention in the Greek resistance and generally appeared indifferent to the fate of the KKE and its fighting arm, ELAS. Indeed, the leader of the Soviet mission, Colonel Popov, advised the Greek Communists to make their peace with the British.[53] The Soviets did provide some limited support to Communist-led resistance groups in Bulgaria and, of course, Yugoslavia. None of that aid filtered through to ELAS. In fact, the relationship of the Greek Communists with their Bulgarian comrades was strained by Bulgarian Communist continuation of the fascist Bulgarian government policy of annexation in Macedonia and western Thrace.[54]

OTHER RESISTANCE GROUPS

The Axis occupation of Greece eventually produced an alphabet soup of Greek resistance organizations in addition to ELAS. Most of those organizations had few supporters and were able to put only small forces in the field. Several restricted their activities to the dissemination of propaganda, intelligence gathering, and occasional sabotage, not attempting to raise armed guerrilla forces at all.

The strongest of the armed resistance groups, other than ELAS, was the Republican Liberal Union (*Ethnikos Dimokratikos Ellinikos Syndesmos*; EDES). EDES was formed in Athens on 9 September 1941 and was thoroughly republican and antimonarchist, but it did attract a few monarchists and other right-wing supporters.[55] The British were instrumental in the development of EDES, hoping it would provide something of a counterweight to ELAS.[56] The Greek government-in-exile was also well disposed to EDES, as the likely "lesser of evils."[57] The nominal leader of EDES was Gen. Nicholas Plastiras, then under detention in France. Over time, the EDES Central Committee and political apparatus in Athens, directed by Gen. Stylianos Gonatas, became increasingly ineffective and estranged from the EDES guerrillas in the mountains, who were led by Col. Napoleon Zervas. Thus, in July 1943, Zervas adopted the name of Greek Nationalist Guerrilla Units (*Ethniki Organosis Ellinikon Andarton*; EOEA) for the military branch of EDES in the field, but both organizations continued to be known as EDES.

Colonel Zervas began recruiting in his native Epirus in June 1942, and by September he had gathered a force of about ninety-eight men. The participation of EDES in a British commando raid on the Gorgopotamos viaduct greatly increased the prestige of EDES and assisted its recruiting efforts. Attractive to professional soldiers by virtue of its apparently moderate political program, EDES grew rapidly to about 500–600 armed men and perhaps another 1,000 trained, but unarmed, men in January 1943. The British provided the necessary weapons, and by the end of March 1943 EDES numbered some 4,000 armed fighters in northern Epirus. In the summer of 1943, Colonel Zervas reorganized EDES along more conventional military lines with eight to ten units, including two regiments of two battalions each.[58] However, Zervas did not attempt to change his tactical doctrine, and EDES remained clearly a guerrilla force. The greatest strength of EDES was in Epirus, although EDES units also operated temporarily in the Peloponnesus, western Thessaly, Roumeli, and even Macedonia. Epirus was a particularly poor district, and most of the logistical support for EDES was provided by the British. When EDES was finally disbanded in the fall of 1944, it had about 12,000 fighters, plus another 5,000 reserves, and was thus about one-fourth the size of ELAS.[59]

Among the other substantial Greek resistance organizations were EKKA, AAA, EOA, ES, EOK, PAO, SNOF, and a number of independent groups under such leaders as Tsaous Andon, Athos Roumeliotis, and Mikhalagas. The National and Social Liberation (*Ethniki kai Koinoniki Apeleftherosis*; EKKA) was a Socialist-oriented group led by Col. Dimitrios Psaros. EKKA operated mainly in the Parnassus Mountains of Roumeli, never exceeded 1,000 men, and was eventually destroyed by ELAS.[60] The Liberation Struggle Command (*Arkhigeion Apeleftherotikou Agonos*; AAA), of which George Papandreou was the political leader, did not survive militarily the defection of Col. Stephanos Saraphis to ELAS, but it continued to function as a political organization.[61] A much smaller but longer-lasting group was formed in Athens by Lt. Col. George Grivas, the former Chief of Staff of the Greek Army's 2nd (Athens) Division.[62] Known as X (the Greek letter *chi*), the secret organization was originally composed of officers of the 2nd Division and was extremely right-wing. The group opposed the Communists much more than it did the Germans. Never very large during the war—perhaps 500–600 members—became an important factor in the civil war of 1945–1949 and after.

The resistance movement in the Peloponnesus was initially dominated by two related right-wing, monarchist organizations: the National Organization of Officers (EOA) and the "Greek Army" (ES).[63] EDES tried but was unable to gain a strong foothold in the Peloponnesus. ELAS was much more successful; it wiped out EOA and ES by October 1943.[64] Neither ELAS nor EDES succeeded in establishing themselves in Crete, where the National Organization of Crete (EOK), under the republican Col. Emmanuel Mandakas, led the resistance.[65]

In northern Greece, there were two prominent guerrilla groups, PAO and SNOF. The right-wing Panhellenic Liberation Organization (*Panellinios Apeleftherotiki Organosis*; PAO) was located in Salonika and put a guerrilla force of about 1,000 men into the field in eastern Macedonia, but ELAS accused PAO of collaboration and eliminated its guerrillas in October 1943.[66] The Slavo-Macedonian National Liberation Front (*Slavomakedonski Narodnoosloboditelniot Front*; SNOF) was somewhat more significant, in that it survived into the period of the civil war of 1945–1949. SNOF, a Communist-inspired organization of Macedonian Slavs led by Gotchev (Ilias Dimakin), was at first affiliated with EAM-ELAS, but the relationship was severed when it became apparent that SNOF was primarily interested in promoting the autonomy of Macedonia within a Communist Southern Slav Federation.[67] SNOF first took the field in November

1943, and at its peak it numbered some 2,000 armed men; in October 1944 ELAS troops attacked Gotchev's bands and forced them over the border into Yugoslavia.[68] An independent band of some 600 men under Tsaous Andon also operated in eastern Macedonia and Grecian Thrace. Known as the United Greek Guerrilla Bands, or as the *Kapetanioi*, Tsaous Andon's men received considerable support from the British and fought the Germans, Bulgarians, and ELAS with equal élan.[69] Other leaders of independent guerrilla forces included Mikhalagas and Athos Roumeliotis, who were little more than bandit chieftains.

On the whole, the proliferation of Greek resistance groups reflected the internal divisions of Greek society; heightened the hatreds among monarchists, republicans, and Communists; and presented the Axis occupation authorities with many opportunities for "dividing and conquering" the resistance movement. ELAS was by far the largest and strongest of the Greek guerrilla forces, with EDES a poor second. However, ELAS, EDES, and the rest expended much more effort, treasure, and blood in fighting each other than they did in fighting the Italians, Germans, or Bulgarians. More importantly, the quarrels ignited during the wartime resistance erupted into flames again in the period 1945–1949.

THE ROLE OF THE BRITISH/ALLIED MILITARY MISSION

Having honored their commitment to defend Greece and having suffered a significant defeat at the hands of the Germans for their trouble, the British were not inclined to surrender their interest in a region they considered to be well within their sphere of action. British interest in the fate of occupied Greece did wane somewhat after the evacuation of Crete in the summer of 1941, but it revived and intensified as planning proceeded for the British counteroffensive at El Alamein. The fact that one of the principal supply lines from Germany to Field Marshal Erwin Rommel's army in North Africa ran through Greece provided the impetus for positive action to contact the Greek armed resistance groups and utilize them to disrupt Axis communications.[70] The existence of the Greek government-in-exile in London under British protection and the well-known preoccupation with the Balkans of Prime Minister Winston Churchill also served to keep interest alive.

In October 1942, three British commando teams (nine officers and three noncommissioned officers, or NCOs) led by Col. (later Brigadier) Edward C. W. "Eddie" Myers, with Maj. Christopher M. Woodhouse as second in command, parachuted into Central Greece with the mission of destroying key facilities on the main rail line between Athens and Salonika. Colonel Myers was able—only with great difficulty and guile—to obtain the assistance of 116 ELAS guerrillas under Aris Velouchiotis, and of forty-five EDES guerrillas under Napoleon Zervas.[71] Bravery and good luck resulted in the destruction of the key Gorgopotamos viaduct on 25 November 1942. Myers' team was to be evacuated, but before that could take place, it received orders to remain in Greece to form the nucleus of a British Military Mission (BMM). Its assignment was to coordinate the activities of the various Greek resistance groups and control the distribution of money, arms, and other supplies that the British Middle East Command was prepared to provide to the guerrillas for use against the Axis occupiers. After another brief flurry of activity immediately preceding the Allied invasion of Sicily in July 1943, Allied interest in Greece waned once again, and Middle East Command was content to advise the Greek guerrillas to husband their resources and reduce their activity. With the invasion of France in June 1944, the Mediterranean theater in general, and Greece in particular, became a backwater, although the British continued to provide some funds and supplies. Nevertheless, the Greek guerrillas continued to conduct ambushes, mine bridges and roads, cut railroads, and destroy Axis telephone and telegraph lines, although their principal efforts were directed toward eliminating their rivals so as to be in a dominant position once the inevitable liberation of Greece finally arrived.

Management of the BMM and delivery of supplies to the Greek resistance groups was entrusted to the British Special Operations Executive–Cairo (SOE-Cairo).[72] SOE-Cairo was the only significant outside source of matériel for ELAS and the other Greek resistance groups. In all, the British delivered to the Greek guerrillas some 5,796 tons of arms and other supplies, of which 85 percent was food and clothing and less than 1,000 tons was arms and ammunition.[73] SOE-Cairo also supplied some 1,230,000 gold sovereigns to the various Greek resistance groups.[74] Most of those funds were provided on the basis of an agreement by which the British pledged to provide one gold sovereign per month per guerrilla plus another gold sovereign for the maintenance of their families.[75] This money was paid to the leaders of the guerrilla groups, who did with it more or less as they pleased. The flood of gold permitted the guerrillas to buy much-needed supplies, but it also fed inflation.

Although later the subject of considerable controversy, the number of weapons supplied by the British to ELAS was actually quite limited, in part because the British were suspicious of the motives of the Communist-led forces.[76] General Saraphis himself later wrote that "during the whole period of its activity, the allies gave ELAS approximately 10 mortars, 100 sub-machine guns, 30 automatic rifles, 3,000 rifles and very little ammunition."[77] Had ELAS proven more amenable to British control, it might have received more weapons and money.[78] After the war, when ELAS' Communist orientation and ultimate aims were known, some observers questioned whether the Allies should have provided any support to ELAS at all.[79] The question became even more sensitive once the "Third Round" of the Greek civil war began in 1945. The only unequivocal answer is that whereas the Allies had been engaged in a struggle to the death with the Axis powers and ELAS had had a potentially effective guerrilla army in the field in an important area, the provision of arms, equipment, and funds to ELAS was both necessary and proper, regardless of the risk that some of those supplies might be used for other purposes.

THE "FIRST ROUND"

In July 1943, the British assembled the leaders of the principal Greek resistance organizations in Cairo to discuss greater cooperation among the various guerrilla forces. The result was the so-called National Bands Agreement, which called for the establishment of a Joint General Headquarters—composed of representatives of the three major guerrilla groups (ELAS, EDES, and EKKA) and the British Military Mission—which would be a part of the British Middle East Command and take its orders from SOE-Cairo. At the time, the various guerrilla organizations reported their strength as: ELAS, 16,000; EDES, 3,000; and EKKA, 400.[80] The Joint GHQ was subsequently established near Pertouli in the Pindus mountains west of Trikkala. The commander of the British Military Mission, Brigadier Myers, did not return to Greece after the July 1943 Cairo conference, and he was replaced by then–Lieutenant Colonel Woodhouse, much to the dissatisfaction of Saraphis and other ELAS leaders, who considered Woodhouse biased toward EDES.[81] In September 1943, several U.S. Army officers, led by Capt. Winston Ehrgott, arrived in Greece to provide liaison with the Greek guerrillas. The British Military Mission was subsequently redesignated the Allied Military Mission (AMM), with Lieutenant Colonel Woodhouse as its commander. Captain Ehrgott was replaced as ranking American officer by Maj. Gerald K. Wines in December 1943.

At about the time of the Cairo meeting, SOE-Cairo was reorganized, British support for the resistance in Yugoslavia shifted from Mihailovitch to Tito, and Siantos replaced Tzimas as the chief political officer at ELAS headquarters in the field. Woodhouse later noted that "the 'first round' of the civil war was the direct result of these changes."[82]

From its very beginning, ELAS had sought to absorb or eliminate the other Greek resistance groups and had achieved some success in that effort. In May 1943, the remainder of AAA was eliminated, and ELAS turned toward its greatest rival—EDES. The Communist-led ELAS was firmly established and held a clear advantage over its rivals in terms of overall numbers and organization, the amount of territory controlled, and the possession of a clearly thought-out program for postwar Greece. ELAS also claimed a moral superiority over its opponents in the Greek resistance movement, accusing its rivals—particularly EDES—of collaboration and plotting with the Axis occupation authorities.[83] The Allied victory in Sicily and the subsequent surrender of the Italians in September 1943 convinced most Greeks that the liberation of their country from the Axis yoke was not far off. The prospect of imminent liberation and the return of the monarchist government-in-exile prompted the leaders of ELAS to strike quickly and decisively to eliminate their rivals and thus be in a better position to dictate the shape of the postoccupation government of Greece. Aris Velouchiotis had long advocated violent action against the rivals of ELAS, but the real "architect" of the campaign to clear away the obstacles to EAM-

ELAS domination of the postoccupation situation was the General Secretary of the KKE, George Siantos.[84]

By September 1943, the reorganization of ELAS bands along conventional lines had been completed, and ELAS strength was about 15,000 fighters and another 20,000 reserves. Secret talks between George Siantos and Dimitrios Psaros, the leader of EKKA, in August and September 1943 ensured the neutrality of EKKA in the conflict between ELAS and EDES.[85] On 12 October 1943, the 8th Epirus Division and other ELAS elements struck against EDES units in the mountains of Thessaly, beginning what came to be called the "First Round" of the Greek civil war. Next, the 16th Thessaly Division, having seized a large quantity of Italian arms and equipment, crossed the Pindus range to strike EDES units in Epirus. At the same time, supporting attacks were made against ELAS rivals in Macedonia and in the Peloponnesus. Given a four-to-one advantage in manpower and the recent windfall of Italian weapons, ammunition, and other equipment, ELAS achieved a good deal of success in the battle against EDES. Zervas lost men, supplies, and territory, and as the size of his recruiting area decreased, his ability to replace his losses also decreased.[86] However, ELAS had overextended its supply lines; also, the Allied Military Mission, fearing a total victory by ELAS, increased its support to EDES. The influx of arms and money enabled Zervas to mount a counteroffensive, and by February 1944 he had regained much of his territory, and a truce—the so-called Plaka Bridge Agreement—ensued. On 12 February 1944, representatives of ELAS, EDES, and the AMM met at the Plaka Bridge, over the Arachthos River in Epirus. The resulting agreement, signed on 29 February 1944, provided for the establishment of well-defined zones of operation for each group in the fight against the Germans, a pledge by each group to refrain from infringing on the other's assigned territory, and a further pledge that all future efforts would be directed against the Germans rather than each other.[87]

Having overestimated their own strength and underestimated both the strength of EDES and the degree to which the Allies would support it, EAM-ELAS had failed to achieve the clear-cut destruction of its most dangerous rival and thereby the unimpeded domination of the political situation in Greece. However, the attack on EDES did not go unrewarded in the political arena. In order to reconcile ELAS and EDES, the British hosted a conference in Lebanon on 17–20 May 1944. The resulting Lebanon Charter of 20 May 1944 provided for the reorganization of the Greek armed forces in the Middle East and the unification of all resistance groups under a "Government of National Unity," headed by George Papandreou.[88] EAM-ELAS was granted a full one-fourth of the cabinet posts in the new government. Thus, the "First Round" was not fought in vain.

The formal structuring of ELAS and the effort to eliminate rivals were parts of a systematic program of the KKE and EAM to establish a full-fledged alternative government in the mountains, a government that, when the time was right, could displace both the puppet collaborationist regime and the royalist government-in-exile and take over the entire country.[89] A major step in that direction was taken with the creation on 1 January 1944 of "People's Committees for Self-Administration" in local areas, followed on 10 March with the establishment at Karpenision of the Political Committee of National Liberation (*Politiki Epitropi Ethnikis Apeleftherosis*; PEEA). The PEEA was intended to be a full-fledged government, which would administer Greece through EAM agencies and preclude Allied restoration of the Greek government-in-exile.[90] The following day, a "Provisional Government of Free Greece" was proclaimed at Viniani, with Col. Euripides Bakirdzis, and later Alexander Svolos, as president.[91] The PEEA/Provisional Government was nominally a "popular front" organization, and the majority of its members were non-Communist. However, since it controlled key positions, EAM—and through it the KKE—was actually in charge.[92] Popular, but well-managed, elections were held for village offices and the *Bouli* (parliament). Many of the non-Communist members subsequently became disillusioned and sought to withdraw, but they were prevented from doing so by the KKE-EAM. In fact, all opposition to the Communist plans for PEEA was brutally suppressed by EAM-ELAS.

After 10 March 1944, the PEEA/Provisional Government relieved ELAS GHQ of many of its logistical and administrative burdens. The ELAS Central Command in Athens was dissolved, and the post of political commissar with field units was abolished.[93] The new PEEA secretary of war took up the former functions of the ELAS Central Command, and the new PEEA secretary for home affairs, George Siantos, the General Secretary of the KKE, provided the necessary political guidance.

The PEEA subsequently attempted to extend its authority to include the Greek armed forces in exile in Egypt. The KKE, acting through the PEEA, infiltrated the Greek armed forces there and precipitated in March 1944 a mutiny that nearly destroyed the Greek Army. The immediate cause of the mutiny was the arrest of a number of Greek officers who had called for a government of national unity based on the PEEA. The revolt was suppressed by loyal Greek Army and Navy elements and the British on 22–23 April 1944, and the mutinous elements of the Greek forces were dispersed.[94] A new brigade, the 3d Mountain, formed from officers and men who had not taken part in the mutiny and commanded by Col. Thrasyboulos Tsakalotos, subsequently fought well under the British Eighth Army in Italy, earning the title of the "Rimini Brigade." Tsakalotos later played a prominent role in the civil war of 1945–1949 as a senior officer of the Greek national army. In 1952, he became Chief of Staff of the Greek Army.

THE REVOLT IN ATHENS AND THE "SECOND ROUND"

In the early fall of 1944, as an Axis withdrawal from Greece became likely, the British sponsored a meeting of the principal Greek factions at Allied GHQ at Caserta, Italy, to coordinate military actions and establish the ground rules for political activity in Greece when the liberation took place. In the resulting Caserta Agreement, signed on 26 September 1944, both EDES and ELAS, as well as the Greek government-in-exile, agreed to place their forces under the command of Lt. Gen. Ronald McKenzie Scobie, the British officer designated to represent the Allied High Command in Greece, for the purpose of driving the Axis out of Greece.[95] ELAS and EDES also agreed to allow the landing of British forces in Greece, to refrain from any attempt to seize power on their own, and to support the return of the Greek Government of National Unity under Papandreou.

The Germans evacuated Athens on 12 October 1944, and by the end of the month they had withdrawn all their forces from Greece. The first British troops under General Scobie arrived in Athens on 14 October 1944. On 17 October 1944, a British and Greek fleet anchored in Phaleron Bay, and the following day the Greek government-in-exile returned to Athens. The small number of elite British troops who took part in the first days of the liberation was augmented at the end of October by the arrival of two brigades of the 4th Indian Division from Italy. It was planned that one of the two Indian brigades would remain in Greece for some time as a garrison force.[96] On 9 November, the first of the regular Greek Army units, the 3d Mountain (Rimini) Brigade, arrived in Athens from Italy. ELAS, and to a lesser extent EDES and the other surviving resistance groups, assumed control of the countryside, but all groups refrained from trying to seize control of the Athens-Piraeus area, in accordance with their previous agreements.

ELAS armed strength at the time of the liberation in mid-October 1944 was 5,240 officers (including *kapetanioi* and political officers) and 43,700 other ranks.[97] As the German forces withdrew, ELAS forces flowed in behind them. Approaching the Albanian frontier, ELAS forces established contact with the Albanian Communist guerrillas under Hoxha; in Macedonia, ELAS drove Gotchev's SNOF guerrillas over the border to take refuge with Tito's partisans; and, following the withdrawal of Bulgarian troops from eastern Macedonia and Grecian Thrace on orders from Stalin, ELAS forces under Euripidis Bakirdzis and Markos Vaphiades moved in quickly. On October 23, ELAS GHQ was moved to Lamia, and ELAS asked to be permitted to assist Tito's partisans against the Germans and to take part in the liberation of Crete and Melos, both of which suggestions were rejected by the British GHQ in Athens.[98]

Almost from the day of its arrival in Greece, the Government of National Unity was in trouble. Papandreou's Liberal Party was weak, and it was clear that his government existed only at the sufferance of the British. There was soon a resurgence of royalists and right-wing groups, and little attempt was made to root out Greeks who had collaborated with the Axis occupation authorities. EAM-ELAS held most of the Greek countryside except for the areas in Epirus and elsewhere held by EDES and the other surviving guerrilla groups; the urban areas of Athens-Piraeus, Salonika, and Patras were occupied by British troops.

Conflict between the monarchist Right and the republican/Communist Left soon became severe, despite the apparent intention of Prime Minister Papandreou to "bind up the war wounds."[99]

Many Greeks who had fought in the resistance felt that their sacrifices were being ignored and that their victory being stolen by the royalists, who had spent the war years in the relative comfort of Cairo and London. The Papandreou government was considered a "cheat," and Papandreou himself was caricatured as a "*papajes*," or "three-card monte sharper."[100] ELAS, EDES, and most of the other important guerrilla groups were at least moderately republican in orientation, whereas the Greek government-in-exile had been connected with monarchism, the Metaxas dictatorship, defeatism, and abandonment of the homeland to the invader. Moreover, many Greeks of leftist sentiment saw little difference between the right-wing adherents of the national government and the equally right-wing elements that had formed the collaborationist government, which had aided the Axis occupation forces.

Three key issues dominated the heated controversy: the demobilization of existing royalist and guerrilla forces, the formation of a new Greek national army, and the treatment of collaborators.[101] The first two issues were related. It was expected, by ELAS at least, that in accordance with the Caserta Agreement both the Greek Army units that had been formed outside Greece and all the guerrilla resistance formations formed inside it would be disbanded and a new Greek national army formed, with equal representation of the former forces. However, the British and rightist elements in the restored Greek government wished to demobilize the guerrillas, particularly ELAS, but retain the royalist Greek Army units and use them as the basis of the new national army, to the exclusion of leftist elements from ELAS.

The issue of how the Greek government was to deal with Greeks who had collaborated with the Axis occupation authorities was even trickier. EAM-ELAS protested in vain the failure of the Papandreou government or the British to take swift and decisive action. Former members of the infamous right-wing Security Battalions, formed by the Germans to control the Greek populace and hunt down guerrillas, were apparently permitted to join the new national armed forces, while former ELAS guerrillas were excluded.[102] Moreover, not only were collaborators not being punished, they were being permitted to take important posts in the restored Greek government. Gen. Theodore Pangalos, a leading propagandist for the Germans, was at large; Stylianos Gonatas, a leader of the political wing of EDES and an avid supporter of the Security Battalions, was being considered for public office; and Brigadier General Katsotas, who had served as minister of war in the quisling Tsolakoglou government, had been named military governor of Attica.[103] As notorious collaborators walked free, leftists who had fought against the Axis occupation were increasingly subject to harassment and arrest by government authorities.

The demand for demobilization of the guerrilla resistance forces, the de facto exclusion of former ELAS officers and men from the new Greek national army, and the lenient treatment of collaborators strengthened the hands of such "hard-liners" in the KKE/EAM-ELAS as Aris Velouchiotis, whose influence had waned with the failure of the "First Round."[104] The attitude of the British and the growing resurgence of right-wing repression in late 1944 seemed to leave few options other than outright armed opposition. However, EAM-ELAS did little to prepare for the coming battle, and the actual outbreak of fighting between the Anglo-Greek government and EAM-ELAS came as something of a surprise to both sides, each of which had badly misjudged the situation and its opponent.[105]

The ELAS Offensive in Athens and Piraeus

The question of demobilization is often credited with having provoked the crisis that led to armed conflict between EAM-ELAS and the Anglo-Greek government forces, but the fundamental factor was the "Greek rightist determination to exploit British support."[106] Prime Minister Papandreou was prepared to compromise, but General Scobie objected strongly to the demobilization of the 3d (Rimini) Brigade. Focused on the problems of maintaining order, Scobie was eager to lessen the potential threat to public order posed by the armed guerrilla armies, and he desired to have available the Greek Army units, such as the 3d Mountain (Rimini) Brigade and the Sacred Battalion, which had proven in Italy their discipline and loyalty to British commanders, to supplement his meager British troop list.[107] On 1 December, the government decreed that all guerrilla groups were to be disarmed by 10 December. On 2 December, the six EAM ministers in the Government of National Unity resigned in protest, and on 4 December Papandreou himself resigned. A new government was formed by Themistocles Sofoulis.

The immediate cause of the fighting was an EAM demonstration in Athens' Constitution Square on Sunday, 3 December 1944, which turned violent when Greek police fired on the unarmed demonstrators, killing fifty (including many women and children) and wounding 250.[108] General Scobie promptly ordered all ELAS units to leave Athens within seventy-two hours, and on the following day he declared martial law. In the early morning hours of 4 December, ELAS "reservists" began operations in the Athens-Piraeus area, attacking Grivas' X forces and taking twenty of twenty-five Athens police stations in the first thirty-six hours. On 5 December, General Scobie committed his British troops to the fray.

For the first three weeks of the fighting in the Athens-Piraeus area, ELAS held the upper hand. General Scobie had underestimated ELAS and found his forces in a very precarious position. By mid-month the situation was desperate: the British held at most only 20 percent of the Athens-Piraeus area; the airfield at Tatoi had been lost, and some 800 Royal Air Force (RAF) headquarters and ground staff personnel were cut off in the northern suburb of Kifissia; the Ka-lamaki airfield was insecure, and the ground routes into Athens were under constant ELAS fire; and the British, denied use of all port facilities, were being forced to bring in supplies and reinforcements over an unimproved landing beach at Phaleron, several miles from the city center. On 11 December, Harold Macmillan, then British resident minister in Greece, noted in his diary that the British had "no secure base anywhere from which to operate."[109]

ELAS fought the battle essentially with the forces in place on 4 December, the only reinforcement being a brigade from the Peloponnesus under Aris Velouchiotis, which arrived on 5–6 December. The ELAS regular forces engaged in the fighting consisted of the 1st (Athens) Army Corps HQ, the 2d (Attica) Division, the 3d (Peloponnesus) Division, the 13th (Roumeli) Division, the Cavalry Brigade, and an assortment of some 10,000 local ELAS "reservists," all under the direct command of the ELAS Central Committee (George Siantos, Gen. Emmanuel Mandakas, and Gen. Michael Hajimikhalis).[110] General Mandakas held the operational field command of ELAS forces in the Athens-Piraeus fighting. The remaining ELAS forces under ELAS GHQ command (General Saraphis) were to be used for "the disbanding of Zervas' and Tsaous Andon's guerrilla forces, frontier security, surveillance of the British garrisons within [their zones] and precautions against landings there."[111]

The principal problem for ELAS commanders was providing sufficient logistical support for their forces. Food was not a particular problem; large quantities were captured from British dumps in and around the city. Arms and ammunition, always a problem for ELAS, were apparently abundant during the early days of the fighting, but as the battle continued ELAS stocks declined rapidly.[112] ELAS fought primarily with rifles, light automatic weapons, and machine guns (some of which had been furnished to the guerrillas by Force 133 and OSS units during the war).[113] Toward the end of December, ELAS forces used large quantities of dynamite to blow up public buildings and private dwellings in the city center, particularly around Omonia Square and along Patissia Street. Apparently the Yugoslavians promised some assistance to ELAS, but if so they never delivered it.[114] Delivery of supplies to ELAS forces in the Athens area from Yugoslavia, while not impossible, would have been difficult, even though ELAS controlled the land routes from the Yugoslavian border into Attica.

The high point of the battle came for ELAS on 18 December, with the seizure of a building in Kifissia that RAF elements had held since the beginning of the fight. Several hundred RAF officers and enlisted personnel were taken prisoner. However, by mid-December General Scobie had received substantial reinforcements from British forces in Italy, and from that point on, ELAS was fighting a losing battle.

The Elimination of EDES

Even as fierce fighting was taking place in the Athens-Piraeus area, General Saraphis' ELAS forces initiated a final drive to eliminate their old enemy, the EDES forces of General Zervas.[115] Zervas' guerrillas at that time held most of

Epirus, including the towns of Arta, Ioannina, Metsovon, and Preveza, as well as the islands of Corfu and Levkas. Saraphis massed three ELAS divisions— the 1st (Thessaly), 8th (Epirus), and 9th (Macedonian)—and on 20 December launched them across the Pindus mountains in a two-pronged attack, with one prong moving via the Metsovon Pass in the north toward Ioannina and Corfu, and another farther south, aimed at Arta and Preveza. EDES, already weakened by its final efforts against the Germans and by the lack of British logistical support, gave way quickly. Arta was taken on 21 December, Ioannina on 23 December, and the island of Levkas on 30 December. Zervas attempted to make a stand at Preveza, but, lacking ammunition and other supplies and unable to recruit replacements for his numerous deserters, he was unable to hold. On 29– 31 December 1944, the remnants of EDES were evacuated by the Royal Navy to Corfu, where they were disarmed and disbanded.[116]

The British Counteroffensive in the Athens-Piraeus Area

Operational control of the British forces in the Athens-Piraeus battle was entrusted to Maj. Gen. John L. I. Hawkesworth, who was transferred from Italy for the purpose. British airborne forces and the remaining brigade of the 4th Indian Division were rushed to Athens, and by 20 December General Hawkesworth had secured his base at Phaleron and had begun an all-out offensive, supported by artillery and aircraft, against ELAS forces in the area.[117] British troops moving north from Phaleron were assisted by the Greek 3d Mountain (Rimini) Brigade, which broke out of its barracks in northern Athens and moved south. In hard house-to-house fighting, the Anglo-Greek forces gradually expanded the area under their control, as the weakened and increasingly dispirited ELAS troops fell back.

The strength of the opposing ground forces at the height of the fighting in the Athens-Piraeus in late December 1944 was as shown in Table 2.2.

Progress was slow, but between 27 and 31 December Hawkesworth's troops gained control of the southern half of the city, although the Athens-Piraeus road remained blocked and British and ELAS forces remained stalemated in Piraeus.[118] On 28 December, the morale of ELAS forces began to break, and on the following day the 13th (Roumeli) Division was overrun. On 31 December ELAS representatives contacted General Scobie to discuss a cease-fire. No agreement was reached, and the British offensive continued.

On Christmas Eve, Prime Minister Churchill and Foreign Minister Anthony Eden flew to Athens for a first-hand look. A conference of British authorities, Greek national government officials, and representatives of EAM-ELAS on 26– 28 December failed to reach agreement on a cease-fire, but it was agreed that Archbishop Damaskinos, the Metropolitan of Greece, should be appointed regent.[119] Archbishop Damaskinos was duly appointed on 31 December, and on 3 January 1945 Gen. Nicholas Plastiras, recently returned to Greece from exile in Paris, was appointed prime minister.

Table 2.2
Strength of Opposing Ground Forces, December 1944

Force	Strength
Greek Government Forces	
3rd Mountain (Rimini) Brigade	4,000
The Sacred Battalion	500
Athens City Police	3,000
"Ξ" Organization	1,000
British Forces	
4th Indian Division (3 infantry brigades)	9,000
Airborne Brigade	2,000
Armored Brigade	1,000
Battalion, Leicestershire Infantry Regiment	1,000
ELAS Forces	
ELAS Regulars	15,000
ELAS "Reservists"	10,000

Sources: Iatrides, *Revolt in Athens: The Greek Communist "Second Round," 1944–1945*, 176; United States, Office of Strategic Services, Research and Analysis Branch, *The Present Balance of Political Forces in Greece*, 3.

The End of the Battle for Athens-Piraeus

By early January 1945, ELAS had destroyed EDES and had gained almost complete control outside Athens. However, in the Athens-Piraeus area, the British, by virtue of their augmented forces, superior logistics, and control of the food supply, had steadily gained the upper hand after a shaky beginning.[120] From 1 to 6 January 1945 the British advanced steadily, threatening to surround ELAS forces remaining in the center of Athens.[121] On the night of 4–5 January, ELAS began a general withdrawal from the Athens-Piraeus area. The evacuation of Piraeus was completed by dawn on 5 January; covered by a determined rearguard, ELAS regular units had cleared Athens by the morning of 6 January, moving northward through Tatoi. The ELAS withdrawal was conducted in good order, and some 15,000 hostages were taken from the city. On 8 January, the British began to pursue ELAS forces to the south toward Corinth and to the north toward Lamia. On 11 January 1945, the ELAS Central Committee requested an armistice, and by 15 January hostilities had ceased. Under the terms of the cease-fire ELAS agreed to evacuate most of southeastern Greece, as well as an area within a twenty-mile radius of Salonika, and to return all ELAS troops to their home areas. It was also agreed that both sides should release all prisoners and hostages. The military defeat of ELAS was accompanied by political defeat, as the EAM coalition of parties began to break up; on 10 January 1945, Dimitrios Stratis' Socialist Party and Elias Tsirimokos' Popular Democratic Union left the EAM coalition.[122] The "Second Round" had been lost. Even so, EAM-ELAS retained control of two-thirds of Greece, and ELAS remained an effective fighting force.

The cost of the revolt in Athens was high for both sides. The British lost some twenty-seven officers and ninety-three other ranks killed, 202 officers and 988 other ranks wounded, and sixteen missing.[123] The actual number of ELAS casualties is unknown, but it was probably quite high. In addition, Greek civilian casualties in the Athens-Piraeus area were heavy. They included some 5,000 persons who were taken hostage by ELAS and subsequently died from exposure, starvation, or summary execution.[124] The Communists were subsequently condemned for the execution and maltreatment of those hostages, but U.S. observers at the time found little to choose between ELAS and the Anglo-Greek forces with respect to the taking of hostages, the maltreatment of prisoners, and even the abuse of Red Cross insignia.[125]

The Varkiza Agreement

Even as the armistice terms were being carried out, ELAS, which had by no means lost its cohesion and which was still well supplied, regrouped its forces and prepared for the resumption of guerrilla warfare. Meanwhile, the political leadership of the KKE and EAM-ELAS prepared for the negotiations that would establish a more permanent reconciliation between EAM-ELAS and the Anglo-Greek government. The negotiations began at a seaside villa in Varkiza, not far from Athens, on 2 February 1945, and by 12 February the opponents had hammered out what came to be known as the Varkiza Agreement.[126] Under the terms of the Agreement and its protocols, martial law was lifted; civil liberties were guaranteed to all Greek citizens; all prisoners and hostages were to be freed; legal prosecution of the December 1944 rebels would be limited to those who had violated the ordinary criminal laws; prosecution of wartime collaborators and war profiteers was to begin at once; ELAS armed forces were to be demobilized within two weeks and were to deposit their weapons in depots that would remain under ELAS control; former ELAS troops, armed with ELAS weapons, were to be included in the new national armed forces; the KKE was recognized as a legal political party and EAM was to be permitted to continue as an organization, although no KKE or EAM representatives would be included in the national government; and a plebiscite on constitutional issues (i.e., the return of the monarchy) and elections would be held within one year.[127] It was also agreed that both the 3d Mountain (Rimini) Brigade and the Sacred Battalion were to be retained on the active rolls, in order that Greece might maintain at least a token force in the continuing war against Germany.[128]

The military protocols prescribing the demobilization of armed resistance forces provided that ELAS was to surrender 41,000 rifles, 2,015 automatic weapons, 163 mortars, and 32 artillery pieces.[129] The OSS reported at the time that ELAS faithfully executed the disarmament provisions of the Varkiza Agreement,

Table 2.3
Arms Surrendered by ELAS under the Varkiza Agreement

Weapon Type	Number Required to Be Surrendered	Number Actually Surrendered
Artillery Pieces	32	100
Mortars	163	219
Heavy Machine guns	315	419
Light Machine guns	1,050	1,412
Light Automatic Weapons	650	713
Rifles and Pistols	41,500	48,953
Antitank Rifles	None	57

Source: Woodhouse, *The Struggle for Greece, 1941–1949*, 104.

and most authorities agree that this was the case.[130] In fact, ELAS handed in more weapons than it was obliged under the Agreement. Table 2.3 provides a comparison of the number of weapons that ELAS was required to surrender and the number actually turned in.

Of course, the weapons turned in by ELAS were its older and less serviceable ones, and a large quantity of weapons and ammunition was cached against the possibility of a resumption of armed conflict.[131] The cached weapons became the nucleus of the armament of the Greek Democratic Army in the "Third Round."

Much to the surprise of the British, EAM-ELAS quickly proceeded to carry out the other terms of the Varkiza Agreement as well, although a few "hard cases," such as Aris Velouchiotis, refused to surrender their arms and fled to the mountains. Many other EAM-ELAS supporters fled to Albania, Yugoslavia, and Bulgaria.[132] By the end of February 1945, ELAS no longer existed. However, the KKE and former members of EAM-ELAS had by no means abandoned their goal of a Greek "democracy" based on Marxist-Leninist principals. With the failure of the "Second Round," the KKE once again reverted to the "soft" policy of attempting to obtain its goals through political means.

CONDITIONS ON THE EVE OF THE "THIRD ROUND"

The Varkiza Agreement of 12 February 1945 provided a temporary respite from open warfare for the first time since the Italian invasion of October 1940, but Greece was a shambles. The country remained politically divided and unstable, subject to the whims and international goals of its powerful Allied liberators and the unresolved rivalries of domestic political groupings—monarchist versus republican, Right versus Left—which went back to the turn of the century. Just below the surface lurked the threat of another attempt by the Communists to impose their political program by force. The most immediate problems, as reported by the OSS, were the formation of a stable government capable of gaining the trust of the majority of the population; the reorganization of the armed forces and civil service; the rehabilitation of agriculture and industry; stabilization of the economic situation, including control of the currency and inflation, unemployment and wages, and restoration of foreign trade; and alleviation of the suffering of the Greek people.[133] A rapid succession of weak governments made it impossible to address the pressing economic and social problems in any constructive way, and the Greek people only eked out a meager existence by virtue of international charity. As one contemporary witness observed, "The situation in Greece in 1945 was such that survival was very difficult. Passions and hatreds were excited. Weaknesses were inevitable and good administration was impossible."[134]

Political Instability

From the summer of 1945 to November of 1946, eight governments attempted to rule in Greece, and all proved incapable of reconciling the virulent political hatreds or mastering the pressing economic and social problems; weakness, incompetence, and corruption were their prevailing characteristics.[135] Gen. Nicholas Plastiras, who had replaced George Papandreou as prime minister on 4 January 1945, was unable to bring order to the political and economic chaos. Following an unsuccessful attempt to prevent the new National Guard from falling totally under the control of right-wing elements, he was replaced by Adm. Petros Voulgaris in the spring of 1945. From that point on, the Greek national government moved steadily to the right, and the Liberals and other centrist groups thus found themselves unwillingly drifting toward alliance with the Left against an increasingly repressive regime. The right-wing royalist Populist Party led by Constantine Tsaldaris was reestablished in Athens on 17 February 1945, under British sponsorship. Many well-to-do Greeks, who had formerly supported the more moderate Venizelist Liberal Party, began to switch their allegiance to the more extreme right-wing groups.[136] The Populists presented the king (whose return from exile they championed) and themselves as the bulwark against hordes of Communists, "Slavs," and "Eamo-Bulgarians" supposedly poised to seize the government by force and enslave the Greek people.[137]

By mid-1945, the situation had become intolerable, particularly for the KKE. In May of 1945, the Allies had found the former leader of the KKE, Nikos Zachariades, in the German concentration camp at Dachau and had returned him to Greece. With apparent ease, Zachariades resumed the leadership of the Greek Communist movement from the men, like George Siantos, who had guided it through the difficult occupation period. Having reluctantly agreed to lay down their arms and abide by the terms of the Varkiza Agreement, the KKE and other leftist groups felt that they had been tricked by the rightist elements that controlled the national government, and they forcefully condemned the growing right-wing oppression of "democrats" and former EAM-ELAS "people's democratic fighters," as well as the failure of the Greek government to deal decisively with wartime collaborators.[138] The substance of leftist complaints was borne out by unbiased American observers and even by official British delegations that visited Greece to examine the situation.[139] Although the KKE remained officially committed to the establishment of a more equitable social order in Greece by peaceful means, in a speech to the Seventh Party Congress of the KKE on 4 October 1945 Zachariades predicted that "if this mess continues, every Greek will have to take to the hills."[140]

In the fall of 1945, following a period in which the regent, Archbishop Damaskinos, held the premiership himself, the aged Liberal politician Themistocles Sofoulis became prime minister, with British support. Sofoulis, whose political career had begun before the turn of the century, resisted the temptation to accommodate Communist complaints during the winter and early spring of 1946. The elections called for by the Varkiza Agreement were finally held on 31 March 1946, under the supervision of an Allied Mission for Observing the Greek Elections (AMFOGE), headed by U.S. major general Harry Maloney.[141] The result was a striking victory for the Right, and the Venizelist Sofoulis was succeeded by Constantine Tsaldaris, the leader of the Populist Party. AMFOGE declared the elections substantially "free and fair" with a high percentage of participation by the Greek electorate, but the KKE and other leftist and even liberal-centrist elements maintained that the election had been accompanied by "rightist terrorism" and that the results were consequently "a fraud."[142]

Prime Minister Tsaldaris persistently pushed the government toward the right. In June 1946, he successfully rammed through the Greek parliament a bill that suspended civil rights and in effect put Greece under martial law. He also pushed for an early plebiscite on the return of King George II to Greece. The plebiscite was finally held on 1 September 1946, and 69 percent of those voting approved the king's return.[143] The Right was victorious on all fronts.

Economic and Social Conditions

Greece's recovery from the devastation of the Second World War and Axis occupation lagged far behind that of the rest of Europe. The OSS reported in February 1945 that "Greece's requirements for economic rehabilitation are so enormous as to imperil the survival of any government."[144] Food, clothing, building materials, seeds and agricultural machinery, livestock, machinery and raw materials for industry, a stable currency, and the alleviation of unemployment—all were lacking. The litany of economic devastation and dislocation left by the war and occupation was long, and there seemed to be little anyone could do to correct the situation. One historian has summed up the situation in a single brief paragraph:

The economic devastation caused by the German occupation was enormous, in the range of $8.5 billion. Over two thousand villages were burnt or razed to the ground. Industry, foreign trade, and exports all came to a standstill. Land communications were thrown into a state of almost complete chaos. Three-quarters of the vessels of the Greek mercantile marine were sunk. The printing press produced enormous numbers of Greek money notes, setting off one of the wildest inflations of modern times and ruining the economy. Shortly after the liberation of Greece, the gold sovereign was equivalent to 170,000,000,000,000 drachmas. The drachma, in fact, had ceased to have any real value as a means of exchange. The resulting distrust of the drachma caused the Greek people to become "incorrigibly gold-minded," and the gold sovereign became the prevalent currency.[145]

The four and a half years of war and occupation had all but destroyed the Greek economy. A significant proportion of the Greek peasantry were refugees in the cities, and agricultural production had fallen to less than 85 percent of prewar levels.[146] Over a million peasants were homeless and lacked the means to cultivate their fields.[147] Foreign markets had been lost. The Axis occupation authorities had stripped Greece of what little modern industrial equipment it had possessed—and what remained was broken, worn out, or simply obsolete.[148] The transportation infrastructure was in total disarray, and the fishing, mining, and forestry industries had been all but destroyed.[149] The government had no reserves, and receipts were minimal. Inflation, speculation, and black market activities were rampant, and the drachma worthless. Unemployment was the rule rather than the exception.

The Greek people, nearly 700,000 of whom were refugees, lacked the basic necessities of life: shelter, food, clothing, and medical care. About 8 percent of the Greek population of seven million had died during the four and a half years of war, ten times the death rate for Britain during the same period.[150] Sanitation conditions were deplorable, and the health of those who had survived the war was imperiled by a resurgence of malaria and tuberculosis, the lack of medicines and medical materials, inadequate diet, and the breakdown of preventive measures. One-fourth of the villages had been burned, and over 100,000 buildings destroyed or heavily damaged.[151] Many rural Greeks had become refugees during the war and occupation; most had fled to the urban areas, which were unable to absorb them. They lived in the most abject poverty, without work or the prospect of improvement in their situation. An equal number, the families of dead or still-serving soldiers, were supported by the state; in all, 34 percent of the Greek population was directly dependent on the national government for the essentials of existence.[152]

Modern Greece had never been able to feed its own population, and the wartime destruction of the Greek transportation infrastructure made the distribution of even the most essential supplies difficult. Famine was narrowly averted in 1945 only by massive aid provided by the Allies and the United Nations Relief and Rehabilitation Administration (UNRRA). In the second half of 1945 alone, UNRRA delivered to Greece some $171 million in goods ($100 million in food, $14 million in seed and agricultural equipment, $21 million in clothing,

$26 million in industrial rehabilitation materials, and $10 million in medical and public sanitation materials).[153] In the first year after the liberation, over 1.7 million tons of food were provided by UNRRA and the Allies; even so, a minimum daily ration of 2,000 calories proved impossible.[154] Without the help of the Allies, the newly formed United Nations, and private assistance from overseas Greeks, "1945 would have been a year of famine. It was instead a year of great misery."[155]

The Resumption of Violence

Political instability in the capital and terrible economic conditions everywhere in Greece provided the background for increased violence throughout the country, motivated both by current hardships and lingering hatreds sparked by the war and occupation. Major Woodhouse notes, "Misery and hardship naturally found an outlet in violence, especially as the provinces were burdened by several thousand unemployed ex-guerrillas whose only training was in the use of arms."[156] Common banditry, a long-standing Greek tradition, increased, and the struggle for mere existence was made more difficult by roaming bands of hungry, angry men. The situation was exacerbated by the continuing conflict between Right and Left. Right-wing groups, such as Grivas' X, sought to root out the former supporters of EAM-ELAS, who retaliated in kind.[157] A few of the EAM-ELAS bands that had refused to demobilize after the Varkiza Agreement, notably that commanded by Aris Velouchiotis, continued to operate in the mountains, the condemnation of the KKE notwithstanding.[158] Thus, by the fall of 1946, large numbers of Greeks, most of whom were liberal patriots and not thugs, once again found themselves in arms against the government in Athens.

The Greeks are a proud and resilient people, inured to hardship and the consequences of political, economic, and social instability. However, the internal conflicts and inequities that the Second World War, the Axis occupation, and the postwar restoration of a repressive rightist government brought to the surface could not long be contained, and some final resolution was imperative. Thus, by the fall of 1946 the stage was set for the final act of the civil war begun by EAM-ELAS three years earlier. The "Third Round" had already begun.

NOTES

1. Floyd A. Spencer, *War and Postwar Greece: An Analysis Based on Greek Writings* (Washington: European Affairs Division, Library of Congress, 1952), 43.

2. Christopher Montague Woodhouse, *The Struggle for Greece, 1941–1949* (London: Hart-Davis, MacGibbon, 1976), 102–103.

3. Edgar O'Ballance, *The Greek Civil War, 1944–1949* (New York: Praeger, 1966), 55.

4. Spencer, 42–43.

5. Hugh H. Gardner, *Guerrilla and Counterguerrilla Warfare in Greece, 1941–1945*

(Draft) (Washington: Office of the Chief of Military History, Department of the Army, 1962), 14–17.

6. Allison Butler Herrick and others, *Area Handbook for Greece*, DA Pam 550–87 (Washington: USGPO, June 1970), 301 [cited hereafter as *Area Handbook*].

7. O'Ballance, 60.

8. Gardner, 17.

9. O'Ballance, 51.

10. Spencer, 43.

11. Stephen Merrill, *The Communist Attack on Greece*, Special Report No. 15, 21st Regular Course, U.S. Strategic Intelligence School (Washington: U.S. Strategic Intelligence School, 28 July 1952), 13.

12. William Hardy McNeill, *The Greek Dilemma: War and Aftermath* (Philadelphia: J. B. Lippincott, 1947), 72–73. The original members of EAM included the KKE, the Agrarian Party of Gavrielides, the United Socialist Party, the Republican Party, the Union of Popular Democracy, the Socialist Party, and elements of the old Liberal Party. Only the Union of Popular Democracy, led by Elias Tsirimokos, and the Socialist Party, which drew its strength from the labor movement, were truly independent of the KKE.

13. O'Ballance, 49–50.

14. Yiannis P. Roubatis, *Tangled Webs: The U.S. in Greece, 1947–1967* (New York: Pella, 1987), 13.

15. *Area Handbook*, 40; O'Ballance, 51; Merrill, 14. Aris ("Ares" or "Mars") Velouchiotis was the nom de guerre of Athanasios Klaras. Trained as an agricultural expert, Klaras was jailed by the Metaxas regime but escaped in the confusion of 1941. He was perhaps the most radical of the ELAS leaders.

16. O'Ballance, 51.

17. Gardner, 18–19 and 43.

18. Ibid., 45.

19. O'Ballance, 75.

20. Gardner, 20.

21. O'Ballance, 82.

22. Stephanos Saraphis had served as an officer in World War I and in the Greek campaigns in Asia Minor. He was exiled after the failed republican coup in 1935 but was allowed to return to Greece in 1940, although he was not permitted to serve again. Saraphis survived the war, only to be imprisoned by the Greek government, and thus he played no role in the civil war of 1945–1949. He told the story of his wartime experiences as commander of ELAS in *Greek Resistance Army: The Story of ELAS* (London: Birch Books, 1951). Saraphis was elected to the Greek parliament in the mid-1950s but was killed on 31 May 1957, when he and his wife were run down on the main road between Athens and Glyfada by a young American airman stationed in Greece. At the time, left-wing elements in Greece claimed that Saraphis' death was part of a right-wing government/CIA plot. I was living in Athens at the time and knew the airman involved, Mike Muselli, quite well. I am convinced the event was just what the authorities said it was—an unfortunate accident caused by inattentive driving on the airman's part and a lack of caution by the elderly Saraphis, who stepped from in front of a bus into the path of the airman's car.

23. O'Ballance, 58–59.

24. Gardner, 19–20. ELAS eventually included sixteen generals, thirty-four colonels, and 1,500 other commissioned officers of the prewar Greek Army.

25. Evangelos Averoff-Tossizza, *By Fire and Axe: The Communist Party and the Civil War in Greece, 1944–1949* (New Rochelle, NY: Caratzas Brothers, 1978), 85; O'Ballance, 59 and 61. Tzimas, who was also known as Vasilis Samariniotis (by which name he is referred to in Saraphis' memoir), was a native of Kastoria and a Slav by ancestry but was educated as a Greek. He became the recognized leader of the Macedonian autonomy movement. In the fall of 1943, he was sent to Tito's headquarters in Yugoslavia as the chief ELAS representative (see McNeill, 263).

26. The administrative and tactical organizations of ELAS are described by O'Ballance (pages 59–74), whose account I have followed closely.

27. Gardner, 104. The ELAS Central Command, not to be confused with the ELAS GHQ in the field, was closely controlled by the EAM Central Committee.

28. Ibid., 34–36.

29. Ibid., 170.

30. Ibid., 47.

31. O'Ballance, 66.

32. Ibid., 61.

33. Ibid., 82.

34. Woodhouse, 58.

35. Gardner, 169.

36. O'Ballance, 71.

37. Gardner, 46–47.

38. Ibid., 47. The British supplied ELAS' rival, EDES, with several mountain guns, which were delivered by sea to EDES forces holding the coast of Epirus.

39. Ibid., 46.

40. Ibid., 134. The situation became so bad that the Germans threatened to shoot any Italian soldier who came in without his weapon.

41. Ibid., 132–34.

42. Woodhouse, 57; O'Ballance, 67; Gardner, 132–34.

43. Gardner, 170.

44. Gardner, 38–39. ELAS had few trained medical personnel, and few civilian doctors were available in the mountains. As a consequence, medical treatment tended to be rather primitive. Survival rates for wounded guerrillas were about the same as they had been for the *andartes* of the War for Independence in the early nineteenth century.

45. Ibid., 53.

46. The principal purpose of EPON was to "mobilize" Greek youth in support of EAM-ELAS for propaganda purposes (see Gardner, 54).

47. O'Ballance, 61–62. In October 1943, EPON was integrated into ELAS proper.

48. Gardner, 55. The *Ipefthirios* ("The Responsible") was the chief EAM local official. Despite its Communist ideological basis, EAM-ELAS did not actively oppose religion, a policy that was expedient in view of the prestige of the village priest in Greek society.

49. O'Ballance, 71.

50. Ibid., 77. O'Ballance (p. 53) notes: "Whilst being slavishly loyal to Soviet ideals to the extent of trying to import Red Army customs, drill and military practices into ELAS, the Greek KKE had no contact at all with Moscow, its former tenuous and unreliable links being abruptly severed by the Axis Occupation of the Balkans."

51. Their principal purpose may have been to make an evaluation of ELAS with a view to providing material aid, but ELAS hopes in that respect were dashed (see

Lawrence S. Wittner, *American Intervention in Greece, 1943–1949* [New York: Columbia University Press, 1982], 8–9). The Russian military mission remained in Greece throughout the 1945–1949 civil war without making any gesture, in word or deed, to support the Communists (see McNeill, 145).

52. John O. Iatrides, *Revolt in Athens: The Greek Communist "Second Round," 1944–1945* (Princeton, NJ: Princeton University Press, 1972), 75, notes that Popov could not supply his own team with vodka, much less supply ELAS with gold or equipment.

53. Woodhouse, 92.

54. O'Ballance, 77; Woodhouse, 90. The Soviet Union declared war on Bulgaria on 5 September 1944, and by 9 September Bulgaria was in Soviet hands and a pro-Soviet puppet government was in power. The Bulgarian Communists soon declared their intention to continue the annexation of the areas of Macedonia and Thrace then under Bulgarian control (see Woodhouse, 93–94).

55. The organization and growth of EDES is discussed in O'Ballance, 53–59, and Gardner, 20–23 and 42.

56. Amikam Nachmani, *International Intervention in the Greek Civil War: The United Nations Special Committee on the Balkans, 1947–1952* (Westport, CT: Praeger, 1990), 2. The British feared that the strength of EAM-ELAS would result in a Communist takeover in Greece. Consequently, British support for EDES was somewhat more generous than for ELAS.

57. Frank J. Abbott, *The Greek Civil War, 1947–1949: Lessons for the Operational Artist in Foreign Internal Defense*, School of Advanced Military Studies thesis (Fort Leavenworth, KS: School of Advanced Military Studies, USACGSC, May 1994), 4.

58. Gardner, 132. As with ELAS, the conventional structure was mostly show, inasmuch as the regiments and battalions never achieved anywhere near the strength or combat power their titles would imply.

59. *Area Handbook*, 301. German estimates of EDES strength were in the range of 7,000–8,000 men; British estimates ranged from 5,000 to 12,000 (with as many as 5,000 reserves). See Woodhouse, 77.

60. Gardner, 22. The political leader of EKKA was Kartalis, a republican.

61. O'Ballance, 58; Gardner, 23. The remnants of the armed AAA forces were destroyed by ELAS in May 1943 (see O'Ballance, 64).

62. McNeill, 89–90. Grivas later became infamous as the leader of EOKA, the Greek nationalist guerrilla force fighting against the British and Turks for *enosis*, the unification of Cyprus with Greece.

63. O'Ballance, 60; Gardner, 22–23.

64. Gardner, 22. The X organization later achieved some degree of success in the Peloponnesus, particularly during the immediate postwar period.

65. O'Ballance, 60.

66. Gardner, 24.

67. O'Ballance, 76–77. Gotchev (also known as Gotsi or Gotseff) was a native of Florina, a Slav by birth and a baker by trade.

68. O'Ballance, 77; McNeill, 264–65.

69. Gardner, 24; Woodhouse, 77.

70. Gardner, 25–26. The Salonika-Athens/Piraeus rail line was estimated to be carrying about 80 percent of Rommel's supplies (see Gardner, 67).

71. Spencer, 44. Velouchiotis was very loathe to risk his fragile force in such hazardous operations (see O'Ballance, 56–57).

72. Gardner, 66–67. SOE-Cairo had a somewhat troubled history; it lacked the authority and resources needed to carry out its mission, was subject to conflicting military and civilian chains of command, and was reorganized a number of times.

73. Woodhouse, 103–104. Of the total, 4,090 tons were delivered by sea and 1,706 tons by air (paradrop).

74. Ibid., 103. ELAS received perhaps half of the total.

75. Ibid., 42. The pledge was part of the National Bands Agreement, concluded at Cairo in July 1943. The gold sovereign had a purchasing power of about five pounds sterling (roughly $100 at 1943 exchange rates).

76. Ibid., 43.

77. Saraphis, 278. These figures are consistent with the overall delivery by the British of less than 1,000 tons of arms and ammunition to all the Greek resistance groups. They also represent less than one-tenth of the number of weapons surrendered by ELAS in 1945 after the Varkiza Agreement, thereby lending credence to Communist claims that they had obtained the greater part of their weaponry from their Italian, German, and Bulgarian enemies (see Woodhouse, 104).

78. O'Ballance, 85–86. The British were not adverse to supporting a Communist-led guerrilla movement per se, as their support of Tito's partisans in Yugoslavia attests.

79. The question is discussed by, inter alia: O'Ballance, 75–76 and 80; Spencer, 86; Woodhouse, 47.

80. O'Ballance, 64.

81. Gardner, 134. Saraphis also opposed Woodhouse because he was not a regular army officer (see Woodhouse, 64).

82. Woodhouse, 56.

83. There is a good deal of evidence to suggest that Zervas and EDES did in fact cooperate with the Germans from time to time in furtherance of their own interests. However, the morally superior pose of ELAS was unwarranted: ELAS, too, often betrayed the plans and movements of its rivals to the Germans, as General Zervas was quick to point out (see Woodhouse, 90).

84. Woodhouse, 56–57.

85. Ibid., 57.

86. O'Ballance, 83.

87. The text of the agreement is given in Iatrides, 291–93.

88. Iatrides, 65.

89. Woodhouse, 58.

90. Ibid.

91. Gardner, 166; United States Military Attaché–Greece (Maj. E. A. Tidmarsh), Intelligence Report R-110–49, ID No. 542941, Athens, 22 March 1949, subject: Organization of the Bandit Forces and Tactics Employed by the Bandits. In File GEOG. L. Greece 370.64 (Guerrillas), General Reference Branch, United States Army Center of Military History, Washington, DC. Bakirdzis, like Stephanos Saraphis, was a former regular officer of the Greek Army. For all practical purposes, the PEEA and the Provisional Government of Free Greece were identical. In the Lebanon Charter of 20 May 1944, EAM agreed to dissolve the PEEA/Provisional Government in the mountains once the EAM ministers took their places in the Government of National Unity (see McNeill, 144).

92. Gardner, 166–67.

93. Ibid., 168. Actually, the political commissars simply assumed military rank and

remained on the staffs of their units. The ELAS Central Command (Committee) was revived in December 1944 to control ELAS forces in the revolt in Athens.

94. The incident is described in McNeill, 127–30, and Merrill, 16–17.

95. Woodhouse, 94–95. In point of fact, ELAS and EDES agreed to place their forces under the direction of the Government of National Unity, with the understanding that the Papandreou government would in turn place them under General Scobie. The exact degree of control ceded to General Scobie was unclear and later became an important point of disagreement between ELAS and the British commander. The text of the Caserta Agreement is reproduced in Iatrides, 311–13.

96. McNeill, 150.

97. Saraphis, 276. The totals do not include ELAS personnel in the Athens area, Samos, or Mytilene (Lesbos), figures Saraphis claimed not to know.

98. O'Ballance, 91.

99. Spencer, 78.

100. Ibid.

101. Ibid., 79.

102. The Germans made particular use of the Security Battalions against ELAS. EAM had requested the Greek government-in-exile to condemn the Security Battalions, which it refused to do. See United States, Office of Strategic Services, Research and Analysis Branch, *The Present Balance of Political Forces in Greece*, Research and Analysis No. 2862 (Washington: Research and Analysis Branch, Office of Strategic Services, 27 February 1945), 28 [cited hereafter as OSS R&A No. 2862].

103. OSS R&A No. 2862, 26. After the end of the "Second Round," on 21 February 1945, twenty-five of the thirty-three Greeks who had served as ministers in the collaborationist government finally went on trial, but the trials were disrupted after only two days by right-wing protests (see OSS R&A No. 2862, 28).

104. C. M. Woodhouse in foreword to O'Ballance, 13–14. The "soft" approach of political infiltration and subversion, as opposed to outright seizure of power by force of arms, was advocated chiefly by George Siantos, the General Secretary of the KKE.

105. William Hardy McNeill in foreword to Iatrides, xi–xii; Spencer, 81.

106. OSS R&A No. 2862, iii.

107. Spencer, 83.

108. OSS R&A No. 2862, 2. The question of which side fired first remains unresolved, although it appears that the initiative was taken by the right-wing Greek police. Some of the casualties resulted from similar incidents of police attacks on civilians on 3–4 December.

109. Quoted in Iatrides, 227.

110. Saraphis, 304.

111. Ibid.

112. United States Military Attaché–Greece (Lt. Col. Sterling Larrabee), Report No. 128, Athens, 4 January 1945, subject: The Battle for Athens, in File GEOG. L. GREECE 370.2 (Athens), General Reference Branch, U.S. Army Center of Military History, Washington, DC.

113. Force 133 was the British Special Operations Executive (SOE) organization in Cairo (later in Bari) which controlled British liaison officers attached to the various Greek and Yugoslav guerrilla groups. The U.S. Office of Strategic Services (OSS) was created in June 1942 and was directed by William J. Donovan. It was the American counterpart of the British SOE. The OSS Special Operations Branch conducted subversion, sabotage,

and intelligence missions in the countries occupied by Axis forces and provided support to resistance movements. OSS operations in Greece began in mid-1943 with the infiltration of some 300 OSS agents into occupied Greece. See I.C.B. Dear (General Editor), *The Oxford Companion to World War II* (Oxford: Oxford University Press, 1995), 379 and 832–835.

114. Iatrides, 225, quoting Nikos Zachariades, *For a Lasting Peace! For a People's Democracy!* (Bucharest: 15 November 1948).

115. Details of the end of EDES are given in O'Ballance, 104–105, and OSS R&A No. 2862, 3. See also United States Military Attaché–Greece (Capt. William H. McNeill, Assistant Military Attaché), Report No. 127, Athens, 3 January 1945, subject: The Campaign in Epirus, 19–30 December 1944, in File GEOG. L. Greece 370.2 (Epirus), General Reference Branch, U.S. Army Center of Military History, Washington, DC.

116. Some 7,000 EDES fighters and 7,000 civilians were evacuated from Preveza and Levkas to Corfu by the British (see U.S. Military Attaché–Greece, Report No. 127).

117. The fighting is described by O'Ballance, 102–104.

118. United States Military Attaché–Greece (Capt. William H. McNeill, Assistant Military Attaché), Report No. 124, Athens, 3 January 1945, subject: British Operations in Athens-Piraeus, 27 December–1 January, in File GEOG. L. GREECE 370.2 (Athens), General Reference Branch, U.S. Army Center of Military History, Washington, DC; O'Ballance, 103.

119. McNeill, 103. Archbishop Damaskinos, who had once been a professional wrestler, held generally republican views, and he had avoided the internecine struggles during the occupation by concentrating on the care of his flock. He was thus a candidate acceptable to both sides (see McNeill, 192–93).

120. OSS R&A No. 2862, 3.

121. The final stages of the battle were reported in United States Military Attaché–Greece (Capt. William H. McNeill, Assistant Military Attaché), Report No. 138, Athens, 7 January 1945, subject: British Operations in Athens-Piraeus, 1–6 January 1945, in File GEOG. L. GREECE 370.2 (Athens), General Reference Branch, U.S. Army Center of Military History, Washington, DC. See also Gardner, 212–13.

122. O'Ballance, 108.

123. Gardner, 213.

124. Ibid.

125. OSS, R&A No. 2862, 6. See also Spencer, 83–85.

126. EAM was represented by Siantos, Partsalidis, and Tsirimokos. Generals Plastiras and Scobie represented the Greek government and the British, respectively. The British resident minister, Harold Macmillan, and the British ambassador to Greece, Sir Reginald Leeper, joined the conference on the last day to break a deadlock (see Woodhouse, 137). The terms of the Varkiza Agreement of 12 February 1945 are summarized in OSS R&A No. 2862 (p. 9). The text of the agreement is reproduced in Iatrides, 320–24.

127. OSS R&A No. 2862, 9.

128. O'Ballance, 112.

129. Woodhouse, 137.

130. OSS R&A No. 2862, 18.

131. See, inter alia: O'Ballance, 114; Merrill, 19; Abbott, 7; Gardner, 215.

132. The number of Communists and other EAM-ELAS *supporters* who fled to neighboring countries is put by Dimitrios G. Kousoulas (*The Price of Freedom: Greece in World Affairs, 1939–1953* [Syracuse, NY: Syracuse University Press, 1953], 149) at

23,000 to Albania, 20,000 to Yugoslavia, and 5,000 to Bulgaria. Abbott (p. 7) puts the total number of ELAS supporters who left Greece "to receive military training in Yugoslavia" at 40,000. O'Ballance (p. 113) puts the number of ELAS *fighters* who crossed over into Albania, Yugoslavia, and Bulgaria at about 4,000. Perhaps another 4,000 former ELAS guerrillas elected to return to the mountains with such unrepentant leaders as Aris Velouchiotis (see M. A. Campbell, E. W. Downs, and L. V. Schuetta, *The Employment of Airpower in the Greek Guerrilla War, 1947–1949*, Project No. AU-411–62-ASI [Maxwell Air Force Base, AL: Concepts Division, Aerospace Studies Institute, U.S. Air University, December 1964], 2–3; Robert W. Selton, "Communist Errors in the Anti-Bandit War," *Military Review* 45, no. 9 [September 1965], 68). Perhaps the best estimate is that of Woodhouse (p. 140), who puts the number of those who fled across the borders at "about 8,000 Greeks and also about 8,000 Slavo-Macedonians in the first phase, followed by nearly 20,000 more people later in the year."

133. OSS R&A No. 2862, iv.

134. Averoff-Tossizza, 148.

135. Nachmani, 5.

136. OSS R&A No. 2862, 12–13.

137. Spencer, 102, Eamo-Bulgarians were those Bulgarians who supported the Communist-dominated National Liberation Front (EAM).

138. Ibid., 92. Brought to trial in the spring of 1945, the most notorious collaborators were exonerated. The depredations of the Axis-supported Security Battalions were excused as the acts of men simply doing "their patriotic duty by the maintenance of law and order in Greece against 'anarchists and terrorists.' "

139. Ibid., 99.

140. Quoted in Woodhouse, 163.

141. Spencer, 94–96. The election observer teams had a mixture of Allied military personnel, but the majority of the observers were drawn from the U.S. 94th Infantry Division, which Maloney had commanded in the European theater. See *Report of the Allied Mission to Observe the Greek Elections* (Department of State Publication No. 2522, Washington: USGPO, 1946).

142. Ibid., 96.

143. Nachmani, 5.

144. OSS R&A No. 2862, 22.

145. Nachmani, 7–8.

146. United States Central Intelligence Agency, *Current Situation in Greece (ORE 28-48)* (Washington: Central Intelligence Agency, 17 November 1948), 7.

147. Stephen G. Xydis, *The Economy and Finances of Greece under Occupation* (New York: Greek Government Office of Information, n.d.), 11.

148. Ibid., 47.

149. Between 1940 and 1945, almost one-fifth of Greece's standing timber (some three million acres) was cut down, and in some areas three-quarters of the forests were destroyed (see Xydis, 47; Nachmani, 2).

150. Nachmani, 1. Not only had innumerable Greeks lost their lives in the four and a half years of war and occupation, but there had also been a great decline in the birth rate (see Xydis, 47).

151. Xydis, 47. In July 1944, it was officially estimated that of the 1,736,000 buildings existing in Greece before the war, 106,000 had been destroyed or damaged. Of course, the December 1945 fighting in the Athens-Piraeus area increased the total substantially.

Averoff-Tossizza (p. 148) put the total of buildings destroyed or damaged at 400,000, nearly one-fourth the total number of prewar structures.

152. Nachmani, 8.

153. McNeill, 205. A large proportion of the goods supplied by UNRRA were siphoned off into the black market or hoarded by speculators, and economic aid provided by the Allies was wasted on useless "foreign missions" or the importation of luxury goods that only the ruling classes could afford (see Nachmani, 5; Dominique Eudes, *The Kapetanios: Partisans and Civil War in Greece, 1943–1949* [New York: Monthly Review Press, 1972], 276).

154. McNeill, 205; OSS R&A No. 2862, 23. The UNRRA provided 1.4 million tons of food, and the Allied Military Liaison provided another 387,000 tons.

155. Averoff-Tossizza, 148.

156. Woodhouse, 162.

157. O'Ballance, 115; Woodhouse, 163. The chief blame for the escalating cycle of violence rested with the right-wing groups, such as X, which reached its peak strength of over 200,000 supporters in January 1946. At the time, the KKE was still officially trying to work within the political system.

158. Woodhouse, 140–41 and 163. Aris Velouchiotis was ambushed by government forces near Arta on 16 June 1945 and apparently killed himself. There is some evidence to support the theory that he was betrayed by the KKE, which had formally denounced him on 12 June, but O'Ballance (p. 115) states that Aris was fingered by X.

3

Internal Conflict in the Greek Communist Party, 1945–1949

One of the most strongly held Cold War myths was the belief in a monolithic, worldwide Communist conspiracy directed from Moscow—uniform in its objectives, organization, and methods, and aimed at the overthrow of democratic states by force of arms. In no case was this belief less true than in the Greek civil war of 1945–1949. Not only did the Greek Communist Party (KKE) receive little or no guidance or material assistance from the Soviet Union, but the KKE was itself in crisis—split into competing factions, each with its own idea of the course to be followed. The rift within the KKE and its military arm, the Greek Democratic Army (GDA), makes the story of the Greek civil war a striking object lesson in what happens to an armed revolutionary movement when it is divided against itself on such basic matters as foreign policy and the organization and employment of its military capabilities.

Formed in 1918, the Greek Communist Party survived the turbulent Greek political environment of the 1920s and 1930s, the Metaxas dictatorship, and the Axis occupation of the Second World War, as well as two previous rounds of civil war. It was organized on traditional Communist principles of hierarchical structure, centralized control and decision making, infiltration of civil and military organizations at every level, and small underground cells in neighborhoods and workplaces. The KKE languished during the pre–World War II period, expanded tremendously in membership and influence during the resistance to Axis occupation from 1941 to 1944, and contracted again following the unsuccessful "Second Round" in December 1944–January 1945. By mid-1946 the KKE, operating openly as a legal political party but under heavy pressure from Greek right-wing elements, had moved toward armed rebellion. Its underground activities were intensified, and in those areas under KKE control, local administrations were established with quasi-governmental fiscal, security, and judicial functions. In December 1947, the KKE set up a Provisional Democratic Government of Free Greece in the mountains of northwestern Greece for the purpose of administering Greek territory under Communist control. This "shadow government" collapsed with the failure of the Communist-led military campaign against the Greek national government in August 1949.

Aside from a lack of genuine mass support, the greatest weakness of the KKE during the period 1945–1949 lay in the degree to which the party was divided by often bitter disagreements over policy and the role of its military arm. This division was exemplified during the "Third Round" by the conflict between the party leader, Nikos Zachariades, a hard-line Stalinist ideologue, and the military leader of the Communist forces, Markos Vafiades, a more pragmatic, "nationalist" leader. The split in the leadership of the KKE/GDA was reflected in the series of key political and military decisions taken after the Varkiza Agreement of February 1945. Within the KKE/GDA, the pro-Cominform (Communist Information Bureau) faction led by Zachariades held the stronger hand.[1] Each successive decision, although bitterly disputed by Vafiades on practical grounds, was shaped by Zachariades' largely theoretical and ideological approach and served either to alienate the Greek Communist rebels from their sources of internal and external support or to force their military forces farther into an ideological mold that made them at once harder to support and less effective. The dominance of Zachariades and the ideologues also led directly to the dismissal of Vafiades and the purge of his supporters—the most able of the GDA's military leaders.

Among the more important of the ill-fated choices made by the KKE leadership were the decisions to support Stalin and the Cominform on the question of Macedonian autonomy and in the dispute with Tito and the Yugoslavian Communist Party. The former cost the KKE/GDA what little popular support it still had among the Greek people and its own fighters. The second alienated their chief supporter, Marshal Tito, and led him finally to cut off all aid to the GDA. The most fateful choice, made in February 1947 but not announced formally until September of that year, was the decision to create a conventional army, with which to challenge the Greek national government directly in an all-out armed struggle for power. The decision to form and fight a conventional force profoundly affected all aspects of the development of the GDA—organization, strategy, and tactics—and placed upon the fragile logistical support system of the GDA a burden it could not sustain. Thus, the internal conflicts within the KKE and GDA led directly to its defeat in the summer of 1949 and the end of the Communist attempt to seize political power in Greece by force.

ORGANIZATION OF THE GREEK COMMUNIST PARTY, 1945–1949

The post–World War II Communist Party of Greece was organized along traditional Communist lines, with a hierarchical structure running from small, often clandestine, cells at the lowest levels, through district and regional organizations, to a centralized directorate, consisting of a Central Committee com-

Figure 3.1
Organization of the Greek Communist Party, 1945–1949

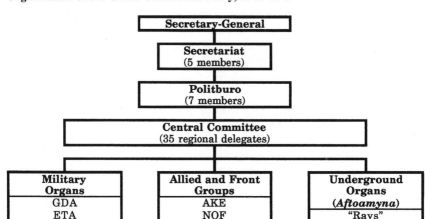

```
                    ┌──────────────────────────┐
                    │     Secretary-General     │
                    └──────────────────────────┘
                      ┌──────────────────────┐
                      │      Secretariat      │
                      │      (5 members)      │
                      └──────────────────────┘
                    ┌──────────────────────────┐
                    │        Politburo          │
                    │       (7 members)         │
                    └──────────────────────────┘
        ┌──────────────────────────────────────────────┐
        │            Central Committee                   │
        │         (35 regional delegates)                │
        └──────────────────────────────────────────────┘
```

Military Organs	Allied and Front Groups	Underground Organs (*Aftoamyna*)
GDA	AKE	"Rays"
ETA	NOF	*Yiafaka*
Local Civil Guard	KOEN	KOSSA
	OENA	
	EPON	
	PDEG	
	KEN	

Source: U.S. Army Command and General Staff College, *Internal Defense Operations: A Case History, Greece 1946–49*, 129, Figure 17.

posed of delegates of the thirty-five regional party organs. The activities of the Central Committee were supervised in turn by a small six or seven-member Politburo, made up of the most important party members, each a leader in his home region. At the very top of the party structure was an even more elite five-member Secretariat, directed by the General Secretary of the KKE. Supporting this formal structure was a large number of allied parties and front organizations that carried out the day-to-day organizing, recruitment, and propaganda work of the party. The general organization of the KKE is shown in Figure 3.1.

Theoretically, major decisions on party policy and discipline were entrusted to the Central Committee meeting periodically in plenary session (known as a "plenum"). In practice, the Politburo, dominated by the General Secretary, ran the party, and the plenums of the Central Committee served to rubber-stamp their decisions. At the Twelfth Plenum of the Central Committee of the KKE, held in Athens on 25–27 June 1945, a new six-member Politburo was elected consisting of Nikos Zachariades as General Secretary and George Siantos, Yiannis Ioannides, Dimitrios Partsalides, Vassilios Bartzotas, and Khryssa Khatzivassiliou as members.[2] From time to time, the party convened a general congress of its members, but these affairs were largely "pep rallies" and showcases for lauding the achievements of the party leadership, real or imagined.

The KKE worked with and through a number of allied political movements and parties, and also a wide range of front organizations incorporating Greek youth, women, labor, and other categories. Among the most prominent of the groups allied to the KKE was the Slavo-Macedonian National Liberation Front (NOF). Several other political groups, including the Communist Organization of Greek Macedonia (KOEN), a Slav-Macedonian organization known as OENA, and the Greek Agrarian Party (AKE), were fully controlled by the KKE.[3] The wartime political front organization, EAM, also continued to function for some time after the Varkiza Agreement of February 1945. The KKE also established front organizations in a variety of social and quasi-political areas. Among the most active were the Democratic Women's Organization of Greece (PDEG) and the National All-Greek Organization of Youth (EPON) KKE organizers were especially active in the Greek labor movement, and the KKE controlled such labor groups as the Seamen's Partisan Committee (KEN) and the Greek Seaman's Union (OENO).[4] The KKE also penetrated the Greek General Confederation of Labor but failed to gain control of its governing body when it was reorganized, with the help of the British Trade Union Confederation, and became a member of the anti-Communist International Confederation of Free Trade Unions.[5]

The KKE also had at its disposal several newspapers and a clandestine radio station, through which party policies, propaganda, and other communications were passed to members and the wider world. Until they were suppressed by the Greek national government in December 1947, when the KKE was made illegal, three daily newspapers published in Athens supported the KKE: *Rizospastis, Eleftheria Ellada*, and *Lafke Phone*.[6] Throughout the civil war, the KKE/GDA also published a number of other periodicals, most of which were printed in Belgrade, Sofia, Bucharest, or Moscow. These included the weekly newspaper of the GDA General Headquarters, *Exsormisis* ("Assault"); a fortnightly newspaper, *Neos Dromos* ("New Day"); and *The Voice of Boulkes*.[7] The clandestine KKE radio station, also known as Eleftheria Ellada (Free Greece) or simply as Radio Markos, appears to have operated from somewhere in Albania, and later in Romania.[8]

In many areas, particularly northern Greece, the KKE was able to rule openly. In those places it performed normal governmental functions, including the administration of justice, taxation, and welfare, in a quite routine manner. In contested areas, the KKE administrative structure was clandestine. KKE administration at the local (village) level was exercised through public councils of three to five members, commonly officials of some front group.[9] In the larger towns, such as Athens and Salonika, local party affairs and sub-rosa, quasi-governmental functions were carried out by local City Committees, or Politburos, such as those in Athens (KOA) and Piraeus (KOP).[10] These City Committees were controlled directly by the Central Committee and were charged with providing the GDA with recruits, information, funds, and other support. The City Committees were generally ineffective as a source of recruits for the GDA, and they ignored repeated calls for uprisings in the towns in support of the GDA.[11] Under constant Greek national government pressure, the City Committees were eventually disbanded by the KKE Politburo. Clandestine KKE branches, or *"rai"* (from the Russian *raion*—district), were also established in each profession, trade, and neighborhood. For example, *rai* were established among industrial workers, civil servants, bank clerks, and military reserve organizations, as well as in different quarters of the major cities.[12] The KKE clandestine organization within the Greek national army, known as the Communist Organization of the Army and Security Corps (KOSSA), gathered information for the GDA and spread dissension among the GNA officers and men.[13] In September 1945, 17 percent of the Air Force, 15 percent of the Army, 5 percent of the Navy, and 2 percent of the Gendarmerie and Civil Police were estimated to be members of KOSSA.[14]

The *Aftoamyna*

Following the decision of the Twelfth Plenum of the Central Committee in June 1945 to proceed with the organization of "mass popular self-defense," many of the clandestine administrative, intelligence, and support organs of the KKE came under control of the "self-defense organization," known as the *aftoamyna*. Created to coordinate defensive actions to protect KKE adherents from "monarcho-fascist terrorism," the overt tasks of the *aftoamyna* included the collection and distribution of information and propaganda; subversion, sabotage and mine laying, recruitment; the the provision of food, shelter, and clothing for the guerrillas; the collection of arms, ammunition, and other military supplies for the GDA; and occasional direct, armed action.[15] The information-gathering and dissemination functions of the *aftoamyna* were particularly important to the KKE/GDA. Information collected by individuals at the local level was processed upward through a series of Centers of Information and Central Centers of Information.[16] The *aftoamyna* appears to have been organized on the typical Communist underground pattern of three-person cells, known as *yiafka*, organized in workplaces or local communities.[17] The total strength of the *aftoamyna* cannot be determined with any certainty, but various sources have estimated that the number of supporters of the Communist insurgency in Greece may have reached as many as 150,000–200,000.[18] However, the number of *active* supporters of the GDA probably did not exceed 50,000 at any time.[19]

In addition to its overt functions, the *aftoamyna* was also charged with internal security, and it appears that certain members, particularly those with established credentials in clandestine organization and "dirty work," formed special secret cells that constituted the successor to the Protective Organization of the People's Fight (OPLA), the KKE secret security and terror apparatus well known for enforcing party discipline and eliminating traitors during the wartime resistance period.[20] This special part of the *aftoamyna* operated under strict rules of operational security. Those chosen to participate were unknown to each other as well as to the other members of their normal *aftoamyna* cell. When a special mission was to be undertaken, an ad hoc group of at least three persons, known as a *synergeia*, was formed by operatives using assumed names and introduced to each other by an agent of the Central Committee. Once their mission was accomplished, they dispersed and changed their names and even their clothing and habits.[21] Among the functions carried out by such teams were the execution of party members condemned by KKE tribunals for collaboration and other offenses, political assassination, intimidation, other acts of terrorism, and surveillance of suspected party members.

The Provisional Democratic Government

A principal objective of the Greek Communists was to gain control over a large area, including a major town in which a formal rebel government could be established. Konitsa was the town most often mentioned as the prospective capital of "free, democratic Greece," but although the GDA came to control a significant portion of northwestern Greece along the borders with Albania and Yugoslavia, it was never able to hold any substantial town long enough to make it the Communist capital. Nevertheless, Zachariades and his backers in the KKE were determined to establish their own government. As Zachariades stated in a speech to the Third Plenum of the KKE Central Committee on 3 September 1947, "the Plenum has ascertained that . . . a Free Greece with its own government is the first step for the salvation of the country."[22]

In fact, the leadership of the KKE/GDA was divided on the issue of the formation of a provisional government.[23] Until his death under suspicious circumstances on 20 May 1947, George Siantos, the deputy leader of the KKE and the principal advocate of the "political" path, had opposed the establishment of a "Free Democratic Government"—either in Greece or outside its borders—on the grounds that it would present the Greek government with the excuse it needed to suppress the KKE and thereby cut it off from its support among leftist organizations at home and abroad. General Secretary Zachariades generally favored the idea of a provisional government, although he shared Siantos' concern about the degree to which the establishment of such a government would disrupt the contacts of the KKE with like-minded groups at home and abroad. For his part, Markos doubted that political action alone would achieve the goals of the KKE, and although he supported the idea of a "Free Democratic Government," he was very wary of its establishment inside Greece. The GDA, he felt, would then be forced to defend its "capital" by positional tactics, which he believed would place it at a disadvantage to the Greek National Army (GNA), which was well supplied with artillery and airpower.[24]

On 23 March 1947, Zachariades met with the Russian and Polish members of the United Nations Commission on the Balkans and apparently received the advice that if the GDA were to "liberate" a small area within Greece and establish a provisional government, that government would be recognized by "friendly" governments, and additional material support would be forthcoming.[25] Three months later, at a meeting of the French Communist Party in Strasbourg in June 1947, Zachariades and Miltiades Porphyrogenis, a member of the KKE Central Committee, floated the idea of a "Free Democratic Government" in Greece and received considerable encouragement.[26] On 16 August 1947, the newly established Democratic Army Radio announced that a "free and independent republic" would be formed and that local elections would be held in the "liberated" areas. However, the establishment of the Provisional Democratic Government of Free Greece (PDGFG) was delayed another five months, its formation being announced by Radio Free Greece on 24 December 1947.

Following the precedent of his model, Stalin, Zachariades did not take any government position but remained General Secretary of the KKE. Markos Vafiades was named prime minister and minister of war. The new provisional government was set up at Pyli, in the vicinity of Lake Prespa, near the intersection of the Greek, Albanian, and Yugoslav borders. Yiannis Ioannides was named deputy premier and minister of foreign affairs. Other members of the first cabinet of the Provisional Democratic Government included Miltiades Porphyrogennis (minister of justice), Petros Kokkalis (minister of public health, education, and welfare), Vassilios Bartzotas (minister of finance), Dimitrios Vlandas (minister of agriculture), and Leonidas Stringos (minister of national economy [supply]).[27]

As expected, the announcement of the establishment of the PDGFG precipitated the official suppression of the KKE and its auxiliary organizations by the Greek national government. The Greek government also offered an amnesty, which, although ignored by most of the Communist fighters, caused considerable anxiety among the leaders of the KKE/GDA.[28] The decision of the United Nations to urge its member nations to withhold recognition was also as expected, but the reaction of the Soviet Union and other "friendly" states came as something of a shock—neither the Soviet Union nor any of its satellites moved to recognize the PDGFG, despite the encouragement given the KKE earlier.[29] To be sure, all of the Balkan Communist states "welcomed" the establishment of the Provisional Government, and in Bulgaria a committee was created to provide it moral and political support, but by this time the Soviet Union was already deeply enmeshed with the problem of an increasingly independent Yugoslavia and appears to have viewed the Greek situation in the overall context of the worsening situation in the Balkans. Unwilling to antagonize the Western powers while the controversy with Tito was unresolved, Stalin bluntly instructed the Yugoslavs to end their support of the Greek Communists, and he himself decided that the Greek rebellion should be ended at once.[30] (Stalin did, however, send a Soviet military advisor, Colonel Yasilefsky, to Markos' headquarters.)[31] In any event, the Provisional Democratic Government was never formally recognized by any sovereign state.

At the Fifth Plenum held at the end of January 1949, Zachariades engineered the ouster of Markos from his positions as premier, minister of war, and commander of the GDA; and Vice Premier Ioannides took over as head of the Provisional Government. Zachariades later assumed the premiership for a short time himself, and between 30 March and 5 April 1949 he radically reorganized the Provisional Government.[32] The number of cabinet posts was greatly expanded, and in an effort to broaden support a number of non-KKE cabinet members were appointed, including two members of the NOF, the support of the Slavo-Macedonian independence movement being particularly sought. The new cabinet lineup, announced by Radio Free Greece on 5 April 1949, included Dimitrios Partsalides (premier), Yiannis Ioannides (vice premier), Petros Roussos (foreign affairs), Dimitrios Vlandas (war), Vassilios Bartzotas (interior), Leonidas Stringos (economics), Kostas Karageorgis (war supplies), and Miltiades Porphyrogennis (justice). There were also several members aligned with parties other than the KKE: Dimitrios Papadimitris (AKE; agriculture), S. Savidis (AKE; cooperatives), P. Avelides (AKE; national economy), Petros Kokkalis (independent; public health and education), G. Tsapakidis (AKE; welfare), Paskal Mitrofski (NOF; food supply), I. Vournas (AKE; transport), Apostolos Grozos (ERGAS; labor), and Kraste Kotseff (NOF; Under-Secretary for National Minorities).[33]

The reorganized Provisional Government, which was to serve scarcely six months before the Greek Communist revolt succumbed to the military power of the Greek national government, was ostensibly a "government of reconciliation," designed to seal the support of those groups the KKE needed. But it also reflected the triumph of the KKE General Secretary Nikos Zachariades over his principal opponent within the Communist movement, Markos Vafiades. Indeed, the very existence of the Provisional Government itself was one of the many points of difference between the two men and their adherents in the internal conflicts that divided the KKE after mid-1945.

INTERNAL CONFLICTS IN THE KKE

Divisions in the Greek Communist Party went back to the origins of the party in 1918. At various times, the fundamental differences of the several factions within the KKE had manifested themselves in open hostility among the members and threatened to destroy the party as an effective force in Greek politics. Urbanism versus ruralism, internationalism versus nationalism, the "Moscow line" versus an "independent Greek line," intellectuals versus fighters—all of these divisions resurfaced with virulence between 1945 and 1949, having been largely suppressed by the need for unity in resisting the wartime occupation of Greece by the Axis powers, and by the providential absence—in captivity and exile—of Nikos Zachariades and many of the Stalinist, internationalist members of the KKE. The return of Zachariades in May 1945 and his seemingly effortless resumption of the leadership of the KKE from George Siantos, the wartime party leader, presaged the resumption of factionalism within the KKE, exacerbated now by the new division between Greek Communists who had passed the war in Axis prisons, in relatively comfortable exile in the Soviet Union, or elsewhere, and those who had borne the burden of organizing and conducting the armed resistance to the Axis occupation and the struggle to overcome right-wing opponents in the resistance movement.

Zachariades Versus Markos

In time, all of the internal dissension in the KKE came to be embodied in the struggle between Nikos Zachariades and Markos Vafiades for control of the organization and employment of the Greek Democratic Army. The two men shared many characteristics. Both were Greeks from Asia Minor, both were long-time, dedicated Communists, and both had been trained in Moscow.[34] However, the two men could not have been more different in temperament, experience, or in their views of the proper course to be followed in achieving the ultimate objective of a "free, democratic Greece under KKE leadership."

Having passed the wartime period of occupation and resistance in Dachau, where he was found by the Allies and returned to Greece by RAF aircraft on 30 May 1945, Nikos Zachariades had been isolated from the spirit of nationalism inherent in the wartime EAM-ELAS resistance movement.[35] By training and inclination a thorough-going Stalinist ideologue, Zachariades resumed control of the KKE in June 1945 and sought to impose ideological discipline and strict adherence to the dictates of Stalin and the Cominform, insofar as these were known to him. This commitment to the party line issuing from Moscow was accompanied by an unquestioning faith in the correctness and general applicability not only of Soviet policy but of Soviet military organization and doctrine as well. As Zachariades himself put it, "any leader in our army without . . . efficient study and familiarization with Stalin's military science . . . is bound to be left behind and will fail sooner or later."[36]

Markos Vafiades, who assumed command of the Communist guerrilla forces in July 1946, was also Moscow trained and a generally orthodox Communist, but he was by temperament far more pragmatic and less ideologically hidebound than Zachariades. Unlike Zachariades, Markos had passed through the fires of the nationalist struggle to free Greece from its Axis oppressors. As the principal EAM-ELAS political officer in northern Greece during the war, he had worked closely with the Slavo-Macedonian Liberation Movement (SNOF) and had developed close ties to Tito and the Yugoslavian partisans. As a result of his wartime experiences, Markos was far more flexible as to party discipline, less tied to Soviet control, and far more attuned to the organizational, strategic, and tactical needs of a guerrilla army engaged with a much larger and better-equipped opponent. His views on military affairs were derived from practical experience unclouded by blind obedience to theories advanced by Russian ideologues for entirely different situations.

The conflict between Zachariades and Markos forced the other leaders of the KKE and GDA to choose sides in the dispute over policy, organization, strategy, and tactics. Many of the Greek Communist leaders supported Zachariades, although Markos attracted some of the clearest thinkers.[37] Among the principal supporters of Zachariades were Yiannis Ioannides, Vassilios Bartzotas, Dimitrios Vlandas, Leonidas Stringos, George Gousias, and Petros Roussos.[38] Markos was generally backed by Andreas Tzimas, Dimitrios Partsalides, George Kikitsas, Kostas Karageorgis, and Khryssa Khatzivassiliou, as well as by George Siantos and John Zevgos until their untimely and suspicious deaths.[39] Early on, Siantos, Partsalides, and Khatzivassiliou had in fact formed a third faction, which favored a "revisionist" policy of seeking to obtain KKE ends through peaceful, political means.[40] Their subsequent support of Markos was consistent with their view in that Markos' proposal for an extended guerrilla war could be seen as less extreme than Zachariades' insistence on an early transition to conventional, all-out warfare.

The political and military differences between Zachariades and Markos were also colored by a degree of personal envy on the part of Zachariades, who was all too aware of his own lack of military qualifications and experience, and who appears to have been jealous of both the wartime reputations earned by some GDA leaders and the popularity of Markos among the rank and file of the GDA.[41] No doubt under Zachariades' influence, the Communist newspaper, *Rizospastis*, and other party organs for some time mentioned Markos only infrequently and with scant detail in articles dealing with the Communist forces. Although Markos had been in the mountains since September 1946, and the order of the day establishing the General Headquarters of the GDA bore the date 28 October 1946 (although perhaps it was actually written some time later), the first mention of Markos in connection with the GHQ did not appear in *Rizospastis* until 18 February 1947.[42] The personal ambition of some members of Zachariades' clique also played a role, in that several of his adherents, themselves veterans of ELAS, desired the prestige and perquisites of commanding larger military formations, such as brigades and divisions.[43]

Great care was taken to prevent the rank and file members of the KKE and GDA from learning of the tremendous rift in the leadership.[44] Only from postwar statements did many of the internal struggles and decisions become widely known. Public announcements were carefully crafted to avoid any hint of dissension or hesitation in the upper echelons of the party and army leadership. For example, GDA orders continued to be issued in Markos' name long after he was officially deposed from his position as commander of the GDA, and his absence from active day-to-day command was explained as due to the effects of a serious illness.[45] Despite the efforts of the KKE leaders, most of the rank and file were aware of the split within the party. For example, one U.S. intelligence report, commenting on the decline in guerrilla morale following Markos' dismissal in early 1949, noted that "seventy per cent of the Bandits are followers of MARKOS, thirty per cent of ZAKHARIADIS."[46]

The Macedonian Question

One issue that had traditionally divided the members of the KKE was the question of Macedonian independence. On this issue too Zachariades and Markos were at odds. As a faithful adherent of Stalin and the Cominform, Zachariades was committed to the idea—long anathema to most Greeks—of an autonomous Macedonia under Bulgarian hegemony. Indeed, Zachariades had been imprisoned by the Greek government in 1926 for advocating the independence of Macedonia.[47] The KKE had abandoned support for an independent Communist Macedonian state in 1936, in the face of massive Greek opposition to the loss of national territory and its Greek-speaking inhabitants.[48] From 1936 to 1949, the KKE policy had been one of guaranteeing Slavo-Macedonian rights within a "democratic" Greece. The KKE had toyed with the idea of a "Union of Soviet Democracies in the Balkans," which would include Greece, Macedonia, Bulgaria, and Serbia. It had been forced, however, to repudiate the so-called Petrich Pact, which was signed on 12 July 1943 at Petrich, Bulgaria, by Yiannis Ioannides for the KKE and by Dushan Daskalof for the Bulgarian Communist Party, it had called for an "independent and autonomous democracy under control of the USSR."[49] However, under Zachariades' influence, the Fifth Plenum of the KKE at the end of January 1949 declared in favor of Macedonian independence. When the Cominform issued a call for an independent Macedonia in February 1949, Zachariades and his followers took up the cry, and Radio Free Greece reported with tacit approval the Cominform resolution favoring Macedonian independence on 1 March 1949.[50]

Although the declaration of the KKE in favor of Macedonian autonomy promised to please Stalin, garner support for the GDA among the Slavo-Macedonian population of northern Greece (and thus improve the GDA's recruiting prospects), and perhaps lead to an increase in Bulgarian support for the GDA, the new policy was essentially a disaster.[51] The Cominform plan for Macedonian autonomy would have placed Macedonia under Bulgarian domination, and adherence to the Cominform policy placed Zachariades in direct opposition to Marshal Tito of Yugoslavia, the principal supporter of the Greek rebels. Both Tito and Georgi Dimitrov, the leader of the Bulgarian Communist Party, favored the idea of an autonomous Macedonia. However, Tito wanted Greek Macedonia to become part of a federation under Yugoslavian auspices, while the Bulgarians intended that it should exist as part of a Greater Bulgaria. KKE support for the Bulgarian position further alienated Tito, who was already edging toward dropping his support for the GDA.[52]

Markos was more circumspect. He understood the KKE's need for the support of Slavo-Macedonian autonomists, who provided a good deal of the GDA manpower in northern Greece, but having had a long relationship with Tito, he recognized the degree to which the existence of the GDA depended on the good will and positive material support of Yugoslavia. Unfortunately, Markos' opposition to the Cominform plan for Macedonian independence earned him little but the hatred of Dimitrov, one of Stalin's pets.[53]

KKE support for Macedonian independence also caused popular support and recruitment for the KKE/GDA among Greeks, already faltering, to decline dramatically. As the historian Evangelos Averoff-Tossizza has noted, the pro-Cominform policy on Macedonia "was to lose for the KKE all of its followers, except those who would blindly obey Moscow's orders. It was to increase the will of the nationalists to crush the rebels as well."[54] Guerrilla morale dropped precipitously. For example, the 135 GDA guerrillas captured at the battle of Langada near Salonika on 1–12 February 1948 uniformly condemned both the pro-Bulgarian policy and the draconian discipline of their commanders.[55] Meanwhile, the morale of Greek government troops was greatly improved. Now the soldiers of the GNA truly had a cause to fight for—the protection of national territory from the despised Bulgarian foe.[56] Zachariades was forced to retreat into ambiguity on the issue and eventually recanted, but the damage could not be undone.[57]

The Tito-Cominform Split

The Macedonian issue was not the only matter involving Yugoslavia over which Zachariades and Markos disagreed. Yugoslavia was the principal supporter of the Greek Communist rebels, providing refuge, training facilities, and much-needed military supplies. Thus, the split between Tito and the Cominform in June 1948 presented the KKE/GDA with a dilemma, and during the summer and fall of 1948 the question preoccupied the Greek rebel leadership.[58] At the Fourth Plenum in June 1948, the KKE drew back from an open condemnation of Tito, and the resolution of the Fifth Plenum in January 1949 was similarly discreet.[59] However, behind the scenes, Zachariades clearly supported the decision of the Cominform against Tito, while the much more pragmatic Markos took every opportunity to avoid giving Tito any excuse for closing his borders to the Greek Communist forces and suspending his material aid to the GDA. Here too Zachariades won out in the end. Relations with Tito soured, and on 10 July 1949 Tito closed the Yugoslavian border and ceased to aid the Greek rebels, which tipped the scales against them and led directly to their annihilation by the GNA the following month. Following the ultimate defeat of the Greek rebellion, Zachariades and others blamed the failure of the Communist revolution in Greece on Tito's withdrawal of support. C. M. Woodhouse, a close observer intimately familiar with the Greek Communist movement, offers the opinion that

Zachariadis' attitude to Tito was inspired by jealousy. He felt that only the accident of being in captivity throughout the war had deprived him of the chance to play a similar or greater role in Greece. Certainly he was mistaken: neither in ability nor in character was he a potential Tito; nor was any other Greek.[60]

The Dispute over Organization, Strategy, and Tactics

The most consequential issue over which Zachariades and Markos differed was the organization and employment of the Greek Communist military forces. In following the line laid down by his Soviet masters, Zachariades was initially reluctant to abandon the policy of political rather than military action adopted by the KKE after Varkiza.[61] Once persuaded that conditions in Greece made armed rebellion the only option, Zachariades became an advocate of organizing the rebel forces along the formal lines of the Red Army and adopting a strategy and tactical doctrine far better suited to the Soviet Army than to a Greek guerrilla army. As Dominique Eudes observed,

for doctrinal reasons the legendary Mountain guerrilla was said to have been tainted with "foreign techniques," while the positional warfare evolved in the Crimea by nineteenth-century imperialism was granted the stamp of revolutionary orthodoxy. The Democratic Army intoxicated itself with resumés of 1930s Russian strategy manuals, while the Americans happily went on colonizing Athens.[62]

Lacking practical military experience of his own, Zachariades was forced to rely on the advice of like-minded (i.e., "politically correct") ELAS veterans with a personal interest in the formation of a conventional military organization; on logistical advisors, who stressed the importance of holding the frontier areas to protect the lines of communications to the neighboring supporters of the rebellion; and on his political commissars, who emphasized the greater degree of party discipline that could be imposed on a conventional military structure.[63] The latter argument in particular appealed to Zachariades, whose view of the desirability of a conventional army was predicated on his perception of the need for greater ideological discipline, a discipline far easier to impose on a conventionally organized force than on scattered, semi-independent guerrilla formations. At the same time, Zachariades' approach was colored by his acceptance of "Stalin's war technique," which promoted a Clausewitzian interrelation of policy, strategy, and tactics, and the employment of all means to achieve the desired strategic outcome. The idea was expounded at some length by Zachariades in his 5–6 March 1949 speech to GDA military leaders, in which he obliquely condemned Markos stating,

He who maintains that the democratic army as a regular one must apply only the tactics of such an army, he deprives the democratic army from its immense reserves in the rear of the enemy (in the villages, and the towns), thus rendering the army unable to win.[64]

At the beginning of the "Third Round," Markos had recognized that the KKE was ascendant in northern Greece and had consequently pressed for immediate aggressive action to take advantage of the tide at its flood.[65] He had worked enthusiastically to shape the GDA into an effective fighting force from mid-

1946 onward, but he was also a pragmatist, and once it became obvious in mid-1948 that the correlation of forces was beginning to favor the Greek government rather than the rebels, he began to advocate a reversion to guerrilla warfare. His doubts about the probable success of a conventional campaign solidified following the disastrous GDA conventional attack on Konitsa in December 1947 and the successful GNA offensive (Operation KORONIS) in the Grammos in the summer of 1948.[66] Although the GDA forces had been able to disengage in the Grammos and retreat through Albanian territory to re-form in the Vitsi, Markos realistically perceived that the GDA was no longer able to defeat the ever-improving GNA forces without direct outside intervention. That, in turn, had become unlikely, since Yugoslavia had been distracted by the split between Tito and the Cominform and could not afford to intervene in Greece. In November 1948, Markos made a pessimistic assessment of the military prospects of the rebels:

Taking into account the existing balance of forces and the means and possibilities open to us, one is led to the conclusion that the Democratic Army is not in a position to overthrow monarcho-fascism by itself in the immediate future; it might be able to do it with direct military aid, which could follow the recognition of the Provisional Democratic Government by friendly countries. This aid does not, however, seem very likely to materialize, as the Democratic Army has not managed to create the necessary conditions and the international situation does not appear to favour such a development, at least for the moment.[67]

Having correctly determined that the GDA had attempted the transition to conventional warfare prematurely, Markos believed the error could be corrected only by a negotiated settlement with the Greek government—a remote possibility unacceptable to most of the rebels—or by the reversion of the GDA to a long-term guerrilla war of attrition, which in itself was problematic and uncertain of ultimate success.[68] Zachariades was far more sanguine about the outcome of a conventional campaign, but in promoting an early transition to conventional organization and tactics he ignored the realities of the Greek situation in favor of a purely theoretical approach. He also ignored the signs that the balance was rapidly shifting to the GNA. As Col. Harvey H. Smith, the U.S. military attaché in Athens, noted in his comments on Zachariades' speech to GDA leaders on 5–6 March 1949,

The guerrilla top-ranking leaders have made strong efforts to organize and equip their forces along modern army lines. Efforts were also made to conduct normal combat operations, rather than adhere to guerrilla type warfare. In so doing, they apparently overestimated their own capabilities and underestimated those of their opponents. Such errors are frequently made by fanatical leadership.[69]

Although Zachariades perceived the escape of the GDA forces from the Grammos in the summer of 1948 as a success, he noted that "out of subjective inability, incompetence, and faults, we did not succeed in concentrating on Grammos the necessary reserves. . . . The monarchofascists were ripe for a decisive blow, despite the overwhelming preponderance they had."[70] He disingenuously blamed the defeat in the Grammos on traitors within the GDA; among others, Yiannoulis, a longtime leader of Communist guerrillas in the Grammos, was indicted, tried, and executed for having betrayed the cause. Zachariades was also greatly encouraged by the successful GDA counteroffensive in the Vitsi in October 1948.[71] Concerned with the growing difficulties of recruitment and encouraged by international events in late 1948 (the Berlin blockade, among other events) to hope for intervention by his Soviet backers, Zachariades was persuaded that the conventional battle should be pushed to an early conclusion. As he stated in his speech to the leading GDA military personnel on 5–6 March 1949,

There is a big discussion going on and much confusion is revealed to be prevailing in this discussion regarding the tactics of the Democratic Army. Which are the correct tactics for us? Guerrilla or Regular Army tactics? This discussion has not been put in the right way, and moreover a comparison between the tactics of a regular army and those of a guerrilla one, do not mean a thing.

As long as our purpose is the liberation of the country, the necessity to build a regular popular and revolutionary army is a political one. It is obvious that we cannot succeed in it with guerrilla groups, since it is completely clear that only a revolutionary army, able to face and destroy the monarchofascist army, can meet such a requirement.

It is the political mission that determines the nature, character and strategy of our army, and it is this same mission that basically determines those tactics which will answer the strategy, serve it, and promote its implementation. This is how the question stands, and there is nothing more to be discussed.[72]

THE TRIUMPH OF ZACHARIADES

The outcome of the conflict between Nikos Zachariades and the adherents of the Cominform on the one hand and Markos Vafiades and the nationalist wing of the KKE on the other was not preordained, but at each successive decision point Zachariades was able to impose his will and his concepts on the KKE and GDA despite strenuous objections from Markos.[73] It thus became apparent rather early that Markos was fighting a losing battle and could expect to be purged. Indeed, it appears that Zachariades first sought to eliminate Markos by ordering an assassination attempt during the retreat from the Grammos in August of 1948.[74] On 20 August, Markos and an escort of ten men, making their way through the mountainous terrain to cross the border into Albania, were followed by another detachment under Polidoros, a GDA officer well known for dispatching troublesome elements within the GDA. Polidoros' detachment caught up with Markos' group only after it had crossed into Albania, and during the ensuing firefight Markos was able to withdraw under covering fire from Albanian frontier guards; he subsequently gained the protection of the Soviet mission in Albania. He later returned to GDA headquarters in Greece, where he continued to oppose Zachariades.

Having failed to eliminate his rival by the most direct method, Zachariades then adopted a more subtle solution, insinuating that the leader of the GDA was suffering from psychological problems of long standing that clouded his judgment and affected his ability to direct the operations of the GDA.[75] Following Markos' peroration on the state of the rebellion in November 1948, Zachariades denounced Markos' "platform" as "defeatist" and "opportunist" (all derogatory terms in orthodox Communist jargon), and on 15 November 1948 he obtained a Politburo vote of no confidence in Markos.[76] Markos continued to hang on, however, and disputes over the correct strategy intensified. On 27 January 1949, Radio Free Greece carried a peace proposal, and less than a week later, at the Fifth Plenum of the KKE Central Committee on 30 January, the decision was taken to relieve Markos as premier and commander of the GDA. The public announcement was made in early February. Markos' position as commander in chief of the GDA, having been refused by his old wartime colleague, George Kikitsas, fell to George Gousias, and the post of premier of the Provisional Democratic Government devolved upon Yiannis Ioannides.[77] Markos and several of his supporters were subsequently expelled from the Central Committee of the KKE, and Markos himself went into exile in Yugoslavia.

The triumph of Zachariades and his clique within the KKE had three important and far-reaching effects on the GDA.[78] First, the decision to support the concept of an independent Macedonia was seen by most Greeks as treason to the Motherland, and both popular support and recruitment for the GDA, already reaching low ebb, were further hampered. Second, the declaration of KKE support for the Cominform in its conflict with Tito persuaded the latter finally to abandon his logistical support of the GDA and to close his borders. Finally, the decision to continue the strategy and tactics of conventional, positional warfare placed the GDA at an ever-increasing disadvantage with respect to the constantly growing and improving GNA. The purge of Markos and his supporters marked the point at which the downward trajectory of the GDA's effectiveness began to accelerate toward its decisive defeat by the GNA in August of 1949.

NOTES

1. The Communist Information Bureau (Cominform) was created in October 1947 with headquarters in Belgrade, Yugoslavia. Its ostensible purpose was to coordinate the activities of the various European Communist parties, but in fact it was the successor of the Communist International (Comintern), suppressed in 1943, as the chief agent for international subversion of the Communist Party of the Soviet Union. See William L. Langer, ed., *An Encyclopedia of World History*, 5th ed. revised and updated (Boston: Houghton Mifflin, 1972), 1164.

2. Dimitrios G. Kousoulas, *Revolution and Defeat: The Story of the Greek Com-*

munist Party (London: Oxford University Press, 1965), 225. The party secretariat consisted of the same individuals, less Bartzotas and Khatzivassiliou.

3. United States Army Command and General Staff College, *Internal Defense Operations: A Case History, Greece 1946–49*, USACGSC RB 31–1 (Fort Leavenworth, KS: United States Army Command and General Staff College, 1 November 1967), 128 and 129, Figure 17.

4. Floyd A. Spencer, *War and Postwar Greece: An Analysis Based on Greek Writings* (Washington: European Affairs Division, Library of Congress, 1952), 109–10.

5. *Internal Defense Operations*, 130.

6. Ibid., 134. After December 1947, *Rizospastis* and *Eleftheria Ellada* continued to be published clandestinely, on an irregular basis and at various places.

7. Military Attaché–Greece (Col. Harvey H. Smith), Intelligence Report R-130-49 (ID No. 548336), Athens, 11 April 1949, subject: Interrogation of Guerrilla (Ex-GNA) Lt. Z. G. ASTRIHADES, 7 ¶3a [in Box 3539, Assistant Chief of Staff, G-2, Intelligence, Numerical Series of Intelligence Document File ("ID Files"), 1944–1955, Record Group 319 (Records of the Army Staff), National Archives II, College Park, MD. The location of similar documents from the "ID Files" will be cited hereafter simply as "in Box *x*, ID Files, RG 319, NA," and on second and subsequent citations such documents will be identified solely by their ID number.

8. *Internal Defense Operations*, 134.

9. ID No. 548336, 7 ¶3a. Local councils were sometimes appointed even for towns yet to come under KKE/GDA control.

10. Stephen Merrill, *The Communist Attack on Greece*, Special Report No. 15, 21st Regular Course, U.S. Strategic Intelligence School (Washington: U.S. Strategic Intelligence School, 28 July 1952), 52.

11. Merrill, 52; *Internal Defense Operations*, 128–29; Edgar O'Ballance, *The Greek Civil War, 1944–1949* (New York: Praeger, 1966), 174–76.

12. *Internal Defense Operations*, 128.

13. Ibid., 134.

14. Merrill, 23.

15. Christopher M. Woodhouse, *The Struggle for Greece, 1941–1949* (London: Hart-Davis, MacGibbon, 1976), 187.

16. Merrill, 52.

17. *Internal Defense Operations*, 134.

18. As reported by *New York Times* on 25 March 1948, 12.

19. The American University, Special Operations Research Office, *Peak Organized Strength of Guerrilla and Government Forces in Algeria, Nagaland, Ireland, Indochina, South Vietnam, Malaya, Philippines, and Greece* (Washington: Counterinsurgency Information Analysis Center, Special Operations Research Office, American University, n.d. [ca. 1965]), 19.

20. *Internal Defense Operations*, 130–31.

21. Ibid., 133.

22. Quoted in Merrill, 32.

23. O'Ballance, 144–45.

24. Ibid., 144. Markos later characterized the establishment of the Provisional Democratic Government as "premature" (see Kousoulas, 348).

25. Evangelos Averoff-Tossizza, *By Fire and Axe: The Communist Party and the Civil War in Greece, 1944–1949* (New Rochelle, NY: Caratzas Brothers, 1978), 214.

26. O'Ballance, 149.

27. Kousoulas, 248; O'Ballance, 159; Dominique Eudes, *The Kapetanios: Partisans and Civil War in Greece, 1943–1949* (New York: Monthly Review Press, 1972), 307.

28. O'Ballance, 149.

29. Eudes, 310.

30. O'Ballance, 159; Eudes, 310.

31. Merrill, 33.

32. Averoff-Tossizza, 334–35.

33. Kousoulas, 266–67; Merrill, 58; Eudes, 347.

34. Kousoulas, 289–90. Zachariades was born in Nicomedia in 1902, studied in Moscow from 1922 to 1925 and again from 1928 to 1931, and was installed as leader of the Greek Communist Party by the Comintern in 1931. Vafiades, usually called Markos, was born in Tosia in 1906, emigrated to Salonika in 1923, became a tobacco worker in Kavalla, joined the KKE in 1927, and served as *kapetanios* of the 10th ELAS Division in Macedonia.

35. Woodhouse, 141. In fact, Zachariades had been "out of circulation" since 1936, when he had been imprisoned by the Metaxas regime.

36. Military Attaché–Greece (Col. Harvey H. Smith), Intelligence Report R-273-49 (ID No. 576384), Athens, 13 July 1949, subject: Guerrilla Strategical and Tactical Problems, 1948 (Speech by N. ZACHARIADES), 12 [in Box 3707, ID Files, RG 319, NA].

37. Woodhouse, 254.

38. Heinz Richter, "The Second Plenum of the Central Committee of the KKE and the Decision for Civil War: A Reappraisal," in Lars Baerentzen, John O. Iatrides, and Ole L. Smith, eds., *Studies in the History of the Greek Civil War, 1945–1949* (Copenhagen: Museum Tusculanum Press, 1987), 187.

39. Woodhouse, 231; Eudes, 288. The wartime leader of the KKE, George Siantos, died under suspicious circumstances on 20 May 1947 while under medical treatment in the Athens clinic of Dr. Petros Kokkalis, who later was named minister of public health, education, and welfare in the Provisional Democratic Government. Zevgos was shot down in the street in Salonika on 23 March 1946.

40. Richter, 186.

41. Eudes, 278.

42. Woodhouse, 193.

43. Robert W. Selton, "Communist Errors in the Anti-Bandit War," *Military Review* 45, no. 9 (September 1965), 75.

44. Eudes, 313.

45. Ibid., 331.

46. Military Attaché-Greece (Col. Harvey H. Smith), Intelligence Report R-133-49 (ID No. 548337), Athens, 11 April 1949, subject: Interrogation of Surrendered Guerrilla Captain Paragiotis MARGARITOPOULOS (17 March 1949), 4 (¶4) [in Box 3539, ID Files, RG 319, NA].

47. Kousoulas, 289.

48. Lawrence S. Wittner, *American Intervention in Greece, 1943–1949* (New York: Columbia University Press, 1982), 271.

49. Merrill, 21.

50. Wittner, 271; William Hardy McNeill, *The Greek Dilemma: War and Aftermath* (Philadelphia: J. B. Lippincott, 1947), 43–44.

51. Wittner, 271–72. Shortly before the KKE declaration of support for an independent

Macedonia, Zachariades, Ioannides, and Vlandas had attended the Fifth Congress of the Bulgarian Communist Party in Sofia in November 1948, where they may well have been promised additional Bulgarian aid in return for a "correct" position on the Macedonian issue. In fact, Bulgarian aid did increase (see Averoff-Tossizza, 319 and 324).

52. Frank J. Abbott, *The Greek Civil War, 1947–1949: Lessons for the Operational Artist in Foreign Internal Defense*, School of Advanced Military Studies thesis (Fort Leavenworth, KS: School of Advanced Military Studies, USACGSC, May 1994), 33.

53. Averoff-Tossizza, 318–19.

54. Ibid., 335.

55. Spencer, 108.

56. McNeill, 43–44.

57. Wittner, 272.

58. Woodhouse, 254.

59. Eudes, 325. In fact, Zachariades managed to get the Fourth Plenum to pass a secret resolution backing the Cominform against Tito (see Woodhouse, 254).

60. Woodhouse, 19.

61. Ibid., 141.

62. Eudes, 313.

63. Selton, 74–75.

64. ID No. 576384, 7.

65. Woodhouse, 142.

66. Woodhouse, 231; O'Ballance, 181.

67. Markos' remarks were subsequently published in August 1950 in *Neos Kosmas*, Volume 8, 476–83 (quoted in Eudes, 337).

68. Kousoulas, 252–53.

69. ID No. 576384, 12.

70. Eudes, 329–30; Zachariades speech to GDA leaders on 5–6 March 1949, as quoted in ID No. 576384, 8.

71. O'Ballance, 181.

72. ID No. 576384, 6–7.

73. Woodhouse, 154. As late as the Fourth Plenum, held at Petra Bouka in the Grammos on 28–29 June 1948, Zachariades was able to prevail upon Markos to present the resolution of the Plenum stating that the end of the "monarcho-fascist regime" was "closer than ever" (see Kousoulas, 253).

74. Eudes, 330–31.

75. Ibid., 338.

76. Woodhouse, 255.

77. Ibid.

78. Selton, 75.

4

The Development of the Greek Democratic Army

The internal divisions of the Greek Communist Party (KKE) profoundly affected all aspects of the development of its military arm—organization, training, recruitment, and logistics as well as strategy and tactics. The organization of the Greek Communist military forces was particularly sensitive to political influence, and many of the decisions affecting military organization taken by the political leaders of the KKE were based on ideological considerations rather than military efficacy. The series of fateful decisions began in the fall of 1945, when the Greek Communist leaders resolved to form a guerrilla force in the mountains to oppose the excesses of the Greek government and right-wing paramilitary forces. The Communist guerrilla bands grew in size and number, and in the fall of 1946 a formal organization was imposed on them, in the form of the Greek Democratic Army (GDA). A civil war of growing intensity ensued. From mid-1947 onward, that war was shaped by the imposition by the General Secretary of the KKE, Nikos Zachariades—over the objections of the GDA military commander, Markos Vafiades—of a policy aimed at transforming the GDA into a conventional military force able to seize and hold territory and to confront the Greek government directly. The impossibility of providing adequate logistical support for a conventional rebel army of 25,000 men and women in the bleak mountains of Greece, and the ill advised defense of rebel base areas against numerically superior government forces plentifully supplied with artillery and air support, brought predictable results. Given the limited resources available, the conventionally organized Communist forces proved unable to achieve the goals set for them and thus ensured the ultimate defeat of the Communist cause. That defeat came in a series of campaigns conducted by the Greek national forces (GNF) in the Grammos and Vitsi mountains in the summer of 1949. Strengthened by massive U.S. economic and military aid, the GNF defeated the GDA decisively and drove its remnants across the northern borders to take refuge in Albania, Yugoslavia, and Bulgaria, thereby ending the threat of a Communist victory obtained by force.

POLITICAL DECISIONS

The key political decisions taken by the leaders of the KKE in the period from February 1945 to August 1949 served to divide the "Third Round" of the Greek civil war into four distinct phases, each of which was marked by significant changes in the development of the Greek Democratic Army.[1] The four phases in the development of the GDA were: a *Self-Defense* phase, from the Varkiza Agreement to the Second Plenum of the Central Committee of the KKE (February 1945–February 1946); a *guerrilla warfare* phase, from the Second Plenum to the decision of the KKE Politburo to form a conventional army (February 1946–February 1947); a *conventional warfare* phase, from the decision to form a conventional army to the dismissal of Markos Vafiades as commander of the GDA (February 1947–January 1949); and a *final* phase, from the relief of Markos to the ultimate defeat of the GDA (February–August 1949).

The First Phase, February 1945–February 1946

The "Third Round" is generally said to have begun with the meeting of the Second Plenum of the Central Committee of the KKE, on 12 February 1946, and the subsequent guerrilla attack on the village of Litochoron on the night of 30–31 March 1946.[2] However, those events were preceded by a preliminary phase, extending from the signing of the Varkiza Agreement on 12 February 1945 to the meeting of the Second Plenum. During this first phase, the Greek Communists focused their efforts on obtaining their objectives by political means, but they prepared for armed insurrection by establishing a self-defense organization, reestablishing control over the remnants of guerrilla groups in the mountains, and taking the basic strategic decision to base any rebellion on the actions of guerrilla forces in the mountains rather than on an uprising in the cities and towns. The tactics employed during the self-defense phase were those of the propagandist, saboteur, and terrorist; armed actions by the Communists were generally on a small scale, uncoordinated, and essentially defensive.

The Varkiza Agreement of 12 February 1945 was followed by dissolution of the armed forces of the KKE and the return of the party to a position of quasi-legality. In April 1945, the Eleventh Plenum of the Central Committee of the KKE met under the guidance of its General Secretary, George Siantos, and decided to focus the efforts of the party on the creation through political means of a bourgeois democratic republic dominated by the KKE, a goal the party had supported since 1934. The policy of the Eleventh Plenum was based clearly on political action within the established framework rather than on armed rebellion. However, in May 1945, the Stalinist Nikos Zachariades returned to Greece and resumed his place as the leader of the KKE. The Twelfth Plenum meeting, in late June 1945, decided to counter the growing oppression of the KKE and other leftist groups by right-wing gangs, abetted by the Greek national government, by creating a self-defense movement, although the principal weapon of the KKE was still propaganda, mass demonstrations and strikes, and occasional sabotage, rather than armed guerrilla operations.[3] This policy was confirmed, and the effort to establish the self-defense groups increased, following the meeting of the Seventh Party Congress of the KKE.

At the Seventh Party Congress in October 1945, General Secretary Zachariades announced that the policy of the Eleventh Plenum with respect to the formation of a bourgeois democracy had been fulfilled and that thenceforth the party would work toward the establishment of a "people's democracy."[4] The new policy assumed that armed action would be required to achieve the party's goals, and on 1 October 1945, the first day of the congress, a Panhellenic Military Committee was formed to study military problems posed by the existing situation. Headed by Nikos Zachariades, the committee consisted of his confederate Yiannis Ioannides, Theodore Makrides (a former ELAS staff officer and the military advisor to the KKE Politburo), and representatives of the KKE provincial organizations. At the committee's second meeting, Zachariades and Makrides proposed that should armed action prove necessary to achieve the party's goals, it should take the form of an armed uprising of KKE adherents in the urban areas rather than of guerrilla forces in the mountains. Such a policy was entirely consistent with Communist theory as expounded by Stalin and the Soviets, who looked to an industrial proletariat (which did not exist in Greece in 1945) rather than the peasants as the mainstay of any successful revolution. As might be expected, Markos Vafiades and the majority of those present opposed such a course of action as impractical under the circumstances and likely to provoke a strong reaction from the British forces still in Greece. Moreover, as Markos had the temerity to point out, the KKE lacked any suitable organized armed infrastructure in the urban areas capable of carrying out Zachariades' plan. Faced with strong opposition, Zachariades quickly dropped the matter, and the Panhellenic Military Committee itself was dissolved. This was the only dispute over strategy and organization that Markos was to win, but it shaped the formation and employment of the Greek Democratic Army until the Politburo decision in February 1947 to convert the GDA to a conventional force.

Although forced to set aside his plan for an armed urban insurrection, Zachariades did not fully accept the idea of a mountain guerrilla war against the Greek national government. Several weeks after the Seventh Party Congress, representatives of the KKE in Macedonia and Thrace reported that they were prepared to field 25,000 armed men; Zachariades made clear to them that the idea was not (at least from his perspective) a realistic program but rather a bluff to force the national government to make political concessions.[5] Throughout the early stages of the civil war, Zachariades and many other leaders of the KKE continued to maintain a negative attitude toward the guerrilla groups in the mountains.

Until February 1946, Communist military operations were restricted for the most part to small-scale raids, sabotage, and defensive actions against raids by right-wing bands and government sweeps. These actions were scattered, uncoordinated, and essentially defensive or retaliatory. By the beginning of 1946, however, the KKE had made considerable progress in preparing for an armed insurrection against the Greek government, should that become necessary and desirable. A supporting self-defense infrastructure (the *aftoamyna*) had been set up and was growing steadily, some control over the independent guerrilla formations in the mountains was being established, and the fundamental decision on the shape of any armed rebellion had been taken. In short, all the elements necessary for a guerrilla war were in place, including such prerequisites of a successful guerrilla campaign as an information network operating in rear areas, caches of weapons and supplies, an unassailable base, political disunity and economic weakness in the country, and widespread sympathy among the population.[6] Only the decision to exploit them remained to be taken.

The Second Phase, February 1946–February 1947

The second phase began in February 1946, with the decision of the Second Plenum of the KKE Central Committee to adopt a more aggressive policy of guerrilla warfare against the Greek government, and it lasted until February 1947, when the KKE Politburo decided to lunge into the creation of a conventional military force and full-scale conventional warfare against the Greek national forces. During the second phase, the KKE continued to try to achieve its objectives through political action while at the same time employing armed guerrilla forces to protect itself. The number and size of the Communist-led guerrilla bands grew, and the KKE imposed upon them centralized control in the form of the GDA and its subordinate headquarters, as the bands themselves were reorganized into companies and then battalions. As the Communist guerrilla army developed, it became more aggressive as well as more successful. Two events pushed the KKE toward an all-out armed insurrection against the Greek government: the success of the right-wing monarchists in the general election of 31 March 1946, and the plebiscite on 1 September 1946, which permitted the return of King George II to Greece on 27 September.[7] Following each of those events, the scope and intensity of GDA operations increased, and by early 1947 the GDA controlled large areas of mainland Greece and was prepared for full-scale civil war.

The decision to adopt a more aggressive program, including increased guerrilla activity, was taken at the Second Plenum of the KKE Central Committee on 12 February 1946.[8] The political decision of the Second Plenum to build up the armed forces of the KKE to resist increasing right-wing oppression is often considered as the beginning of the civil war proper. In reality, the Second Plenum did not make a definitive decision to pursue an armed conflict but rather decided to pursue a "dual strategy" of continued political action coupled with a build-up of military capability.[9] The decision of the Second Plenum thus represented a compromise between those members of the party who wanted to continue the policy of political action followed since the Varkiza Agreement and those who wanted to proceed immediately to an armed rebellion. Accordingly, the KKE and its military arm continued to seek reconciliation while completing "the technical-organisational military preparation for the progressive reinforcement of the armed struggle of the people."[10]

The gradual transformation of the uneasy, intermittently violent, relationship between the KKE and the Greek Right into an all-out armed conflict was not entirely the fault of the Communists. As Heinz Richter has noted, "The civil war did not come as a result of the decision or the acts of the KKE; it was rather the outcome of a process set in motion by the terrorist acts of the extreme right."[11] In fact, the actions of the KKE during the second phase can be seen as still primarily defensive in nature:

The Central Committee decided gradually to build up armed resistance where local conditions made it possible, allowing the groups of persecuted communists to defend themselves with arms, without giving the British any opportunity to intervene. Thus the last stage of self-defence was reached, but the important point is that the military action decided upon was of a clearly *defensive* nature.[12]

As the second phase came to a close at the end of January 1947, the advantages all seemed to lie with the GDA. In a remarkably short time, Markos had organized the independent guerrilla bands into a coordinated, disciplined military force; the strength of the GDA had expanded; and the aggressive guerrilla strategy and tactics of the GDA had clearly carried the day, with large areas of Greece, especially along the critical northern border, coming under Communist control. However, the tide was about to turn against the rebels.

The Third Phase, February 1947–January 1949

The February 1947 decision of the KKE Politburo to emphasize the military struggle while still maintaining the cover of a legal political policy marked the effective beginning of the third phase. The Third Plenum of the KKE Central Committee in September 1947 confirmed the decision to seek the goals of the KKE by armed insurrection, as well as the fateful decision to form a conventional army and undertake conventional operations against the Greek national forces. The third phase—marked by the establishment of the Provisional Democratic Government of Free Greece in December 1947, the efforts of the GDA to transform itself into a conventional army in the course of operations, and the growing power and operational skill of the GNF—constituted the main, offensive period of the civil war. Despite the considerable achievements of the GDA in the military sphere, the third phase ended on 31 January 1947, with the

decision of the Fifth Plenum to dismiss Markos Vafiades from his political and
military offices.

The successive decisions of the KKE political leadership during the third
phase led to two interlocking developments, both of which served to put the
GDA at an increasing disadvantage to the GNF.[13] The establishment of the
Provisional Democratic Government carried with it the necessity of seizing and
holding territory, thereby forcing the comparatively weaker GDA to engage in
conventional positional warfare for which it was ill equipped. At the same time,
the decision to abandon guerrilla organization and tactics in favor of the formation of a conventional army operating along conventional lines not only
brought the GDA into direct and sustained confrontation with the constantly
improving GNF but created requirements for manpower and logistical support
that could not be met with the resources available to the GDA.

On 13 May 1947, the General Secretary of the KKE, Nikos Zachariades,
informed his mentor Stalin that "the Politburo of the Central Committee of the
KKE at its meeting in the middle of February 1947 came to the conclusion that
the democratic movement, although still taking full advantage of all legal possibilities, ought to consider the armed struggle as the most important."[14] However, decisive action to engage the Greek national government in an all-out
armed confrontation did not take place until after the meeting of the Third
Plenum of the KKE Central Committee in mid-September 1947, by which time
the futility of political measures and the growing strength of the Greek government and its right-wing terrorist allies, backed by British and American aid, was
threatening to exterminate gradually the Left.[15] The Third Plenum met on 12–
15 September 1947, with only six of the twenty-five regular members in atten-
dance, and presented Markos and the other advocates of guerrilla warfare with
a fait accompli. After some preliminary remarks, Zachariades announced that

we have decided to shift the centre of gravity of Party activities towards the politico-
military sector, with a view to turning the Democratic Army into a force that will ensure
the establishment of a Free Greece in the shortest possible time, starting with all the
northern regions.[16]

Shorn of its rhetoric, Zachariades statement was a declaration of his intent to
reform the GDA along conventional organizational lines and to launch it on a
campaign of operations in which it would be required to confront the GNF
directly in battles to seize and hold terrain. In so doing, the militarily inept
political leader of the KKE, mesmerized by the model of the Soviet Army and
the desire to impose a higher standard of party discipline, ignored the increasing
difficulties of recruiting for the GDA, his own failure to mobilize the party's
members in the urban areas in support of the GDA, and the logistical burden
such a conventional force would impose.[17]

Markos, who had already (on 4 August 1947) drafted his realistic views on
the organization and employment of the GDA for presentation to the Plenum,

at once opposed the decision to reorganize the GDA along conventional lines and to engage the GNF in battles for the control of towns and terrain.[18] Convinced that Zachariades' decision, taken without the consideration of the full membership of the Central Committee, was both premature and motivated by ideological rather than sound military reasoning, Markos vehemently argued against the decision, but in the end he was forced to yield, thus marking "the beginning of his fall into disfavour and the beginning of the end for the Democratic Army."[19]

On 15 January 1948, the principal Greek Communist political and military leaders met at Pyli, on Lake Prespa, to review the situation in the light of the failure of the new Provisional Democratic Government to gain international recognition and of the abortive attack on Konitsa in December 1947, and to lay out the operational plans for the coming year. The failure of the attack on Konitsa had convinced Markos that a reversion to guerrilla warfare was necessary, even though final victory could not be achieved by guerrilla operations alone but must necessarily be accompanied by outside intervention. Zachariades, on the other hand, remained convinced that the GDA, as then constituted, could win the war by itself. The result of the Pyli conference was an apparent compromise between the views of Zachariades and those of Markos.[20] The conversion of the GDA to a conventional force would continue, but the attempt to seize and hold a capital for the Provisional Government was to be postponed, and it was agreed that for the time being the GDA would continue to employ the large-scale guerrilla tactics of disrupting government communications, attacking isolated government outposts and convoys, and raiding towns for men and supplies. It was also agreed that the efforts to improve the training of the GDA and to spread the battle to new areas should be continued. Although able to carry his points in many respects, Markos was again forced to concede publicly that the decisions of the Third Plenum were correct.[21]

The expulsion of Tito from the Cominform on 28 June 1948 prompted the convocation of yet another plenum of the KKE Central Committee. Meeting at Petra Bouka in the Grammos on 28–29 June 1948, the Fourth Plenum, with only ten of its twenty-five members present, proposed to reexamine the decisions of the Third Plenum. It concluded, as Zachariades intended, that the course adopted in September 1947 had been correct and that victory over the "monarcho-fascists" was closer than ever.[22] With a crucial battle going on nearby, Markos was once again compelled to set aside his doubts about the existing policy and appear to give it his loyalty.

Despite the decision to shift the focus to military action, hope for a political solution was not entirely abandoned; throughout the third phase the leaders of the KKE/GDA from time to time announced their willingness to resolve the conflict through negotiation. In September 1947, the KKE proposed a cease-fire contingent upon the formation of a government of reconciliation that would include the Left, but the offer was spurned by the Greek government, which viewed it as mere Communist propaganda.[23] The offer to negotiate was renewed by the KKE leadership on 7 April 1948 and was again dismissed by the So-phoulis government.[24] On 31 May 1948, Democratic Army Radio broadcast yet another offer, this time in the name of General Markos, who announced his willingness to discuss peace proposals, provided "the democratic life of the people is unreservedly secured, that national independence and autonomy be insured without any foreign intervention, and that the people alone and free may decide their future."[25] This effort, too, came to naught; the government sensed that the balance of power was changing as American aid increased and Com-munist solidarity appeared to be crumbling.[26] Despite the consistent rejections, the KKE/GDA renewed its offer to negotiate later in 1948 and again in January 1949. In late April 1949, the so-called "Gromyko Proposals" were presented to the United Nations, only to be rejected by the Greek government as an attempt to garner public sympathy for the rebels and to forestall an imminent govern-ment military victory.[27]

The Fourth Phase, February–August 1949

The fourth and final phase of the Greek civil war of 1945–1949—a phase that began at the end of January 1949 with the decision of the Fifth Plenum to dismiss Markos Vafiades as prime minister of the Provisional Democratic Gov-ernment and commander in chief of the GDA, and ended with the decisive defeat of the GDA in the Grammos and Vitsi in August 1949—was something of an anticlimax. By the end of January 1949, the Greek Communists had established a provisional government and had created a regular military force with a strength of some 25,000 combatants. The force was composed of artillery, cavalry, sig-nal, engineer, transportation, antitank, and antiaircraft artillery units as well as substantial intelligence and logistics systems. The GDA controlled most of the mountainous region in the interior and a strip of territory extending for some 500 miles along the borders of Greece, in which were located its headquarters, bases, and logistical centers. However, the crucial political and military decisions that would contribute to the ultimate failure of the armed Communist insurrec-tion had already been taken. Eight months after the dismissal of Markos and many of the better commanders, the GDA lay in ruins, in large part because of its own internal defects and the faulty doctrines imposed upon it by Nikos Zachariades. Any hope of a Communist victory was then abandoned; the end of the armed rebellion was acknowledged by the Sixth Plenum of the Central Committee of the KKE in October 1949.

The Fifth Plenum of the KKE Central Committee met on 30–31 January 1949 in the Vitsi. Encouraged by the recent success of the GDA at Karditsa, Naousa, and Karpenision, Zachariades forced the dismissal of Markos Vafiades from his political positions and military command.[28] The decision was announced pub-licly on 4 February 1949; Markos' "resignation" was attributed to "ill health." Khryssa Khatzivassiliou, who was suffering from leukemia, was expelled from the Central Committee along with Markos, and several of the best GDA commanders were relieved and took refuge in Yugoslavia. General Kocha Popovic, Markos' Yugoslavian advisor, was also dismissed. Only Kostas Karageorgis remained—for the time being—to oppose Zachariades in the top ranks of the KKE/GDA.

Several other major decisions, all equally harmful to the GDA, were also taken at the Fifth Plenum. First, the plenum confirmed that the conversion of the GDA to a conventional army would continue and that it would be used to seize and hold territory. Second, at Zachariades' urging, the KKE cast its lot with Stalin and the Cominform in the condemnation of Tito and the Yugoslavs, thereby alienating the GDA's most generous supporter. Third, and perhaps most significantly, the Fifth Plenum approved Zachariades' plans to support the formation of an independent Slavic Macedonian state, long anathema to patriotic Greeks and since 1934 to Greek Communists as well. Adopted in part for ideological reasons and because Stalin desired it, the decision to support an independent Slavo-Macedonian regime under Bulgarian domination was motivated as well by the need for recruits for the GDA, which at this stage in the civil war could only come from the Slavo-Macedonian activists in northern Greece. It was taken, however, at the cost of whatever support for the KKE/GDA remained among Greek patriots. In effect Zachariades was proposing to trade the support of some 1.5 million Macedonian Greeks for the less certain support of 80,000 Slavs.[29] As Woodhouse has written, "Zakhariadis was master of the KKE, both in policy and strategy . . . [but he had also become] . . . the political prisoner of NOF, which was increasingly the mouth-piece of the Bulgarian Communists."[30]

Zachariades' true motives in forcing such clearly dysfunctional decisions remain unclear. Perhaps he genuinely believed that with active intervention by the Soviet Union and its satellites a GDA victory was still possible, or he might have been following Stalin's instructions in sacrificing the GDA in order to end the rebellion and facilitate the Soviet Union's political agenda.[31] On 5–6 March 1949, he called together the leading political and military instructors of the GDA to review the situation. His speech to the group, subsequently published in the April 1949 issue of the monthly *Democratic Army*, revealed his optimistic assessment that the failure of the government operations in the Grammos and the Vitsi and the GDA successes at Karditsa, Naousa, and Karpenision had resulted in "the financial, political, military and morale crisis of the enemy[,] . . . proved by the fact that he was obliged to change his army leadership and politically reform his government."[32]

Zachariades' optimism was ill founded. On 4 April 1949, the North Atlantic Treaty was signed. The Soviet Union, reacting to the new evidence of Western strength, ended the Berlin blockade on 12 May and at the same time opened a dialogue with the United States and Great Britain to discuss the situation in Greece, with a view to bringing the civil war to an end.[33] Closer to home, the Greek national forces, although shaken by the success of the GDA attacks on urban areas in December 1948 and the first two months of 1949, were growing stronger than ever. By the beginning of 1949, the Greek government had already received from the United States over $170 million in military aid, including by September 1948 some 140 aircraft, 3,890 guns and mortars, 97,000 rifles, and 10,000 motor vehicles; significant allocations had been made for 1949.[34] The GNA had increased to over 168,500 men, most of whom were well equipped with new American weapons and other hardware. Moreover, the reappointment of Gen. Alexander Papagos as commander in chief of the GNF on 21 January 1949 led to rigorous measures to rid the GNF of inept and lackadaisical commanders, tighten discipline, and improve morale.[35] To aid General Papagos, the National Defense Council was reorganized and given full authority over Greek economic and military resources; General Kosmos was appointed Chief of the General Staff, and Gen. Constantine Ventiris was recalled to serve as inspector-general.

At the same time the morale of the GDA rank and file was falling fast, and GDA recruiting, long dependent on force, was becoming extremely difficult. The loss of good leaders, the decreasing effectiveness of the intelligence and logistical support system provided by the *aftoamyna*, and the decline in support from Albania, Bulgaria, and Yugoslavia, all foreshadowed the final result. Already by the end of April 1949, a GDA officer in Roumeli could record in his diary, "No food for over forty-eight hours! Can't remember when we last had bread: perhaps a month! No rations: nothing to be had."[36] The decline in morale was accompanied by a decline in the level of discipline, despite the draconian measures enforced by Zachariades. Rape, robbery, and brutality became a common feature of GDA operations, and the high ideals of the struggle were lost to sight. Still, almost to the very end, the junior officers and soldiers of the GDA remained faithful to the cause and convinced of its ultimate triumph. The dismissal of Markos was carefully concealed for some time from the rank and file, who continued to believe that thousands of international volunteers would soon arrive to help them achieve the final victory.[37]

ORGANIZATION OF THE GREEK DEMOCRATIC ARMY

Many former ELAS guerrillas refused to accept the terms of the Varkiza Agreement of February 1945 and continued to hold out in the mountains, where they were augmented by dissident such minority groups as the Macedonian Slavs, volunteers seeking to escape from the ever-increasing right-wing terror campaign, and individuals simply hoping to find adventure and relief from the poverty and dullness of village life.[38] There were perhaps as many as two hundred of these unreconciled guerrilla bands, most of them located in the remote areas of Roumeli, Macedonia, Epirus, and the Peloponnesus. In the spring of 1945 the number of guerrillas in such bands was estimated to be 5,000 in Greece plus another 6,000 armed Slavo-Macedonian veterans along the frontiers.[39]

As the oppression of ELAS veterans and other leftist elements by the Greek national government and right-wing terrorists increased, the number and size of the Communist-led guerrilla bands increased. The pool from which new guerrilla bands could be formed was quite large; by the fall of 1945 the total number of KKE adherents throughout Greece was estimated to be between 35,000 and 40,000, and some 8,000–10,000 ELAS veterans had fled to the mountains or taken refuge with their families in Albania and Yugoslavia.[40] Many of the former ELAS members who had fled to neighboring countries were assembled in KKE-sponsored camps, such as that at Boulkes in Yugoslavia, where they were indoctrinated and received training to return to Greece as cadres for the Communist guerrilla forces.

During the first, defensive phase of the "Third Round," the Communist guerrillas were organized tactically into small, independent, highly mobile, and easily supported bands (*omathes*) of seven to ten men.[41] Led by self-appointed *kapetanioi*, almost all the guerrillas were volunteers, and they were armed with a hodgepodge of light weaponry left over from the wartime resistance period. During the course of 1945, the Greek national forces (GNF) discovered a large portion of the weapons hidden by the Communists at the time of the Varkiza Agreement, including all the artillery; however, large quantities of rifles, automatic weapons, light machine guns, and small arms ammunition remained available to the Communist guerrillas.[42] The small, independent bands focused on survival, and they established secure hideouts, lines of communications, and sources of supply among the population. Their actions were primarily defensive in nature, but from time to time they undertook offensive operations. Such operations were initiated by the isolated guerrilla formations on their own and generally had quite limited objectives, such as harassing police outposts, obtaining weapons, food, and other supplies, or countering the actions of right-wing groups. Employing characteristic guerrilla "hit and run" tactics, the bands at first acted independently without central coordination, but they eventually began to expand and coordinate their activities; they had considerable success in terrorist attacks on isolated villages and gendarmerie posts.

Although the various guerrilla bands in the mountains were ostensibly independent, there was little doubt that the KKE exercised a degree of control over their formation and employment. However, the agencies of the Greek government (and later its American ally) were unable to conceive that the political and military direction of the Communist-led forces was solely a Greek affair. Although definitive proof was never forthcoming, they assumed that the Greek Communist guerrillas were directed and coordinated by a higher headquarters composed of Greeks, Yugoslavs, Bulgarians, and Albanians, probably located in Skoplje, Yugoslavia.[43] The assumption was based on the idea that such international coordination would be necessary to provide bases and supplies and to facilitate border crossings. This chimera was probably a result of the 15 December 1945 meeting in Petrich, Bulgaria, attended by members of the KKE Central Committee and representatives of the Yugoslavian and Bulgarian general staffs, at which Yugoslavia promised to support the formation of a Greek Communist army.[44]

Creation of the Greek Democratic Army

As the conflict increased between the KKE and the right-wing gangs supported by the government in the first half of 1946, so did the number and size of Communist-led units in the field. The small autonomous bands of the first phase were grouped into sixty to eighty–man companies during the second phase and were later reorganized into full-fledged battalions, brigades, and divisions (during the third phase, after February 1947). In July 1946, Nikos Zachariades, the KKE General Secretary ordered Markos Vafiades to the mountains to coordinate the expanding activities of the Communist guerrillas. Apparently, the appointment of Markos to head the Communist military arm was made by Zachariades, without consultation with other members of the KKE hierarchy, but the appointment was confirmed by the Central Committee in August.[45] Markos proceeded immediately to gain control over the independent Communist-led bands and to impose formal standards of discipline and tactical doctrine, as well as to establish the intelligence, communications, and logistical infrastructures required by a larger, formally organized guerrilla army.

On 28 October 1946, Markos announced the establishment of a Greek Democratic Army (*Demokratikos Stratos Ellados*; GDA) and of its general headquarters in the field, the GDA General Command (*Gheniko Archighio*).[46] A substantial portion of the all-Greek General Command was actually located at the GDA training camp at Boulkes in Yugoslavia, having been formed there during Markos' visit in September 1946.[47] Markos' field headquarters in Greece was relatively mobile; it maintained contact by radio with the Boulkes base, Yugoslavian authorities in Skoplje and Belgrade, and subordinate headquarters.[48] The GDA field headquarters was originally located in Roumeli, but Markos eventually settled on the wild and remote mountain area in northwestern Greece, on the border with Albania and Yugoslavia near Lake Prespa, as the permanent site. The GDA General Command displaced to the village of Lykorrahi, where, protected by the Grammos and Vitsi mountain ranges, it remained until the end of the civil war. By the fall of 1948, the GDA General Command had developed fully. It was organized generally along British-Greek lines, with a "General Staff" combined with directorates to oversee various functions, as shown in Figure 4.1.[49]

The Supreme War Council

In the spring of 1948, the KKE leadership created a Supreme War Council as a conduit for transmitting the political and military decisions of the party to the GDA.[50] The council consisted of the members of the KKE Politburo with the addition of several high-ranking GDA officers who were not members of the inner circle of party leadership. As of October 1948 the members of the Supreme War Council included Nikos Zachariades (General Secretary of the KKE); Gen. Markos Vafiades (prime minister, minister of war, and commander in chief, GDA); Lt. Gen. George Gousias (deputy commander in chief, GDA);

Figure 4.1
Greek Democratic Army GHQ, October 1948

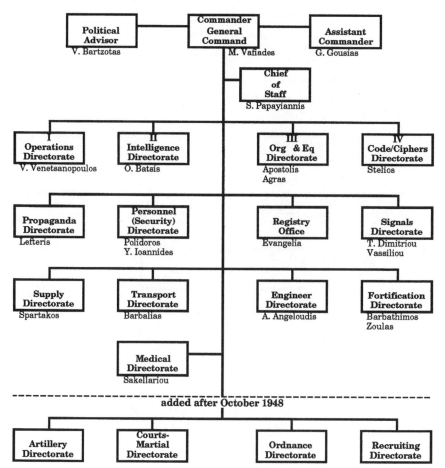

Lt. Gen. George Kikitsas (commander, GDA forces in eastern Macedonia/ western Thrace); Lt. Gen. Kostas Karageorgis (commander, GDA forces in southern Greece); Maj. Gen. Vasilios Bartzotas (minister of finance/political advisor, GDA General Command); Maj. Gen. Dimitrios Vlantas (deputy political advisor, GDA General Command); Col. Stefanos Papayiannis (chief of staff, GDA General Command); and Lt. Col. Polidoros (head of GDA General Command Security Directorate).[51] The Supreme War Council met monthly, but additional meetings were not uncommon. In addition to the regular members, other KKE/GDA political and military figures were summoned to attend depending upon the subject under discussion, either to express their opinions or answer for shortcomings. The meetings were usually presided over by Zachariades, who

Figure 4.2
Greek Democratic Army Area Headquarters, 1946–1947

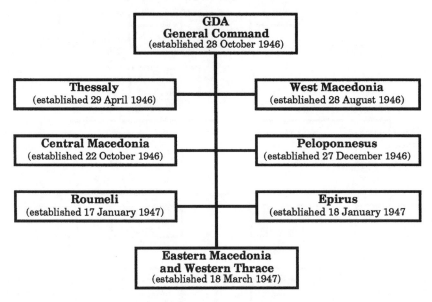

normally dominated the proceedings. In effect the real decisions continued to be made by the Central Committee and Politburo of the KKE.[52]

Area Headquarters

Initially, the guerrilla units of the GDA were coordinated by four mobile headquarters, one each for western Macedonia, eastern Macedonia and Thessaly, Roumeli, and the Peloponnesus. Following the creation of the GDA General Command, seven subordinate regional commands, known as *archighia* (area headquarters) were created to control GDA forces in the various geographical regions. By March 1947, the structure of the area headquarters was as shown in Figure 4.2.

The area headquarters, each of which had a commander, a political commissar, a logistics officer, and supporting personnel, remained fairly mobile, and they relocated when the operational situation demanded. Their functions were to provide intelligence, logistical, and other services; to transmit the orders of GDA General Command; and to control the GDA forces within their assigned region.[53] The forces subordinate to each area headquarters included a varying number of tactical units, liaison units, and area units. The regular tactical units of the GDA included saboteur and sniper teams, independent companies, battalions, and later brigades and divisions. The liaison units were composed of six to eight men and operated directly under an echelon headquarters controlling one of the twenty-five separate administrative sectors, each consisting of a num-

Figure 4.3
Reorganization of GDA "Echelon" Headquarters, 27 August 1948

Old "Echelon" Headquarters	→	New Divisional Headquarters
Thessaly	→	1st Division
Roumeli	→	2nd Division
Peloponnesus	→	3rd Division
Epirus	→	8th Division
West Macedonia	→	9th, 10th, and 11th Divisions
East Macedonia and West Thrace	→	7th Division (formed 5 September 1948)
Central Macedonia	→	6th and 15th Divisions (formed in December 1948)

ber of villages, into which Greece was divided.[54] The liaison units exercised some control over the static area units in their sector and also provided guide and courier services for the more mobile tactical units. Area units were local organizations of fifty to sixty highly armed personnel and provided control over their assigned area and support for other GDA elements.

On 27 August 1948, the minister of war of the Provisional Democratic Government issued an order that abolished the area headquarters and transferred their functions to division headquarters, as shown in Figure 4.3. The new divisional commands retained most of the territorial responsibilities of the former area headquarters, and in fact they generally replicated both the numerical designations and assigned zones of the ELAS divisions of the resistance period.[55] The boundaries of the areas for which each division was responsible were somewhat flexible, and in fact the area controls themselves were somewhat loosely defined. At the meeting of KKE/GDA leaders at Pyli on 15 January 1948, two "echelon" (*klimakia*) headquarters were reestablished to control GDA forces in southern Greece and eastern Macedonia–western Thrace.[56] The motive for reinstituting the echelon headquarters was, in part, to diminish the influence of Markos' on the direction of the GDA.[57] Echelon General Headquarters, Southern Greece (KGANE), controlled the 1st, 2d, and 3d Divisions in Thessaly, Roumeli, and the Peloponnesus respectively. Echelon General Headquarters, Eastern Macedonia and Western Thrace (KGAKAMT), controlled the 6th and 7th Divisions. The remaining divisions in the critical northern border areas from Epirus east to the Axios River (the 8th Division in Epirus and the 9th, 10th, and 11th Divisions in western Macedonia) were controlled directly by GDA General Command. GDA units in the Kaimaktsalan, Paikon, Vermion, Pierria, Olympus areas (i.e., that part of central Macedonia focused on Salonika) were controlled by the 15th Division.

Tactical Organization

Following the decision taken at the Second Plenum in February 1946 to pursue more aggressive guerrilla operations against the government, and with the return to the mountains of veteran Communist cadres from the training camps in Albania, Yugoslavia, and Bulgaria, the small autonomous bands established in 1945 and early 1946 grew steadily. They were reorganized, beginning in April 1946, into autonomous companies (*syngrotimata*) of sixty to eighty men, grouped in two or three platoons of two sections each.[58] These autonomous companies were initially controlled by the regional *aftoamyna* organization, and they sometimes cooperated on a specific operation but then dispersed. Eventually, two or three such companies came under the control of a designated sub-command. The identification of these GDA guerrilla units was haphazard: some were numbered, some took the name of their commander or area of operations, and some took whatever designation caught their fancy. Their armament consisted of a variety of light infantry weapons, mostly in good condition. By the fall of 1946, they had added some light mortars and heavy machine guns. Initially, each unit had its own small base area, from which it drew whatever supplies and other support it could, and the guerrillas concealed themselves easily and were largely self-supporting. But by early 1947 there were some one or two hundred active Communist-led guerrilla units in the field, and as the units grew in size and the number of units increased, they required larger established bases and increasing amounts of logistical support.[59]

The decision of the KKE Politburo in February 1947 to transform the GDA into a conventional army capable of opposing the Greek national forces in battles to seize and hold terrain was confirmed by the Third Plenum in September 1947 and the Fourth Plenum in June 1948, over the protests of the GDA commander in chief. The conversion process began in the spring of 1947 and was essentially complete by the end of 1948. However, the conversion cost the GDA in terms of mobility, flexibility, and the ability to practice tactical infiltration, and it did not provide compensating increases in firepower.[60] Despite the best efforts of the KKE/GDA leadership, the GDA remained primarily a light infantry force with relatively few heavy weapons or support personnel. Moreover, it placed heavy burdens on the limited GDA logistical system. While GDA units had good firepower at short range, they had virtually no long-range firepower. What little artillery the GDA did have was used to defend its base areas and to harass Greek government forces in towns and villages; thus its military value was negligible.[61]

Between October 1946 and March 1947 the autonomous guerrilla companies were grouped into battalions, each of which had a strength of two to four hundred officers and men and was organized with three to five companies, each of which in turn had three to four platoons of three to four sections each.[62] Cadres to man the new headquarters were provided from Boulkes or the other training centers outside Greece. By mid-1947, there were sixty-five to seventy such battalions inside Greece. Some twenty battalions—over 5,000 of the best GDA fighters—were in the so-called "Frontier Corner" (where the borders of Greece, Albania, and Yugoslavia met), guarding the GDA Central Command headquarters and the passes on the lines of communications into Greece from Albania and Yugoslavia. There were also twenty-four battalions in Macedonia and

Thrace and a few being re-formed just over the border. The remainder were in Thessaly and the Peloponnesus.

In the fall of 1947, the battalions began to be organized into light brigades of 700–1,300 men, beginning first in the critical western Macedonian region.[63] The changeover then progressed to the whole of Epirus and Thessaly and subsequently to the Roumeli area, central Greece, and the Peloponnesus. The formation of heavier brigades followed. The next step was the organization of the brigades into five small divisions, each of which was normally authorized two brigades of three battalions each. The first GDA division was formed in May 1948, although the formal order imposing a divisional structure on the existing brigades was not issued until 28 August 1948.[64] The process accelerated in September 1948, so that by the end of the year there were eight GDA divisions, which controlled some twenty-three brigades, forty-two battalions, twenty-five double companies, and eighteen independent companies.[65] By December 1948, two additional divisions were in the process of formation: the 15th Division in the Sinaiatsikon-Ventzia region and the 6th Division, commanded by Petris, in the Axios-Nestos area.

The GDA formations were largely battalions, brigades, or divisions in name only. The conversion of the GDA into a conventional force significantly increased its requirements for qualified commanders and staff officers and for support personnel as well as for riflemen, all of whom grew scarcer as the war progressed. Authorized strengths of GDA units at every level were eventually established, but the authorized number of men and amounts of equipment were seldom achieved. In any event, the authorized strength of GDA divisions was lower than that of the opposing GNA divisions and lacked an adequate array of organic support units.[66] Moreover, GDA divisions were seldom employed as such. Brigades were authorized over 1,500 men but each normally had only about 800 men, while battalions, authorized 400 to 500 men, mustered only 200 to 250.[67] The GDA light infantry brigade was authorized 1,209 officers and men and 124 mules organized into a headquarters company, a demolitions (heavy weapons) platoon, two standard infantry battalions, and one light infantry battalion. The light infantry battalion was authorized 239 officers and men and six mules organized into a headquarters section and three seventy-four-man companies, each with a headquarters squad, a heavy machine gun squad, and two thirty-man platoons.[68] Figure 4.4 shows the authorized strength in men and equipment for standard GDA infantry units of various sizes. Detailed organizational diagrams for the various types and sizes of GDA units are to be found in Appendix B.

The conversion of the GDA from a guerrilla force into a conventional army was accompanied by the adoption of a standard uniform and a system of rank insignia. On 21 January 1948, insignia of rank for GDA officers were prescribed by an order of the GDA General Command, and the wearing of insignia of rank by officers promoted by the General Command was made compulsory. The GDA insignia scheme was a cross between the Greek and Soviet systems. Junior

Figure 4.4
Authorized Strength of GDA Infantry Units

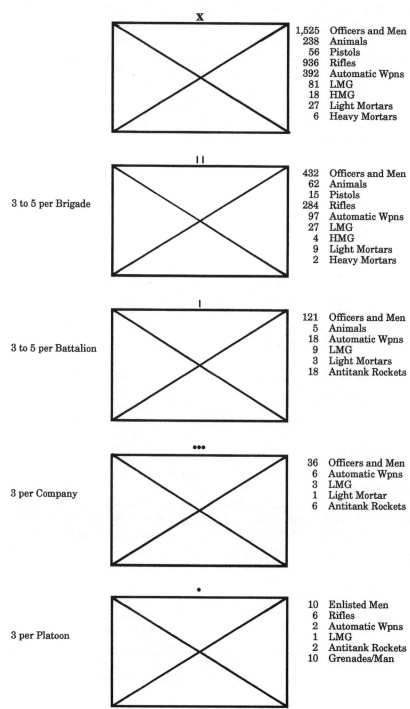

X

1,525	Officers and Men
238	Animals
56	Pistols
936	Rifles
392	Automatic Wpns
81	LMG
18	HMG
27	Light Mortars
6	Heavy Mortars

I I

3 to 5 per Brigade

432	Officers and Men
62	Animals
15	Pistols
284	Rifles
97	Automatic Wpns
27	LMG
4	HMG
9	Light Mortars
2	Heavy Mortars

I

3 to 5 per Battalion

121	Officers and Men
5	Animals
18	Automatic Wpns
9	LMG
3	Light Mortars
18	Antitank Rockets

•••

3 per Company

36	Officers and Men
6	Automatic Wpns
3	LMG
1	Light Mortar
6	Antitank Rockets

•

3 per Platoon

10	Enlisted Men
6	Rifles
2	Automatic Wpns
1	LMG
2	Antitank Rockets
10	Grenades/Man

officers (lieutenants and captains) wore one to three silver stars on a plain epaulet; senior officers (majors, lieutenant colonels, and colonels) had one to three gold stars on an epaulet with a central red (pink) stripe; and general officers wore gold epaulets with a central red stripe and one to four gold stars larger than those of senior officers.[69]

Supporting Arms and Services

The GDA began to employ artillery pieces, primarily in defense of the base areas in northwestern Greece, at the end of 1947. On 1 April 1948, the Greek General Staff reported thirty-seven GDA guns, of which twenty-one were still unconfirmed.[70] By 10 January 1949, the GDA had some seventy-two pieces in service, including two 105 mm howitzers, twenty-four 75 mm mountain guns, four 65 mm mountain guns, eight 37 mm antiaircraft guns, and thirty-four 26 mm antiaircraft guns.[71] At the peak in mid-1949, before the final GNA offensive in the Grammos and Vitsi, the Greek General Staff estimated GDA artillery strength at fifteen 105 mm howitzers, forty-five to forty-seven 75 mm mountain guns, thirty-one 20 mm or 37 mm antiaircraft guns, thirty-eight 20 mm or 37 mm antitank guns, three antitank guns of various calibers, and two to twelve 120 mm mortars.[72]

GDA artillery was organized in independent batteries, troops, and sections.[73] By 1949 there were nine batteries. Normally, a GDA artillery battery consisted of two troops, each with 125 officers and men, fifty-eight mules, four guns, two heavy machine guns, and a basic load of 300 rounds. Each troop was organized with two thirty-five-man sections, each of which was divided into two seventeen-man gun squads with one gun and nine mules. Each GDA brigade was also authorized an antitank gun group, equipped with 20 mm or 37 mm antitank guns, and an antiaircraft artillery group, consisting of one officer, nine gunners, nine ammunition carriers, and nine heavy antiaircraft machine guns (20 mm or 37 mm). For the most part, the GDA employment of artillery was ineffective, due to an inability to concentrate the guns and the lack of sufficient stocks of ammunition. Consequently, as noted, most of the available GDA artillery was used in the defense of the base areas in northwestern Greece.

In addition to infantry and artillery units, the GDA also organized and employed two cavalry units of brigade size and several smaller cavalry detachments, assigned to various headquarters.[74] One cavalry brigade of some 350–400 men was located in Thessaly and the other, of 200–250 men, in the Vitsi/Siniatsikon area. In general, the GDA employment of cavalry was limited by the number of suitable horses available and the difficulties of providing forage. The GDA also formed two field engineer battalions, which were employed under the control of the GDA General Command to assist the combat units by repairing roads and bridges, laying mines, and constructing field fortifications.[75] One battalion was located in the Grammos base area, the other in the Vitsi base area. Engineer sections reinforced combat units during movements and operations.

The dispersion of GDA units made effective communications a necessity; the Communist forces used radios, telephones, and messengers.[76] Once the GDA had been supplied with signal equipment by its outside supporters, radio communications were established between the GDA General Command and its subordinate divisions and brigades, as well as with the echelon headquarters, GDA bases in the neighboring countries, and Yugoslavian authorities in Skoplje and Belgrade. Eventually, sufficient radios were acquired to link all battalions, area units, and independent formations, as well as some information centers and local party headquarters. However, telephones were the primary means used to link most GDA units operating in areas where commercial lines existed or landlines could be established. Runners were also used extensively, particularly in the mountain regions, when units were on the move, or when extra reliability and security were required. A 280-man signal battalion directly subordinate to the GDA General Command was formed at the end of 1948, and a training school was established under the Signal Directorate of GDA General Command to train radio operators and technicians. The GDA signal school had an enrollment of 100 to 120 students at any one time. The GDA General Command Signal Directorate also supervised workshops for the repair and maintenance of signal equipment. The GDA Signal Battalion included an Interception Section of eight to ten radio operators, who monitored GNA transmissions and implemented GDA deception plans by interfering with GNA radio nets. Despite great efforts, however, the lack of adequate signal capabilities plagued the GDA throughout the civil war period.[77]

Support of the GDA tactical units was provided by the two types of area units: Popular Civil Guard and "home defense." One of the first general orders issued by Markos' new headquarters (Decree No. 10) created a Popular Civil Guard (*Laiki Politophylaki*; LP) to maintain order in areas that came under GDA control.[78] These uniformed units, composed of reliable men, were enjoined to "believe in the aims of the GDA, behave well to the people, and be firm and conscientious in the performance of their duties."[79] The Popular Civil Guard organization in the Peloponnesus was typical. In January 1949, it consisted of a headquarters (the Command of the Popular Civil Guard of the Peloponnesus, commanded by one Babbalias) controlling several subcommands, which were subdivided into sections, with one section for each municipality.[80] For example, the Argolis-Corinthia (Liakas) Subcommand, located at Mazeika, had sections based on Alea, Arfara, and Trikkala.

In those areas not under "permanent" GDA control, the functions of the Popular Civil Guard were performed by "home defense" units. Both types of area units were static formations composed of fifty to sixty lightly armed personnel, and they were coordinated and integrated into the GDA military chain of command by the liaison units.[81] Employed either alone or in conjunction with other GDA forces, the area units controlled their assigned area, exposed government agents, participated in the impressment and training of recruits, collected and stored local supplies and transport, treated and cared for the sick and wounded, gathered and forwarded information, and served as messengers. On rare occasions, an area unit might be required to conduct defensive operations to protect its bases or supply caches, but the principal purpose of such units was to support GDA tactical forces. They assumed logistical responsibility for the GDA tactical units operating in or passing through their assigned areas. During GNA counterguerrilla sweeps, the GDA area units often dispersed in small detachments and remained hidden until the sweep was completed.

TRAINING AND PARTY DISCIPLINE

Many of the officers and men of the GDA were veterans of ELAS and had learned what they needed to know "on the job," but the GDA did have an effective program of officer, NCO, and individual combat training, as well as some specialist training.[82] The standard of training attained was adequate for most soldiers and quite good for officers of all ranks. At any given time, the number of men and women in training, both inside Greece and in the neighboring Communist countries, was about 8,000.[83] Most officer training as well as a good deal of the individual and specialist training was conducted at GDA training camps in Albania, Yugoslavia, and Bulgaria, but the GDA General Command ran an officer training school and conducted a four-month course for political commissars. Each echelon (later division) headquarters had its own NCO school and also conducted training for junior officers. Some basic individual combat training was conducted at GDA bases in Greece. Recruits were often given about twenty days of individual combat training, which was focused on the use of small arms, the use of terrain, and political indoctrination. Officer training included a basic course, an intensive two-month platoon commanders course, a six-month senior officers course, and a political course. The basic course and platoon commanders course covered both guerrilla and conventional tactics, urban warfare, and attacks on fortified positions, but they emphasized mountain operations and such topics as ambushes, the attack of outposts, sabotage, and the use of mines. The senior officer course added instruction in tactics, map reading, topography, camouflage, air cover, demolitions, sand-table exercises, and lessons learned by Soviet and Yugoslav guerrillas in World War II, but apparently there was no review of Greek guerrilla operations in World War II. The political course was mandatory for all senior officers and covered Marxist theory, the works of Lenin and Stalin, the history of the Russian Bolshevik movement, and political economy. Specialist training was provided for communications personnel (radio operators), saboteurs, and nurses.

Political Indoctrination

GDA political indoctrination and "enlightenment" activities involved a variety of media, including radio broadcasts, newspapers and magazines, books and pamphlets, and the direct efforts of the political commissars.[84] In the large urban centers, the political commissar was normally a civilian under the direct supervision of the KKE Politburo, but the political commissars in provincial towns were often drawn from the ranks of the GDA's political commissars. In the early stages of the "Third Round," the KKE consciously downplayed political indoctrination to attract a wider spectrum of recruits and supporters. Until the end of 1947, the political indoctrination of the Communist military personnel was entrusted to the *kapetanios* who shared the command of each unit. However, as the GDA grew in size and the decision to form a conventional force was taken, the party and GDA leaders increased the emphasis on political reliability. The political and military disputes between the factions headed by Zachariades and Markos Vafiades obviously made the imposition of party discipline and "correct thinking" more necessary, from Zachariades' point of view. The increasing proportion of forced recruits also argued for more stringent ideological controls. In January 1948, Zachariades established within the GDA a system of political commissars based on that of the Soviet Army. Reliable men were chosen, given four months of intensive schooling at GDA General Command, and assigned to all levels of command down to platoon level.[85] The number of political commissars in the GDA expanded from only eighteen at the end of 1947 to some 700 in 1948.[86]

At division level, the political indoctrination was the responsibility of the Personnel Directorate, under the direction of a major (the political commissar) and a staff of eight to ten officers (an assistant commissar and officers responsible for biographical data, women, youth, towns, and counterintelligence).[87] At brigade and battalion level, there were usually two officers, or an officer and a warrant officer, to perform the functions of the political commissar. The quality of the men appointed as political commissars varied widely, since the post of commissar obviously required extraordinarily dedicated and disciplined Communists—ideally, ones who had suffered for the cause, were popular with the men but objective and unsentimental, and were not too fond of women or entertainment, qualities which were probably in short supply.[88]

Internal Security

Internal security, counterintelligence, and the maintenance of party discipline were matters of the first importance to the KKE and consequently to the GDA. Consequently, the euphemistically named Personnel Directorate was perhaps the most influential staff section of the GDA General Command.[89] Originally under the direction of a Lieutenant Colonel Polidoros, the Personnel Directorate later came under Yiannis Ioannides, one of Nikos Zachariades' strongest supporters. The primary function of the Personnel Directorate was to maintain internal security within the GDA and also within the KKE itself. Files were maintained on every officer and NCO as well as some political leaders, and the agents of the Personnel Directorate rendered regular reports on the conduct of officers and men as well as the state of their morale. Orders and reports were examined with a view to detecting deviations from party and army policies and fixing responsibility for failures. The Personnel Directorate also monitored the morale of units of the Greek national forces. Among its other major functions were the maintenance of liaison with authorities in the Soviet Union and the satellite countries with respect to the support provided to the GDA, and the supervision of the political indoctrination program of the GDA, which was carried out by a system of political commissars at every echelon of command.

CONCLUSION

Markos Vafiades was dismissed as prime minister of the Provisional Democratic Government and as commander in chief of the GDA at the Fifth Plenum on 31 January 1949. Yiannis Ioannides took his place as prime minister, and for a short time Zachariades himself took direct command of the GDA while remaining General Secretary of the KKE. The post of commander in chief was subsequently offered to Markos' old wartime comrade, George Kikitsas, who refused it. Political reliability rather than military acumen being the primary consideration, George Gousias, one of Zachariades' strongest supporters, was then named commander in chief. A former printer, Gousias was no Markos Vafiades. As the author of an article in *Time* magazine put it in May 1949, "There were still no songs about the new guerrilla commander[,] . . . whose mustache is considerably less impressive than his predecessor's."[90]

In the early spring of 1949 the GDA was organized into a general headquarters and two subordinate regional headquarters controlling nine infantry divisions, three separate infantry brigades, two cavalry brigades, nine artillery batteries, the Officers' School Brigade, a signal battalion, two engineer battalions, three transport battalions, and two stretcher-bearer battalions, as shown in Figure 4.5. As the GNA campaigns gathered steam in the spring and summer of 1949, the formal organization of the GDA began to disintegrate. The 1st and 2d Divisions were decimated by GNA in Agrafa-Roumeli during the withdrawal from Karpenision in February–March, and during April–June the remaining GDA guerrillas in the Peloponnesus, Samos, and Kefallinia were mopped up by government forces.[91] Heavy casualties, the loss of capable leaders, and persistent pursuit and harassment by government forces reduced the size and broke the cohesion of GDA units. The remnants of divisions, brigades, and battalions had to be pieced together in ad hoc formations, lacking men and weapons. At the same time, the *aftoamyna* suffered heavy losses and in many areas ceased to exist at all, thus depriving the GDA of intelligence, recruiting services, and logistical support.

At its peak in mid-1948, the GDA numbered slightly more than 25,000 fighters in Greece, perhaps another 20,000 in the neighboring states, and 50,000 active supporters. The logistical requirements of such a force under conditions of guerrilla warfare were not extraordinary. However, Zachariades' ill-considered deci-

Figure 4.5
Greek Democratic Army, Early 1949

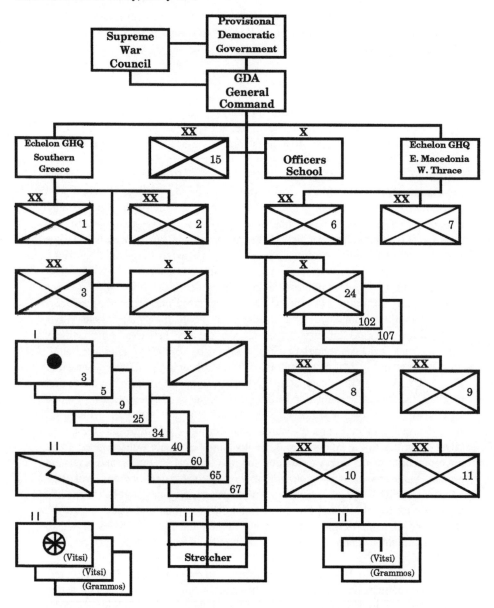

sion to proceed in 1947 from guerrilla warfare to conventional, positional warfare, meant that the GDA would not be able to sustain itself from internal sources alone. The remoteness and chronic poverty of the areas of operations, the economic devastation left by the Axis occupation (and the resistance to it) in World War II, and the overall paucity of internal resources made the support of conventional forces, even a force as small as 25,000 fighters, impossible. Although the GDA probably could have continued guerrilla operations almost indefinitely, the shift to conventional organization and positional warfare from mid-1947 failed to take into account the limited manpower and logistical resources available and thus required resources that could only be obtained from external sources.

NOTES

1. Most authors divide the period from February 1945 to August 1949 into only three phases. The three traditional phases are most clearly established by John O. Iatrides in "Civil War, 1945–1949: National and International Aspects," in John O. Iatrides, ed., *Greece in the 1940s: A Nation in Crisis* (Hanover, NH: University of New England Press, 1981), 199. Iatrides names the phases "Unplanned Insurrection," "Transition," and "Planned Insurrection." In "The Varkiza Agreement and the Origins of the Civil War" (in Iatrides, ed., 179), Heinz Richter accepts Iatrides' three phases but calls them "Unarmed Self-Defense," "Armed Self-Defense," and "Offense." Other authors define the phases differently. Dimitrios G. Kousoulas (*Revolution and Defeat: The Story of the Greek Communist Party* [London: Oxford Univ. Press, 1965], 240 note 6) divides the civil war into three periods: March–September 1946, October 1946–March 1947, and April 1947–August 1949. The authors of *Peak Organized Strength of Guerrilla and Government Forces in Algeria, Nagaland, Ireland, Indochina, South Vietnam, Malaya, Philippines, and Greece* (Washington: Counterinsurgency Information Analysis Center, Special Operations Research Office, American University, n.d. [ca. 1965], 18–19) offer yet a third phasing: Spring–Fall 1946 ("Bandit"), Fall 1946–mid-1948 ("Guerrilla"), and mid-1948–August 1949 ("Positional and Conventional").

2. See, for example, Christopher M. Woodhouse, *The Struggle for Greece, 1941–1949* (London: Hart-Davis, MacGibbon, 1976), 169.

3. Stephen Merrill, *The Communist Attack on Greece*, Special Report No. 15, 21st Regular Course, U.S. Strategic Intelligence School (Washington: U.S. Strategic Intelligence School, 28 July 1952), 23.

4. The events of the Seventh Party Congress are described by Heinz Richter in "The Second Plenum of the Central Committee of the KKE and the Decision for Civil War: A Reappraisal," in Lars Baerentzen, John O. Iatrides, and Ole L. Smith, eds., *Studies in the History of the Greek Civil War, 1945–1949* (Copenhagen: Museum Tusculanum Press, 1987), 184–87.

5. Ibid., 185.

6. Iatrides, "Civil War," 197.

7. George T. Mavrogordatos, "The 1946 Election and Plebiscite: Prelude to Civil War," in Iatrides, ed., 187.

8. The plenums of the KKE Central Committee began a new numerical sequence

with the return of Nikos Zachariades as General Secretary. Thus, the Second Plenum in February 1946 followed the Twelfth Plenum of June 1945.

9. On several occasions Stalin had advised the KKE leaders to adopt such a "dual strategy" (see Merrill, 24–25, and Ole L. Smith, "Self-Defence and Communist Policy, 1945–1947," in Lars Baerentzen, John O. Iatrides, and Ole L. Smith, eds., *Studies in the History of the Greek Civil War, 1945–1949* [Copenhagen: Museum Tusculanum Press, 1987], 160 note 5).

10. Woodhouse, 170.

11. Richter, "Varkiza Agreement," 179.

12. Smith, "Self-Defence," 166.

13. Iatrides, "Civil War," 210.

14. Quoted from the 14 December 1947 edition of *Avgi* by Smith ("Self-Defence and Communist Policy," 175). The decision was apparently taken with the understanding that both the Soviets and the Yugoslavs would provide the necessary material help.

15. Smith, "Self-Defence," 160.

16. Quoted from *Neos Kosmos*, no. 8 (August 1950), 478, by Dominique Eudes, *The Kapetanios: Partisans and Civil War in Greece, 1943–1949* (New York: Monthly Review Press, 1972), 302.

17. Eudes, 303.

18. Woodhouse, 211–13.

19. Eudes, 303.

20. Woodhouse, 226.

21. Eudes, 309.

22. Kousoulas, 253; Eudes, 327–28.

23. Edgar O'Ballance, *The Greek Civil War, 1944–1949* (New York: Praeger, 1966), 155; Merrill, 65.

24. Lawrence S. Wittner, *American Intervention in Greece, 1943–1949* (New York: Columbia Univ. Press, 1982), 264.

25. Quoted by O'Ballance, 170. O'Ballance notes that Markos' offer, which was subsequently confirmed by Zachariades, was prompted in part by the anxiety of the Greek Communists over the deteriorating relationship between the Cominform and Marshal Tito.

26. O'Ballance, 170. At the same time, the Greek government was pursuing negotiations to normalize relations with both Albania and Bulgaria. On 7 June 1948, it decided to enter peace negotiations with Albania, and on 13 June it accepted a Bulgarian offer to resume diplomatic relations.

27. Merrill, 66.

28. The actions of the Fifth Plenum are discussed by Eudes, 340–41; Woodhouse, 262; Merrill, 57; Kousoulas, 262–63; and O'Ballance, 185–86.

29. Kousoulas, 263; O'Ballance, 186.

30. Woodhouse, 262.

31. Eudes, 332.

32. Quoted in United States Military Attaché-Greece (Col. Harvey H. Smith), Intelligence Report R-273-49 (ID No. 576384) Athens, 13 July 1949, subject: Guerrilla Strategical and Tactical Problems, 1948, 9 [in Box 3707, Assistant Chief of Staff, G-2, Intelligence, Numerical Series of Intelligence Document File ("ID Files"), 1944–1955, Record Group 319 (Records of the Army Staff), National Archives II, College Park, MD. The location of similar documents from the "ID Files" will be cited hereafter simply as

"in Box *x*, ID Files, RG 319, NA," and on second and subsequent citations such documents will be identified solely by their ID number.

33. Woodhouse, 271–72.

34. O'Ballance, 187; Woodhouse, 247; M. A. Campbell, E. W. Downs, and L. V. Schuetta, *The Employment of Airpower in the Greek Guerrilla War, 1947–1949*, Project No. AU-411-62-ASI (Maxwell Air Force Base, AL: Concepts Division, Aerospace Studies Institute, United States Air University, December 1964), 12 [cited hereafter as *Employment of Airpower*].

35. Frank J. Abbott, *The Greek Civil War, 1947–1949: Lessons for the Operational Artist in Foreign Internal Defense*, School of Advanced Military Studies thesis (Fort Leavenworth, KS: School of Advanced Military Studies, USACGSC, May 1994), 26–30 passim; *Employment of Airpower*, 12; Woodhouse, 247.

36. Quoted by Woodhouse, 267.

37. Woodhouse, 267–68; Eudes, 332.

38. Hugh H. Gardner, *Civil War in Greece, 1945–1949*, incomplete draft (Washington: Office of the Chief of Military History, Department of the Army, n.d.), "Sources of Guerrilla Manpower" (unpaginated) [cited hereafter as Gardner draft].

39. Iatrides, "Civil War," 199–200. The most famous leader of unreconciled ELAS veterans was Aris Velouchiotis, who was killed in a government ambush on 16 June 1945.

40. Merrill, 23.

41. Kousoulas, 240 note 6.

42. Iatrides, "Civil War," 200.

43. Merrill, 34–35.

44. O'Ballance, 121.

45. Smith, "Self-Defence," 171; Evangelos Averoff-Tossizza, *By Fire and Axe: The Communist Party and the Civil War in Greece, 1944–1949* (New Rochelle, NY: Caratzas Brothers, 1978), 177.

46. The Greek Communist military force was originally referred to as the Republican Army; the title of Greek Democratic Army was adopted in December 1946 (see O'Ballance, 121).

47. O'Ballance, 122.

48. Iatrides, "Civil War," 211; O'Ballance, 126.

49. On the organization of the GDA General Command in late 1948 see United States Military Attaché-Greece (Col. Harvey H. Smith), Intelligence Report R-666-48 (ID No. 507127), Athens, 13 November 1948, subject: Preliminary Interrogation Report of Captured Bandit, Major REPA, Assistant Intelligence Officer, MARKOS' HQ, 4–6 [in Box 3286, ID Files, RG 319, NA]; Greek General Staff, Intelligence Directorate, Study (Ref. No. F8206/95/2–12-50), Athens, 12 February 1950, subject: Guerrilla Warfare—The Organization and Employment of Irregulars, Chart A [in file "GEOG. L. GREECE 370.64 (Guerrillas)," General Reference Branch, United States Army Center of Military History, Washington, DC] [cited hereafter as Greek General Staff, *Guerrilla Warfare*]; and United States Military Attaché-Greece (Capt. Charles M. Conover), Intelligence Report R-124-49 (ID No. 544879), Athens, 31 March 1949, subject: GDA Director of Engineers [in Box 3520, ID Files, RG 319, NA]. The first incumbent listed in Figure 4.1 was in place in October 1948 (as reported by Major Repa, the Assistant Intelligence Officer of Markos' headquarters, who was captured by the GNA near Florina on 24 October 1948), the second as of 15 December 1948 (see United States Military Attaché-Greece [Maj. Harold

A. Tidmarsh], Intelligence Report R-110-49 [ID No. 542941], Athens, 22 March 1949, subject: Organization of the Bandit Forces and Tactics Employed by the Bandits, 5 [in file "GEOG. L. GREECE 370.64 (Guerrillas)," General Reference Branch, United States Army Center of Military History, Washington, DC] [cited hereafter as ID No. 542941]).

50. On the Supreme War Council see Kousoulas, 267; Merrill, 57; Greek General Staff, *Guerrilla Warfare*, 49; and ID No. 542941, 4.

51. As revealed under interrogation by Major Repa (see ID No. 507127), 4; ID No. 542941, 4.

52. ID No. 542941, 4; Eudes, 332.

53. Extract-Summary of the Report of Maj. Gen. Stephen J. Chamberlin to U.S. Army Chief of Staff, 20 October 1947, 2 [in file "GEOG. L. GREECE 370.02 (Civil War)," General Reference Branch, United States Army Center of Military History, Washington, DC] [cited hereafter as Chamberlin Report].

54. Chamberlin Report, 2; J. C. Murray, "The Anti-Bandit War [Part II]," *Marine Corps Gazette* 38, no. 2 (February 1954), 52. The sectors were administrative zones and did not control tactical operations.

55. ID No. 542941, 4; Gardner draft, "The Insurgent Organization."

56. The creation and organization of the echelon headquarters are described in Woodhouse, 226; Greek General Staff, *Guerrilla Warfare*, 121–22 and Chart A; ID No. 542941, 4; Gardner draft, "The Insurgent Organization"; and ID No. 523063, 4.

57. Woodhouse, 226.

58. The organization and employment of the *syngrotimata* are described in Merrill, 55; Gardner draft, "The Insurgent Organization"; O'Ballance, 143; Averoff-Tossizza, 176; and Kousoulas, 240 note 6. Each autonomous company was led by a commander and a political commissar (*kapetanios*).

59. E. E. Zacharakis, "Lessons Learned from the Anti-Guerrilla War in Greece (1946–1949)," *Revue Militaire Générale* 7 (July 1960), 182; O'Ballance, 143; Averoff-Tossizza, 179.

60. *Employment of Airpower*, 19–20.

61. Murray, "The Anti-Bandit War [Part II]," 51.

62. The organization of GDA battalions is described in Gardner draft, "The Insurgent Organization"; Chamberlin Report, 2; Merrill, 55; and O'Ballance, 151.

63. The organization of GDA brigades and divisions is described in Gardner draft, "The Insurgent Organization"; Merrill, 55; Murray, "The Anti-Bandit War [Part II]," 53; O'Ballance, 182; ID No. 542941, 4; and Greek General Staff, *Guerilla Warfare*, 49.

64. Woodhouse, 231.

65. United States Military Attaché-Greece (Capt. Charles M. Conover), Intelligence Report R-1-49 (ID No. 523063), Athens, 4 January 1949, subject: Guerrilla Order of Battle—Strength, Organization and Disposition, 4 and 12 [in Box 3390, ID Files, RG 319, NA]; United States Military Attaché-Greece (Capt. Charles M. Conover), Intelligence Report R-90-49 (ID No. 538917), Athens, 2 March 1949, subject: Guerrilla Order of Battle—Strength, Organization and Disposition, 4 [in Box 3482, ID Files, RG 319, NA]; and United States Military Attaché-Greece (Col. Harvey H. Smith), Intelligence Report R-130-49 (ID No. 548336), Athens, 11 April 1949, subject: Interrogation of Guerrilla [Ex-GNA] Lt. Z. G. ASTRIHADES, 7 [in Box 3539, ID Files, RG 319, NA].

66. Gardner draft, "The Insurgent Organization"; Murray, "The Anti-Bandit War [Part II]," 53.

67. Greek General Staff, *Guerrilla Warfare*, 49; Gardner draft, "The Insurgent Organization"; Averoff-Tossizza, 254.

68. ID No. 542941, Enclosures 2–4; Gardner draft, Charts B and C.

69. United States Military Attaché-Greece (Lt. Col. Albert B. Seitz), Intelligence Report R-462-48 (ID No. 474894), Salonika, 28 June 1948, subject: Order of the Democratic Army dated 21 January 1948, 2 [in Box 3074, ID Files, RG 319, NA].

70. United States Military Attaché-Greece (Capt. W. R. Cory), Intelligence Report R-319-48 (ID No. 458904), Athens, 26 April 1948, subject: Guerrilla (Bandit) Order of Battle, 10 [in Box 2966, ID Files, RG 319, NA].

71. United States Army Group, Headquarters, Joint United States Military Advisory and Planning Group-Greece, Operations Report, APO 206 [Athens], 28 January 1949, subject: JUSMAPG Operations Report No. 50 (190001–252400 Jan. 49), Annex No. 2 (Intelligence Report for period 190001–252400 Jan. 49, dated 26 January 1949), 5–6 [Item 4, Case 8, Section I-B, Book I, P&O Division, 091 Greece, RG 319, NA].

72. Gardner draft, Chart A; ID No. 589129.

73. The organization of the GDA artillery is described in Greek General Staff, *Guerrilla Warfare*, 50, 121–22, and Chart A; ID No. 542941, enclosure 5; Gardner draft, Chart E; and Murray, "The Anti-Bandit War [Part II]," 53. Detailed organizational diagrams for GDA artillery units are in Appendix B.

74. Greek General Staff, *Guerrilla Warfare*, 50; ID No. 542941, 7.

75. Greek General Staff, *Guerrilla Warfare*, 50; ID No. 548336, 7.

76. GDA communications are described in Greek General Staff, *Guerrilla Warfare*, 50; ID No. 542941, 11; and Gardner draft, "Communications."

77. United States Army Command and General Staff College, *Internal Defense Operations: A Case History, Greece 1946–49*, USACGSC RB 31-1 (Fort Leavenworth, KS: United States Army Command and General Staff College, 1 November 1967), 130–31.

78. Amikam Nachmani, *International Intervention in the Greek Civil War: The United Nations Special Committee on the Balkans, 1947–1952* (New York: Praeger, 1990), 13.

79. Ibid.

80. United States Military Attaché-Greece (Col. Harvey H. Smith), Intelligence Report R-87-49 (ID No. 529461), Athens, 3 March 1949, subject: Information from Bandit [Anastassios KYRIAKZIS] Captured in ARGOS, PELOPONNESE 19 January 1949, 7 [in Box 3470, ID Files, RG 319, NA].

81. Greek General Staff, *Guerrilla Warfare*, 49; Chamberlin Report, 2; Gardner draft, "Supply and Services."

82. GDA training is described in Chamberlin Report, 3–5; O'Ballance, 151; and Gardner draft, "Training."

83. O'Ballance, 142.

84. Political indoctrination in the GDA and the role of the political commissar are described in Gardner draft, "Political Commissars."

85. ID No. 542941, Enclosure 1.

86. Woodhouse, 223.

87. ID No. 542941, Enclosure 1.

88. Gardner draft, "Political Commissars."

89. The GDA Personnel Directorate is described in Gardner draft, "Internal Security."

90. *Time*, 23 May 1949, 27.

91. Kousoulas, 266. The survivors of the 2d Division, some 1,500 men and women, did not reach the Grammos until the end of March, after a harrowing trek through the mountains and a narrow escape from being surrounded by Government forces near Metsovon (see Eudes, 346–47).

Nikos Zachariades, General Secretary of the
Greek Communist Party.

General Markos Vafiades, Commander in
Chief of the Greek Democratic Army.

Headquarters of the Greek Democratic Army at Lykorrahi, January 1948.

A Communist guerrilla band in the mountains, January 1948.

Two Greek Communist fighters, July 1947. The male guerrilla is wearing a U.S. Army issue uniform blouse. The female guerrilla is wearing a British-style battledress jacket. Both guerrillas are carrying British Sten Mark 2 submachine guns.

Communist guerrillas at breakfast near the Plain of Ardea in Macedonia, January 1948.

Greek Democratic Army command post near the Plain of Ardea in Macedonia, January 1948.

View of the town of Konitsa, December 1947. The American school of agriculture is in the foreground.

Communist-held height in the Grammos, July 1948.

5

The Greek Democratic Army: Manpower and Logistics

Manpower and logistics were the twin Achilles' heels of the Greek Democratic Army (GDA), and the political and military decisions that shaped the organization of the GDA during the civil war of 1945–1949 also established its requirements for men and matériel. The adoption of Nikos Zachariades' plan for the conversion of the GDA to a conventional force and the subsequent defensive battles to carve out a Communist-controlled domain in the mountains of northwestern Greece placed on the slender manpower base and fragile logistical structure of the GDA a burden that they could not sustain. It led directly to the defeat of the GDA by the Greek government forces, which had the advantages of plentiful manpower and a logistical system backed by American aid.

Even without the added requirements imposed by the conversion to a conventional army, the GDA faced daunting challenges in recruiting and retaining sufficient manpower and in providing the necessary logistical support. The size of the GDA was the principal determinant of its logistical requirements, and the success or failure of operations as well as organizational initiatives were dependent on the success of the GDA in recruiting combatants and auxiliaries, and in avoiding losses through desertion, surrender, wounds, and death on the battlefield. Given the small pool of manpower upon which they were able to draw and the many excellent reasons for avoiding service in the Communist army, the GDA was under constant pressure to provide even the minimum numbers of combatants and support personnel required.

Obtaining and distributing the supplies and services needed by the GDA was an equally challenging task. The difficult terrain and severe climate of the principal area of operations in the mountains of northwestern Greece increased requirements for food, forage, clothing, and fuel, and it impeded the distribution of supplies. The lack of staff skills and experience in large-scale logistics, as well as the lack of necessary technical skills at lower levels, produced inefficiency and waste. The destruction during the World War II occupation and subsequent civil war had reduced the internal resources of Greece—in any event, a poor and underdeveloped country—to such a degree that a guerrilla army was hard pressed to obtain locally even its most basic needs, such as food, clothing, and medical supplies, either by purchase or forced requisition. Consequently, the GDA was obliged to depend on outside support, which was tenuous at best. Finally, the GDA was faced with an opponent constantly growing in strength and logistical capability—thanks to the generous support of the United States— and thus increasingly effective in destroying the bases and logistical infrastructure of the GDA and interdicting the GDA's lines of communications.

In the end, the Greek Communist forces were simply unable to recruit and retain the manpower or to obtain and distribute the food, arms, ammunition, or other supplies required by a large conventionally organized military force engaged in almost continuous heavy action, either from internal resources or with the assistance of outside supporters. Whether or not the GDA could have sustained a smaller guerrilla army, as Markos Vafiades argued, and prolonged the civil war long enough for the Greek government to flag and seek a negotiated settlement is problematic. The fact remains that the success of Nikos Zachariades in imposing his vision of a Soviet-style conventional army and a strategy of positional warfare doomed the GDA, and thus the Communist cause, to defeat.

STRENGTH OF THE COMMUNIST FORCES, FEBRUARY 1945–AUGUST 1949

The manpower of the GDA came from two sources, volunteers and forced recruits. From February 1945 to the end of the civil war in August 1949, a considerable number of volunteers were found to fill the ranks of the GDA, although as the position of the GDA deteriorated in late 1948 and 1949 the numbers of volunteers declined. Volunteers were motivated by several considerations: dedication to the idea of a new Communist society in Greece, the desire among Macedonian Slavs to create an autonomous Macedonian state, the need to escape right-wing terrorism or punishment for civil offenses, the desire for adventure and relief from the monotony and poverty of life in the rural villages, and, among many of the veterans of ELAS, habituation to the free life of the mountain guerrilla.[1] The recruitment of volunteers was carried out mainly through the local Greek Communist Party (KKE) cells and liaison units (yia-faka), but some young men and women simply wandered into the mountains to find the guerrilla bands on their own.

The majority of the recruits for the GDA, particularly as the conflict wore on, were obtained by forced recruiting. As early as October 1947, American and Greek national authorities estimated that up to 60 percent of the GDA regular forces were being recruited by force, 25 percent were dedicated Communists, and the remaining 15 percent included individuals who enlisted in the GDA for adventure, to escape punishment for civil crimes, or other reasons.[2] The Greek national government made an issue of the forced recruitment of men for the

Table 5.1
GDA Recruitment, October 1948–June 1949

Month	Recruits
October 1948	3,600
November 1948	1,920
December 1948	1,848
January 1949	1,500
23 February–1 March 1949	1,500
May 1949	720
June 1949	100

Sources: Compiled from JUSMAPG monthly operations reports, Greek General Staff estimates, and
    U.S. Military Attaché–Greece reports.

GDA, although its own methods were not substantially more enlightened.[3] As
Gardner points out, while 60 percent of the GDA force may have been recruited
by force, "there is no evidence to indicate that anything like 60 percent of the
guerrillas were held in the ranks of the Democratic Army against their will."[4]
The desire of captured rebels to present themselves as unwilling conscripts is
understandable. As Floyd A. Spencer has noted,

It became the habit of the dissidents who later went over to the government side to claim
that they had been conscripted, that they would never have remained with "the red
wolves" had not they and their families been threatened with death. This may have been
true in many cases, but a corporal who has found it difficult to keep his raw recruits
from disappearing off a level parade ground into the nearby woods will find it hard to
understand by what wizardry the communist commissars kept their conscripts from disappearing over a long period of months in the Greek mountains.[5]

From the point of view of the individual conscript, there was in fact much to
be said for being forcibly inducted into the guerrilla ranks rather than into the
Greek national forces (GNF). For one thing, the discipline and lifestyle of the
mountain guerrilla was more attractive than service in the GNF. In any event,
recruits on both sides had ample opportunities to escape should they so desire;
perhaps 50 percent of forced recruits gained their freedom in a matter of days,
although occasionally the GDA apprehended a deserter and publicly executed
him *"pour encourager les autres."*[6]

The success of GDA recruiters and impressment gangs varied depending upon
the success or failure of GDA operations. Between 1 December 1947 and 1
March 1948, the GDA pulled in 5,580–5,829 new recruits, an average of 1,860–
1,900 per month over a three-month period.[7] From 1 April to 1 October 1948,
the total number of new GDA recruits was 20,500, or about 1,800 per month.[8]
As the war ground toward its end, the GDA encountered increasing difficulty
in replacing its heavy casualties. Table 5.1 shows the monthly recruitment fig-

ures for selected months from October 1948 to June 1949, when the GNA final campaign began.

GDA Combatant Strength

The total strength of the GDA included active combatants—members of the GDA strictly speaking, including headquarters and logistical personnel; auxiliaries—members of the various branches of the self-defense (*aftoamyna*), including liaison units (*yiafka*) and area (Popular Civil Guard and home defense) units; reserves in the friendly neighboring countries, including the wounded and support personnel; and those who simply shared the goals of the KKE/GDA and were kindly disposed. One might also add the numerous Albanians, Yugoslavians, Bulgarians, and others who actively worked in their own countries to support the GDA.

Female guerrillas (*andartisses*) served as combatants in the Communist guerrilla bands from the earliest stages of the "Third Round." A relatively high percentage of the GDA active force comprised women; by March 1949, about 20 to 25 percent of the GDA combatants were women.[9] During the desperate final battles in the Grammos and Vitsi in the summer of 1949, the percentage of female combatants in some units rose to as high as 50 percent.[10] The percentage of women in supporting units was, of course, higher. One estimate placed the percentage of women in the two GDA transport battalions under Barbalias at 90 percent.[11] Since women were normally not subject to GDA impressment, it may be assumed that most of the women in the GDA were dedicated volunteers. In general, women were utilized for administrative and logistical tasks, but some did participate in active combat, and for the most part they were well motivated, brave, and good fighters.[12] Many of the female members of the GDA paid a high price for their patriotism, being abused sexually by their male comrades and subsequently ostracized, in accordance with Greek mores.[13]

The maximum strength of the regular GDA combatant forces during the period from February 1945 to August 1949 cannot be determined with any precision, and all figures for GDA recruitment, supporters, reserves, and casualties—whether reported by the Greek national government or the Greek Communists themselves—must be considered suspect, as having been "cooked" for political purposes.[14] The best estimates are that GDA combatant strength averaged about 23,000 during the height of the civil war in 1948–1949 and peaked in April 1948 at about 26,210 active fighters inside Greece, plus another 20,000 reserves (including recruits in training) in the neighboring countries and about 50,000 active auxiliaries.[15] Recruiting and logistical considerations limited the GDA to about 25,000 as the maximum number that could be supported on a sustained basis, and in fact GDA strength averaged about 23,000 during most of 1948 and 1949.[16] In all, as many as 100,000 men and women may have served actively in the GDA.[17] Table 5.2 provides an estimate of GDA combatant

Table 5.2
GDA Combatant Strength in Greece, 1946–1949

Date	Total	Pelopon-nesus	Central Greece, Crete, and Islands	Epirus-Western Macedonia	Eastern Macedonia-Western Thrace
Second Phase: February 1946–February 1947					
March 1946	2,500				
June 1946	3,000				
July 1946	4,000				
August 1946	5,500				
October 1946	6,000				
December 1946	9,285				
"Early 1947"	11,390	400	8,140	1,700	1,150
Third Phase: March 1947–February 1949					
March 1947	13,000				
April 1947	14,250				
Summer 1947	18,000				
September 1947	13,610				
October 1947	17,000		3,000	8,500	5,000
November 1947	19,420				
December 1947	20,350				
January 1948	22,250				
February 1948	24,140				
March 1948	25,000	1,000	9,450	9,450	5,100
April 1948	26,210	3,000	8,800	10,400	4,010
May 1948	25,610				
June 1948	23,300				
July 1948	24,180	2,500	4,940	10,490	6,250
August 1948	21,100				
September 48	23,720				
October 1948	25,480				
November 1948	25,000	3,300	1,720	13,080	6,900
December 1948	24,000	3,300	1,620	11,080	8,000
January 1949	23,210	3,000	2,020	10,390	7,800
Fourth Phase: February–October 1949					
February 1949	24,090	1,600	5,370	11,120	6,000
March 1949	21,810	1,000	7,780	7,250	5,780
April 1949	19,820	100	4,830	9,750	5,140
May 1949	20,240	50	5,650	9,880	4,660
June 1949	18,270	130	2,840	11,280	4,020
July 1949	17,635	80	1,270	12,855	3,430
August 1949	10,105	0	1,735	5,610	2,760
September 1949	3,580	0	1,490	590	1,500
October 1949	1,910				

Sources: Based on JUSMAPG, Greek General Staff, and U.S. Military Attaché–Greece reports and other sources.

strength in Greece at various dates from the beginning of 1946 through December of 1949.

The active strength of the GDA at the beginning of the second phase was about 2,500; by July 1946, when Markos was assigned to take command, there were about 4,000 Communist-led men and women under arms. By the time the creation of the GDA was announced in late October, the total had risen to 6,000, and by the end of the second phase in February 1947 it had increased to nearly 12,000, having been greatly augmented by ELAS veterans returning from the training camps in Albania and Yugoslavia.[18] At the time the formal decision was made to convert the GDA to a conventional force in September 1947, the size of the GDA stood at about 17,000 men and women.

Markos estimated that a force of some 50,000 to 60,000 armed guerrillas would be needed to achieve the objectives of the KKE.[19] In retrospect, such a large force probably could not have been raised, and even if it had been, could not have been adequately supported logistically. In any event, the progress of the GDA toward assembling such a large force was retarded rather than assisted by the policies and actions of the KKE leadership in the cities. For some time after Markos assumed command of the Communist forces in July 1946, the KKE refused to mobilize its urban cadres for service with the guerrilla units in the mountains, and party members continued to be instructed to answer the draft calls of the national government, although it was known that all suspected Communist sympathizers were placed in concentration camps as soon as they reported for induction.[20] By January 1947, Markos was beginning to sense that his chance of raising a 50,000-man force would slip away unless the party leaders in Athens and Salonika agreed to mobilize.[21]

Markos' repeated calls for mobilization of the urban cadres were denied in part perhaps because of a lingering belief in the orthodox Communist shibboleth of a revolution based on an urban industrial proletariat. The Salonika politburo, controlled by Vasilios Bartzotas (a "Zachariades man"), replied to one of Markos' calls for reinforcement with the declaration, "We will support you with the means at our disposal. But the essential thing is the day to day struggle of the proletariat and the people to supply their own needs. Above all, we must never forget that we are struggling for reconciliation."[22] Dimitrios Vlantas went so far as to tell the party faithful in Piraeus, "Those who want to take to the mountains are cowards, running away from the real revolutionary struggle in the towns and in the factories."[23]

Although the decision had been taken to proceed with the development of a rebel army, many of the leaders of the KKE remained unconvinced that the time was yet ripe or that a guerrilla army in the mountains was the proper form for the insurrection to take. Zachariades himself appears to have been among the chief doubters. The instructions he gave to Markos in July 1946 severely restricted the rapid and effective development of the Communist military forces. Zachariades insisted that recruitment must be voluntary; no defection by complete units of the GNA should be accepted; the Communist forces must attack only the "monarcho-fascist" bands, not the regular forces of the Greek govern-ment; the Communist forces should remain on the defensive; and reconciliation was to remain the party line.[24] The restriction on accepting the wholesale de-fection of GNA units was particularly unfortunate in that many of the govern-ment troops were sympathetic to the KKE. Markos ignored these restrictive instructions whenever possible, and, left to his own devices, he proceeded to organize his forces as best he could under the circumstances. Fortunately, guer-rilla morale during this period remained high, and the attractions of the guerrilla life and fighting for "a just cause" continued to draw significant numbers of volunteers.[25] However, the number of volunteers was insufficient to fill out the rapidly growing GDA force structure, and increasingly the GDA had to rely on forced recruitment to provide the number of common soldiers required.

The members of the various Communist guerrilla bands were almost all vol-unteers in 1945 and 1946, but by November 1946 Markos was already experi-encing problems with desertion, and forced recruiting had begun.[26] By mid-1947, the majority of GDA recruits (about 60 percent) were being acquired by force. However, the recruitment rate in 1947–1948 averaged only about 1,800 per month, and casualties exceeded accessions.[27] In 1948, for example, the GDA intake of recruits was about 24,000, but during the same period the GDA suf-fered 19,126 casualties. Obviously, a 50,000-man army could not be assembled under such conditions.

Finding enough qualified officers to lead the growing GDA was another prob-lem. Of course, many of the GDA officers were veterans of ELAS. Among the more prominent were Ypsilantis, Lassanis, and George Kikitsas in Macedonia and George Gousias, a Zachariades supporter and practically the only prominent party member to take the field, in Roumeli.[28] Markos himself had been a political commissar in ELAS rather than a line officer, but he had taken an active part in operations and had a flair for military matters, which he developed by asso-ciation with General Bakirdzis, his partner in the leadership of the Macedonian Corps, and other former regular officers of the Greek Army.[29] Although many former officers of ELAS found their way into leadership positions in the GDA, the policies of the KKE leadership tended to exclude experienced men in favor of "reliable" party members. KKE policies, enunciated by Zachariades, dis-couraged the accession of former regular officers of the Greek Army, even those who were veterans of ELAS and proven Communists.[30] This rather odd restric-tion, which deprived the GDA of much-needed military expertise, appears to have been the work of Theodore Makrides, the only former regular officer on the KKE Central Committee, who, however, never played a prominent role in the organization and employment of the GDA.[31] In any event, after Varkiza many former ELAS officers were reintegrated into the Greek National Army, and in September 1946, eighty-six of the less "reliable" senior ex-officers of ELAS—including its former commander, Stephanos Saraphis, and Markos' mentor, Bakirdzis—were rounded up and incarcerated on the islands by the Greek national government.[32] The practical effect of the ill-considered KKE policy and of the government action was to limit the contribution of professional soldiers to the organization and employment of the GDA.[33] There were no professional officers at all in the GDA General Command, and the direction of the GDA at every level was often in the hands of amateur soldiers or, at best, of reserve officers with experience in guerrilla warfare during the occupation.

Despite the opposition of some KKE leaders, the combat strength of the GDA grew rapidly during 1947. At the beginning of the third phase in March 1947 the number of active GDA combatants was about 13,000; by October 1947 the number had increased to some 17,000, with another 10,000 men and women in training or held in reserve in Albania, Yugoslavia, and Bulgaria.[34] At the end of 1947, following the abortive attack on Konitsa, the GDA could muster 20,350 "regulars." GDA strength peaked in April 1948 at 26,210 combatants (3,000 in the Peloponnesus, 8,800 in central Greece and the islands, 10,400 in Epirus and western Macedonia, and 4,010 in eastern Macedonia and western Thrace) and subsequently stabilized at about 24,000.[35] The overall strength of the GDA fell to 21,100 in August 1948 with the GNF summer offensive in the Grammos, but it recovered to 24,000 in December 1948 (3,300 in the Peloponnesus, 1,620 in central Greece, 11,080 in Epirus and western Macedonia, and 8,000 in eastern Macedonia and western Thrace). As the GNF cleared the rebels from southern Greece, the proportion of Slavo-Macedonians in the GDA grew rapidly. In 1948 11,000 out of 25,000 GDA combatants were Slavo-Macedonians; by mid-1949 the proportion had increased to 14,000 out of less than 20,000.[36]

At the time of Markos' dismissal, the Greek Democratic Army had reached the limits of its development, although its peak strength had been reached a year earlier in April 1948. In February 1949 the GDA numbered some 24,090 male and female combatants (5,370 in central Greece, 11,120 in Epirus and western Macedonia, 6,000 in eastern Macedonia and western Thrace, and 1,600—soon to be reduced to less than 250—in the Peloponnesus). However, once GNA operations began in the late spring of 1949, GDA casualties mounted, recruiting became ever more difficult, and the number of GDA combatants began to fall rapidly: to 21,810 in March and 19,820 in April; and then up slightly to 20,240 in May only to dive to 18,270 in June; 17,635 in July; 10,105 in August; and 3,580 in September at the end of Operation TORCH and of the civil war itself.

GDA Auxiliaries and Reserves

The auxiliaries of the GDA included the members of the "self-defense" (aftoamyna)—the liaison units (yiafka), the Popular Civil Guard and home defense personnel, and others who worked actively for the KKE and GDA. The number of such individuals was large, but that number is even more difficult to estimate than the number of active GDA combatants, in part because the supporting infrastructure was largely clandestine. Estimates vary from 70,000 to 200,000, the lower figure probably being closer to the mark.[37] Western intelligence estimates from the early days of the "Third Round," posited that some 700,000 adults, or about 10 percent of the entire Greek population, considered themselves leftists, and that 150,000–200,000 of these were prepared to take an active role in antigovernment activities.[38] The proportion of supporters to active combatants can perhaps be extrapolated from the fact that in December 1948–March 1949, the Greek national forces in the Peloponnesus killed, captured, or accepted the surrender of some 4,512 GDA combatants and arrested over 6,700 members of the *aftoamyna*, 4,000 of them on 28 December 1948 alone.[39] The ratio was probably somewhat higher in areas dominated by the GDA, such as the border zones in northern and northwestern Greece.

The reserves available to the GDA, located for the most part outside Greece, varied from time to time. Some 4,000 Greek veterans of ELAS took refuge outside Greece immediately after the Varkiza Agreement in February 1945, and their numbers increased significantly in 1945–1946.[40] In early 1948 the Greek General Staff estimated the number of GDA reserves at 22,300, including 9,150 in Albania, 7,500 in Yugoslavia, and 5,650 in Bulgaria, plus another 5,000–6,000 in training inside Greece, of whom 80 percent were armed.[41] The need for GDA replacements due to the GNF offensive in the summer of 1948 reduced the available reserves outside Greece to only 10,000, of whom about half were fit for service: 3,700 (2,700 wounded) in Albania, 3,300 in Yugoslavia, and 3,000 in Bulgaria.[42] By 30 June 1949 the number had increased to 15,500 (including noncombatants): 6,500 in Albania, 4,000 in Yugoslavia, and 5,000 in Bulgaria.[43] On 10 July 1949, Marshal Tito closed the borders of Yugoslavia to the Greek Communist rebels, and some 4,000 GDA combatants in Yugoslavia were cut off from the main GDA forces in Greece.[44] Another 2,500 GDA fighters in Bulgaria and 2,500 in eastern Macedonia and western Thrace were also isolated, a further reduction of about 30 to 35 percent of the total GDA strength at the time.[45]

GDA Casualties

As the overall size of the GDA increased and it became more directly engaged in prolonged operations with the GNF, GDA casualties increased accordingly. In 1947, GDA casualties totaled 18,303 (8,453 killed, 5,378 captured, and 4,472 surrendered). During the government offensive in the Grammos and Vitsi in the summer of 1948 alone, the GDA lost 1,210 (900 killed, 217 captured, and 92 surrendered), plus wounded in a proportion of about three men wounded for every man killed.[46] In the course of 1948, GDA losses amounted to 32,898 (15,727 killed, 8,915 captured, and 8,256 surrendered), or about one and a half times the average total strength of the GDA during the year.[47]

Estimates of total GDA casualties during the civil war range between 50,395 and 83,925, with the most likely figures being those provided by Laiou: 24,235 killed, 9,871 captured, and 16,289 surrendered.[48] The number of GDA wounded during that period cannot be estimated accurately but may have been on the order of two to three men wounded for every man killed.[49] As might be expected, the official Joint U.S. Military Advisory and Planning Group–Greece (JUSMAPG) estimate was somewhat higher: 38,421 killed, 23,960 captured, and 21,544 surrendered.[50] Greek national government figures estimate the total number of casualties suffered by the GDA between June 1945 and March 1949 at 70,027, of which 28,992 were killed, 13,105 were captured, and 27,931 surrendered.[51] During the same period the Greek national forces (including the gendarmerie and civil police) lost 10,927 killed, 23,251 wounded, and 3,756 missing. From 1946 to early 1949, the GDA lost an average of around 1,500 men per month.[52] At the height of the civil war, the GDA lost a monthly average of 2,500 personnel killed, captured, or surrendered, and by mid-1949 GDA losses were such that it was no longer possible to replace them even by forced recruiting.[53] Table 5.3 shows the JUSMAPG monthly estimates of GDA casualties from 1947 through the end of the civil war period.

LOGISTICAL ORGANIZATION OF THE GREEK DEMOCRATIC ARMY

Apparently, the Greek Democratic Army did not subscribe to any particular, well-defined set of principles for logistical organization and operations; at least, no published statements of such have come to hand. In general, we can assume that insofar as any principles were applied at all, they were probably adaptations of Soviet Army doctrine. The chief characteristic of the GDA logistical support organization appears to have been an overlapping of clandestine civilian agencies with the overt logistical apparatus of the GDA itself. In both cases, the logistical agencies were generally static and operated on an area-support basis rather than supporting a specific mobile unit, although each GDA tactical unit, of course, had its own organic logistical structure that moved with the unit. Moreover, the organization of support for the guerrilla fighters varied from region to region, the organization in the Peloponnesus being somewhat different from that in the Grammos and Vitsi.

Generally, the responsibility for logistics in the GDA was shared by the military commander and his political counterpart, the *kapetanios*, or political commissar, at all levels. At the highest level—that of the KKE Politburo and Central Committee and the Provisional Democratic Government—the logistical support of the Communist military forces was entirely in civilian hands. In fact, considering the key role played in GDA logistics by the *aftoamyna*, one might say that GDA logistics at every level was dependent on civilian agents.

Higher-Level Logistical Organization

Following the usual Communist principle of centralized direction by the party hierarchy of all important matters, the KKE Politburo and Central Committee played a dominant role in the support of the GDA. The KKE General Secretary, Nikos Zachariades, and other high-ranking party members frequently traveled

Table 5.3
GDA Casualties, 1947–1949

Period/Date	Total	Killed	Captured	Surrender
Total 1947	18,303	8,453	5,378	4,472
January 1948	1,890	835	609	446
February 1948	1,770	731	553	486
March 1948	3,426	1,459	968	999
April 1948	3,029	1,371	1,059	599
May 1948	3,759	1,301	1,527	931
June 1948	2,462	1,304	579	579
July 1948	3,346	1,817	690	839
August 1948	3,231	1,896	634	701
September 1948	3,299	1,831	635	833
October 1948	1,963	1,012	332	619
November 1948	2,033	891	588	554
December 1948	2,690	1,279	741	670
Total 1948	32,898	15,727	8,915	8,256
January 1949	2,963	1,375	657	931
February 1949	3,901	1,846	1,264	791
March 1949	5,376	1,894	2,219	1,263
April 1949	3,978	1,924	1,034	1,020
May 1949	3,343	1,161	1,133	1,049
June 1949	2,907	927	1,199	781
July 1949	1,922	653	696	573
August 1949	4,697	2,588	1,543	566
September 1949	1.355	551	442	362
October 1949	1,087	173	450	464
November 1949	577	100	194	283
December 1949	372	96	126	150
Total 1949	32,478	13,288	10,957	8,233
Total 1947–1949 (per table)	83,679	37,468	25,250	20,961
War Total (per JUSMAPG)	83,925	38,421	23,960	21,544
June 1945–March 1949 (per Greek General Staff)	70,027	28,992	13,105	27,931
War Total (per Laiou)	50,395	24,235	9,871	16,289

Sources: Based on *JUSMAPG—Brief History*, 24. Note that the total of the JUSMAPG monthly figures for the period 1947–1949 do not agree with the JUSMAPG total figures for the war given at the end of the table. This discrepancy is probably due to later adjustment of the monthly figures. See also Laiou, "Population Movements," 55–58 (Table 1); Iatrides, "Civil War," 390 note 79; and O'Ballance, *The Greek Civil War, 1944–1949*, 192.

outside Greece to solicit support and arrange for the supply to the GDA of all types of logistical support, and it is safe to assume that no arrangements were made without the approval of the party leadership. Within the Provisional Democratic Government, the minister for war bore the primary responsibility for the organization, support, and employment of the GDA. Important roles were also played by the ministers of national economy, finance, agriculture, food supply, labor, and transport. The exact division of responsibility and authority is unclear, but the minister of war supply—an office held after 5 April 1949 by Kostas

Karageorgis—presumably focused on matters concerning the supply of the GDA and the provision of labor, transport, and other services. It appears likely that decisions regarding taxation in kind and requisitioning on the population were also the concern of the war supply ministry.

At the level of the GDA General Command, several staff officers exercised general staff supervision, and in some cases operational control, over the various logistical functions and units of the GDA.[54] The Organization and Equipment Directorate, under its director Apostolis (later Agras), was concerned with general questions of organization and equipment, including the establishment of tables of organization and equipment. The Central Supply Directorate, headed by Major Spartakos, dealt with rations, forage, clothing, and other equipment. The Director of Central Ordnance oversaw the acquisition, storage, maintenance, and distribution of arms and ammunition. The Central Transportation Directorate, under Barbalias, coordinated GDA transportation services and oversaw the operations of the three GDA regular transport battalions. Medical evacuation and treatment, as well as direction of the two GDA stretcher-bearer battalions, came under the Central Medical Directorate, headed by Dr. (Lieutenant Colonel) George Sakellariou, Signal equipment and its maintenance were the responsibility of Capt. Takis Dimitriou, who headed the Signal Directorate. The construction of fortifications was managed by the Directorate of Fortifications, under Engineer Colonel Barbathimios (later Zoulas), and the Directorate of Engineering, under Colonel Angeloudis, was responsible for the construction and maintenance of routes, supply facilities, and camps.

A significant role in the coordination of the delivery of supplies from friendly Communist states was played by the so-called "Personnel Directorate" (Section IIa; actually the GDA Security Service [YSA]), which was under the direction of Lt. Col. Polidoris and later of Yiannis Ioannides.[55] The Personnel Directorate also oversaw the logistical as well as the intelligence functions of the liaison units (*yiafaka*), including those established in the neighboring states to facilitate support. The approval of the Security Service was required before supplies and equipment could be issued to units.[56] The area (echelon) headquarters, each of which had a logistics officer as well as a commander and a political commissar, provided intelligence, logistical, and other services; transmitted the orders of GDA General Command; and controlled the GDA forces within their assigned region.[57]

Role of the *Aftoamyna*

The main organization responsible for the support of the GDA was the Greek Communist self-defense organization, known as the *aftoamyna*.[58] At its peak strength in mid-1947, the *aftoamyna* counted as many as 50,000 active members, aided on occasion by perhaps another 250,000 sympathizers.[59] Under constant pressure from the police and military forces of the Greek government, the destruction of the *aftoamyna*—and thus the GDA support system—became a primary target during the last two years of the war, and the effectiveness of the clandestine *aftoamyna* declined as its cells, caches of supplies, and routes were uncovered and destroyed by the GNF. For example, between December 1948 and March 1949, the *aftoamyna* in the Peloponnesus was almost entirely wiped out by the government forces, in Operation PIGEON.

The exact ratio of support personnel to combatants in the GDA is not well established. The Greek General Staff apparently accepted as "an established fact" that the GDA, like other armies, maintained a ratio of four supporters for every combatant, but the U.S. military attaché in Athens considered the Greek General Staff estimate to be excessive and tending to make the guerrilla enemy appear more formidable.[60] The U.S. military attaché did, however, accept that combatants formed about 40 percent of the total strength of the GDA (a ratio of 1.5 supporters to every combatant). This appears reasonable, in that at the peak some 25,000 GDA combatants were supported by about 50,000 members of the *aftoamyna*, some of whom did not have functions directly related to the logistical support of the GDA (for example, the OPLA terrorist teams).

The liaison units (*yiafaka*) played a key role in the logistical support of the GDA. The liaison units were composed of six to eight men and operated directly under the area (echelon) headquarters, but they were ultimately responsible to the GDA Security Service (YSA), which was directed by the Personnel (Security) Directorate of the GDA General Command.[61] Each liaison unit was responsible for a sector consisting of several villages.[62] The liaison units coordinated the logistical activities of the static area units in their sector and reviewed supply requisitions submitted by tactical units. They also provided guide and courier services for the more mobile tactical units. The tax collection functions performed for EAM/ELAS by ETA during the resistance period were assumed by the liaison units during the civil war of 1945–1949, and the liaison units handled the disbursement of funds to the area units and individual KKE cells (*yiafka*) for the purchase of supplies. This was confirmed by Major Kronos, the commander of the 2d Battalion of the Parnassos Brigade, whose notebooks were recovered by the GNF after he was killed during operations in the Balikon Mountains at the end of March 1948.[63] Kronos' notebook contained copies of directives from the GDA General Command to subordinate units and referred to transfers of gold through liaison unit channels for the purchase of food, radio parts, and other supplies. Kronos also indicated that his own 212-man battalion included fourteen women and was augmented by twelve kitchen workers and twelve members of the *aftoamyna*, probably detached from the area unit responsible for his area of operations.

The GDA area units (Popular Civil Guard and "home defense")—static formations composed of fifty to sixty lightly armed personnel—provided the core of the logistical support for the GDA. Coordinated by the liaison units, the area units, in addition to their security, intelligence, and recruiting functions, collected and stored local supplies, provided transport services, and treated and cared for the sick and wounded. On rare occasions, an area unit might be required to conduct defensive operations to protect its bases or supply caches, but the principal purpose of such units was to support GDA tactical forces. This was accomplished by assuming logistical responsibility for the GDA tactical units operating in or passing through their assigned area. During GNA counter-guerrilla sweeps, the GDA area units often dispersed in small detachments and remained hidden until the sweep was completed, sometimes leaving behind small saboteur groups to destroy matériel that could not be carried to safety and had to be abandoned.[64] After mid-1947 the GDA received the bulk of its arms, ammunition, food, and other supplies from outside suppliers, and the focus of area unit activities shifted to local storage and distribution of supplies rather than their collection.

The *aftoamyna* organization in the Peloponnesus appears to have been some-what different from that elsewhere in Greece, the supply service being attached to, but strictly speaking separate from, the Popular Civil Guard (area) units. An order of the headquarters of the GDA Achaia-Ilias Group in the northwestern Peloponnesus, dated 28 June 1948, provided that the echelons of the Provincial Supply Service should be attached to the various subcommands of the provincial Popular Civil Guard, and that the various supply and hiding teams would, in the case of government action, follow the sections of the Popular Civil Guard in their area, taking care to ensure the safety of pack animals and cattle.[65] The hospital was to be dissolved in the case of government action; the seriously ill and wounded guerrillas were to be taken to secret hiding places, accompanied, if possible, by one or two good "fighter nurses." Lightly ill and wounded guer-rillas were enjoined to follow their unit or the nearest element of the Popular Civil Guard. The Popular Civil Guard units were instructed to maneuver within their area so as to avoid government troops, to report the meeting places they intended to use, and to return to their own area as soon as possible.

Another snapshot of the organization of the *aftoamyna* support system as it existed in the Peloponnesus in late 1948 and early 1949, just before its destruc-tion by the GNF, was provided by Anastassios Kyriazis, the chief of the KKE Center of Information at Lirki, who was captured near Argos on 19 January 1949 by elements of a Greek National Army (GNA) commando group.[66] During his interrogation, Kyriazis revealed that the GDA Argolis-Corinthia Group was served by a Central Supply Service located in the village of Mazeika and com-manded by a Captain Kokoris. The Central Supply Service was organized with four subordinate provincial supply echelons with elements in every village: Ech-elon Argolis, with headquarters at Tatsi, was commanded by Kostas Marousis; Echelon Corinthia, with headquarters at Sofiana, was commanded by Gerode-mos; Echelon Aigialia, with headquarters at Peristera, was commanded by Fi-lipos; and Echelon Kalavrita, with headquarters at Kazeika, was commanded by Gotsis. Kyriazis also related that special supply-hiding teams had recently been organized in the Argolis-Corinthia area, because local supply administrators were unable to hide the supplies under their control; one team in the Argolis area was unsuccessful due to haste, and another attempted to hide some 3,000–

3,500 *okas* (8,400–9,800 pounds; 1 oka = 2.8 pounds) of wheat in a cave but left many of the bags outside.

Two organizations important to the logistical support of the Communist guerrillas early in the "Third Round" were soon absorbed into the *aftoamyna*. The logistical support organization of ELAS during the Resistance period, ETA (*Epimeletis tou Andarte*), was disbanded at the time of the Varkiza Agreement in February 1945, but by July 1945 it had been revived and was engaged in the recovery of arms and ammunition from secret dumps and delivering them, along with other supplies, to the Communist guerrilla bands scattered in the mountains and in the camps over the northern borders.[67] Leftists in the towns of Volos and Naousa provided the initial personnel complement of the new ETA, but by the end of the summer of 1945 ETA had been reestablished over large areas of Greece. The development of the *aftoamyna* after February 1946 resulted in the supercession of ETA by the system of liaison units (*yiafaka*) and area units, which assumed the functions originally performed by ETA. The United Panhellenic Youth Organization (*Eniaia Panellinios Organosis Neolaias*; EPON), the KKE youth organization, also played an important role in the logistical support of the GDA in the early phases of the civil war. Just as during the resistance, the young men and women of EPON were given some basic military training and were attached in small groups to the various guerrilla units, for which they performed such essential housekeeping tasks as office work, cooking, the distribution of supplies, and service as messengers and guides.[68] Eventually, EPON was integrated into the GDA supply and service units, just as it had been absorbed into ELAS during the resistance period.

Unit Logistical Organization

Most of the logistical support of the GDA tactical units was provided on an area basis by the area units, coordinated by the liaison units controlling the sectors, and the organic logistical structure of the GDA divisions, brigades, battalions, and companies appears to have been quite small. In fact, the GDA divisions, formed quite late in the war, do not appear to have had any standard logistical organization at all.[69] However, each division was probably organized with a supply unit of battalion size, which included the division's organic transport and operated the division's tactical supply and ammunition dumps; distributed arms, ammunition, food, and other supplies to subordinate units; and performed whatever other logistical activities were required, presumably under the direction of one or more logistical staff officers from the division headquarters. Each division surely had its own field medical unit and was probably also allotted a company from one of the two GDA stretcher-bearer battalions, the platoons being further attached down to the division's brigades. Some GDA divisions also appear to have had an attached liaison unit to provide contact with the supporting liaison and area units; in 1949 the 1st, 2d, and 6th Divisions each had an area unit dedicated to its support. The divisional liaison units probably operated under the control of the (divisional) political commissar (*kape-tanios*), who is known to have played an important role in logistical activities at every level.

The situation is somewhat clearer with respect to the GDA brigades, for which standard tables of organization and equipment were prescribed.[70] The standard 1,525-man GDA infantry brigade included a supply platoon, consisting of twenty officers and men and thirty mules as well as an attached stretcher-bearer platoon of twenty officers and men. The supply platoon of the GDA light brigade was slightly smaller, with seventeen officers and men and thirty mules. The support structure for the standard 432-man GDA infantry battalion was apparently contained within the twenty-one-man Headquarters Group, which was authorized twenty horses and nine mules. GDA artillery troops (batteries) were authorized an ammunition section of twenty-three officers and men and twenty-two mules, capable of transporting three hundred shells. Each artillery section (two guns) had an ammunition squad of twelve men and eleven mules, capable of transporting 150 shells. Personnel and animals to provide other logistical services (food, small arms ammunition, etc.) were included in the troop/section headquarters.

Presumably, a headquarters staff at division, brigade, and battalion level included one or more officers responsible for logistical matters, and at company level there was probably one or more officers or NCOs concerned with them. At every level, dedicated personnel were required to manage and care for the unit's organic complement of animals (238 for a brigade, sixty-two for a battalion, five for an infantry company, and eighteen for a heavy weapons company). At lower levels, logistical functions may have been performed as an additional duty, under the direction of the political commissar (*kapetanios*), by personnel primarily charged with other duties.

INTERNAL SOURCES OF SUPPORT

Compared with most other guerrilla movements, the GDA was strapped for internal resources, and the supply of the GDA was a struggle throughout the civil war. Modern Greece had been a poor country in the best of times; the destruction of World War II, occupation, resistance, and of the first two rounds of civil war had left the country devastated, its industry and commerce prostrate, and agricultural production at a low level. Moreover, the GDA operated primarily in the mountains, which were sparsely populated and devoid of all but the smallest amounts of food or other supplies. Nevertheless, the GDA seized every opportunity to provide itself with supplies by voluntary and forced donations, purchase on the open market, taxation in kind, requisitions on the local population, and raids on towns and villages as well as on government arsenals and military units. However, the uncertain support of the civilian population, particularly after the announcement of the KKE's policy supporting the independence of Macedonia, coupled with aggressive government measures to separate the GDA from its civilian supporters, eventually required the GDA to depend on outside support for almost all of the logistical support required for the bulk of its forces in the barren Grammos-Vitsi stronghold near the Albanian and Yugoslavian borders. The smaller GDA contingents elsewhere in Greece continued to rely, with decreasing success, on local procurement, particularly of food and clothing, although by the end of the war the remaining units in central Greece and the Peloponnesus were also almost entirely dependent on the deliveries of arms and ammunition from outside sources.

For the first two and a half years of the civil war—until the autumn of 1947—the Communist guerrillas were able to supply most of their requirements for small arms, light automatic weapons, and the associated ammunition from stocks left over from matériel obtained from the Allies or captured from the Italians, Germans, and Bulgarians during the resistance period and not surrendered under the terms of the Varkiza Agreement. As Communist guerrilla operations intensified, these original stocks were supplemented by a variety of arms, ammunition, food, clothing, medical supplies, and other equipment stolen or captured from the Greek government forces. Guerrilla raids often had as a primary objective the looting of government and civilian storehouses, hospitals, businesses, and private homes. Livestock, for example, was carried off and placed in the care of friendly peasants in guerrilla-controlled areas, thereby solving the GDA's most difficult food requirement—fresh meat.

Insofar as supplies of food, clothing, medical supplies, and other items were available on the Greek market and the funds were available to purchase them, the GDA obtained a small proportion of its requirements through actual purchase. However, the inherent scarcity of supplies of all kinds and increasing government surveillance and restrictions eventually made this method of little practical value. The GDA, unlike the Viet Minh in Indochina, did not engage in substantial internal manufacture of the materials needed to conduct a war—the raw materials, machinery, and expertise were simply lacking. However, the GDA did develop in its base areas, particularly in the Grammos and Vitsi strongholds, a variety of small shops to manufacture and repair clothing, shoes, and other equipment, to bake bread and preserve other foodstuffs, and to manufacture antipersonnel mines and some other weaponry. The production of such facilities was limited, however, and in any event it could not have met the demands of a conventionally organized army of substantial size.

In areas under its control, the KKE/GDA imposed a system of taxation in kind, which did produce some food, clothing, and other supplies. However, the inherent poverty of the Greek population, the relatively barren areas under GDA control, and the depopulation of key areas seriously limited the amount of matériel which could be obtained by such methods. About the only commodity in good supply was labor; the GDA obtained the manpower it required for construction, transport, and other tasks through voluntary and forced participation by the local populace in the areas in which it operated.

Regardless of the zeal and ruthlessness of GDA tax collectors, only so much could be gathered by forced or voluntary contributions from the Greek peasants, and for their own reasons some KKE leaders were unwilling to force their followers in the urban areas to contribute substantially to the support of the GDA fighters in the mountains. In 1945 and 1946, enthusiasm for the Communist guerrillas among the civilian population was relatively high, inasmuch as they were seen as protectors against the depredations of the royalist government and the right-wing terrorist bands. There was probably far more support for the Communist guerrillas than the Greek government was willing to admit in its official estimates. Gardner cites a figure of 15 percent as the amount of disaffection in the Greek National Army (GNA), and notes that if the 15 percent figure were applied to the Greek population as a whole (then about 7.5 million), there would have been over a million leftist sympathizers.[71]

The degree to which the Greek population cooperated freely with the Communist guerrillas was reflected in the debriefing of Francis L. McShane, an American civilian engineer captured by the guerrillas on 10 November 1948 near Tripolis in the Peloponnesus.[72] McShane, who was well treated, was given a "tour of Free Greece" before being released on 21 November. The U.S. military attaché in Athens reported that "the villagers impressed McShane as being caught in the middle: the bandits were here today and had to be supplied with food and mules; tomorrow the GNA would take the remaining mules; either way they lost."[73] McShane also related that (in the words of the U.S. military attaché) "the bandits simply entered a house, asked for food and/or lodging and there was no question about giving it to them. McShane never saw them pay for any food that they got."[74]

However, as the civil war dragged on, large segments of the Greek populace lost their zeal for supporting the rebels, particularly once the ideologically motivated and pro-Soviet policies of Zachariades came to overshadow the nationalist focus of Markos and his clique. Zachariades' support of Stalin and the Comintern in their dispute with Tito, and most particularly his pro-Bulgarian policy of support for an independent Macedonia, significantly reduced support for the KKE/GDA among patriotic Greeks. Moreover, the growing strength of the Greek government caused many mildly proleftist Greeks to reevaluate the probable outcome of the civil war and to abandon what has been called a strategy of "re-insurance," whereby Greek citizens subject to the alternating control of the GDA and government forces, including government civil servants and prominent businessmen, refused to take any action that might result in reprisals should the Communists emerge victorious.[75]

THE IMPACT OF GOVERNMENT RESETTLEMENT OPERATIONS

In addition to the underlying poverty, lack of agricultural and manufactured goods, and uncertain support of the civilian population, a severe constraint upon the ability of the GDA to obtain supplies from sources within Greece was the government policy of removing the population from contested areas and by the general flow of refugees to the major towns under government control. The intensification of guerrilla operations after February 1946 created large numbers of refugees in areas subject to guerrilla raids and government counteraction. In order to deprive the Communist guerrillas of support, the Greek government adopted a number of measures, including curfews, stationing GNA or government militia units in the villages, and depriving guerrilla-dominated villages of their share of the food, clothing, and medical supplies distributed under the aegis of the United Nations Relief and Recovery Agency (UNRRA).[76] In the course of 1946, the government adopted a more drastic policy of forced evacuation of the population from villages in areas occupied by the GDA or otherwise considered to be insecure. The purpose of this policy, which remained in effect officially until November 1947 and in practice even longer, was to disrupt the *aftoamyna* and deprive the guerrillas of intelligence, recruits, logistical support, and labor. The forced evacuation policy was focused on areas with the greatest concentration of GDA activity and support within Epirus, Macedonia, Roumeli, and central Greece. The number of refugees or displaced persons grew rapidly with the beginning in April 1947 of Operation TERMINUS to clear Roumeli.[77] By mid-February 1948, the "official" government count included some 485,000 displaced persons; by January 1949, the total reached 666,374.[78]

Although the policy of forced evacuation caused many peasants to join the guerrillas, it was very successful in breaking up the GDA infrastructure and thus impeding its efforts to gather information, recruits, and supplies.[79] The removal of large numbers of peasants from the land resulted in both a serious reduction in the number of potential GDA recruits and an acute food crisis in the areas occupied by the GDA. By 1949 hunger had become the constant companion of many Communist guerrillas. Dimitrios Vlantas, a senior GDA officer, later wrote that "the greatest difficulty which our troops faced during enemy operations was hunger, as a result of the evacuation of the peasants and their concentration in the towns."[80]

In contrast to the great success of the forced evacuation policy as a tactical measure, it had a number of drawbacks for the government. In the first place, the policy was viewed with some distaste by Greece's Western allies, both on humanitarian grounds and for practical economic reasons. The enormous number of refugees—or "displaced persons," as the Greek government preferred to call them—crowded into the urban areas and, lacking the means or opportunity to engage in productive work, constituted a serious drain on the already devastated Greek economy. The dimensions of the refugee problem are clearly shown in Table 5.4.

To nearly half a million refugees in late 1947 must be added well over 1.6 million indigent persons, and the numbers of both increased until eventually over one-quarter of the entire Greek population was being supported directly by the government.[81] The direct and indirect costs of supporting such large numbers of unproductive citizens were enormous. Under pressure from its American ally,

Table 5.4
Number of Greek Refugees by Area, January 1947–September 1949

Area	Jan 1947	Jun 1947	Oct 1947	Dec 1947	Mar 1948	Jan 1949	Jul 1949	Sep 1949
Macedonia	7,500	86,021	173,284	202,003	239,047	254,534	233,376	168,196
Thrace	2,500	8,943	19,194	53,527	52,018	58,100	62,215	51,144
Epirus	–	3,145	10,000	14,855	30,304	112,560	113,425	67,266
Cent. Greece	9,100	22,263	78,784	150,669	184,758	221,161	254,624	222,560
Peloponnesus	–	180	3,500	9,319	8,080	18,164	18,550	795
Islands	–	–	50	–	2,928	1,855	2,007	7,753
Total	18,900	120,532	284,812	430,373	517,135	666,374	684,197	517,714

Sources: Based on Laiou, "Population Movements," 74 (Table II.5), and Enclosure 2 to ID No. 589130.

on 9 November 1947 the Greek government issued instructions to suspend the forced evacuation policy and begin the process of repatriation of refugees to their native villages.[82] Unofficially, forced evacuations continued in certain areas even as the repatriation program slowly gathered steam. Still, nearly 50,000 refugees had been returned to their home villages by the time the repatriation program was officially suspended on 11 August 1949.[83] Despite the government order to suspend the repatriation program, however, it continued, and by December 1949 the number of displaced persons had fallen to 207,191.[84]

From the GDA perspective, the government's forced relocation policy was a net loss, but it did have the effect of removing children and other unproductive persons from the areas in which the GDA was obliged to support civilian populations as well as guerrilla forces. The understandable desire to reduce the number of people in GDA-controlled areas who could not contribute to the war effort but required food, clothing, shelter, and medical attention produced one of the most controversial acts of the civil war—the *paidomazoma*, or evacuation of large numbers of children from the Communist-controlled areas to camps and homes in the Soviet Union and satellite states.[85] The guerrilla radio service acknowledged the existence of the program on 11 March 1948; it gave the rationale that the children faced malnutrition and other dangers in the areas subject to government military action.[86] The Greek government and many Western governments characterized the removal of the children as "kidnapping," and charges were also made that the abducted children were being given military training and returned to Greece as GDA combatants.[87] The actual number of children sent away by the Communists is unknown, but the government claimed that the total was about 28,000, of whom only about 10,000 were ever returned.[88] Regardless of the numbers or motives involved, the policy of removing children from their parents was viewed by most Western observers as reprehensible and a sign of the devilish evil of Communism; the issue continues to excite strong feelings. It should be noted that not all of the children were removed from their families by the Communists; the Greek government actively practiced the removal of children from guerrilla-controlled areas. In fact, Queen Frederika played a prominent role in one such program, and in 1948 alone some 14,700 children were removed to government "colonies."[89]

SUPPLY OF THE GREEK DEMOCRATIC ARMY

The Greek Communist guerrilla lived a frugal life, as much from habit and natural inclination as from necessity. His food was plain and his clothing and equipment relatively simple. His needs and expectations for medical supplies and comfort items were limited, and he had few motor vehicles or other heavy equipment requiring fuel or spare parts, although both forage and fuel for cooking and heating were needed in substantial quantities. The number of artillery pieces and other heavy weapons in the GDA was small, and the use of even small arms ammunition was fairly restrained.

Throughout the civil war, the Greek General Staff apparently believed that the Communist forces were successful in meeting logistical needs, although it did recognize that the GDA experienced difficulties in providing supplies to units in areas far from the border regions and that the formation of a conventional army would result in great supply difficulties.[90] In fact, the supply requirements of the GDA did increase substantially as the conversion of Markos' guerrilla army into Zachariades' conventional army progressed. At the same time, the GNF, under pressure from Gen. James A. Van Fleet, increased the tempo of operations and tried to keep the GDA engaged continuously. This, of course, added to the quantities of ammunition and other supplies required by the GDA, decreased the time and opportunity for gathering such supplies from the area of operations, and interfered substantially with the movement of matériel across the borders and from the base areas to GDA units operating elsewhere in Greece. GDA transport requirements were also increased by the larger number of casualties requiring evacuation. The GNF's adoption of the strategy of "staggered offensives," conducted so as to exert continuous pressure on the GDA, also heavily damaged the GDA logistical infrastructure resident in the *aftoamyna*, further reducing the ability of the GDA to meet its ever-increasing logistical needs.

Rations

The guerrilla diet was simple and spare. Bread, milk, olives, cheese, and lamb or goat meat constituted the bulk of what was required. Fresh fruits and vegetables were provided when available. Certain essential items, however, such as sugar, coffee, tobacco, and particularly salt, were hard to obtain and often lacking.

Except in the border regions, and particularly during the early phases of the war, the GDA's requirements for foodstuffs were met by local procurement, sometimes by purchase but more often by taxation in kind or straight-forward requisition from the civilian population. This was not a particularly effective means of providing the foodstuffs required, as most areas of Greece were not especially fertile and produced barely enough for the subsistence of the local population alone. Problems of local procurement of foodstuffs were less severe in the plains of eastern Macedonia, western Thrace, and Thessaly, which are relatively fertile. As the size of the GDA grew, it became increasingly difficult to meet ration requirements by local procurement, however determined and harsh the collection methods, and the GDA increasingly had to rely on food provided by its outside supporters and laboriously transported to the GDA units in various parts of the country.

At times, particularly later in the war, the GDA went hungry or subsisted on what it could take from government troops. For example, on the eve of the attack on Florina, the commander of the GDA 425th Infantry Battalion encouraged his men by saying,

Boys, since we shall enter Florina tomorrow and, since we are all like one family, we must say that they may have the Americans aiding them but we also have the Peoples Democracies and above all "the uncle with the big mustache" [presumably Stalin]. Hold on to your hunger for a while till we enter Florina where we shall eat, drink and entertain ourselves for a month.[91]

The weight of the daily GDA ration is not known, but based on the Korean, Indochinese, and Algerian experience, it can reasonably be estimated at between three and four pounds/man/day.[92] Thus, in gross terms, using the higher figure of four pounds/man/day, a full-strength GDA infantry battalion of 432 men would have required 1,728 pounds (nearly one short ton) of rations per day. A minimum of 95,560 pounds (48.78 short tons) of food per day would have been required in February 1949 for the total GDA combatant complement of 23,890 guerrillas, exclusive of headquarters and support personnel, auxiliaries, and dependents, of whom there were a considerable number.

Forage

The transport system connecting the GDA bases in Greece with each other and with the bases in the neighboring countries relied heavily on animal transport, almost exclusively mules. Forage requirements for animals employed in military operations are notoriously high, particularly with respect to bulk. Forage was a particular problem for the GDA, especially during the long winters in the mountains, and GDA animals were no doubt chronically underfed. The contemporary U.S. forage requirements were ten pounds of grain, fourteen pounds of hay, and 0.125 pounds of salt per horse or mule per day.[93] North Korean and Chinese Communist animals in Korea apparently subsisted on a total of twelve pounds per day.[94] The terrain and other conditions being roughly the same, the Korean estimate of twelve pounds/animal/day of feed and forage can reasonably be applied in the Greek situation. Thus, a "standard" GDA infantry battalion, which was authorized at full strength sixty-two horses and mules, would require on a daily basis not less than 744 pounds of forage.

Clothing and Other Equipment

The GDA guerrilla's personal clothing and equipment were basic, usually consisting of a woolen uniform with overcoat and boots, a knife, a blanket, a weapon and ammunition, and perhaps a small haversack containing a cup, mess kit, and a few personal items. Few of the GDA's clothing and equipment requirements could be met by purchase or requisition on local markets; most such matériel was captured from the GNF, particularly the village defense forces. A great quantity was also provided by the GDA's outside supporters, particularly in the later stages of the war. Even so, the GDA was generally well supplied with clothing and normal camp equipment. Indeed, during the early part of the war, the individual equipment of the guerrilla was somewhat better than that of the government soldier, although the Greek National Army had the advantage with respect to unit equipment such as tents, stoves, and tools.[95] The GDA fell behind only after U.S. aid began to reach the GNF in massive proportions.

Normally, the regular soldiers of the GDA wore a mixture of Greek national, British, and even U.S. uniform items. An order of the GDA General Command, dated 18 November 1947, prescribed that the "standard" field uniform of the GDA should consist of a Greek-type rather than a British-type blouse, British trousers, and a British field cap.[96] The usual material was wool, although some U.S. and British summer kakhi uniform items were to be seen. Order No. 587 also directed that uniforms be cut in three sizes. Heavy boots or shoes were worn, and in winter GDA troops were usually provided with a heavy woolen overcoat and gloves. Boots and shoes were quickly worn out on the rocky Greek terrain and were often in short supply. Thus it was not unusual, at least early in the war, for the guerrillas to go unshod. Officers generally wore the same type clothing as their men, although they were permitted to wear the Greek Army–type officer uniform, and breeches instead of trousers. Senior officers were authorized to wear high boots.

Even after the GDA was well along in the process of conversion to a conventional army, its requirements for most major items of equipment (Class IV supplies)—other than individual and crew-served weapons—were small.[97] There were few motor vehicles, generators, or similar pieces of heavy equipment, but GDA requirements for signal matériel (radios, telephones, wire, spare parts, etc.), harness and animal pack saddles, and barrier materials were still substantial. Most GDA construction was accomplished using local materials, primarily wood, but the intense efforts to fortify the Grammos and Vitsi base areas did involve the use of a good deal of barbed wire and other construction materials, which were obtained principally from the neighboring countries.

Overall, the GDA daily requirements for individual clothing and equipment (Class II supplies) did not reach the levels provided for U.S. forces at the same period. The same was true for such Class IV supplies as fortification materials and other engineer items. The contemporary U.S. planning factors were 5.74 pounds/man/day for Class II and 12.6 pounds/man/day for Class IV.[98] Communist forces in Korea were estimated to have needed only about 15 percent of the U.S. requirement.[99] If the same factor is applied to the GDA, the daily Class II requirement for a 432-man GDA infantry battalion would have been 372 pounds and the Class IV requirement 816.5 pounds, of which about 471.7 pounds would be for engineer construction materials alone.

Medical Supplies and Services

The GDA medical service was directed by Dr. (Lt. Col.) George Sakellariou, but there were few trained doctors anywhere in the GDA.[100] Most wounded or sick guerrillas found themselves under the care of nurses. Many nurses had completed the two-month nursing course conducted by GDA General Command or at the division headquarters, but many of them were little more than practitioners of folk medicine. The GDA medical services were generally adequate— even if somewhat primitive—in the base areas along the northern borders and in the field hospitals just over the borders, but in some areas, particularly southeastern Greece and the Peloponnesus, the medical facilities available to the GDA were scarcely better than those that had been available to the ELAS guerrillas during the resistance period.[101] However, the GDA did make heroic efforts to evacuate the wounded from the battlefield and to provide them with necessary treatment and postoperative care. Medical supplies were scarce even in countries supporting the GDA, and guerrilla military operations frequently had the objective of raiding some government hospital or dispensary for medical supplies.

The principal GDA medical facilities were in Albanian, Yugoslav, or Bulgarian territory. The most gravely wounded were in some cases transferred to other Communist countries or even to the Soviet Union for definitive treatment. In Greece itself, there were several field hospitals and aid stations in the base areas close to the border, and these were fairly well equipped with instruments and medical supplies. The guerrillas elsewhere in Greece enjoyed less-well-equipped facilities, often no more than a straw pallet in a cave and the attention of some caring, but unskilled, attendant.

Evacuation from the battlefield and from aid stations within Greece to the GDA field hospitals in Albania, Yugoslavia, and Bulgaria was usually accomplished by stretcher-bearer units, of which the GDA boasted two battalions.[102] One battalion, commanded by Fokas, was in the Vitsi, and the other was based in the Grammos. Each battalion had a strength of about two hundred, of whom three-quarters were women. The battalions were dispersed for operations in such a way that at brigade level there was usually a stretcher-bearer platoon, with smaller contingents at lower levels. The area units of the *aftoamyna* were also responsible for providing support in the evacuation and temporary care of sick and wounded guerrillas. Wounded guerrillas were carried to the field aid stations by litter bearers from their unit, and from there by personnel of the stretcher-bearer battalions. Those who were only lightly wounded generally were treated and convalesced in Greece; the more seriously wounded were evacuated to the hospitals in the neighboring countries.

Fuel

Inasmuch as the GDA possessed little or no motor transport within Greece, its requirements for motor fuel were negligible. Albanian, Yugoslavian, and Bulgarian motor vehicles utilized in support of the GDA were presumably fueled at bases within those countries and from stocks maintained by their governments.[103] If the GDA required little in the way of fuel for motor vehicles, its existence in the mountains did require a considerable amount of heating and cooking fuel, primarily wood. The contemporary U.S. planning figure (theater-wide, for Europe) was 8.5 pounds/man/day of heating and cooking fuel.[104] Given the harsh conditions in the Greek mountains, one may safely assume that the U.S. standard fairly represents the GDA requirement. Thus, a 432-man GDA infantry battalion would have required on the order of 3,672 pounds of fuel per day (about 1.84 short tons).

Arms and Ammunition

The Greek government and its American ally went to great lengths to demonstrate that the Soviet Union and its satellites were the principal sources of arms and ammunition for the Communist guerrillas in Greece. Both the United Nations Commission of Investigation Concerning Greek Frontier Incidents and the United Nations Special Committee on the Balkans (UNSCOB), though failing to communicate directly with the guerrillas themselves, asserted that such was the case.[105] In November 1946, a Greek National Army Ordnance committee reported that weapons captured from the guerrillas had been examined and had been found to be of Slavic or Russian origin; this it cited as proof that the Yugoslavians were supplying the Communist guerrillas.[106] On the other hand, during a two-month tour of GDA-held territory, Simone Teris, a correspondent of the Paris Communist newspaper *Humanité*, reported seeing a variety of British, German, and American weapons. She commented, "It would be difficult for the Commission [i.e., the UN Commission of Investigation] to assert bare-facedly that the soldiers of the Democratic Army were armed by Soviet, Yugoslav or Bulgarian weapons."[107]

The claim that the Greek Communist guerrillas were being supplied by the Soviet Union or its satellites was manifestly untrue, at least in the early part of the war and as far as small arms and light automatic weapons were concerned. During the first phase of the civil war, the small, scattered Communist guerrilla bands were obliged to find their own weapons and ammunition. Subsequently, during the second and into the third phase, the GDA appears to have obtained the greater part of its small arms, light automatic weapons, and associated ammunition from stocks held by ELAS at the end of the resistance period. Most of the armaments that ELAS had accumulated had been turned over by the Greek Army, captured from the Italian, German, and Bulgarian occupation troops, or provided by the Allied liaison teams.[108] A few of the weapons obtained by ELAS were of Soviet manufacture or design, probably acquired from Tito's Yugoslavian partisans.[109] Although ELAS surrendered a large quantity of such arms and ammunition at the time of the Varkiza Agreement, substantial quantities of the material in better condition were carefully hidden away for later use. Estimates of the number of weapons hidden by ELAS at the time of the Varkiza Agreement range from 20,000–40,000 items, but apparently all of the heavier weapons (artillery, heavy mortars, etc.) were surrendered.[110] Dimitrios Kousoulas, who personally observed the packing and movement of weapons to ELAS hideouts, claimed that only the most worthless weapons were turned in.[111] In any event, about half of the weapons hidden by ELAS were subsequently discovered by Greek government forces, and Markos Vafiades, the commander of the GDA, later claimed that the weapons surrendered under the Varkiza Agreement were used by the Greek government to arm the right-wing bands that oppressed the ELAS veterans and other left-wing groups.[112] As late as March 1948, most of the GDA weapons captured by the GNF bore manufacturing dates before 1944, lending credence to the idea that the principal source of GDA small arms and light automatic weapons was the stock captured by ELAS or left behind by the Italian, German, or Bulgarian troops during and after the occupation.[113]

The capture of arms and ammunition from the Greek government forces was yet another major source of guerrilla weaponry. Markos maintained that most of the GDA armament was obtained by capture from the GNF, particularly the village defense forces, and that Greek government claims that the rebels were being provided the bulk of their weapons by the Soviets were false.[114] In fact, a substantial proportion of the GDA's weapons and ammunition were seized in ambushes and raids, stolen from government depots, or obtained from village defense units armed by the government. Some had only to be picked up—GNF troops were notoriously lax in supply discipline and frequently left ammunition in abandoned positions.[115]

As the war progressed and the GDA established sources of supply in the neighboring Communist countries, the proportion of light weapons, particularly machine guns and mortars, supplied from Communist sources increased, and almost all of the GDA's heavy weapons (artillery, heavy mortars, antiaircraft and antitank guns, and even flamethrowers) were supplied by the GDA's outside supporters.[116] In the winter of 1948, UNSCOB observers and Greek government authorities began to find large stores of Soviet and Eastern European weapons. Up to that time most of the guerrilla weapons recovered had been of German, British, or Italian manufacture. Guerrilla prisoners and defectors also claimed that their supporters would soon provide them with airplanes, tanks, heavy artillery, and antiaircraft guns.[117] Probably about 75 percent of the small arms and all of the mortars, antitank weapons, and artillery were obtained from Balkan sources, while the remaining 25 percent were of British, German, or Italian origin and had been held for some time.[118] The proportion of small arms in GDA hands received from Communist sources after 1945 was perhaps no more than 10 percent, although some 50 percent of the GDA's heavy weapons and mines were received from outside sources.[119]

The number and types of weapons available to the GDA by the end of the war is indicated by the list of arms and ammunition captured by government forces during the Grammos phase of Operation TORCH, 24–31 August 1949, the last battle of the war. The items seized by the GNF in the Grammos—in addition to large quantities of artillery, mortar, and small arms ammunition and mines—included fourteen artillery pieces, seventeen antiaircraft guns, seven antitank guns, 147 heavy mortars (81 mm type), forty-five light mortars (60 mm type), two antiaircraft machine guns, ninety-nine heavy machine guns, 538 light machine guns, sixty-six miscellaneous automatic weapons, 2,701 rifles, two range finders, ten antitank rockets, and two mine detectors.[120] In fact, the stocks of artillery and small arms ammunition found by GNA troops in the Grammos and Vitsi were limited, perhaps due to heavy expenditure, the inability to build up sufficient stocks, and a reduction in the amounts being provided by the Yugoslavs; in contrast, antiaircraft and antitank ammunition, which had not been heavily drawn on, remained in plentiful supply.[121]

The problem for the GDA was not the number of weapons available but rather their distribution, the perpetual scarcity of ammunition and spare parts, and the multiplicity of types, which complicated weapons training, maintenance, and the supply of ammunition. As the war went on, the GDA attempted to solve the problem of heterogeneous weaponry by shifting the older Italian weapons to the *aftoamyna*, equipping the better units—particularly those defending the Grammos and Vitsi—principally with German weapons, and equipping the bulk of the GDA with British or German rifles and light automatic weapons.[122] The success of these attempts at standardization was minimal, and until the end of the war most GDA units were equipped with a hodgepodge of weapons of Italian, German, British, U.S., French, Soviet, Bulgarian, Greek, and Czechoslovakian origin.[123] The diversity of GDA weaponry is reflected in the report of weapons captured by the GNA 15th Mountain Division during the month of August 1948. Among the items taken were one French machine gun, one German light machine gun, one British light machine gun (Bren), four British submachine guns (Sten), one German antitank rifle, one French automatic rifle, ninety-seven Italian rifles, twenty-one German Mauser rifles, fourteen British rifles, eleven Greek Mannlicher rifles, three Bulgarian rifles, three French rifles, three Turkish Mauser rifles, and one Russian rifle.[124]

The GDA was apparently never short of small arms, and even recruits in training were supplied with individual weapons.[125] However, local shortages existed from time to time due to the difficulties of distribution and the perpetual shortage of spare parts.[126] Once formal tables of allowances for the various GDA

Table 5.5
Weapons on Hand in GDA 588th Battalion, July 1948

Number	Weapon	Origin/Type
9	Pistols	
180	Rifles	British, German, Italian
58	Automatic Weapons	British, German, Italian, U.S.
49	Light Machine guns	British, German, Italian
4	Light Mortars	British, German
4	Heavy Mortars	German, Italian, Canadian
8	Light Machine gun Spare Barrels	
392	grenades	British, German, Polish
6	Antitank Mines	German (Teller)
20	Antipersonnel Mines	"Schuh"-type
47	"Bazookas"	two types; probably German *Panzerfaust* and British PIAT
105,920	Rounds of Small Arms Ammo	British, German, Italian, U.S.
355	"Big" Mortar Rounds	German, Italian, Canadian; probably 81mm type
208	"Small" Mortar Rounds	British, German; probably 60mm type

Source: ID No. 494972, 1–3.

units were worked out, the allocations of weapons were fairly generous, with a high proportion of automatic weapons. The typical GDA infantry squad of ten men was armed with one light machine gun, two automatic weapons, one or two sniper rifles, four or five rifles, a few pistols, ten hand grenades, and two antitank rockets.[127] A 432-man GDA infantry battalion was authorized fifteen pistols, 284 rifles, ninety-seven automatic weapons, twenty-seven light machine guns, four heavy machine guns, nine light mortars, and two heavy mortars.[128] A 1,525-man GDA brigade was authorized fifty-six pistols, 936 rifles, 392 automatic weapons, eighty-one light machine guns, eighteen heavy machine guns, twenty-seven light mortars, and six heavy mortars.[129]

Of course, GDA units were never at full strength in either personnel or equipment. The actual armament of a GDA infantry battalion is reflected by a document found in the Grammos area in early September 1948.[130] It lists the arms and ammunition on hand in July 1948 in the GDA 588th Battalion, then assigned to the 14th Brigade, 10th Division. At the time the document was prepared, the 588th Battalion had a strength of fifteen officers and 245 enlisted personnel. The armament of the 588th Battalion in July 1948, shown in Table 5.5, reflects how heterogeneous GDA armament remained, even toward the end of the war. As the U.S. military attaché commented in his report on the armament of the 588th Battalion,

Supply and maintenance difficulties must be continuous and considerable, in order to maintain three types of rifles [British, German, and Italian], five types of machine guns

[Bren, Brenda, Fiat, German, and Vickers], and five types of mortars [two German, British, Canadian, and Italian] in operation.[131]

Colonel Smith also noted that the ratio of automatic weapons per man is greater in the GDA battalion than in the standard GNA battalion but also that the advantage was probably more than offset by the inefficiency resulting from heterogeneous types found in the GDA battalion.

Since most of the GDA's ammunition in the later part of the war was imported from the neighboring Communist countries and brought in over extremely difficult terrain, ammunition was often scarce and was always carefully husbanded. Usually, the GDA guerrilla rifleman carried twenty to thirty rounds, and 200–300 rounds were carried for each machine gun.[132] There was a significant difference in ammunition requirements for GDA units in the main Grammos-Vitsi base area and those elsewhere in Greece, those of the former being substantially greater, due to the concentration in the defended base areas of most of the GDA heavy (artillery, antiaircraft, and antitank) weapons.[133]

The ammunition supply problem was greatly increased by the multiplicity of calibers and types of weapons employed, but on some occasions the GDA planners and supply operators were apparently quite successful in overcoming these difficulties.[134] Officers of the GNA 8th Infantry Division reported that in the battle of Konitsa (December 1947), the guerrillas apparently had unlimited ammunition of all types; some dead guerrilla riflemen were found to be carrying 1,000 rounds, and guerrilla machine gun positions were found with 7,000 rounds in place.[135] The captured GDA weapons were reported to be old but serviceable, indicating that the guerrillas had received some maintenance training.

Late in the war, the GDA General Command prescribed the basic load for various types of weapons. The types, quantities, and weight of the official (theoretical) allowance for a 432-man GDA infantry battalion is shown in Table 5.6. The authorized basic load of a GDA infantry battalion amounted to nearly six short tons, or approximately eighty mule loads under ideal conditions. Assuming that a GDA battalion would have only half its authorized number of personnel, animals, weapons, or ammunition on hand at any given time, the total would still amount to 5,900 pounds, or approximately forty mule loads. Since a full-strength GDA infantry battalion was authorized only sixty-two animals, the logistical tail of the GDA was clearly short indeed, even in theory.

Using contemporary U.S. planning figures, it is also possible to calculate the approximate daily ammunition requirement for a full-strength, 432-man GDA infantry battalion. The U.S. planning figure (theaterwide, Europe) was 3.64 pounds/man/day.[136] A simple calculation would thus give an estimate of the daily ammunition requirement of a GDA infantry battalion as 1,572.5 pounds (about 0.79 short tons). However, the U.S. planning figure includes an allowance for supporting artillery, antiaircraft artillery, and rear-area personnel and thus is not a particularly accurate indicator of the actual requirements of a front-line GDA infantry unit. It is, however, possible using another method, to arrive at

Table 5.6
Weight of Authorized Ammunition Basic Load for 432-Man GDA Infantry Battalion

Item	Quantity	Weight Per Round in lbs	Total Weight in lbs
Pistol (.45 cal) Cartridges	750	.055	41.3
Rifle (.30 cal) Cartridges	23,450	.086	2,016.70
Automatic Rifle (.30 cal) Cartridges	9,100	.075	682.5
Light Machine gun (.30 cal) Cartridges	5,400	.077	415.8
Heavy Machine gun (.50 cal) Cartridges	12,000	.370	4,440.0
Heavy (81mm) Mortar Rounds	144	9.700	1,396.8
Light (60mm) Mortar Rounds	432	4.500	1,944.0
Antitank Rockets (3.5–in.)	31	9.380	290.8
Handgrenades (U.S. fragmentation)	270	2.120	572.4
Total			11,800

Sources: Enclosure 4 to ID No. 542941; *FM 101–10*, August 1949, ¶¶108–109 (pp. 259–62). Weight
per piece based on U.S. weapons of the period.

a more accurate estimate. Table 5.7 indicates that the daily ammunition requirement for a full-strength GDA infantry battalion amounted to about 0.55 short tons (about eight mule loads), or about 2.56 pounds/man.

At the beginning of the "Third Round," the Communist guerrillas and the government forces were evenly matched with respect to artillery and other heavy weapons, neither side having any substantial number of such weapons. American aid to the GNF soon shifted the advantage in long-range, indirect fire to the government; the GDA scrambled to catch up but never succeeded in matching the artillery firepower of the government forces.[137] Although the guerrillas eventually obtained a number of artillery pieces, heavy mortars, and antiaircraft and antitank guns as well as mines, grenades, and radios from their outside supporters, the numbers were never large; the supply of ammunition and spare parts remained difficult, employment in the mountainous terrain difficult, pieces vulnerable to massive counterbattery and air attack, and fire direction skills limited.[138] As a consequence, GDA artillery support was restricted primarily to the Grammos and Vitsi base areas, for which the valuable weapons could be kept in nearby Albania or Yugoslavia or evacuated there quickly in case of need.[139] The GDA had no tanks or self-propelled artillery pieces, although at the beginning of January 1949 the Greek General Staff reported that the GDA had six armored cars in the border region near Lake Prespa.[140] In February 1949 a surrendered GDA lieutenant, Zafirios Aristinides, also reported having seen one destroyed armored car near Vronderon and another moving toward Florina.[141]

Until the end of 1947, the GDA had few artillery pieces or other heavy weapons, but between November 1947 and April 1948 the GDA apparently received a number of artillery pieces, mortars, and antiaircraft guns, most of which were subsequently employed in the defense of the northern base areas.[142] The most common type of GDA artillery piece was the 75 mm Skoda mountain

Table 5.7
Estimated Daily Ammunition Expenditure for 432-Man GDA Infantry Battalion

Item	No. of Wpns in Unit	Rds per Wpn per Day	Total Rounds per Day	Weight Per Round	Total Weight in lbs
Pistol (.45 cal) Cartridges	15	.3	4.5	.055	.25
Rifle (.30 cal) Cartridges	284	6.0	1,704.0	.086	146.6
Automatic Rifle (.30 cal) Cartridges	97	20.0	1,940.0	.075	145.5
Light machine gun (.30 cal) Cartridges	27	50.0	1,350.0	.077	104.0
Heavy Machine gun(.50 cal)Cartridges	4	20.0	80.0	.370	29.6
Heavy (81mm) Mortar Rounds	2	20.0	40.0	9.700	388.0
Light (60mm) Mortar Rounds	9	5.0	45.0	4.500	202.5
Antitank Rockets (3.5–in.)	54	estimated 5.0		9.380	46.9
Handgrenades (fragmentation)	270	estimated 20.0		2.120	42.4
Total					1,106

Sources: Enclosure 4 to ID No. 542941; *FM 101–10*, August 1949, ¶112 (p. 267). Calculated using the "Protracted Period" estimate. The estimate does *not* contain an allowance for antitank and antipersonnel land mines, which were used extensively by the GDA.

gun (pack howitzer), which had a range of 10,200 meters.[143] Other types included German, Italian, British, and Soviet makes, the 120 mm mortars being of the Soviet pattern. The antiaircraft weapons were all of the 20 mm or 37 mm automatic-weapon type. By January 1949 the GDA was reported to have on hand fifteen 105 mm howitzers, forty-five 75 mm pack howitzers/field guns, thirty-one 20 mm/37 mm antiaircraft guns, two 75 mm antitank guns, thirty-eight 20 mm/37 mm antitank guns, and twelve 120 mm mortars.[144] By comparison, the number and types of weapons in use by the GNA at the same time included 175 25-pounder guns, forty-one 5.5-inch field guns, eight 75 mm pack howitzers, fifty 3.7-inch howitzers, eighty-three 6-pounder guns, eighty-two 40 mm guns, forty-nine 4.2-inch mortars, 446 3-inch mortars, 1,045 81 mm mortars, 1,020 60 mm mortars, sixty-six U.S. Sherman medium tanks, fifty-four British Centaur light tanks, two U.S. M-8 armored cars, twenty-three U.S. Greyhound armored cars, 216 South African scout cars, 261 Ford Lynx scout cars, and 191 Bren gun carriers.[145]

By virtue of its greater bulk and weight, artillery ammunition—a necessity for any conventionally organized military force—posed a tremendous logistical problem for the GDA in terms of storage, handling, and transportation. Table 5.8 shows the estimated daily ammunition expenditure for the GDA artillery park at its peak.

Mines were a favorite weapon of the GDA guerrilla; they have been called "the most effective single weapon in the guerrilla arsenal."[146] Mines were apparently available to the GDA in quantity, probably from leftover German World War II stocks. The most common types were the Teller antitank mine, the so-called "Schuh" mine (a wooden box antipersonnel mine of German origin), S mines, and various improvised types.[147] Antitank mines could be used indiscriminately, since the GDA had no motor vehicles. Table 5.9 shows mine statistics for several months in 1948–1949.

Table 5.8
Estimated Daily GDA Expenditure of Artillery Ammunition

Weapon	Number of Weapons	Rounds/ Day/ Weapon	Total Rounds	Weight of Round in lbs	Total Weight in lbs
105mm Howitzer	15	45	675	49.00	3,307.5
75mm Pack Howitzer	45	25	1,125	22.00	2,475.0
20mm/37mm Antiaircraft Gun	31	20.0	620	.44	272.8
75mm Antitank Gun	2	2	4	21.85	87.4
20mm/37mm Antitank Gun	38	6.0	228	1.61	367.1
120mm Mortar	12	20	240	35.06	8,414.4
Total					14,924

Sources: *FM 101-10*, August 1949, ¶108 and ¶112; Weiner and Lewis, *The Warsaw Pact Armies: Organization—Concept of War, Weapons, and Equipment*, 191, 229, and 231. Calculated using the "Protracted Period" estimate. Weight of round data used is for Soviet-type weapons (20 mm antiaircraft gun, 37 mm antitank gun, and 120 mm mortar) or nearest U.S. equivalent weapon (105 mm and 75 mm howitzers and 75 mm recoilless rifle for 75 mm antitank gun). Rounds/weapon/day for antiaircraft and antitank weapons is estimated. This estimate assumes all weapons were in service, which was certainly not the case.

Overall Logistical Requirements

On 8 February 1949, at the time Markos Vafiades was relieved as commander of the GDA, the conversion of the GDA to a conventional army was well advanced, and Nikos Zachariades and his supporters were basking in the glow of the GDA's successes at Karditsa, Naousa, and Karpenision. The defeat at Florina was still a week away; the government drive in the Peloponnesus had not yet been concluded; and the aggressive GNA campaigns of the spring and summer of 1949 were still some time in the future. The overall size of the GDA within Greece at that time was 23,890 combatants, to which must be added, of course, a considerable supporting infrastructure, dependents, and associated animals.[148] The bulk of the Communist forces—perhaps 90 percent—were ranged along the northern borders. Some gauge of the logistical requirements of the GDA at the peak of its development at the beginning of February 1949 can be obtained by a few simple calculations, using the hypothetical 432-man GDA "standard" infantry battalion as a benchmark. Based on the daily requirements for various classes of supply noted above, the overall daily resupply requirement for a full-strength GDA infantry battalion, around February 1949, would be as shown in Table 5.10.

Thus, a full-strength GDA infantry battalion would require a daily resupply of about 4.22 short tons, or approximately 19.6 pounds per man.[149] Of course, GDA units were never at full authorized strength. However, even if we assume a GDA infantry battalion was at half strength, theoretically it would still have needed about 2.1 short tons of supplies per day, or about twenty-nine mule loads. In February 1949, there were some fifty-eight GDA infantry battalions, sixteen double companies, and twenty-one independent companies, or roughly

Table 5.9
GDA Use of Mines, 1948–1949

Period	Detected by GNF		Damaged or Destroyed by Mines			
	Anti-tank	Anti-personnel	Military Vehicles	Civilian Vehicles	Railroad Trains	Wheeled Carts
Jun 1948	587	2,062				
Oct 1948	915	1,939				
Nov 1948	620	1,430				
Dec 1948	262	524	39	14	4	
Jan 1949	302	565	31	6	8	
May 1949	918	522	30	14	6	7
Jun 1949	243	766	20	3	3	12

Sources: ID No. 589129; ID No. 523063; ID No. 538917.

seventy-two battalion equivalents. Thus, for infantry forces alone, the GDA in February 1949 would have required approximately 151.9 short tons of supplies per day, or about 2,025 mule loads. To this must be added ammunition and other supplies required for headquarters, artillery, antiaircraft artillery, and logistical forces, as well as auxiliaries and dependents.

Military expert J. C. Murray has estimated that if the GDA had consumed supplies at the same rate allowed in planning figures for U.S. troops, their daily requirements would have exceeded a million pounds, or some 400 2.5-ton truckloads.[150] Actually, the GDA's daily consumption was probably closer to half of that. Using the modified U.S. planning figures discussed above, and considering the 23,890 combatants of the GDA but leaving aside the supporting infrastructure (*aftoamyna*) and dependents, the overall daily resupply requirements of the GDA on 8 February 1949 would have been as shown in Table 5.11.

GDA BASES IN GREECE

The principal logistical facilities supporting the GDA were located close to the Greek border in Albania, Yugoslavia, and Bulgaria. However, the GDA created a number of substantial base areas within Greece, particularly in the Grammos-Vitsi stronghold and other border regions. Smaller regional bases were also established throughout the country to support GDA forces operating in various areas. Despite his obvious respect for Tito and the fact that he had to rely on Albania, Yugoslavia, and Bulgaria to supply the bulk of his war matériel and to provide the logistical facilities required, Markos was no fool, and he sought to create his own complex of bases inside Greece to support the operations of the GDA even if his socialist allies proved unreliable. These bases were well dispersed and sited so as to facilitate the operations of GDA units. Major GDA bases were located along the Greek borders in Mourgana, Grammos, Vitsi, Kaimaktsalan, Beles, Boz Dag, Khaidou, and Evros; in the Pieria-Olympus, Agrafa, Roumeli, Othris, Kallidrhomon, and Parnassos regions of central Greece; and in all of the mountain ranges of the Peloponnesus.[151] Except for the Grammos-Vitsi stronghold areas, the GDA was not committed to a last-ditch

Table 5.10
Daily Resupply Requirements for a Full-Strength GDA Infantry Battalion, ca. 1949

Class of Supply	Pounds
Class I (Rations)	1,728
Class I (Forage)	744
Class II (Clothing and Equipment)	372
Class III (Fuel)	3,672
Class IV (Engineer Supplies)	817
Class V (Ammunition)	1,106
Total	8,439

defense of their bases, preferring instead to remain relatively mobile and to evacuate the bases rather than become decisively engaged with government troops.

The vital nature of the GDA's bases in the border regions as entrepôts for equipment and supplies from the neighboring Communist countries was well recognized by the leaders of the Greek national forces, whose strategy was based on cutting off the GDA from its outside suppliers by overrunning and destroying the GDA's base areas. Soon after assuming command of the GNF, Gen. Alexander Papagos told his subordinates, that

If they [the guerrillas] fail in ensuring their supplies from the neighboring states—and these supplies come from those frontier bases—their war potential will soon expire. Moreover, those frontier bases constitute their refuge in case of need. . . . Finally, wherever, by progressive clearing, we reach the frontier, especially in vital areas for the bandits (areas of supply from neighboring states) we must ensure the occupation and control of those areas in order to deprive them progressively of these supplies.[152]

The Grammos-Vitsi Stronghold

The first Communist guerrilla bases in Greece, other than caches of matériel hidden at the time of the Varkiza Agreement in February 1945, were established in September 1946 by Markos in the border regions having easy access to both the safety of and sources of supply in neighboring countries. As the GDA expanded and guerrilla operations were initiated in Roumeli, the Peloponnesus, and other areas remote from the northern borders, bases were established in the various operational areas, usually in remote mountain locations. The border base areas, particularly those in the Grammos and Vitsi mountains adjacent to the Albania and Yugoslavian borders, were subsequently further developed to serve as receiving and distribution points for supplies and equipment from the neighboring Communist countries.

The GDA logistical facilities in the Grammos and Vitsi were initially quite

Table 5.11
Overall GDA Daily Resupply Requirements, 8 February 1949

Month	Recruits
October 1948	3,600
November 1948	1,920
December 1948	1,848
January 1949	1,500
23 February–1 March 1949	1,500
May 1949	720
June 1949	100

NB: Calculated at four pounds/man/day for Class I; twelve pounds/animal/day for forage (2,000 animals); 0.86 pounds/man/day for Class II; 8.5 pounds/man/day for Class III; 1.89 pounds/man/day for Class IV; and 3.64 pounds/man/day for Class V. Note that Class II and IV planning figures are only 15 percent of the U.S. standard.

primitive, but in time they were developed into major logistical base areas, with protected storage for food, clothing, arms, ammunition, and other supplies. The base areas also included workshops for the manufacture and repair of arms and equipment, such as tailor and cobbler shops, armories, and saddlers, as well as post offices and medical facilities. For example, one surrendered GDA lieutenant told his government interrogators that the GDA had tailor, shoemaker, and armorer workshops, a tannery, and a base post office at Mikrolimni; 300-man training camps at Plati and Lefkona; an officers' school at Pyxos; a POW camp at Plati; and an eighty-bed hospital, directed by Colonel Petropoulos (a former GNA second lieutenant medical officer), at Vronteron—the site (in February 1949) of the GDA General Command headquarters.[153] Other field hospitals in Greece were located in the village of Pyxos and along the valley extending from Antathotov to Pyxos.[154] These facilities provided support to the guerrillas within the base areas and forwarded supplies to the GDA units located elsewhere in Greece. The operation of the GDA logistical facilities in the Grammos-Vitsi base areas, as elsewhere in Greece, was apparently entrusted to the area units, although the staff sections of GDA General Command probably exercised close supervision of the principal stocks.

As the GDA logistical facilities expanded, they became impossible to conceal, and the GDA consequently was obliged to fortify the Grammos-Vitsi region and conduct a position defense to prevent the penetration of government troops and the destruction of the guerrilla bases. Field fortifications were constructed, minefields were laid, and artillery and antiaircraft guns were installed to defend the vital GDA base areas. Eventually, the major portion of the GDA's combat manpower was located in the Grammos-Vitsi stronghold, and because the supply of arms and other matériel from Albania and Yugoslavia were vital to the continued viability of the GDA everywhere in Greece, government operations into the

Grammos-Vitsi region were resisted strongly and, until the spring of 1949, with a high degree of success.

Workshops, Supply Depots, and Other Support Facilities

The GDA maintained a number of logistical facilities scattered throughout Greece. The Pindus Mountains from Metsovon to the Gulf of Corinth and the range of mountains extending from Vermion to Pelion, in particular, provided a number of areas suitable for guerrilla bases. Bases there were protected by rugged mountains yet close enough to the populated plains so that the guerrillas could leave their hiding places, strike, and return to the safety of their bases during the course of a single night.[155] Usually, these facilities were located in wooded areas away from inhabited villages and roads and were protected by small forces of guerrillas that could delay government forces long enough for wounded guerrillas to be evacuated and vital equipment and supplies either removed to a safe location or hidden. In the GDA-controlled areas, these logistical complexes could be quite large. One guerrilla of the GDA 53d Brigade surrendered on 30 December 1948 and revealed that large stores of food and clothing were located in the village of Filippaioi.[156] He reported the existence there of about 2,000 pairs of Czech shoes and boxes of cotton and woolen clothing brought from the Grammos as well as clothing workshops, spinning mills, weaving mills, and looms for the making of clothing. Thirty-five to forty women were employed in these shops. Workshops for the making of "Schuh" mines, flashlights, and dry batteries and stores of food containing large quantities of cereals, corn, peas, and rye were also located in Filippaioi.

The majority of GDA supplies were stored by the area units for distribution to GDA tactical units as required, and each guerrilla unit established its own temporary dumps or caches of food, water, ammunition, fuel, tools, and other essential items.[157] These field storage locations in a unit's operating area were usually small, temporary, and relatively mobile, being taken up if the unit was reassigned to another location. Food was often stored in houses on the outskirts of villages, and ammunition in the open along both sides of roads on the slopes of hills. GDA divisions and brigades also maintained tactical dumps of food and ammunition. Battalions drew food from the supply center (dump) of their brigade, which in turn obtained food for one to two days at a time from divisional dumps, the supplies being transported on organic mules, by carts, or, in areas near the border, by trucks.

The GDA forces in the Peloponnesus were nearly independent with respect to supply, although essential items such as ammunition were received from Albania and Yugoslavia by sea or via the Grammos-Vitsi base area and the tortuous line of communication through the Pindus Mountains. GDA bases were established in the various mountainous areas controlled by the guerrillas, and secure supply facilities were set up throughout the Peloponnesus. Withal, the GDA forces in the Peloponnesus remained relatively mobile, carrying only essential supplies and depending on the *aftoamyna* infrastructure to store and issue most supplies and services.[158] Instructions issued by the headquarters of the GDA forces in the Mainalon Mountains north of Tripolis on 22 August 1948 provided for the construction of two secret supply shelters in each subcommand area.[159] Each shelter was to contain stocks of food and water, and the subordinate units were cautioned to locate the shelters in strategically unimportant areas unlikely to be overrun by the GNA and to keep their location unknown to local shepherds and other civilians.

GDA TRANSPORT

The main battles of the Greek civil war, particularly after mid-1948, were fought in remote, wild mountain areas, nearly devoid of roads, shelter, or population. Due to government control of the existing roads, most guerrilla movements were conducted at night on foot or horseback over precipitous mountain trails, often in foul weather. GDA ground transport of supplies was limited, both by the terrain and by the availability of porters and pack animals, which required large amounts of forage. The resupply of guerrilla units by sea was restricted by effective sea denial by the Royal Hellenic Navy (RHN) and by the location of the guerrilla units, which were usually in mountainous areas away from the coasts. The aerial delivery of supplies to the guerrillas was negligible. Overall, the GDA's transport requirements exceeded its transport capabilities by a fair margin.

GDA Transport Requirements

The daily transport requirement for GDA units outside the border strongholds was probably on the order of one to two pounds per man per day.[160] While such quantities were insignificant on an individual basis, in the aggregate they constituted a substantial demand for what little transport the GDA could muster, and the supplies, no matter how small in volume, were critical to the guerrillas. Murray has estimated that the guerrillas in south and central Greece would have required about fifty to a hundred mule loads of supplies per day, with the average distance carried being about 120 miles from the base areas on the northern borders.[161] Without regard to losses, the number of animals required would have been between 700 and 1,400, and the turnaround time about two weeks.[162] But in fact, the GNA and Royal Hellenic Air Force (RHAF) intercepted numerous mule columns and destroyed large numbers of animals with their loads. However, based on the overall GDA daily resupply requirement in February 1949 of 237.66 short tons (see Table 5.11), some 3,169 mules or 159 2.5-ton trucks would have been required to meet all of the GDA's daily transport requirements. With probably fewer than 1,500 mules available, the GDA's transport requirements clearly exceeded its capabilities, even though a portion of the requirements might have been satisfied by porters or even trucks.

Ground Transport

The majority of the Communist forces were deployed along Greece's borders with Albania, Yugoslavia, and Bulgaria, and thus could be resupplied with relative ease from those countries. However, the GDA forces located in the interior, in the Peloponnesus, and on the islands were much more difficult to supply and were consequently much more vulnerable to government interdiction. Insofar as equipment and supplies provided by the GDA's outside supporters reached these forces, they did so by ground transport—primarily pack mule convoys and porters, many of whom were women, although occasionally the GDA was able to use trucks captured from the GNF or supplied by outside sources.[163] The internal ground transport routes used by the GDA ran principally along the spine of the Pindus range, the northern end of which lay in the Grammos-Vitsi base area.[164] Another major route ran from the Kaimaktsalan region via Mounts Vermion, Olympus, and Pelion to the Agrafa-Roumeli area.[165]

Within Greece, nearly all GDA supply movements were carried out by either porters or pack animals, both of which were limited in the amounts they could carry and the distances they could travel without rest.[166] The GDA liaison and area units were responsible for the provision of both porters and pack animals. The three GDA regular transport battalions (two in Vitsi and one in Grammos), equipped primarily as pack outfits, handled major requirements and reinforced locally acquired resources as necessary. The number of porters employed by the GDA is unknown, but at any given time late in the war as many as 1,400 mules may have been involved in the internal movement of GDA supplies.[167] Pack animals were rather scarce and difficult to maintain, due to their very substantial forage requirements; in winter the GDA was forced to farm out a large number of its pack animals and horses to peasants in the more temperate valleys and plains, where more forage was available.[168] Nevertheless, some GDA mule trains were quite large. In early January 1949 a 400-mule convoy under Agrafiotis successfully resupplied the GDA 1st and 2d Divisions in preparation for their attack on Karpenision, despite an all-out effort by the RHAF to locate and interdict the column, an effort that was stymied by poor flying weather.[169] However, not all GDA mule convoys were as large or so successful. On 8 January 1949 the GNA ambushed a GDA cavalry unit led by Stephos; the guerrillas lost eight men killed, sixteen loaded mules killed, and forty loaded mules captured.[170]

Guerrilla lines of communications were maintained and improved by detachments from the two engineer battalions available to the GDA General Command. Although forced to operate in rugged, unimproved areas, the GDA had not the manpower, engineering skill, or equipment to do much more than improve the mountain trails, erect temporary bridging, and try to keep the entire network in a basic state of repair. Major road construction projects were not attempted.[171] In any event, motor roads were not a high priority, as the GDA had little motor transport available within Greece—although the U.S. military attaché in Athens reported two battalions of motor transport, totaling about a hundred trucks, in the Vitsi area in March 1949.[172] The reported vehicles were probably being used to shuttle supplies from Albania to GDA storage sites just inside the Greek border.

Water Transport

Despite the extensive coastline of Greece and the Greek seafaring tradition, only limited use was made of coastal vessels in supplying the GDA detachments located far from the border areas. In the first place, most of the GDA guerrilla units were located in mountain areas remote from the coast. Moreover, the trans-shipment of cargo from boats to mules or vice versa was onerous and time consuming. In any event, the Royal Hellenic Navy was very effective at inter-dicting seaborne traffic, particularly attempts to resupply the Communist forces in the Peloponnesus by sea.[173] Markos was successful in obtaining a few small ships from Albania to move supplies for the GDA. The Communist guerrilla navy—known during the resistance period as ELAN—was revived on a small scale in 1947, but the new ELAN restricted its activities to the Adriatic coast of Greece and the Gulf of Corinth.[174] The guerrillas were also reported to have obtained an old Italian submarine from Albania in March 1948 and to have used it in the Adriatic.[175]

The GDA forces in the Peloponnesus depended almost entirely on arms and ammunition forwarded to them from the Grammos-Vitsi base area along the slow and difficult ground line through the Pindus Mountains. Consequently, numerous attempts were made to resupply the GDA in the Peloponnesus by sea, using *caiques*, or small ships, sailing from Albanian or Yugoslavian ports. In April 1948, the U.S. naval attaché in Rome reported that a special section of the Yugoslavian naval headquarters at Split was charged with the organization and transport of war matériel to the GDA.[176] The special section was reported to be directed by Yugoslavian navy captain Ivan Lovetich, who had two Greeks and a Russian as liaison officers. The delivery of supplies was reported to be accomplished by three old Yugoslavian submarines, which loaded at night in various small ports near Split. The attaché noted that Yugoslavia was known to have only one prewar submarine at the time but that Yugoslavia might have acquired several Italian midget submarines left in Yugoslavia at the end of World War II. He also mentioned that Russian submarines were frequently re-ported in various Mediterranean ports.

In July 1948 the GDA attempted to test the feasibility of moving supplies by *caique* from Albania to the Peloponnesus, but the shipment of twenty-two tons, including 500 *panzerfaust* antitank rockets, 200 machine guns, and a large quan-tity of ammunition, never reached the guerrillas.[177] A short time later, on 6 September 1948, the RHN corvette *Polemistis* intercepted a small, 250-ton *caique* and chased it into the bay of Fokianos, southeast of the town of Leon-idion.[178] The *Polemistis* received fire from both the *caique* and guerrilla positions on shore but succeeded in hitting the *caique*, which blew up, with no survivors.

It was subsequently determined that the *caique* had been loaded with some 2,000 German rifles, 100 machine guns, 3,000 mines, and substantial amounts of ammunition, hand grenades, and Communist printed propaganda at the Albanian port of Durrës (Durazzo, the ancient Dyrrhachium), which was quite close to the important GDA training centers and supply bases at Souht and Shijak, west of Tirana. The crew had been composed of GDA guerrillas, but the captain had been an Albanian, Hassan Moustafa. Other attempts were more successful. Between 10 and 20 August 1948, a vessel loaded at Valona (now Vlorë), Albania, with three German machine guns and 10,000 rounds of machine-gun ammunition, 120 Bren guns with spare parts, more than 200 British-made antitank rockets, and 1.5 million rounds of small arms ammunition landed its cargo for the GDA near Kyparissia.[179] The last major attempt to resupply the GDA guerrillas in the Peloponnesus by sea before their defeat by the GNF in Operation PIGEON took place in November 1948. A *caique* loaded with some 1,500 rifles, 100 machine guns, more than 1,000 mines, and a large quantity of other weapons and explosives was intercepted and sunk by an RHN vessel.[180]

Despite the vigilance of the Royal Hellenic Navy, supplies for the GDA were also moved across the Aegean Sea. On 12 April 1948, the U.S. naval attaché in Athens reported Turkish sources as stating that Soviet vessels probably carrying supplies for the Greek guerrillas were passing through the Bosphorus without pilots and presumably transshipping their cargoes somewhere in the Greek islands in the Aegean.[181] In the same month, his counterpart in Rome reported that many small craft from the Dodecanese Islands were calling at the Italian ports of Brindisi, Bari, and Gallipoli with merchandise for sale on the Italian market and then loading at night and in secrecy with supplies for the Greek rebels.[182]

Air Transport

Markos hoped to form a GDA air force, with aircraft from Yugoslavia and Bulgaria. Although two small airstrips were built in the area near Lake Prespa and a call for pilots, experienced crew, and ground-support personnel was issued, the aircraft were never received, and no guerrilla air force was ever formed.[183] One low-rated intelligence source reported that a guerrilla air force existed, with ten fighters, eight bombers, and a complement of ninety officers and 140 enlisted personnel, but no evidence was ever found to support that claim.[184] The airfields apparently did exist—they were attacked by the RHAF in March 1948—but the use to which they were put is unknown.[185]

The Greek government was constantly concerned about the potential resupply of the Communist rebels by air from the surrounding Communist states. Reports of unidentified aircraft in Greek airspace were plentiful, and the GDA guerrillas no doubt received aerial deliveries on an irregular basis, but there is little solid evidence to indicate that the GDA received regular or substantial amounts of supplies by air. A guerrilla captured in the Peloponnesus in January 1949 alleged that no attempts had been made to resupply GDA forces in the Peloponnesus by airdrop, a statement that confirmed the opinion of the U.S. military attaché in Athens at that time.[186] On the other hand, there is good reason to believe that the GDA guerrillas in northern Greece did receive some supplies from their outside benefactors by air. In July 1948 the U.S. military attaché in Turkey forwarded a map found on the body of a Bulgarian colonel, Boris Ganev, who was killed in the hijacking of a Bulgarian civil airliner that was forced to fly to Turkey.[187] The map was marked with what appeared to be routes to be flown and drop zones for the aerial resupply of the Greek guerrillas from Bulgaria. Potential or actual drop zones, underlined or circled on the map, included areas near Alexandroupolis, Negrita, Edhessa, Vere, Florina, Bitolj, and three remote mountain sites. The information on Colonel Ganev's map was never confirmed, and most airdrops to the GDA guerrillas, if they occurred at all, were probably on the order of that reported by a captured GDA guerrilla interrogated in May 1948: "On 5 March 1948, at 0200 hours, in the district north of Amalias, an aircraft dropped to my unit fifteen rifles, military uniforms, and a sack of sugar."[188] The assistant U.S. air attaché in Athens, First Lt. Robert B. English, commented on the report that it was the "first instance in which a guerrilla [had] admitted air supply" and that there had been "numerous reports of unidentified aircraft over the Peloponnesus which have been disregarded due to much commercial air traffic in the Gulf of Corinth corridor."[189]

CONCLUSION

The political decisions taken by Nikos Zachariades and the leaders of the KKE between February 1947 and February 1949 seriously hampered the ability of the GDA to attract willing fighters and support them adequately. Zachariades' plan to convert an effective Communist guerrilla army into a conventional force and to use it in direct confrontation with the superior Greek national forces imposed on the GDA manpower requirements that it could not meet. As Nachmani has written,

Holding territory and manning field positions increased the demands on the GDA's manpower. Establishing a regular army required growing numbers of administrative auxiliaries and noncombatants for repair-shops, printing works, military police, the military legal system, medical personnel, officers for liaison with the civilian population, and so on. The heavy casualties inflicted on the GDA, the additional demands of conventional warfare, and the Greek government's intentional evacuation of hundreds of thousands of people from areas susceptible to falling into Communist hands all deprived the guerrillas of crucial manpower.[190]

Not only did the attempt to form a conventional army increase GDA manpower requirements, but Zachariades' other policies made it impossible to exploit fully the small manpower pool available to the Communists. The attempt to enforce party discipline on military personnel and civilians by the use of terror reduced support for the KKE and GDA among the Greek population, and the decision to support the creation of an independent Slavic Macedonia at the expense of some 1.5 million Greeks living in Macedonia resulted in the loss of what little sympathy remained for the Communist cause.

The increased size and formal structure of a conventional army also imposed logistical burdens that the limited resources and fragile support structure of the GDA could not carry, even with outside assistance. Moreover, Zachariades' decision to side with Stalin and the Cominform in their dispute with the independent-minded Tito alienated the GDA's principal logistical supporter. The logistical requirements of the GDA were substantial, particularly once the decision to form and fight a conventional army was put into effect. However, the internal resources available to satisfy those requirements were limited. The organic GDA logistical organization was small and generally inexperienced, and the deficiency of numbers and expertise limited the expansion of logistical services as the size of the GDA increased and the nature of its operations changed from small-scale guerrilla attacks to positional defense. The dependence of the GDA on the *aftoamyna* for the collection, storage, and distribution of supplies and the provision of transport and other services also became a liability once the Greek government forces began aggressively to root out and destroy the guerrilla infrastructure.

In any event, the ability of the *aftoamyna* to meet the needs of the GDA was constrained by the limited agricultural and industrial resources of post–World War II Greece, particularly in the desolate mountain areas controlled by the guerrillas. In the early years of the civil war of 1945–1949, the Communist rebels were able to meet their requirements for arms and ammunition from stocks accumulated by ELAS during the World War II resistance period and by matériel captured from the GNF, but as the GDA increased in size and transformed itself into a more or less conventional army, it was forced to rely increasingly on its friendly Communist neighbors not only for heavy artillery, antiaircraft guns, antitank guns, communications equipment, and mines with which to defend its vital base areas along the northern borders of Greece, but for food, clothing, medical supplies, small arms, and small arms ammunition.

NOTES

1. Hugh H. Gardner, *Civil War in Greece, 1945–1949*, Incomplete draft (Washington: U.S. Army Center of Military History, n.d.), "Sources of Guerrilla Manpower" (unpaginated) [cited hereafter as Gardner draft]; United States Army Command and General Staff College, *Internal Defense Operations: A Case History, Greece 1946–49*, USACGSC RB 31-1 (Fort Leavenworth, KS: United States Army Command and General Staff College, 1 November 1967), 131. Slavo-Macedonian volunteers formed an important segment of the overall strength of the GDA, and at one point they constituted almost two-thirds of the total GDA strength (see Frank J. Abbott, *The Greek Civil War, 1947–*

1949: Lessons for the Operational Artist in Foreign Internal Defense, School of Advanced Military Studies thesis [Fort Leavenworth, KS: School of Advanced Military Studies, U.S. Army Command and General Staff College, May 1994], 33).

2. Extract-Summary of the Report of Maj. Gen. S. J. Chamberlin to U.S. Army Chief of Staff, 20 October 1947, 2–3 [in File "GEOG. L. GREECE 370.02 (Civil War)," General Reference Branch, United States Army Center of Military History, Washington, DC] [cited hereafter as Chamberlin Report]; United States Military Attaché–Greece, Intelligence Report R-188-48 (ID No. 448978), Athens, 16 March 1948, subject: Estimate of the Situation, 14–15 [in Box 2900, Assistant Chief of Staff, G-2, Intelligence, Numerical Series of Intelligence Document File ("ID Files"), 1944–1955, Record Group 319 (Records of the Army Staff), National Archives II, College Park, MD] [the location of other documents from the "ID Files" will be cited hereafter simply as "in Box *x*, ID Files, RG 319, NA," and on second and subsequent citations such documents will be identified solely by their ID number]; M. A. Campbell, E. W. Downs, and L. V. Schuetta, *The Employment of Airpower in the Greek Guerrilla War, 1947–1949*, Project No. AU-411-62-ASI (Maxwell Air Force Base, AL: Concepts Division, Aerospace Studies Institute, United States Air University, December 1964), 17 [cited hereafter as *Employment of Airpower*]. John O. Iatrides, "Civil War, 1945–1949: National and International Aspects," in John O. Iatrides, ed., *Greece in the 1940s: A Nation in Crisis* (Hanover, NH: Univ. of New England Press, 1981), 207–208.

3. Gardner draft, "Sources of Guerrilla Manpower."

4. Ibid.

5. Floyd A. Spencer, *War and Postwar Greece: An Analysis Based on Greek Writings* (Washington: European Affairs Division, Library of Congress, 1952), 100.

6. Gardner draft, "Sources of Guerrilla Manpower."

7. ID No. 448978, 8 and 14.

8. United States Military Attaché–Greece (Maj. Harold A. Tidmarsh), Intelligence Report R-698-48 (ID No. 515268), Athens, 10 December 1948, subject: Review of GNA Operations during the Summer of 1948, 5 [in Box 3341, ID Files, RG 319, NA].

9. United States Military Attaché–Greece (Capt. Charles M. Conover), Intelligence Report R-90-49 (ID No. 538917), Athens, 2 March 1949, subject: Guerrilla Order of Battle—Strength, Organization and Disposition, 11 [in Box 3482, ID Files, RG 319, NA]; Robert W. Selton, "Communist Errors in the Anti-Bandit War," *Military Review* 45, no. 9 (September 1965), 76.

10. Amikam Nachmani, *International Intervention in the Greek Civil War: The United Nations Special Committee on the Balkans, 1947–1952* (New York: Praeger, 1990), 22.

11. ID No. 538917, 11.

12. Evangelos Averoff-Tossizza, *By Fire and Axe: The Communist Party and the Civil War in Greece, 1944–1949* (New Rochelle, NY: Caratzas Brothers, 1978), 254–55; Edgar O'Ballance, *The Greek Civil War, 1944–1949* (New York: Praeger, 1966), 151.

13. Nachmani, 11.

14. Angeliki E. Laiou, "Population Movements in the Greek Countryside during the Civil War," in Lars Baerentzen, John O. Iatrides, and Ole L. Smith, eds., *Studies in the History of the Greek Civil War, 1945–1949* (Copenhagen: Museum Tusculanum Press, 1987), 55.

15. Iatrides, 213; Selton, 71. Frontline strength generally included combatants in units, the staff, and regular logistical personnel but not recruits undergoing training.

16. J. C. Murray, "The Anti-Bandit War [Part I]," *Marine Corps Gazette* 38, no. 1 (January 1954), 18; Nachmani, 22; Gardner draft, "Sources of Guerrilla Manpower."

17. Iatrides, 213.

18. The GDA was also reinforced at the end of October 1946 by the return of a band of 100 to 200 Slavo-Macedonian NOF guerrillas under Gotchev (Ilias Dimakis) and their political commissar Pascalis Mitropoulos (see U.S. Military Attaché–Greece [Lt. Col. Allen C. Miller II], Intelligence Report R-461-46 [ID No. 329020], Athens, 4 December 1946, subject: Monthly Estimate of the Situation [November 1946], 9–10 [in Box 2166, ID Files, RG 319, NA]).

19. O'Ballance, 130; Iatrides, 211.

20. Iatrides, 205; Averoff-Tossizza, 204–205.

21. Dominique Eudes, *The Kapetanios: Partisans and Civil War in Greece, 1943–1949* (New York: Monthly Review Press, 1972), 277 and 294.

22. Ibid., 274.

23. Ibid.

24. Christopher M. Woodhouse, *The Struggle for Greece, 1941–1949* (London: Hart-Davis, MacGibbon, 1976), 183.

25. William Hardy McNeill, *Greece: American Aid in Action, 1947–1956* (New York: Twentieth Century Fund, 1957), 41.

26. O'Ballance, 130–31.

27. ID No. 515268, 5.

28. Woodhouse, 184.

29. O'Ballance, 123.

30. Nachmani, 13. GDA General Command Decree No. 11 ("Decree on Officer Corps") established who would be considered an officer in the GDA.

31. Woodhouse, 183.

32. Ibid. Saraphis was a potential rival to Markos as commander in chief of the GDA, even though he was not a Communist. However, his assistance was not solicited, and in any event he was closely watched by the government and spent most of the period 1945–1949 in government prisons (see O'Ballance, 123).

33. Ibid.

34. Estimate of General Chamberlin on 20 October 1947 (Chamberlin Report, Summary ¶1, 1). Chamberlin also put the GDA recruitment rate at that time at about 1,000 per month and forecast that the strength of GDA regular forces would probably exceed 25,000 during the winter of 1947–1948, with 60 percent of the force being composed of conscripts.

35. Woodhouse (pages 222–23) notes that a Soviet source puts the maximum strength of the GDA at about 30,000, the discrepancies in the numbers being due to how one counts the reserves available in the neighboring countries.

36. Woodhouse, 262.

37. The smaller figure is based on the estimate of the U.S. military attaché–Greece that the ratio of GDA combatants to supporters was on the order of 2:3 (see ID No. 515268, 7). The larger figure is probably derived from the number of males of voting age in the three elections between 1949 and 1954 who indicated that they were favorably disposed toward the Communists (see Murray, "The Anti-Bandit War [Part I]," 19).

38. Iatrides, 197.

39. O'Ballance, 188–89; Letter, Director, JUSMAPG (Lt. Gen. James A. Van Fleet) to Director, Plans and Operations Division, General Staff, U.S. Army, Athens, 27 January 1949, subject: Appointment of General Papagos as Greek Commander-in-Chief [Case 10, Item 4, in Box 541 ("091 Greece"), Plans and Operations Division, Decimal File, 1949–February 1950, Record Group 319 (Records of the Army Staff), National Archives II, College Park, MD); *Employment of Airpower*, 17; Murray, "The Anti-Bandit War [Part I]," 18–19.

40. Murray, "The Anti-Bandit War [Part I]," 19.

41. ID No. 448978, 14; United States Military Attaché–Greece (Maj. H. A. Tidmarsh), Intelligence Report R-337-48 (ID No. 461019), Athens, 28 April 1948, subject: Quasi-Military Forces—Greek Guerrillas, 3 [in Box 2979, ID Files, RG 319, NA].

42. United States Military Attaché–Greece (Capt. Charles M. Conover), Intelligence Report R-1-49 (ID No. 523063), Athens, 4 January 1949, subject: Guerrilla Order of Battle—Strength, Organization and Disposition, 4 [in Box 3390, ID Files, RG 319, NA].

43. United States Military Attaché–Greece (Capt. C. R. Meltesen), Intelligence Report R-298-49 (ID No. 589129), Athens, 8 August 1949, subject: Guerrilla Order of Battle—Strength, Organization and Disposition, 4 [in Box 3781, ID Files, RG 319, NA].

44. *Employment of Airpower*, 18.

45. Murray, "The Anti-Bandit War [Part I]," 19.

46. ID No. 515268.

47. Selton, 76; O'Ballance, 177. GNA casualties during the same period were about 20,000.

48. Laiou, 55–58 Table I.

49. Joint United States Advisory and Planning Group–Greece, Reports and Records Section, *JUSMAPG—Brief History, 1 January 1948 to 31 December 1949*, Mimeo (Athens: Reports and Records Section, JUSMAPG, 3 February 1950), 24; O'Ballance, 192.

50. Iatrides, 390 note 79.

51. O'Ballance, 192.

52. Murray, "The Anti-Bandit War [Part I]," 19.

53. United States Military Attaché–Greece (Maj. Harold A. Tidmarsh), Intelligence Report R-110-49 (ID No. 542941), Athens, 22 March 1949, subject: Organization of the Bandit Forces and Tactics Employed by the Bandits, 12 [in File "GEOG. L. Greece 370.64 (Guerrillas)," General Reference Branch, U.S. Army Center of Military History, Washington, DC]. Murray ("The Anti-Bandit War [Part I]," 20) notes that in the last six months of the civil war GDA casualties averaged 4,000 men per month, while GDA recruitment brought in an average of only 1,000 men per month. Based on the figures given in Tables 5.1 and 5.3, a more accurate statement for the period January–June 1949 would be an average monthly loss of 3,748 versus an average monthly gain of only about 887 (estimated).

54. Outlined in United States Military Attaché–Greece (Col. Harvey H. Smith), Intelligence Report R-666-48 (ID No. 507127), Athens, 13 November 1948, subject: Preliminary Interrogation Report of Captured Bandit, Major REPA, Assistant Intelligence Officer, MARKOS' HQ, 4–6 [in Box 3286, ID Files, RG 319, NA]; J. C. Murray, "The Anti-Bandit War [Part IV]," *Marine Corps Gazette* 38, no. 4 (April 1954), 60.

55. ID No. 542941, 8; ID No. 507127, 5.

56. ID No. 542941, 8.

57. Chamberlin Report, 2; Averoff-Tossizza, 204.

58. The nomenclature of the various Greek Communist auxiliary formations involved

with the logistical support of the GDA is very confusing. The general term used to describe the Communist self-defense apparatus, including the clandestine KKE cells in towns and villages, was *aftoamyna*. The individual three-man KKE cells were often called *yafka*, a Russian word meaning "clandestine meeting place," "safe house," or "refuge" (see Edward R. Wainhouse, "Guerrilla War in Greece, 1946–49: A Case Study," *Military Review* 37, no. 3 [June 1957], 22). The term *yiafaka* (also spelled *yiafka* or *yiafkes*) was used in three senses. First, it referred to the general KKE/GDA apparatus concerned with territorial administration. Second, it was used specifically for the GDA liaison units. Third, and perhaps most ambiguously, it was used to refer to the GDA area units (Popular Civil Guard and "home defense"), which provided the core of the GDA support system in the countryside. For the sake of clarity, the term *yiafaka* is used herein only for the liaison units; the other organizational entities are called by their English titles. One further complication arises from the use of the acronym ETA for the first and third senses of *yiafaka*.

    59. O'Ballance, 142.

    60. ID No. 515268, 7–9.

    61. ID No. 542941, 8.

    62. Chamberlin Report, 2; Murray, "The Anti-Bandit War [Part II]," *Marine Corps Gazette* 38, no. 2 (February 1954), 52. The sectors were administrative zones and did not control tactical operations. Liaison units were also located in the friendly neighboring countries to coordinate activities in support of the GDA.

    63. United States Military Attaché–Greece (Maj. Harold A. Tidmarsh), Intelligence Report R-325-48 (ID No. 460460), Athens, 28 April 1948, subject: Translation of Diary Notes of Guerrilla KRONOS, 2 [in Box 2975, ID Files, RG 319, NA].

    64. Message No. L-3927, Director, JUSMAPG, to Chief, Plans and Operations Division, U.S. Army General Staff, Athens, 27 August 1949, 5 [Item 35, Case 4, Book I, Section I-A, file "091 Greece (Incoming Messages)," Box 541, Plans and Operations Division Decimal File, 1949–February 1950, RG 319, NA].

    65. United States Military Attaché–Greece (Col. Harvey H. Smith), Intelligence Report R-57-49 (ID No. 529461), Athens, 2 February 1949, subject: Guerrilla Group Leader's Order to His Supply & Intelligence Services (PELOPONNESUS), 1–4 [in Box 3427, ID Files, RG 319, NA]. The order was signed by Lt. Col. K. Bassakidis. The Achaia-Ilias Group was composed of 200 to 300 guerrillas and was probably located in the Erymanthos Mountains area.

    66. United States Military Attaché–Greece (Col. Harvey H. Smith), Intelligence Report R-87-49 (ID No. 536782), Athens, 3 March 1949, subject: Information from Bandit (Anastassios KYRIAZIS) Captured in ARGOS, PELOPONNESE, 19 January 1949, 6–7 [in Box 3472, ID Files, RG 319, NA].

    67. The revival and role of ETA in the "Third Round" are described by O'Ballance, 121 and 151–52. The process by which ETA was absorbed into the *aftoamyna* is unclear, and O'Ballance, for one, seems to confuse the ETA with the area units.

    68. O'Ballance, 61–62.

    69. At least, I have found no organizational diagrams or descriptions of the authorized logistical elements of any GDA division among the materials I have reviewed for this study.

    70. See Appendix B for the authorized structure of the GDA infantry brigade and battalion and for the GDA artillery troop and section.

    71. Gardner draft, "Supply and Logistics."

72. United States Military Attaché–Greece (Capt. Charles M. Conover), Intelligence Report R-89-49 (ID No. 536784), Athens, 1 March 1949, subject: Statement of Francis L. McShane, American Engineer Captured by Bandits, 1–8 [in Box 3470, ID Files, RG 319, NA].

73. Ibid., 3.

74. Ibid., 7.

75. United States Military Attaché–Greece (Col. Harvey H. Smith), Intelligence Report R-188-48 (ID No. 448978), Athens, 16 March 1948, subject: Estimate of the Situation, 40 [in Box 2900, ID Files, RG 319, NA].

76. Laiou, 64.

77. Ibid., 75.

78. ID No. 448978, 37–38; Laiou, 74 Table II.5; United States Military Attaché–Greece (Lt. Col. James R. Weaver), Intelligence Report R-357-49 (ID No. 589130), Athens, 31 August 1949, subject: Rehabilitation of Greek Refugees, Enclosure 2 (Distribution of Refugees by Areas–1949) [in Box 3781, ID Files, RG 319, NA].

79. Laiou, 63.

80. Quoted in Dimitrios G. Kousoulas, *Revolution and Defeat: The Story of the Greek Communist Party* (London: Oxford Univ. Press, 1965), 259 note 9.

81. ID No. 448978, 37–38. In November 1947, the "official" number of refugees was around 400,000, and the "official" number of indigent persons was 1,617,132. By 1949, perhaps 18 percent of the rural population of Greece were refugees (see Laiou, 62).

82. Laiou, 67 and 89.

83. ID No. 589130, 1. The exact number of repatriated refugees at the end of July 1949 was 49,378.

84. Laiou, 74 Table II.5.

85. Lars Baerentzen, "The 'Paidomazoma' and the Queen's Camps," in John O. Iatrides, Lars Baerentzen, and Ole L. Smith, eds., *Studies in the History of the Greek Civil War, 1945–1949* (Copenhagen: Museum Tusculanum Press, 1987), 127–57; United Nations, General Assembly, *Report of the United Nations Special Committee on the Balkans*, General Assembly, Official Records: Third Session, Supplement No. 8, A/574 (Lake Success, NY: United Nations General Assembly, 1948), and subsequent reports of the UNSCOB (listed in the Selected Bibliography).

86. Averoff-Tossizza, 260–61.

87. United Nations, General Assembly, *Report of the United Nations Special Committee on the Balkans*, General Assembly, Official Records: Fourth Session, Supplement No. 8, A/935 (Lake Success, NY: United Nations General Assembly, 1949), 15.

88. Averoff-Tossizza, 261; Woodhouse, 208–209.

89. O'Ballance, 169.

90. ID No. 542941, 12; Memorandum for Record prepared by Lt. Col. Theodore J. Conway, Athens, 1 October 1947, subject: Briefing Presented by Brigadier General Maniadakis, Greek General Staff, Logistics Annex, 2 [in file "091.41-092. Greece, 1 January 1946–31 December 1948," Box 225, Assistant Chief of Staff, G-2, Project Decimal Files, 1946–1948, RG 319, NA].

91. Quoted in HQ, JUSMAPG, JUSMAPG Operations Report No. 56, Athens, 11 March 1949, Enclosure 1 (Information Record, 19 February 1949) to Annex 2 (Intelligence Report for period 020001–082400 March 1949, 4 March 1949), 6 [Item 8, Case

8, Book II, Section I-B, file "091 Greece," Box 541, Plans and Operations Division Decimal File, 1949–February 1950, RG 319, NA].

92. Murray ("The Anti-Bandit War [Part IV]," 58) estimated the daily GDA ration at three pounds. The contemporary U.S. planning figure (theaterwide, Europe) was 7.17 pounds/man/day (see *Department of the Army Field Manual 101-10: Staff Officers' Field Manual—Organization, Technical, and Logistical Data* [Washington: Headquarters, Department of the Army, August 1949], ¶126 [p. 303]).

93. *FM 101-10*, August 1949, 224.

94. See Charles R. Shrader, *Communist Logistics in the Korean War* (Westport, CT: Greenwood, 1995), 95.

95. Chamberlin Report, 5.

96. GDA General Command Order No. 587, 18 November 1947, reproduced in United States Military Attaché–Greece (Lt. Col. Albert B. Seitz), Intelligence Report R-450-48 (ID No. 474977), Salonika, 23 June 1948, subject: Order of Democratic Army of Greece, 18 November 1947 [in Box 3074, ID Files, RG 319, NA].

97. In contemporary U.S. Army usage, there were five classes of supply: Class I—rations and forage; Class II—individual clothing and equipment, most medical supplies, and general supplies, such as tentage; Class III—petroleum products; Class IV—major items of equipment, such as individual and crew-served weapons, tracked and wheeled vehicles, spare parts, communications gear, health and comfort (post exchange) items, and construction materials; and Class V—ammunition, pyrotechnics, and explosives of all kinds.

98. *FM 101-10*, August 1949, ¶126 (p. 303). The U.S. planning figures are for the European environment and represent the theaterwide requirement (i.e., an allowance has been made for both frontline and rear-area forces). Note that the Class II planning figure includes medical supplies.

99. Shrader, 96. The level of combat intensity was approximately the same in Korea, 1950–1953, and in Greece, 1949.

100. The GDA medical service is described in Gardner draft, "Medical Service," based on information in ID No. 542941, 11–12.

101. Gardner draft, "Medical Service."

102. ID No. 542941, 11–12.

103. The contemporary U.S. planning figure (theaterwide, Europe) was 11.4 pounds/man/day of petroleum, oils, and lubricants (POL) for motor vehicles (see *FM 101-10*, August 1949, ¶126 [p. 303]). Near-contemporary consumption estimates for similar Soviet-type motor vehicles in Korea was seven gallons of gasoline per truck per day (see Shrader, 97).

104. *FM 101-10*, August 1949, ¶126 (p. 303).

105. Nachmani, 121.

106. United States Military Attaché–Greece (Lt. Col. Allen C. Miller II), Intelligence Report R-452-46 (ID No. 329019), Athens, 3 December 1946, subject: Weapons Carried by Armed Bandits in Greece [in Box 2166, ID Files, RG 319, NA].

107. Quoted by Nachmani, 121.

108. Stephen Merrill, *The Communist Attack on Greece*, Special Report No. 15, 21st Regular Course, U.S. Strategic Intelligence School (Washington: U.S. Strategic Intelligence School, 28 July 1952), 53; Iatrides, 201–202.

109. Murray, "The Anti-Bandit War [Part II]," 56.

110. Iatrides, 387 note 3.

111. Kousoulas, 225.

112. Iatrides, 201; Eudes, 285–86.

113. ID No. 448978, 8.

114. Eudes, 285–86.

115. Murray, "The Anti-Bandit War [Part IV]," 58.

116. Nachmani, 61.

117. Ibid.

118. O'Ballance, 153.

119. Iatrides, 212–13.

120. Message No. L-3993, Director, JUSMAPG, to Chief, Plans and Operations Division, U.S. Army General Staff, Athens, 10 September 1949, 3–4 [Item 39, Case 4, Book I, Section I-A, file "091 Greece (Incoming Messages)," Box 541, Plans and Operations Division Decimal File, 1949–February 1950, RG 319, NA].

121. Murray, "The Anti-Bandit War [Part II]," 56.

122. ID No. 542941, 11; Murray, "The Anti-Bandit War [Part II]," 56.

123. ID No. 448978, 8.

124. JUSMAPG Detachment, TAC HQ, XV Mountain Division, Kastoria, 31 August 1948, subject: Monthly Report as of 2400 hours, 31 August 1948, ¶3e [in file "319.1—Operations Reports—XV Mountain Division (Greek), 1948," JUSMAPG General Decimal File, Box 48, Record Group 334 (Records of Interservice Agencies), NA].

125. O'Ballance, 153.

126. Murray, "The Anti-Bandit War [Part II]," 56.

127. JUSMAPG Operations Report No. 56, Enclosure 1 to Annex 2, 3; ID No. 542941, 11 and Enclosure 4; Greek General Staff, Intelligence Directorate, Study (Ref. No. F8206/95/2-12-50), Athens, [12 February 1950], subject: Guerrilla Warfare—The Organization and Employment of Irregulars, Chart C [in file "GEOG. L. Greece 370.64 (Guerrillas)," General Reference Branch, U.S. Army Center of Military History, Washington, DC] [cited hereafter as Greek General Staff, *Guerrilla Warfare*].

128. ID No. 542941, Enclosure 4; Greek General Staff, *Guerrilla Warfare*, Chart C.

129. ID No. 542941, Enclosure 2; Greek General Staff, *Guerrilla Warfare*, ¶125 and Chart C.

130. United States Military Attaché–Greece (Col. Harvey H. Smith), Intelligence Report R-625-49 (ID No. 494972), Athens, 23 September 1949, subject: Armament & Ammunition, 588 Guerrilla Battalion, 14 Brigade, GRAMMOS Area, July '48 [in Box 3201, ID Files, RG 319, NA].

131. Ibid., 3.

132. Murray, "The Anti-Bandit War [Part IV]," 58.

133. Ibid.

134. O'Ballance, 152–53.

135. United States Military Attaché–Greece (Maj. Harold A. Tidmarsh), Intelligence Report R-42-48 (ID No. 432477), Athens, 21 January 1948, subject: Battle of Konitsa, 5 [in Box 2786, ID Files, RG 319, NA].

136. *FM 101-10*, August 1949, ¶126 (p. 303).

137. By the summer of 1948, the GNA had received a number of U.S. 75 mm pack howitzers, and a battery was organized for each division (see Murray, "The Anti-Bandit War [Part II]," 59).

138. Murray, "The Anti-Bandit War [Part II]," 59. The GDA began to receive heavy weapons from Albania and Yugoslavia before the end of 1948 (see Iatrides, 212).

139. O'Ballance, 153; Iatrides, 212.

140. HQ JUSMAPG, JUSMAPG Operation Report No. 47 for the period 290001 December 1948–042400 January 1949, Athens, 5 January 1949, Annex 2 (Intelligence Report), ¶1g [Item 1, Case 8, Book I, Section I-B, file "091 Greece," Box 541, Plans and Operations Decimal File, 1949–February 1950, RG 319, NA].

141. JUSMAPG Operations Report No. 56, Enclosure 1 to Annex 2, 8.

142. Greek General Staff, Guerrilla Warfare, 49; ID No. 448978, 15. The guerrillas in central Macedonia, for example, had only four 75 mm Skoda pack howitzers before January 1948.

143. ID No. 542941, 11.

144. Greek General Staff, Guerrilla Warfare, 49–50; Gardner draft, Chart A; ID No. 589129.

145. ID No. 448978, 1–2.

146. Murray, "The Anti-Bandit War [Part II]," 56.

147. ID No. 523063, 11.

148. Message No. L-2668, Director, JUSMAPG, to Chief, Plans and Operations Division, U.S. Army General Staff, Athens, 12 February 1949, 4 [Item 4, Case 4, Book I, Section I-A, file "091 Greece (Incoming Messages)," Box 541, Plans and Operations Division Decimal File, 1949, RG 319, NA].

149. Murray ("The Anti-Bandit War [Part IV]," 58) estimated the GDA requirement (less artillery ammunition) at five pounds/man/day (three pounds of food, one pound of equipment, and one pound of ammunition). Woodhouse (p. 224) repeats Murray's estimate. Note that Murray does not attempt to account for the very considerable amount of fuel and engineer supplies obviously required by the GDA.

150. Murray, "The Anti-Bandit War [Part IV]," 58.

151. JUSMAPG—Brief History, 5–6.

152. Dispatch No. 143 (ID No. 535689), United States Ambassador to Greece (Henry F. Grady) to Secretary of State, Athens, 17 February 1949, subject: Transmittal of Statement of General Papagos at Meeting of War Council, February 5, and a Memorandum Setting Forth Position of U.S. Concerning Size of Greek Armed Forces, Enclosure 1 (Statement of General Papagos), 3 and 5 [in Box 3463, ID Files, RG 319, NA].

153. United States Military Attaché–Greece (Col. Harvey H. Smith), Intelligence Report R-130-49 (ID No. 548336), Athens, 11 April 1949, subject: Interrogation of Guerrilla (Ex-GNA) Lt. Z. G. ASTRIHADES, 5 [in Box 3539, ID Files, RG 319, NA]. Lt. Zafirios Astrihades surrendered to the GNA 2d Infantry Division near Florina on 11 February 1949. He was a former GNA lieutenant who had been captured by the GDA on 20 September 1948 and had subsequently served with the GDA near Lake Prespa.

154. ID No. 507127, 6.

155. Murray "The Anti-Bandit War [Part IV]," 55.

156. HQ JUSMAPG, JUSMAPG Operations Report No. 48 (050001–112400 January 1949), Athens, 14 January 1949, Annex 2 (Intelligence Report for period 050001–112400 January 1949, dated 12 January 1949), 6 [Item 2, Case 8, Book I, Section I-B, file "091 Greece," Box 541, Plans and Operations Division Decimal File, 1949–February 1950, RG 319, NA].

157. ID No. 542941, 18; ID No. 548336, 4–5.

158. United States Military Attaché–Greece (Col. Harvey H. Smith), Intelligence Report R-647-48 (ID No. 500489), Athens, 13 October 1948, subject: Guerrilla Instructions

on Construction of Supply Shelters—PELOPONNESE, 2 [in Box 3237, ID Files, RG 319, NA].

159. Ibid., 1.

160. Murray, "The Anti-Bandit War [Part IV]," 59.

161. Ibid. Murray assumed that there were some 5,000 guerrillas in the areas concerned.

162. Ibid.

163. Gardner draft, "Supply and Logistics."

164. Murray, "The Anti-Bandit War [Part IV]," 55; Selton, 70–71.

165. JUSMAPG Operations Report No. 48, Annex 2 (Intelligence Report), 7.

166. A seasoned porter can carry a load of 65–80 pounds a distance of about ten to fifteen miles during a twelve-hour period, and the average load for a pack mule is 130–200 pounds (see Shrader, 136). The figures cited are based on the Communist experience in Korea and assume relatively level terrain. Almost all movement of supplies in Greece was carried out in extremely rugged, mountainous terrain, sometimes over ridges inaccessible to even pack animals, so lower limits are perhaps more applicable there. Throughout this study, calculations are based on 65 pounds as the average load for a porter and 150 pounds as the average load for a pack mule.

167. Woodhouse, 225.

168. ID No. 542941, 11.

169. Message No. L-2437, Director, JUSMAPG, to Chief, Plans and Operations Division, U.S. Army General Staff, Athens, 15 January 1949, 2 [Item 1, Case 4, Book I, Section I-A, file "091 Greece (Incoming Messages)," Box 541, Plans and Operations Division Decimal File, 1949, RG 319, NA]; Message No. L-3577, Director, JUSMAPG, to Chief, Plans and Operations Division, U.S. Army General Staff, Athens, 9 July 1949, 1 [Item 29, Case 4, Book I, Section I-A, file "091 Greece (Incoming Messages)," Box 541, Plans and Operations Division Decimal File, 1949, RG 319, NA].

170. Message No. L-2437, 2.

171. As part of its efforts to promote the creation of a shadow government during the World War II resistance period, ELAS had proposed to build a road from Macedonia to Roumeli along the spine of the Pindus Mountains. As Woodhouse (p. 58) has noted, "The mountains had only been intersected from east to west: a route from north to south would have been invaluable in the 'third round' of the civil war, though it served little purpose in a guerrilla campaign. The Allied Military Mission was asked, but declined, to provide assistance for the project."

172. ID No. 542941, 11.

173. Gardner draft, "Supply and Logistics." At the end of 1948 the RHN had some 115 ships including one cruiser, ten destroyers, and two submarines (see O'Ballance, 188 note 1).

174. O'Ballance, 163.

175. Ibid. O'Ballance does not provide a source for this report.

176. United States Naval Attaché–Italy, Intelligence Report R-65-48 (ID No. 465199), Rome, 20 April 1948, subject: Jugoslavia/Greece—Navy—Operations—Movement of Vessels (Delivery of War Materiel to Greek Rebels Organized by Jugoslav Navy Headquarters in Split and Effected by Jugoslav Submarines), 2 [in Box 3007, ID Files, RG 319, NA].

177. ID No. 536782, 6–7. Iatrides (page 212) states that the GDA officer in charge of the operation was executed for his part in the failure.

178. Details of the *Polemistis* incident are provided by Averoff-Tossizza, 299–300, and in ID No. 536782, 6–7. Leonidion, on the east coast of the Peloponnesus and on the southwestern side of the mouth of the Gulf of Argolis, was apparently a favorite GDA landing place.

179. United States Military Attaché–Greece (Maj. Harold A. Tidmarsh), Intelligence Report R-96-49 (ID No. 538916), Athens, 8 March 1949, subject: Memorandum to UN-SCOB from the Greek Government Concerning Aid to Guerrillas, 10 [in Box 3482, ID Files, RG 319, NA].

180. Kousoulas, 261; Eudes, 339.

181. United States Naval Attaché–Greece, Intelligence Report GR-37-48 (ID No. 464690), Athens, 12 April 1948, subject: Greece—Naval Section—JUSMAPG Report, ¶1 [in Box 3004, ID Files, RG 319, NA].

182. United States Naval Attaché–Italy, Intelligence Report R-68-48 (ID No. 465039), Rome, 20 April 1948, subject: ITALY/GREECE—Commerce, Shipping—Movements of Foreign Commerce Vessels [in Box 3006, ID Files, RG 319, NA].

183. ID No. 448978, 6-a and 28–29.

184. Ibid., 29.

185. *Employment of Airpower*, 10.

186. ID No. 536782, 7–8.

187. United States Military Attaché–Turkey (Maj. M. S. Tyler, Jr., USAF), Intelligence Report R-491-48 (ID No. 481662), Adana, 19 July 1948, subject: Supply of Greek Guerrillas by Bulgaria, 2 [in Box 3119, ID Files, RG 319, NA].

188. United States Military Attaché–Greece (First Lt. Robert B. English, Assistant Air Attaché), Intelligence Report R-399-49 (ID No. 467816), Athens, 29 May 1948, subject: Air Supply to Guerrilla Units [in Box 3025, ID Files, RG 319, NA].

189. Ibid.

190. Nachmani, 21.

6

The Greek Democratic Army: External Support

To be successful, a guerrilla movement needs two things above all: the support of the population and a reliable source of outside logistical support. For a time during the civil war of 1945–1949, the Greek Communist guerrillas enjoyed both, but in the long run neither the support of the population nor outside logistical support proved as solid as the Greek Communist Party (KKE) and the Greek Democratic Army (GDA) wished. Both were eroded by the counteraction of the Greek government, the changing international situation, the self-interest of the parties involved, and the counterproductive policies of the Greek Communist leadership. Contrary to both the hopes of the Greek Communists and common perceptions among their opponents, the Soviet Union provided little or no direct support of any kind, and it even acted to impede the support of the Communist rebellion in Greece. On the other hand, the Communist regimes on the borders of Greece—Albania, Yugoslavia, and Bulgaria—motivated by long-standing quarrels with the Greek government, ethnic considerations, and territorial ambitions as well as by ideological affinity with the Greek Communist rebels, provided refuge, money, advice, material aid, and secure facilities that were crucial to the continuation of the rebellion. The amounts of supplies and other support provided by Albania, Yugoslavia, and Bulgaria were substantial, but the three Communist countries had problems of their own, both political and material, which precluded their direct intervention and limited the support they were willing or able to provide.[1] The other Soviet satellite nations also provided aid to the Greek guerrillas, if in lesser amounts, and the guerrillas even found Western suppliers willing to sell them war matériel.

Yugoslavia was the most generous supplier of the GDA. The expulsion of Yugoslavia from the Cominform in June 1948 and the subsequent declaration of the KKE, under Zachariades' guidance, in favor of the Cominform alienated Marshal Tito and led to the cessation of Yugoslavian support and the closing of the Yugoslavian border to the guerrillas in July 1949. At the same time, the support of Albania and Bulgaria became less reliable, in part because both Albania and Bulgaria wished to retain the amity of Stalin and the Cominform, and in part because they feared that their resources might be required for their own defense in the event Stalin turned against them, as he had against Yugoslavia. Nevertheless, with Yugoslavia out of the way, the interests of both Albania and Bulgaria were well served by continuing to support the GDA, and the two nations did so until it became absolutely clear, in the late summer of 1949, that the GDA was about to be defeated by the Greek national forces (GNF).

THE UNITED NATIONS AND THE SITUATION IN GREECE

Both sides in the Greek civil war of 1945–1949 received massive support from outside sources. International relations specialist Amikam Nachmani has noted that "few if any twentieth-century civil wars involved greater foreign intervention than that in Greece."[2] The exact dimensions of the massive support provided to the Greek government by Britain, the United States, and other Western powers is well known, but the magnitude of the support provided by the Communist states to the Greek Communist rebels, as well as the mechanisms by which such support was rendered, remain somewhat obscure. As the assistant U.S. military attaché in Athens noted in March 1949, "It is difficult to obtain full information on the organization by the northern neighbors of aid to the armed bands and therefore estimates are bound to be far lower than the actual figures."[3] Considerable confusion also arises from the difficulty of sorting out whether the support provided to the guerrillas came from official government sources or from the so-called "committees for assistance to the Greeks" that were formed in all of the Balkan states. However the "committees" could not have operated in Albania, Yugoslavia, Bulgaria, or elsewhere in the Soviet bloc without official government and party sanction, and in any event, military supplies such as ammunition and artillery pieces could have been provided only from government stocks.[4] As one experienced team of American investigators commented, "The aid which the government receives from abroad is open, legal, wholesale; that which Leftist guerrillas receive is clandestine, illegal, difficult to appraise with accuracy, but none the less significant."[5]

In the absence of any extensive body of surviving GDA documents and because of the continued closure of the archives of the Balkan states, most of the details of the support provided to the Greek guerrillas by Albania, Yugoslavia, Bulgaria, and the other Soviet satellites are derived primarily from the reports of the two United Nations (UN) commissions sent to Greece between 1946 and 1951: the United Nations Commission of Investigation Concerning Greek Frontier Incidents (December 1946–September 1947) and the United Nations Special Committee on the Balkans (UNSCOB) of October 1947–December 1951.[6] Neither commission was able to carry out full investigations in the areas controlled by the Greek Communists or in Albania, Yugoslavia, or Bulgaria, and consequently the reports of both commissions were incomplete, often inaccurate, and often biased toward the Greek government.

The United Nations Commission of Investigation Concerning Greek Frontier Incidents

The situation in Greece was brought before the United Nations Security Council three times in 1946. In January 1946 the Soviet Union raised the question of the continued British presence in Greece, and in September the Ukrainian foreign minister alleged that the actions of the Greek government in the Balkans constituted a serious threat to peace. Both Communist initiatives came to nothing, being vetoed in the Security Council. On 30 November 1946 the Greek representative at the UN asked the Security Council to consider—under Articles 34 and 35(1) of the UN Charter—the situation on Greece's northern borders and the support being provided to the Greek Communist guerrillas by Albania, Yugoslavia, and Bulgaria. On 3 December 1946 the Greek prime minister, Constantine Tsaldaris, petitioned the Secretary-General of the United Nations, Trygve Lie, to consider an investigation of the situation on Greece's northern borders, and on 19 December the Security Council voted to establish a United Nations Commission of Investigation Concerning Greek Frontier Incidents.[7] Surprisingly, the Soviet Union did not exercise its veto; both the Soviet Union and Poland were represented on the commission, whose eleven members were all then serving on the UN Security Council. The other members of the commission were Australia, Belgium, Brazil, China, Colombia, France, Syria, the United Kingdom, and the United States. The commission conducted a seven-month investigation, during which it held ninety-one meetings, examined the testimony of 270 witnesses, and accumulated some 20,000 pages of evidence. The commission completed its three-volume, 767-page report on 23 May 1947 and submitted it to the UN Security Council on 27 June. A subsidiary group of the commission continued to gather evidence in Greece until September 1947. Unlike its successor, UNSCOB, the commission was able to carry out investigations in Albania, Yugoslavia, and Bulgaria, and the Polish and Soviet representatives on the Commission in fact met with Markos and Kikitsas on 20 March 1947 to obtain the views of the Communist leadership.[8]

Based on the evidence collected, eight of the participant members of the UN commission concluded that both the Greek government and its northern neighbors had contributed to the numerous border incidents, documented in detail by the commission, and that Yugoslavia (and to a lesser extent Albania and Bulgaria) had in fact provided refuge, facilities, supplies, and other support to the Greek Communist rebels and had permitted the guerrillas to cross their borders freely and to fire on Greek Army troops from their territory.[9] The commission urged Albania, Yugoslavia, and Bulgaria to refrain from aiding the Greek guerrillas; asked all of the parties involved to settle their differences through diplomatic channels; and recommended that the United Nations form a commission to monitor the situation on a continuing basis.[10] The French delegate expressed significant disagreement with some aspects of the report, and the Polish and Soviet representatives rejected the majority report altogether. The issue then proceeded to a stalemate in the Security Council, as various resolutions were debated and vetoed by one side or the other between 27 June and 19 August 1947. The existence of the Commission of Investigation was ended by a double Soviet veto on 17 September 1947.

The United Nations Special Committee on the Balkans (UNSCOB)

With consideration of the Greek question stymied in the Security Council, the matter was brought before the UN General Assembly, and on 21 October 1947, on a vote of forty to one with eleven abstentions, the General Assembly approved a resolution calling upon Albania, Yugoslavia, and Bulgaria to refrain from aiding the rebels and to join with Greece in seeking a peaceful settlement of their differences. The resolution also provided for the establishment of a UN Special Committee on the Balkans to continue the investigation and render reports on the situation. The UNSCOB consisted of representatives of Australia, Brazil, China, France, Mexico, the Netherlands, Pakistan, the United Kingdom, and the United States. Poland and the Soviet Union were offered seats on the committee, which they refused to fill.

The primary mission of the UNSCOB observers was to gather information regarding border incidents and the support provided by outside sources to the Communist rebels in Greece. Accordingly, UNSCOB established its headquarters at Salonika on 1 December 1947 and deployed five observer groups to gather information. Each observer group was composed of four observers and auxiliary personnel, including interpreters provided by the Greek government—which gave the UNSCOB its full cooperation, to the extent of providing (well-prepared) witnesses as well as details regarding the support received by the Communist guerrillas from outside sources. Albania, Yugoslavia, and Bulgaria, on the other hand, refused to cooperate or to allow UNSCOB to enter their territories.

Strictly speaking, UNSCOB was an unarmed observer operation rather than a peacekeeping force of the type subsequently deployed by the UN in the Sinai, the Gaza Strip, the Congo, West Irian, Cyprus, the Golan Heights, Lebanon, and elsewhere. As one writer has noted, "While peacekeeping troops control and protect certain areas and sites (borders, demilitarized zones, infrastructure buildings, and so on) and constitute a buffer between the rival sides, the unarmed observers investigate, report, and occasionally supervise."[11] After fifty years the difference remains unclear in practice, and as with more recent UN observer and peacekeeping operations, UNSCOB experienced a certain degree of "mission creep" to accommodate the various interests of the member states. Largely as a result of U.S. influence, UNSCOB came to be a means of publicizing the situation and thus something of a deterrent force, in that its mere presence in the area was thought to impede outside support to the rebels. The Australian members of UNSCOB saw its function as one of conciliation and urged the UNSCOB observers to act whenever possible to reconcile the parties. The Greek government had hoped that UNSCOB would take an active role in shutting down the traffic across its borders and became incensed when the UNSCOB observers stuck to their charter as impartial observers.

In point of fact, UNSCOB was not particularly impartial—it was after all a creature of the United States, which was its principal proponent and paymaster. From the U.S. point of view, the primary function of the UNSCOB was to keep the situation in Greece from spinning out of control, thereby preventing the need for the direct intervention of U.S. armed forces and the consequent possibility of a direct armed confrontation between the United States and the Soviet Union or its satellites. Indeed, as Amikam Nachmani, an expert on UNSCOB, has noted, "The establishment of UNSCOB was a product of the U.S. conviction that the Greeks were incapable of managing their own affairs"; the Truman Doctrine—as it was implemented in Greece—aimed at restoring economic stability, providing a better-trained and better-equipped army to fight the guerrillas, and using the UN to "guarantee that the conflict would remain a civil war and not turn into a Balkan or global conflict."[12] The British, on the other hand, had opposed the creation and operation of UNSCOB, precisely because it relieved the Greek government of the need to solve its own problems and provided a means for the United States to avoid the commitment of troops to Greece.[13] In this respect the UNSCOB was entirely successful; its presence modulated the actions of both the GDA's outside supporters and the Greek government and thus prevented the escalation of what was essentially a civil war into an international armed conflict.

The UNSCOB observer teams were composed principally of American and British personnel and received most of their financial and logistical support from the United States.[14] Observers were selected on the basis of their knowledge of Greek, their physical fitness, and their mental toughness and impartiality. Most were unmarried, and many were field-grade officers and veterans of World War II. The equipment supplied by the United States included vehicles, communications equipment, and transport aircraft and crews. Substantial efforts were made to train the observer teams and to provide them with guidelines for carrying out their mission. For example, the UN produced a series of handbooks for the observers containing standard forms for recording incidents, questions to ask of witnesses, and the format for reports. The handbooks contained detailed instructions on the reporting of such logistical matters as "the hospitalization of guerrillas and their subsequent return to Greece and the transport of arms, munitions, and foodstuffs through foreign territory . . . routes, the composition of convoys, the attitude of authorities, and the procedure of crossing the frontier."[15]

The UNSCOB observers gathered information from a variety of sources, including "direct observation and investigation, interrogation of witnesses, reconstruction of incidents on sand tables, and studying official statements, the press, and monitored radio broadcasts."[16] The Australian members opposed "active observation," and consequently UNSCOB observers based their conclusions largely on the interrogation of witness supplied by the Greek government liaison officers. Lacking any cooperation from Albania, Yugoslavia, or Bulgaria, and often prevented from carrying out their investigations in government-controlled border areas as well as in GDA territory, the UNSCOB observers still gathered a great deal of information on border incidents and other aspects of the outside support being provided the rebels. Indeed, the level of detail was sometimes ludicrous, the theft of a single mule, the identification of weapons, or the border crossings of innocent peasant herdsmen often receiving extraordinarily detailed examination.[17] On the other hand, the reports rendered by the UNSCOB observers contained little of substance regarding the organization of outside support for the rebels or the methods by which such matériel was assembled, stored, or delivered.

Also, the information obtained by UNSCOB was tainted, in that the observers were of necessity forced to rely upon witnesses presented by the four principals (Greece, Albania, Yugoslavia, and Bulgaria). Since only the Greek government was prepared to cooperate, the practical result was that almost all the witnesses interrogated by the UNSCOB teams were identified—and most likely carefully coached—by the full-time Greek liaison officer to the Special Committee. The evidence was thus slanted toward the Greek government's point of view. Nevertheless, the conclusion that the Greek Communist guerrillas were being aided in many ways by Greece's northern neighbors was undeniable, a fact that scarcely warranted a detailed investigation spread over several years.

UNSCOB provided to the UN General Assembly a series of interim reports, which were published at various times between June 1948 and the end of 1951. The reports cited numerous incidents in which Albania, Yugoslavia, and Bulgaria had permitted the Greek guerrillas to cross their borders and to fire on Greek government troops from over the borders, and in which they had supplied arms, ammunition, food, clothing, and other military equipment as well as transport, medical care, and financial support. The UNSCOB reports fully supported the Greek government position, and in fact at least one American historian has alleged that "the State Department virtually wrote the UNSCOB report." This assertion was based on a detailed list of conclusions provided to the U.S. representatives on the UNSCOB on 13 May 1948, conclusions that were "framed so that desirable recommendations would flow naturally" from them.[18] In fact, although the UNSCOB reports were "a mixture that combined the observers' findings, the delegates' 'horse trading,' and their governments' pressures and views," the reports of the observer teams themselves were unbiased, although often incomplete by virtue of the lack of Communist input.[19]

The conclusions of the UNSCOB Interim Report covering the period 21 October 1947 to 16 June 1948 were representative of those found in the other interim reports.

It appears to the Special Committee that the Greek guerrillas have received aid and assistance from Albania, Bulgaria and Yugoslavia; that they have been furnished with war material and other supplies from those countries; that they have been allowed to use the territories of Albania, Yugoslavia and Bulgaria for tactical operations; and that after rest or medical treatment in the territories of Albania, Bulgaria and Yugoslavia their return to Greece has been facilitated. The Special Committee further finds that moral support has been given to the guerrillas through government-controlled radio stations, the existence of the broadcasting station of the Greek guerrillas on Yugoslav soil, and the systematic organization of aid committees. This assistance has been on such a scale that the Special Committee has concluded that it could not have been given without the knowledge of the Governments of Albania, Bulgaria and Yugoslavia.[20]

In a supplementary report covering the period from 17 June to 10 September 1948, the UNSCOB noted that it was

fully convinced that the guerrillas in the frontier zones: (1) have been largely dependent on external supply. Great quantities of arms, ammunition, and other military stores have come across the border, notably during times of heavy fighting. Strongly-held positions of the guerrillas have protected their vital supply lines from Bulgaria, Yugoslavia and, in particular, from Albania. In recent months, there has been less evidence of receipt of supplies from Yugoslavia by the guerrillas; (2) have frequently moved at will in territory across the frontier for tactical reasons, and have thus been able to concentrate their forces without interference by the Greek Army, and to return to Greece when they wished; and (3) have frequently retired safely into the territory of Albania, Bulgaria and Yugoslavia when the Greek Army exerted great pressure.[21]

On the whole, the UN Commission of Investigation and UNSCOB did a creditable job of documenting the support provided to the Greek Communist guerrillas by outside sources, but neither body was successful either in bringing about a reconciliation of the parties or in limiting the amount of support provided. Indeed, the only limits to such support arose from the national and ideological interests of those states providing aid and from changes in the international political situation between 1946 and 1949.

THE ROLE OF THE SOVIET UNION

The contemporary Western perception of the civil war in Greece was that the rebellion had been fomented and was supported by the Soviet Union in order to extend Communist domination in the Balkans and to secure such Soviet objectives as unimpeded access to the Mediterranean Sea, further Soviet expansion in the Middle East, and the discomfiture of the Western powers. In retrospect, it is clear that such a perception was largely the product of the developing Cold War paranoia and a consequent false interpretation of the situation. But at the time, the United States, Britain, and other Western democracies were prepared to accept the myth of an ever-expanding monolithic Communism directed from the Kremlin and operating in accordance with a well-designed, unchanging plan. In the case of Greece, nothing could have been farther from the truth. Stalin and the Soviet Union were extremely cautious and declined to provide any substantial direct material support to the Greek Communist guerrillas. Indeed, the evidence now available clearly indicates that Stalin desired an early termination of the Greek rebellion lest it provoke a direct confrontation between the Soviet Union and the United States, and that he attempted, without much success, to impede the support of the Greek rebels by the Balkan Communist states, each of which had its own reasons for disregarding his instructions.

The Communist insurrection in Greece was entirely homegrown, but the Greek Communists—both the Stalinist ideologues led by Zachariades and the pragmatic nationalists led by Markos—anticipated that Stalin would place at their disposal the resources of not only the Soviet Union but the entire international Communist movement—if only they began the rebellion, demonstrated success in battling the Greek national forces, gained control of a certain amount of Greek territory, established a provisional government, or achieved any of a number of goals that would prove the viability of their movement. In the end they were disappointed. Soviet diplomatic support proved lukewarm at best before disappearing altogether, and there is no credible evidence that the Soviet Union provided any direct material aid. As Woodhouse has written, the Greek Communists did not go into action at Stalin's behest; "Indeed, they had difficulty in guessing what his behest was."[22]

In fact, the handwriting was on the wall, but the Greek Communists refused to read it. The minimal importance Stalin assigned events in Greece to the Soviet Union and international Communism had been clearly revealed during the Second World War and immediately afterward. The Soviet Union had provided no material aid to ELAS, either during the resistance or in the first two "rounds" of the civil war in Greece.[23] Indeed, both British and American observers at the time of the ELAS insurrection in Athens in December 1945 were compelled to admit that the Soviet Union had acted in a perfectly correct manner, eschewing any aid to the Greek Communist rebels. During the "Second Round" in December 1944, Petros Roussos, a member of the KKE Central Committee, had attempted to reach Moscow to plead for Soviet assistance but was arrested by the Soviets and returned to Greece, his return being followed in a matter of days by a telegram from Moscow condemning KKE policy and the insurrection then in progress. At Yalta in February 1945, Churchill had been delighted at the apparently negative attitude of Stalin toward the rebellion in Greece and his refusal to offer the Greek Communists any aid. Although the Soviet Union had refused to send a representative to the meeting at Petrich in December 1945, where Yugoslavia and Bulgaria promised aid to their Greek comrades, the Greek

Communists continued to hope that Stalin would provide the material aid they required.[24]

The Soviet attitude did not change after the KKE took the decision in February 1946 to defend itself more aggressively against the royalist Greek government and right-wing thugs.[25] When a KKE delegation led by Dimitrios Partsalidis visited Moscow in April 1946 to obtain support, it was told in no uncertain terms to concentrate on political action and to "wait and see."[26] In August 1946 Yiannis Ioannides, then the KKE's liaison officer in Belgrade, sought permission to travel to Moscow to present the KKE's case for Soviet aid, but he was refused permission and was instructed instead to submit his written request through Georgi Dimitrov, the leader of the Bulgarian Communist Party. He did so, citing the dire need of the Greek Communist movement for aid of all kinds. The reply came through Dimitrov in November 1946, and it too was entirely negative, counseling continued mass struggle through lawful means. On 31 December, Dimitrov told the Greek comrades that the aid they had requested would probably not be forthcoming.[27] Even Stalin's most faithful Greek follower, Nikos Zachariades, the General Secretary of the KKE, was unable to obtain any satisfaction from his mentor. Zachariades, who "commanded no respect in Moscow, least of all with Stalin personally," saw Stalin in the Crimea in April 1946, wrote him a long letter in January 1947, and saw him again in May 1947.[28] None of Zachariades' appeals produced any tangible support for the rebellion in Greece, but the KKE leadership nevertheless continued to beg for help, and its appeals became increasingly pathetic. A KKE letter of 6 October 1947 requested a typewriter with twenty ribbons and a can of printer's ink, pled for permission to join the Cominform, and reminded the Russian comrades that winter was approaching and that the GDA desperately needed clothing, boots, outer garments, and tents.[29]

The opposition of Stalin and the Soviet Union to the Communist rebellion in Greece is known largely through the comments of the Yugoslavians, who experienced a good deal of Soviet pressure to end their own support of the KKE/GDA. Tito's close associates Svetozar Vukmanovich-Tempo, Edvard Karadelj (the Yugoslavian foreign minister), and Milovan Djilas, as well as Tito's biographer, the journalist Vladimir Dedijer, were among those who later published details of Soviet opposition to the Greek rebellion.[30] Djilas, one of Tito's trusted associates, noted that "the Soviet Government took no direct action over the uprising in Greece, practically leaving Yugoslavia to face the music alone in the United Nations."[31] Elsewhere Djilas reported that in a meeting with Yugoslavian representatives on 9–10 February 1948, Stalin had indicated his concern that the revolution in Greece could not succeed and that in any case Britain and the United States would not permit their lines of communications in the Mediterranean to be cut; thus the Greek insurrection had to be "rolled up" as soon as possible.[32] Yet another indication that Stalin intended to remove himself as far as possible from the Greek Communist cause came in November 1948, when Miltiades Porphyrogenis, the minister of justice in the Provisional Dem-

ocratic Government of Free Greece, referring publicly to the support being received from "the freedom-loving peoples of the world headed by our great friend
and defender, by the land of Socialism, the Soviet Union," received so scathing
a rebuke from Stalin that four years passed before any leader of the KKE dared
mention the possibility of outside support.[33]

Stalin's policy toward the Communist rebellion in Greece has been characterized as a "twin-track policy" of proclaiming publicly his sympathy for and
support of the Greek Communist rebels while at the same time privately working
to soothe Western anxieties and minimize Western disapproval.[34] That policy
was shaped by a number of factors, including Stalin's perception that Greece
was outside his sphere of influence, his concern about the dangers of antago-
nizing the Western powers, and his preoccupation with the situation in Yugoslavia and the other Balkan states. In 1950, Svetozar Vukmanovich-Tempo, the
liaison officer between Tito and ELAS during the resistance period, set forth
the reasons for Stalin's attitude quite clearly:

The leadership of the Soviet Union had no interest whatever in the victory of the people's
revolutionary movement in Greece, because Greece was geographically remote from the
Soviet Union (hence intervention of the Soviet Army was out of the question), and
because it was outside the sphere of interest of the Soviet Union (by agreement between
the Governments of the Soviet Union and the western imperialists).[35]

For reasons known only to him, Stalin adhered to the so-called "percentage
deal" made with British prime minister Winston Churchill in October 1944 and
subsequently confirmed at the Yalta Conference in 1945.[36] Stalin and Churchill
had agreed on the degree of influence each should have in the Balkans in the
postwar period; in the case of Greece, Britain would have a 90 percent "interest"
and the Soviet Union only a 10 percent "interest." Stalin subsequently proved
uncharacteristically faithful to the bargain throughout the period of the Greek
civil war, so much so in fact that Churchill remarked at the time of the ELAS
insurrection in Athens in December 1944, "I am increasingly impressed . . . with
the loyalty with which . . . Stalin has kept off Greece in accordance with our
agreement."[37]

Stalin was prepared to take advantage of events in the Balkans, but he remained extremely careful to avoid provoking an open conflict with the West
over Greece, a place too remote for direct Soviet intervention and not central
to Soviet interests. One evidence of his caution was the attitude taken by the
Soviet Union toward the two UN commissions sent to investigate the situation
in Greece. The Soviet Union and its Polish satellite actively participated in the
first, and although they refused to take part in the second, Stalin was careful to
pressure the Greek guerrillas to refrain from kidnapping or otherwise harming
the UNSCOB observers.[38] In the Soviet view, "observation and publicity" were
preferable to the armed intervention of the United States, an intervention that
could potentially involve the Soviet Union in a direct confrontation with its

powerful Cold War opponent.[39] By the same token, Stalin was careful to exclude Greek Communists from the meetings that led to the formation of the Cominform in October 1947, lest their presence upset the international community.[40] The international situation was delicate, and Stalin as well as Tito and the leaders of the French and Italian Communist parties were not eager to connect themselves too closely with events in Greece.[41]

Always—and especially after June 1948—the Soviet Union was much more concerned with other matters in the Balkans, particularly the threat of independent nationalism expressed by Tito and Yugoslavs.[42] The rebellion in Greece, despite the slavish Stalinism of Zachariades and his dominant clique within the KKE/GDA, represented for Stalin something of the centrifugal nationalist spirit that motivated the Yugoslavs and threatened to endanger the carefully constructed buffer he had erected against the West. For that reason alone, Stalin may have viewed the destruction of the Greek Communist insurrection with equanimity.[43] The repeated declarations of Stalin and his minions of their intention to abandon the Greek Communists to their fate were perhaps intended as a warning for Tito and the other satellite leaders of what would happen to them should the Soviet Union decide that they were either unimportant to Soviet global or regional interests or should they adopt too independent and too nationalist a policy.

Nevertheless, the temptation for the Soviet Union to play a more active role in the Greek civil war must have been strong. Ideological affinities aside, the United States attributed a number of motives to what was perceived in Western capitals as deep Soviet involvement in the Greek situation. Among these were the traditional Russian drive to dominate in the Balkans; the long-standing Russian desire for an unrestricted outlet to the Mediterranean; the desire to control the eastern Mediterranean as a means of ensuring Soviet access to Middle East oil supplies; and even an effort to distract the Western powers from Soviet moves elsewhere and to engage them in a war of economic attrition.[44] Moreover, until the announcement of the Truman Doctrine in March 1947 and the subsequent massive economic and military aid to Greece, Greece was vulnerable, the Communist guerrillas were achieving a great deal of success, and Soviet intervention would have been relatively cheap.

Convinced at the outset that the Soviet Union stood four-square behind the insurrection in Greece, the Greek government and its American ally only very slowly came to understand that the Greek Democratic Army was not receiving—and would not receive—any direct assistance from Moscow. The usual U.S. position was that noted in a State Department report dated 17 April 1948: "It is reasonable to assume that all action in support of Markos takes place with the prior knowledge and approval of Moscow and with the participation of Soviet coordinators on the spot."[45] Throughout most of the Greek civil war, American intelligence agencies "appeared to believe that searching for evidence linking the Greek guerrillas directly to Moscow was futile and unnecessary. There was ample proof that the guerrillas received aid and comfort from

Greece's communist neighbors and that the KKE was in contact with 'international communism.' "[46] However, an April 1948 Central Intelligence Agency (CIA) assessment of the opportunities for the Soviets to exploit the situation in Greece acknowledged that

with careful regard for U.S. reaction, however, the USSR and the Satellite States will avoid any open and inescapable commitment to Greece. No Soviet or Satellite forces, as such, will enter the country, nor are the USSR and the Satellite States likely to grant formal recognition to the Communist government, at least not until Communist control of Greece is apparently assured.[47]

One month later, a member of an American law firm representing the Greek government also acknowledged to the U.S. State Department that the GDA was not receiving the level of support it desired from outside sources and that Stalin was apparently not pushing for a Communist victory in Greece.[48] Some Western analysts saw the dismissal of Markos Vafiades from his posts of leadership in the KKE and GDA as a further indication of the Kremlin's desire to back away from armed insurrection in Greece, in favor of the old political tactics.[49] By October 1948, the authors of a CIA assessment of continuing satellite aid to the Greek guerrillas were willing to concede that

the Kremlin (hence also Albania, Yugoslavia, and Bulgaria) was unwilling to risk further world censure by furnishing aid to the guerrillas in the amount necessary to enable them to disrupt the Greek nation sufficiently to bring about an early overthrow of the regime, and that Markos would accordingly be allowed to "wither on the vine."[50]

To be sure, there were sporadic reports of the involvement of Soviet military personnel in providing support to the Greek Communist guerrillas. Most of these reports, such as those of Soviet liaison officers assisting in the movement of supplies to the rebels from the Yugoslavian port of Split, or of a Soviet Army colonel coordinating the distribution of supplies received by air in Tirana, remained unconfirmed. Even representatives of the Greek government were compelled to acknowledge that reports of Russians fighting alongside the Greek rebels were in error, and at no time during the civil war did the Greek government ever claim to have killed or captured any Soviet military personnel serving with the Communist guerrillas.[51] In February 1949 the Greek charge d'affaires in Moscow discussed with his American counterpart recent reports of "Russians" wounded in the Greek civil war arriving in Rumania for medical treatment; he expressed his confidence that there had been no recruiting among the Greek population in the Soviet Union and that any Russian-speaking Greek rebels had probably been recruited in Greece from among the 3,000 Greeks expelled from the Soviet Union in 1938 and returned to Greece.[52] Moscow apparently did send a few observers, but for the most part they stayed over the borders.[53] On balance, the U.S. military attaché in Athens in 1947, Col. Harvey H. Smith, was at least partially correct when he stated, "I don't think there is any doubt but that the Soviet Union is backing Albania and Yugoslavia in training the bandits. But they are not across the border directing operations."[54]

There were also frequent reports of material assistance being provided by the Soviet Union directly to the Greek guerrillas, but these reports also remained unconfirmed. Such reports included the sending of gold and banknotes of various types to the guerrillas. Also, KKE Central Committee members Petros Roussos and Leonidas Stringos were reported to have met in Slimnitsa in July 1948 to discuss the question of supplies with a Russian general, who is alleged to have told them that the Soviet Union considered it important that the insurrection in Greece continue and that supplies for the GDA would be included in shipments by sea from the Soviet Union for the Albanian army. The likelihood of any Soviet officer making such a statement in July 1948 is extremely low, given Stalin's known desire to liquidate the rebellion in Greece due to the growing problem with Yugoslavia. However, contemporary U.S. naval intelligence reports mentioned Soviet ships in the Aegean apparently loaded with supplies for the Greek guerrillas, and Russian submarines were frequently reported in various Mediterranean ports and may have been used for clandestine resupply of the Greek rebels.[55] Reports of the delivery of supplies for the Greek guerrillas by Russian aircraft were also common. One such report claimed that on 21 August 1948 aircraft loaded with 150 boxes of Russian medical supplies had arrived in Sofia for onward movement to the Greek guerrillas via Tirana and Koritsa.[56] A similar report stated that fifteen Soviet cargo planes had arrived in Tirana from Rumania on 15 August 1948 loaded with various types of war matériel ostensibly for the Albanian army. Other examples of Soviet movement of supplies by air to the GDA in northwestern Greece were also reported. Supposedly, the GDA received significant quantities of supplies from the Soviet Union in the Lake Prespa region in the fall of 1948, in preparation for the subsequent major attack on Florina. While it is likely that the Soviet Union did in fact provide Albania, Yugoslavia, and Bulgaria with funds and matériel that subsequently found their way to the Greeks, there is no credible evidence to support the many reports that the Russians engaged in direct support of the GDA. All the reports alleging Soviet support of the GDA, including those just noted, were extremely hazy, and there is no good reason to believe that any of them contained more than a kernel of truth.

Of course, the Soviets did provide some degree of diplomatic and propaganda support for the Communist rebellion in Greece. Such support was cheap, expected of the Soviet Union as the leader of the worldwide Communist movement, and thus largely pro forma. In any event, the public pronouncements of the Soviet government and its diplomatic representatives must be seen in the context of the Cold War and of Soviet relations with Yugoslavia and the other satellite nations. In many cases, the message was more anti-Western than pro-KKE, and often the real purpose was to send a message to Yugoslavia or to one of the other Soviet satellites. In point of fact, Soviet diplomacy was always designed to aid the Soviet Union, not the Greek insurgents. The refusal to recognize the Provisional Democratic Government of Free Greece after December 1947 is just one example, and the judicious use of the Soviet veto in the UN Security Council, as in the case of its not being employed against the creation of the UN Commission of Investigation, is another. Moreover, as Soviet concern with Tito's independent line increased, the Soviets stepped up efforts to minimize the situation in Greece. In 1949 the Soviet Union initiated a drive for a negotiated settlement of the Greek question in the UN and the conclusion of a peace, even at the expense of the KKE.[57] To that end, Stalin also applied pressure on both Albania and Bulgaria to reduce their support of the GDA, even as he had previously advised Tito to suspend his support of the guerrillas.

OUTSIDE SUPPORT FOR THE GREEK DEMOCRATIC ARMY

Albania, Yugoslavia, and Bulgaria were united by a common ideology, were on generally good terms with each other, and—even though their specific national interests were not entirely compatible—looked with favor on the idea of a fellow Communist state on their southern borders.[58] To that end they were prepared to provide the Greek Communist rebels with sanctuary; training, medical, and supply facilities; and a variety of supplies and logistical services, as well as free transit of their borders and, on occasion, covering fire from their frontier posts. Although the question of Communist solidarity was involved, each of the Communist states that provided—or declined to provide—assistance to the Greek Communists did so on the basis of its own interests. This is perfectly clear in the case of the Soviet Union and in the case of the French and Italian Communist parties, which were vying for legitimacy and power at home, wished to avoid the impression that they were responsible for armed insurrections elsewhere, and wanted to focus Communist attention and resources on their own struggles. Being both more remote and more secure, other Soviet satellite states, such as Rumania, Hungary, Poland, Czechoslovakia, and East Germany, could and did provide token assistance to their Greek comrades.

The national interests of Albania, Yugoslavia, and Bulgaria were directly involved in the Greek situation, and substantial support for the Communist guerrillas in Greece served their interests well as a means of putting pressure on the Greek government. Each of Greece's northern neighbors had long-standing ethnic, religious, political, economic, or territorial disputes with the Greek government.[59] The victory of the Greek right wing in January 1945 and the passing of all three of Greece's northern neighbors into the Communist camp by the end of 1946 added the dimension of ideological conflict to already strained relationships. Old mutual fears of territorial encroachment and even outright invasion were revived in the postwar period and were intensified by the support provided by Albania, Yugoslavia, and Bulgaria to the Greek Communist rebels. Although by March 1948 the Greek government was prepared to resume normal relations with Bulgaria, Hungary, and Rumania, the Greek people remained hostile to those Communist countries as well as to Albania and Yugoslavia, due to the widespread belief that they were giving aid to the Greek Communist guerrillas.[60]

Of course, the interests of both the Greek government and the three principal supporters of the KKE/GDA changed over time, and the outside support received by the Greek Communist guerrillas changed accordingly. The fact that Albania, Yugoslavia, and Bulgaria as well as Rumania and Hungary continued to support the Greek Communist guerrillas long after Stalin had made clear his desire to terminate the rebellion in Greece can only be seen as evidence of the mythical nature of a monolithic worldwide Communist conspiracy directed from Moscow, and of the inability of the Soviet Union to control every action of its satellite states. Yugoslavia, in particular, continued to support the GDA despite repeated Soviet warnings, and it discontinued that support only when the KKE leadership made clear that it intended to side with the Cominform and Stalin in their dispute with Tito. Both Albania and Bulgaria were weaker and thus more subject to Soviet influence, but they too acted on what they perceived as their own interests to continue to support the Greek guerrillas in defiance of Soviet guidance, until it became obvious that the GDA was doomed by Operation TORCH in the summer of 1949, and until the purge of national Communist leaders, such as Enver Hoxha in Albania and Georgi Dimitrov in Bulgaria, had well begun.

The Meeting at Petrich (December 1945)

Despite the growing oppression of the royalist government and right-wing terrorist groups in the months after the Varkiza Agreement of February 1945, the KKE leadership was hesitant to return to armed action to protect its adherents and establish a "democratic" regime in Greece, in part because it was uncertain as to the aid that it might be able to obtain from its Communist comrades outside Greece.[61] The decision of the Second Plenum of the Central Committee to adopt a more aggressive policy of armed self-defense came in February 1946, but only after the KKE leaders had received indications that the neighboring Communist countries would indeed provide support.[62] The clearest evidence of the intentions of Yugoslavia and Bulgaria was provided during a meeting of representatives of the KKE Central Committee with Yugoslavian and Bulgarian military officers at Petrich, on the Greek-Bulgarian border, on 15 December 1945.[63] At the Petrich meeting, both Yugoslavia and Bulgaria promised substantial assistance should their Greek comrades elect to launch an armed rebellion. Marshal Tito detailed a senior Yugoslavian officer, Alexander Rankovitch, to work out the details of Yugoslavian aid, and the Yugoslavs proposed that all such efforts should be coordinated centrally.[64]

The exact degree to which Albania, Yugoslavia, and Bulgaria coordinated their activities in support of the Greek guerrillas is not clear, but the Greek government and its Western allies assumed that the effort was centrally directed by a headquarters outside Greece. On 26 August 1948, A. Dalietos, the Greek Liaison Service representative to the chairman of the UN Special Committee on the Balkans, submitted a letter that, in commenting on the UNSCOB report of 30 June 1948, stated,

Numerous facts, insufficiently stressed by the Special Committee, enable one to build up a picture of the master plan governing the aid furnished to the guerrillas by the northern neighbours.

Indeed, if the facts are examined as a whole, it becomes clear that a sort of offensive alliance exists. Bands which seek refuge in Albania often re-appear with the same men and the same leaders in areas of Greek territory bordering on another State. Thus the guerrillas can not only make frequent use of the territory of neighbouring countries but they are also able, when strategic considerations require it, to move from one State to another behind the iron curtain in order to take the Greek Army in the rear in sectors where its strength is temporarily reduced.[65]

Even after the Petrich meeting in December 1945 and the subsequent KKE decision in February 1946 to move toward armed rebellion, the promises of support from the Greeks' Communist comrades remained vague and ambiguous. The Yugoslavian and Czech Communist Parties offered further vague promises of support after the KKE boycott of the Greek general election on 31 March 1946, but the French and Italian Communist Parties responded negatively to any suggestion of an armed uprising in Greece.[66] In fact, the Yugoslavians soon made good on their offers of support, by accepting several thousand ex-ELAS guerrillas and their families as refugees and allowing them to establish a number of refugee camps and supply centers on Yugoslavian territory, notably at Boulkes, northeast of Belgrade. The situation improved following a tour of Balkan capitals by Markos in 1946, during which the GDA's outside supporters promised more facilities and greater quantities of matériel in return for KKE agreement on certain issues involving the correction of borders and the status of minorities.[67]

The Bled Conference (August 1947)

The Petrich agreements were confirmed and expanded during a meeting of Markos with Albanian, Yugoslavian, and Bulgarian military representatives at Bled, in Yugoslavia, at the beginning of August 1947.[68] By that time, the formation of the GDA was well advanced, and the GDA had already demonstrated some ability to face the Greek government forces successfully, thereby justifying the investment of its outside supporters in arms, ammunition, food, and other equipment and in training, supply, and medical facilities for the rebels. The participants at the Bled meeting agreed that

1. The Albanian, Yugoslavian, and Bulgarian armies would provide the GDA with instructors, supplies, arms, and other equipment, including trucks and radios, and the Hungarian and Rumanian governments would be asked to help as well.

2. The Albanian, Yugoslavian, and Bulgarian general staffs would organize a rear defense, to include infantry, artillery, and aircraft, to protect the GDA in the border areas and from cross-border pursuit by the GNF, and to intervene directly against the GNF, if such action promised to be decisive.

3. Albania would provide a naval base for the use of the GDA, presumably as a port of embarkation for supplies to be moved by sea.

4. Military representatives of the Albanian, Yugoslavian, and Bulgarian governments would establish contact with the "Greek Democratic Government" as soon as it was established.

5. An "international legion" would be formed to fight alongside the GDA in Greece.[69]

The participants in the Bled conference also agreed to establish a Balkan Joint Staff (BJS), consisting of military representatives of the four principals, the purpose of which would be to coordinate operations and logistical support for the GDA. To obtain the other concessions, Markos was obliged to accept the guidance of the BJS, which was dominated by the Yugoslavs, in the person of one General Popovic.[70] Markos was also forced to accept BJS approval of senior GDA appointments and removals.[71] The BJS was in fact established, but its methods and the extent of its actual influence on GDA organization and operations is unclear. Apparently, Markos resisted many of the measures proposed by Popovic and the BJS, and in any event Zachariades sent Popovic away in February 1949, when Markos was dismissed as commander of the GDA.[72]

The announcement of the establishment of the Provisional Democratic Government of Free Greece in late December 1947 did not produce the appearance of the military representatives of Albania, Yugoslavia, and Bulgaria promised in the Bled agreements, nor did it produce formal recognition by any government, Communist or otherwise. However, the announcement was followed by an intensification of efforts in Albania, Yugoslavia, and Bulgaria to provide the Greek guerrillas with moral, political, and material support, and in all three Communist states there were organized national committees for aid to the "Greek Democratic People"; considerable sums of money were collected for the rebels.[73]

Yugoslavia

There were several reasons why Marshal Tito and the Yugoslavs were willing to support the guerrillas in their struggle against the Greek government, chief among them being Yugoslavia's territorial ambitions with respect to Macedonia. Greek-Yugoslavian relationships had long been complicated by traditional Yugoslavian desires for an outlet on the Aegean, to be achieved by Yugoslavian annexation—or alternatively, the independence under Yugoslavian hegemony—of the more than 80,000 ethnic Slavs in Greek Macedonia. Many of these Slavs were hostile to the Greek government and cooperated with the Greek Communists in the hope of gaining their independence.[74] Tito perceived that his territorial ambitions with respect to the Slavic population of Macedonia might be "more likely to be realized in a Greece ruled by Markos or Zachariades than in one dominated by the traditionally Slavophobic right."[75] Closely connected with the desire to gain control of "Aegean Macedonia" was a broader objective of forming a Balkan federation, dominated by Yugoslavia.[76]

Of more immediate moment, however, was Tito's fear of Western—specifically British—"imperialist" moves with respect to the Balkans in general and Yugoslavia in particular. Tito saw the British intervention in the "Second Round" of the Greek civil war in December 1944 as yet another step in a British plan to dominate postwar Yugoslavia, the Churchill-Stalin "percentage deal" in October 1944 having been an earlier indication of British intentions. In the light of such an assessment of Yugoslavia's strategic situation, a strong Communist guerrilla movement in northern Greece was seen by Tito as an effective buffer, especially if the guerrillas were successful.[77]

Tito also no doubt felt a certain ideological solidarity with the Greek Communists and a sense of responsibility to foster the advance of Communism in general.[78] The relationship between Tito's partisans and the Greek guerrillas of EAM/ELAS during the resistance period had been generally good, although there had been some difficulties over control of SNOF (Slavo-Macedonian Liberation Front) bands by ELAS and over the question of "Aegean Macedonia." Cooperation between Tito's partisans and ELAS was initiated with the visit of Svetozar Vukmanovich-Tempo to northern Greece in the summer of 1943, but much to the disgust of the ELAS commander, Gen. Stephanos Saraphis, the Greek guerrillas received no arms or other supplies from the partisans, despite repeated requests. The commander of the GDA, Markos Vafiades, had been a high-ranking ELAS officer in northern Greece during the resistance period, but there is nothing to suggest that he had a close relationship with the Yugoslavian Communists at that time. In fact, as a nationalist he had opposed Yugoslavian ambitions with respect to Macedonia, and he had directed operations against dissident SNOF forces in northern Greece in 1944.

The Yugoslavian authorities were more comfortable with Markos' guerrilla-oriented strategy than with the conventional army strategy advocated by Nikos Zachariades, the General Secretary of the KKE. Ideologically, Tito and Markos were natural nationalistic bedfellows, while Zachariades was a confirmed Stalinist internationalist. Moreover, Markos seems to have had a clearer concept of who supported the GDA and who did not, and he realized that the Communist insurrection in Greece could not succeed without Tito's support.[79] In any event, by the fall of 1946 whatever animosities may have existed between Tito and Markos had been forgotten, and the Yugoslavs seemed willing to provide whatever facilities and supplies the GDA might require. Following the Petrich meeting in December 1945, Yugoslavia began to provide the Greek Communist guerrillas with a variety of training and logistical support. The Yugoslavian military authorities maintained close contact with the GDA, and a Yugoslav mission, consisting of Gen. Peko Dapchevic and a small staff, was attached to Markos' GDA General Command.[80]

In its first report to the UN General Assembly in 1948, UNSCOB pointed to Yugoslavia as the principal supporter of the Greek Communist guerrillas, and it continued to do so until early 1949.[81] In time, Markos and the GDA came to rely heavily on Yugoslavian aid and the transit of material through Yugoslavia to Albania and thence to the Greek guerrillas. The material assistance provided by Yugoslavia to the Greek Communists included transport, motor vehicles, antiaircraft guns, machine guns, rifles, mines, ammunition, food, clothing, and timber.[82] The overall dimensions of such aid is not known, but one Yugoslavian writer, Vladimir Dedijer, claimed that Yugoslavia provided some 2,000 German heavy machine guns, 3,500 other machine guns, 35,000 rifles, 7,000 German *panzerfaust* antitank rockets, 10,000 land mines, clothing for 12,000 men, and thirty wagons of food.[83] According to Dedijer, the Soviet Union provided thirty antiaircraft guns (which remained in Yugoslavia), Hungary supplied three or four truckloads of medical supplies and a liaison officer, Rumania sent 2,000 blankets, and Czechoslovakia (or Hungary) donated a collection of recordings of Russian war songs.[84] The time span over which this aid was delivered is unclear. In addition, in October 1947 Yugoslavia and Bulgaria provided the GDA with fifteen 105 mm howitzers and forty-five 75 mm guns, which were subsequently deployed to defend the Grammos-Vitsi stronghold.[85]

In Yugoslavia, as in other Communist countries, committees were formed to collect food, money, clothing, medical supplies, and other matériel for the Greek guerrillas.[86] The lead in these activities was taken by state-approved trade unions, youth groups, women's associations, and veterans groups; "Committees of Assistance" were formed in the various regions of Yugoslavia. UNSCOB estimated that by March 1948 the value of the matériel collected totaled about $150,000.[87] Yugoslavian authorities were also active in recruiting for the GDA, particularly among the Macedonian separatist groups sponsored by Yugoslavia. In early 1948 the Yugoslavian Army encouraged "volunteers" from among its noncommissioned officers to serve with the GDA, probably as trainers.[88] Guerrilla units were also allowed to take refuge in Yugoslavia, maneuver on Yugoslavian territory, and even to support their forces in Greece by fire from Yugoslavia.[89] Yugoslavian support included the use of the state-controlled Radio Belgrade for proguerrilla announcements and commentary as well as permission for the GDA to establish its own Radio Free Greece near Belgrade.[90] In addition, the Yugoslavian government provided diplomatic support for the Greek rebels in the UN and elsewhere, and it was reported to have made a loan of some 250 million dinars to support the GDA.[91] It is not clear whether the loan represented credits toward the cost of facilities and supplies provided by Yugoslavia, or a cash loan.

Another important aspect of the aid provided to the Greek Communist guerrillas by the Yugoslavians was medical care for the sick and wounded. In late 1948–early 1949, the main GDA medical facility in Yugoslavia was located at Katlanska Banya, a spa site near Skoplje.[92] Sick and wounded guerrillas received treatment and convalesced at Katlanksa Banya and then returned to Greece to fight again. After the first months of 1949, wounded guerrillas were held in Yugoslavia only a short time before being evacuated on to Bulgaria or Rumania. In November 1949 the Yugoslavian State radio in Belgrade claimed that Yugoslavian hospitals had treated 6,317 wounded guerrillas, at a cost of over eighty million dinars.[93]

Beginning in 1945, the Yugoslavian authorities made available to the KKE/GDA a large number of headquarters sites, reception and refugee centers, training camps, supply depots, and other military facilities. These bases were apparently constructed and maintained by the Yugoslavian government, which also supplied their inhabitants with food, clothing, fuel, and other necessities. The first major GDA base to be established in Yugoslavia—and by far the largest—was at Boulkes.[94] In the aftermath of the Varkiza Agreement in February 1945, thousands of former ELAS guerrillas and their families took refuge in Albania, Yugoslavia, and Bulgaria. The flow of Greek refugees seeking to escape right-wing oppression in Greece increased in 1946, and a group of about 3,000 ex-ELASites went to the Yugoslavian town of Tetovo, where they stayed for a short time before moving on to Novis Iva, a village abandoned by its prosperous German-speaking community during World War II. Eventually, the group, led by Andreas Tzimas, moved to Boulkes, a Yugoslavian army camp in the loop of the Danube River northwest of Belgrade. The Boulkes camp had been occupied by Germans and consisted of some 600 buildings on about 20,000 acres.[95]

The decision of the Yugoslavian government to permit the expansion of what was essentially a refugee camp into a full-fledged guerrilla base was apparently taken in March or April 1946, following Zachariades' visit to Yugoslavia on his way home from a Communist meeting in Prague.[96] Boulkes, supplied and supervised by the Yugoslavians but under the direct control of the KKE/GDA, soon expanded into a major GDA headquarters, reception, training, and indoctrination center. In June 1946 there were 3,000 Greeks at Boulkes, and the numbers grew quickly to 11,000 in January 1947, 22,500 in January 1948, and 25,000 in December 1948.[97] One British journalist who visited Boulkes in 1947 described it as "an entire Greek town" rather than just a military camp.[98] Boulkes gave the appearance of a well-planned Soviet-style commune, with euphemistically named "departments" responsible for various functions.[99] The Boulkes camp was also linked by radio to both the KKE Central Committee in Athens and the GDA General Command field headquarters in northwestern Greece, as well as to GDA liaison units (*yiafaka*) in Tirana and Sofia. It also included an active printing plant, which published several periodicals and other propaganda materials for the KKE/GDA.[100]

A reception and training center as well as a logistical base, the Boulkes camp also became an indoctrination center where the Greek guerrillas lived under constant, and often severe, party surveillance and discipline. Dominique Eudes, no friend of the Stalinist clique within the KKE, described Boulkes as "more a concentration camp for Stalinist indoctrination than for military training and assembly."[101] The Stalinist camp commandant, Pechtasidis, assisted by a 300-man armed Security Service Group (YTO) headed by a 48-year-old former regular Greek Army officer, *Kapetanios* Alexis, ran roughshod over the guerrilla fighters and their commanders. He used "police state" methods of terror, denunciation, and controls so strict that individuals were not permitted to visit the latrines alone at night.[102] Dissidents were closely watched, and not a few were eliminated. Those who wished to leave Boulkes were often arrested for disloyalty and treated harshly.

Conditions in the Boulkes camp were described in detail by one former ELAS guerrilla, George Zafiris, who testified that he withdrew to Albania after the unsuccessful ELAS revolt in Athens in December 1944.[103] After a stay in an Albanian camp for Greek refugees at Rubig, Zafiris and a group of 300–400 other Greeks drew food and clothing from the Albanian government at Tirana and moved to Boulkes by truck in October 1945. Zafiris related that there was a good deal of tension in the Boulkes camp between the former EAM-ELAS men and the Macedonians belonging to NOF until the spring of 1946, when the NOF guerrillas were removed to a camp of their own near Skoplje. At Boulkes, Zafiris was taught Communist theory and military tactics. Zafiris was not sympathetic with the Stalinist regime at Boulkes, and in September 1946, he escaped to the Allied Control Commission in Bucharest and was subsequently repatriated to Greece.

Additional details on the organization and operation of the Boulkes camp were provided by Etstathios Papagranides, a Greek civilian who was captured by Greek and Serbian bandits near Grannitsa on 5 November 1946. He was taken to Boulkes, where, being suspect for his political beliefs, he worked in the tuberculosis sanitarium for six months before being incarcerated in the camp prison.[104] During the time Papagranides was at Boulkes, the camp population included about 1,850 KKE party members and Communist (ex-ELAS) guerrillas, including three hundred women, who were either wives of the party members and guerrillas or party members themselves. There were also 1,300 hostages, principally individuals who had refused to join the guerrillas. Other inmates included 1,150 tuberculosis patients and other invalids, and three hundred civilians captured in Greece by the ELAS guerrillas between the liberation and the general election of 1946. The party members and guerrillas were divided into about thirty groups, each of which was supervised by a group leader, known as a *korarchis*, who was assisted by several other party members. Everyone in the camp was dressed in military uniforms provided by the Yugoslavians, and couriers came regularly from Greece. Security was strict, only approved reading material was permitted, and Communist indoctrination sessions were conducted regularly. Papagranides reported having seen Zachariades when he visited the camp in March 1946 and made a short speech, but he recalled that Zachariades had made a bad impression, because he did not speak directly to anyone.

Aside from its usefulness as a center of Communist indoctrination, Boulkes was a major GDA training base. Courses were conducted for both junior and senior officers as well as the *andartes*, and there was also a course for political commissars.[105] Training was conducted using Yugoslavian and Soviet field manuals provided by the Yugoslavian Army. Beginning in the spring of 1946, Greek guerrillas trained at Boulkes were returned to Greece to form the cadres for the expanding GDA.[106] Trained and armed at Boulkes, groups of as many as 1,500 guerrillas crossed the Yugoslavian border into Greece to fight for the GDA. Throughout the Greek civil war, right up to July 1949, when Tito closed his borders to the Greek guerrillas, the Boulkes camp remained the largest and most active GDA base outside the Grammos-Vitsi stronghold.

The GDA facilities in Yugoslavia included a number of other training camps, hospitals and first-aid evacuation centers, radio stations, and supply centers.[107] Training camps were located at Debar, Dubrovnik (for officer courses at the Yugoslavian Naval Academy), Kamenitsa, Koumanovo, Matejitsa, Prilep, Skoplje, Slokvitsa, Strumitsa, Tetovo, Torza, and Veles. In addition to the main GDA medical facility at Katlanska Banya, near Skoplje, GDA had hospitals at Bitolj (Monastir), Bogomila, Boulkes, Kanikan, Koumanovo, Moetsi, Nokolitse, Palaga, Palanka, Skoplje, Tetovo, and Valadovo, and first-aid evacuation centers were located at Huma and Ljubojna. The GDA supply centers in Yugoslavia were at Bezani, Bitolj, Derbigan, Doumen, Dragos, Gradenitsa, Huma, Mujin, Petrovaradin, Prilep, Skotsivir, Sovits, and Strumitsa.

Geographically, Yugoslavia occupied a critical position with respect to supplying the Greek Communist guerrillas. In addition to supplies from Yugoslavia, Yugoslavia handled the transshipment of large amounts of cargo for the Greek guerrillas from Czechoslovakia, Bulgaria, and other Communist countries. A large portion of the matériel provided by the various Soviet satellites that entered Greece after January 1949 crossed at various points on the Greek-Albanian frontier, but except for some limited shipments by sea and air, Albania itself was isolated from the other satellite states, and everything had to pass through Yugoslavia.[108]

Greece's border with its northern neighbors Albania, Yugoslavia, and Bulgaria was about the same length as the Western Front in World War I from Switzerland to the North Sea. That portion of the border abutting Yugoslavia runs for some two hundred kilometers, the greater part of that distance along the rugged Beles and Kaimaktsalan (Vorros Onos) mountain chains in the east and the northern extension of the Vermion Mountains in the west. There are few passes through these mountains, and wheeled vehicle traffic is barred except through the two most important passes—the Monastir Gap, a broad and easy route from Prilep and Bitolj (Monastir) into western Macedonia, and the Vardar Gap, through which flows the Vardar (Axios) River farther east. Minor routes crossed the frontier in the vicinity of Lakes Doiran and Lake Prespa. Map 2 shows the routes from Yugoslavia into Greece used for the movement of supplies for the GDA.

The movement of supplies for the GDA from Yugoslavia into Greece was accomplished both by land and by sea. UNSCOB observers identified three main ground routes.[109] The first began at Bogomila and ran via Prilep and Bitolj (Monastir) to Ljubojna and thence along the eastern shore of Lake Prespa to Laimos and on to Ayios Germanos and Plati in the Vitsi. This was the major route by which guerrilla forces in the Vitsi received supplies from Albania as well as Yugoslavia. It connected to two routes to the interior of Greece that began in the foothills of the mountains south of the loop in the Aliakmon River: northeast to the Kamvounia and Pierria Mountains, and to Mount Pelion via Mounts Olympus, Ossa, and Mavrounion. Between January and June 1948, ammunition from the Yugoslavian depot in Bitolj was moved regularly along this route by trucks or mules. Boats of over one ton loaded with arms from Albania and Yugoslavia regularly crossed Lake Little Prespa and connected with routes beginning on Yugoslavian territory and running via Mikrolimni to Vadohorion. The second major land route led from Skotsivir on the Crna Reke across the Kaimaktsalan to the Ardhea plain around Loutraki. Beginning at Valadovo, this route continued to the Khalkidiki Peninsula via Korona and Mounts Kroussia, Vertsiko, and Kerdylia. The third major land route, used primarily to supply guerrillas in the Beles Mountains, began at Strumitsa near the intersection of the Bulgarian, Yugoslavian, and Greek borders and divided in the Beles into two branches. One branch ran to Lithoto and Kavalaris and the other along the northern shore of Lake Doiran to the area known as the Korona Salient, where the guerrillas abandoned large amounts of supplies and equipment in June 1948.

Caiques and other small ships sailing from Albanian or Yugoslavian ports were also used to deliver equipment and supplies to the Greek rebels along the Adriatic coast and in the Peloponnesus. The U.S. naval attaché in Rome reported in April 1948 that a special section of the Yugoslavian naval headquarters at Split, directed by a Yugoslavian navy captain (Ivan Lovetich), assisted by three liaison officers, two Greek and one Russian, was charged with the organization and transport to the GDA of supplies, which were supposedly delivered by three old Yugoslavian submarines loaded at night in various small ports near Split.[110]

Yugoslavian support of the GDA was complicated by Tito's estrangement from the Soviet Union and the Cominform. Yugoslavian and Soviet goals with respect to Greece were not in consonance, and the Yugoslavs received repeated warnings from Moscow to terminate their support of the GDA.[111] Assessing his own interests in Greece, Tito chose to continue to provide refuge, facilities, and supplies to the Greek Communists even after his expulsion from the Cominform in June 1948, but at a steadily decreasing level. He ended all support and closed the Yugoslavian borders to the GDA only after the KKE under the leadership of Zachariades publicly announced a policy supporting the Cominform against Yugoslavia.

Map 2
GDA Bases in Yugoslavia and Entry Routes from Yugoslavia into Greece

Until late 1947, the Yugoslavian authorities were confident that they could support the Greek guerrillas without any adverse effect on their own situation.[112] However, the announcement of the formation of the Provisional Democratic Government of Free Greece in December 1947 aroused significant consternation in the West, and Tito began to act more cautiously, lest his support of the Greek rebels involve Yugoslavia in some direct confrontation with Britain or the United States. The failure of the GDA to take Konitsa also influenced Tito's attitude, casting doubt on the ultimate success of the Greek Communist insurgency.[113] Nevertheless, Yugoslavian support continued at a relatively high level throughout the first half of 1948. On 22 March 1948, about the same time the split between Tito and the Cominform began to take tangible shape, the U.S. ambassador in Yugoslavia sent to the State Department his analysis of the situation.

The Yugoslav Government is furnishing aid and assistance to the Greek guerrillas at the present time economically, through its Committees of Assistance; diplomatically, by its semi-official attentions to various Markos agents; militarily, through logistical and other support; and in the field of public opinion, by the extension of its propaganda facilities. ... these acts in the aggregate come close to a de facto recognition of the [Provisional Democratic Government of Free Greece].[114]

Stalin had long been suspicious of Tito's independent line in Yugoslavia and feared that Tito's nationalist spirit might infect the other Soviet satellite states. The conflict between Tito and Stalin began to reach crisis proportions in early 1948.[115] On 17 March 1948, after Yugoslavia and Albania had concluded an agreement, the Soviets sent a condemnatory letter to the Yugoslavian Central Committee, and similar messages followed in May. In essence, the Soviets challenged Tito to an ideological debate before the delegates to the Cominform, a form of trial that Tito wished to avoid. The scheduled meeting of the Cominform took place in Bucharest in June 1948, and on 28 June the assembled delegates condemned Yugoslavia for betraying Marxism-Leninism and for a host of other "crimes," including "nationalism," "cozying up to the imperialists," and the purge of Soviet "specialists"—whose function had been to control Yugoslavian affairs and spy on the Yugoslavians in the interest of the Soviet Union—from the Yugoslavian administration.

The condemnation of Tito by the Cominform in June 1948 presented both the Yugoslavs and the Greek Communists with a dilemma. Tito was inclined to continue his support of the GDA, if for no other reason than to ensure the good will of the KKE in his confrontation with Stalin. However, with Yugoslavia isolated from the other Communist states, several factors induced him to reduce his support for the Greek rebels.[116] In the first place, he now became preoccupied with his own situation and had to consider some sort of accommodation with the Greek government in order to be able to concentrate on protecting Yugoslavia from any Soviet-sponsored military action. Then too, he was compelled to husband his resources for his own use; he would need massive amounts of military equipment and supplies if Yugoslavia was attacked by the Soviet Union or its satellites.

The loss of Soviet and satellite economic support had serious economic consequences for Yugoslavia. Most of Yugoslavia's trade had been with the Soviet satellite nations, and that trade declined so precipitously after June 1948 that by the spring of 1949 Yugoslavia was almost entirely cut off from deliveries of machinery, fuel, medicine, and other items essential for its economy.[117] Consequently, Tito became more inclined to consider the possibility of accepting aid from the West, which had been offered at various times in the past.[118] Cessation of Yugoslavian support for the GDA was, understandably, a precondition for any Western aid to Yugoslavia. Thus, in mid-1948 Tito began to scale back the amount of aid being provided to the GDA. It should be noted that Tito's decision to reduce Yugoslavian support for the Greek guerrillas, however, came before either his firm decision to seek Western aid or the formal declaration of the KKE in favor of the Cominform.[119]

Despite the many reasons for terminating Yugoslavian aid to the Greek guerrillas, several factors led Tito to continue to support the Greek Communist guerrillas for over a year after his break with the Cominform. In the first place, he was under considerable pressure from his supporters among the Macedonian separatists to continue aid to the rebellion in Greece, which appeared to offer the best chance for the achievement of their own goals.[120] The need to prepare the Yugoslavian people for any change in policy and the desire to have at least one Communist group friendly to him also played a part.[121] It also appears that Tito continued to provide aid to the Greek rebels precisely because Stalin opposed it.[122]

For their part, the leaders of the KKE/GDA were presented with a serious problem by the Cominform break with Tito. If they supported Tito, their principal supplier, they would probably be cut off by the other Communist states, including Albania and Bulgaria, which were also providing significant assistance to the GDA. If, on the other hand, they sided with the Cominform, Tito would surely end his support for the Communist insurgency in Greece. For over a year after the Tito-Cominform split, the KKE/GDA leadership refrained from open expressions favoring either side in the dispute; indeed, the KKE was the only Communist party that failed to side immediately with the Cominform in its condemnation of Yugoslavia. However, the issue widened the split within the upper ranks of the KKE/GDA; Markos and his supporters, including the Slavo-Macedonian elements within the GDA, argued against any open condemnation of Tito, whereas Zachariades and the Stalinist bloc within the KKE/GDA were eager to demonstrate their solidarity with Stalin and the Cominform.[123] Discussion of the situation among the rank and file of the GDA was forbidden as the two factions argued over what to do. The dismissal of Markos on 8 February 1949 signaled the shift toward a pro-Cominform policy among the leadership of the KKE/GDA, but still no overt action was taken, for another five months.

The practical effects on the GDA of the break between Tito and the Soviets and of Tito's consequent decision to reduce aid to the GDA began to be felt almost at once. Although the Greek government continued to claim as late as the beginning of February 1949 that outside support for the GDA was increasing, as early as in the fall of 1948 UNSCOB observers in Greece were reporting a decline in Yugoslavian assistance to the Greek Communist guerrillas, and as time went on such reports multiplied.[124] The various aid committees formed in Yugoslavia to provide assistance to the Greek guerrillas apparently ceased operations before January 1949, and material aid from Yugoslavia became scanty after March.[125] Radio Free Greece was moved from Belgrade to Bucharest in early 1949.[126] In April 1949 the U.S. military attaché in Athens reported that "reinforcements and foodstuffs continue to be transported from Albania. From Yugoslavia, only foodstuffs, though not from Tito's Government."[127] By June 1949 Yugoslavian aid for the GDA had all but disappeared, although the Yugoslavian authorities continued to permit the Greek guerrillas to maneuver on Yugoslavian territory and to allow shipments from Bulgaria and elsewhere to transit Yugoslavia en route to Greece.[128] There was also a simultaneous reduction in the number of guerrillas moving from training camps, particularly Boulkes, into Greece.[129]

Following the dismissal of Markos in February 1949, the KKE decided secretly to support the Cominform in its dispute with Tito but to withhold any public disclosure of that policy. However, on 6 July 1949 Radio Free Greece broadcast the charge that the Yugoslavian authorities had permitted Greek national forces to maneuver on Yugoslavian territory for attacks on the GDA in the Mount Kaimaktsalan area.[130] On 14 July another Radio Free Greece broadcast denounced two NOF members, Gotsi and Keramitzieff, as traitors and "Tito's agents," further alienating the GDA's Slavo-Macedonian contingent as well as Tito and the Yugoslavians.[131] On 3 August, just as the final phase of the Greek government offensive in the Grammos-Vitsi was about to begin, Zachariades attacked Yugoslavia, calling Tito a "foul and cunning enemy" and charging that the Yugoslavians had stabbed the GDA in the back.[132]

Tito was already annoyed that the KKE had announced its support for the pro-Bulgarian plan for an "independent" Macedonia; the charges of aiding the GNF in battle against the Greek Communist guerrillas proved to be the last straw. The Yugoslavian population had by now been prepared and the Slavo-Macedonians placated; Tito concluded that he had little to lose by soliciting Western economic aid.[133] On 10 July 1949, four days after Radio Free Greece had broadcast its accusations, Marshal Tito announced in a speech at the Istrian town of Pola the closure of the Yugoslavian border to the Greek guerrillas, stating that the action was required

because of numerous incidents, because of the deaths of several Yugoslavs during these incidents, and finally, because of the false news broadcast by DAG [Democratic Army of Greece] according to which the Greek army had been authorized to cross the border to attack the enemy.[134]

Tito also had another good reason for closing his borders to the Greek guerrillas. Already in late June 1949, in the course of negotiation with the British for economic aid, he had promised that he would close the border and end his support for the Communist insurgents in Greece. Thus, his announcement at Pola was greeted with satisfaction in London and Washington, and no doubt it improved his chances of concluding some arrangement with the Western powers to repair the economic damage done by the split with the Cominform.

On 21 July UNSCOB reported that the closure of the Yugoslavian border had in fact taken place; that fact was confirmed by Kardelj, the Yugoslavian foreign minister, on 23 July.[135] The closure of the Yugoslavian border and the complete cessation of aid from Yugoslavia was a serious blow to the GDA, which was then engaged in its most serious battle—to retain control of its Grammos-Vitsi stronghold. The reduction in receipts of arms, ammunition, and other supplies could not have come at a worse time. The closure of the border also deprived the GDA of some 4,000 combatants in Yugoslavia, and it cut off 2,500 guerrillas in Bulgaria and another 2,500 in eastern Macedonia and western Thrace, just when they were needed to help defend the Grammos-Vitsi base.[136] Communications between the Kaimaktsalan-Beles and Grammos-Vitsi base areas were also interrupted, and the transit of supplies from Bulgaria and the other Communist states through Yugoslavia to Albania and thence to the Greek guerrillas was curtailed. However, although distant from the main battle in the Grammos and Vitsi, both Bulgaria and Romania increased their support of the GDA.[137] The slow reduction of Yugoslavian aid after June 1948 no doubt weakened the GDA, but the closure of the Yugoslavian border and the complete cessation of Yugoslavian assistance were blows from which the GDA could not recover.

Albania

With the withdrawal of German forces from Albania in 1944, Gen. Enver Hoxha, the leader of the Albanian partisans, established a Communist government that subsequently received diplomatic recognition by Britain and other powers. King Zog was deposed in January 1946, and a People's Republic was established. For ideological reasons, Hoxha and the Albanian People's Republic were prepared to support the Communist rebels in Greece; refugees from the rightist terror in Greece in 1945–1946 were received and cared for, small amounts of food and other supplies were provided, and the Albanian government permitted the GDA to establish camps near the frontier and to pass freely across the Greek-Albanian border to conduct guerrilla operations in Greece.

Albanian support for the Greek Communists was strengthened by continuing animosity between the Albanian and Greek governments and the apparent willingness of the Greek Communists to resolve differences equitably. Greek hatred of the Albanians, whom they referred to as "unlettered goat thieves," went back for centuries. Throughout the Greek civil war period Greece and Albania remained technically at war, diplomatic relations having been severed in 1940 when Albania assisted the invasion and subsequent occupation of Greece by Italy.[138] The Greek and Albanian governments were also at odds over mutual territorial claims in northern Epirus. The refusal of the Greek government to allow the emigration of the remaining members of the Chams, an Albanian Moslem tribe from southern Epirus that had cooperated with the Italians and fled to Albania at the end of World War II, and the existence of some 34,500 Greek-speaking inhabitants of northern Epirus (Albania) only intensified the conflict.[139]

General Hoxha, like Marshal Tito in Yugoslavia, was greatly concerned over the possibility of a Greek invasion of Albania backed by the Western powers. A strong antigovernment Communist guerrilla movement based in the Greek-Albanian border area was thus no doubt seen by Hoxha as a useful strategic buffer. His fears were not unwarranted. By the summer of 1949 Greek bitterness over Albanian support of the Greek Communist rebels, combined with the long-standing Greek desire to incorporate northern Epirus and a desire for revenge over Albania's World War II actions, led briefly to consideration of plans for a full-scale Greek invasion of Albania. These plans were stifled only by the strong opposition of the United States, the paymaster of the Greek military forces.[140] Public sentiment in Greece remained strong for eliminating Albania as a base for the Communist guerrillas, and even after the defeat of the GDA in Operation TORCH, Greek National Army leaders such as the Deputy Chief of Staff, Lieutenant General Kitrilakis, were eager to invade Albania or to create a nationalist guerrilla movement in Albania to overthrow the Communist government.[141]

Like Yugoslavia, Albania provided the Greek Communist guerrillas a wide range of support, including free transit across its borders and permission to maneuver on Albanian territory as well as occasional supporting fire; training bases, hospitals, and other facilities; recruiting and the collection of food, money, and clothing; arms, ammunition, and supplies of all types; and, in the case of Albania most significantly, transport.[142] The Albanians also provided refuge for the families of GDA guerrillas during GNA clearing operations in the border areas and maintained stocks of rations for the use of GDA dependents.[143]

By early 1949, the majority of GDA forces were concentrated in the Grammos and Vitsi base areas, which were in rugged, relatively barren terrain. UNSCOB observers rightly surmised that a large military force could not have been maintained in that area without outside support and that most of that external support was being channeled through Albania.[144] The UNSCOB observers in the area of the Greek-Albanian border reported that the support given by Albania to the Greek guerrillas included the supply of arms, ammunition, transport, signalling equipment and facilities and, to a lesser extent, clothes and food. It noted particularly the extensive use of mines by the guerrillas in the frontier area and the fact that the guerrillas were often engaged with their backs to the frontier in prolonged battles involving very heavy expenditure of ammunition . . . [and that] . . . a constant supply of ammunition was arriving from Albania.[145]

The matériel provided to the GDA through Albania also included artillery. For example, the delivery of three artillery pieces, probably 75 mm guns, to the Vitsi via Zemiak, Biglitsa, and Krystallopygi was reported in November 1948, and on 1 April 1949 sixteen guns were delivered to the GDA from Biglitsa.[146]

The free use of the Albanian borders was of significant tactical value to the GDA, and on numerous occasions it mounted attacks in safety from Albanian territory, to which the guerrillas fled once an operation was completed.[147] The GDA's fortified positions in the border area also extended in some places across the border into Albanian territory, as UNSCOB reported, noting that the "guerrillas made extensive use of Albanian territory during the [August 1948] Grammos operation for gun positions, rest and communications . . . [and] machine gun and mortar positions, trenches and other military emplacements which had been used by the guerrillas, were observed on the Albanian side of the frontier."[148] That the Albanians permitted such actions and provided significant material support to the guerrillas was no secret to the Greek government, which repeatedly complained of Albanian perfidy, or to the UNSCOB observer teams, who reported frequent such incidents. One example occurred during operations in the Mourgana pocket in early April 1949, when "the simultaneous observation by the group of heavy traffic along the Argyrokastron-Kokovic road and the testimony of witnesses, led the Special Committee to conclude definitely that the guerrillas in the Mourgana pocket were receiving logistical support from Albania on a very large scale."[149]

As was the case in Yugoslavia, Albanian trade unions and other quasigovernmental associations took the lead in the often compulsory collection of money, food, clothing, and other supplies for the Greek guerrillas. Collections for the GDA had already been going on for some time before the Albanian National Committee for Aid to the Greek Democratic People was formed in February 1948. Radio Tirana reported on 3 January 1948 that such collections already totaled over 630,000 *leks*.[150] The Albanian government also permitted the KKE/GDA to establish a radio station, which began broadcasting on 17 July 1947 from a site near Tirana. The state-controlled Albanian press and radio service also regularly issued communiqués and appeals on behalf of the guerrillas.[151] The Albanian authorities were active in recruitment of Greeks and Cham tribesmen in Albania for service with the GDA, and official Albanian orders for enlistment were administered and enforced by Albanian police units.[152] Albanian peasants also provided various services to the guerrillas. The proximity of the Greek guerrillas bases in the Grammos and the ease with which crossing of the Albanian border could be effected made it possible for the GDA to maintain large herds of sheep, cattle, and mules in the Albanian border regions for immediate use by the guerrillas. The size of such herds, which were cared for by Albanian peasants, was substantial; herds as large as 40,000 sheep and 3,000 mules were reported.[153]

There were also numerous reports of Greek guerrillas receiving medical treatment in Albanian facilities. The main GDA medical facility in Albania was at Koritsa; numerous Greek guerrillas were treated in hospitals at Elbasan and Moskhopolis; a major GDA convalescent center and rest camp was located at Souht; and special surgery, eye tests, and X-ray examinations were conducted in Tirana.[154] It appears to have been standard procedure for wounded guerrillas to be moved within Albania on Albanian Army vehicles escorted by Albanian soldiers. For example, one captured GDA guerrilla, Georgios Apostolidis, a twenty-three-year-old farmer, revealed under interrogation that he had been wounded at Alevitsa during the battle for the Grammos in April 1947 and had been carried by his comrades to Palaiochorion and thence to Slimnitsa, where he had joined fourteen other wounded guerrillas.[155] They stayed at Slimnitsa for four days until around 17 April 1947, when they were moved by mule across the border into Albania escorted by two healthy guerrillas. The wounded men were then loaded on trucks at Bozigrad and escorted by Albanian soldiers to the GDA hospital at Koritsa. After five days at Koritsa Apostolidis was returned by truck to the improvised guerrilla hospital at Slimnitsa, where he remained until the end of June 1947. He subsequently returned to fight again in the Grammos.

Given the poverty of Albania and its dependence on outside aid for its own civilian economy and military forces, it is certain that the aid received by the GDA from Albania originated elsewhere in the Soviet bloc.[156] Between 1 September and 15 December 1948 alone, the Soviet Union reportedly shipped some 38,000 tons of matériel to Albania, a part of which was perhaps intended for the Greek guerrillas. During 1949, Soviet shipments to Albania averaged about $1.5 million worth of goods per month. Most of the tonnage delivered consisted of grain, but there were also 133 ZIS trucks, 221 automobiles, two 75-ton railroad engines, a few rail cars, 6,000 tons of rails, 2.5 million square meters of textiles, 3,000 pieces of agricultural equipment, 10,000 tons of chemical fertilizer, medical supplies, 1,000 tons of coal, some sugar, and $310,000 worth of petroleum products. Analysts of the Central Intelligence Agency estimated that between 1 January and 15 August 1949 about sixty ships from Communist bloc nations arrived in Albanian ports to discharge some 250,000 tons of cargo. They noted that a definite correlation had been made in the past between the intensity of GDA operations in Greece and the numbers of Soviet bloc ships calling at Albanian ports. In December 1949 the CIA also estimated that in 1948 the combined total of Albanian grain production and imports had totaled about 313,000 metric tons, of which only about 223,000 metric tons had been required for Albanian consumption. Of the surplus of 90,000 metric tons, 7,000 metric tons would have met the annual grain requirements of the Greek guerrillas, both those in Albania and those in Greece.[157]

In April 1949 the U.S. military attaché in Athens reported on the publication in London on 21 April 1949 of an article by the diplomatic correspondent of the Continental News Service outlining the support provided to the Greek guerrillas by the various Cominform countries and channeled through Albania.[158] The author of the article alleged that "Albania . . . remains the main source of reinforcement and base for the attacks of the Greek communist bands" and that the greatest part of the supplies for the Greek guerrillas arrived in Albania by air from Hungary, in accordance with an agreement signed in March 1949 for the establishment of a regular weekly air service between Budapest and Tirana. The agreement was reportedly intended to supersede the other—far more frequent—flights for dropping supplies to the guerrillas. Such deliveries were reported by Albanian refugees in Yugoslavia as having taken place in February–March 1949, when despite bad weather, Soviet aircraft from Hungary landed at Koukes airfield, or dropped by parachute, cases containing weapons and ammunition, three or four times per week. The clearing of the airfield and the collection of air-dropped packages was accomplished by Albanian personnel, and the matériel was placed on Albanian military trucks under the supervision of Colonel Vasilenko, the Soviet commander of the airbase at Koukes, and Captain Konikolis, the GDA representative.

The Continental News Service correspondent also reported that the new arrangement for delivery of supplies from Hungary began at the end of March 1949, with the delivery of "gifts" to the Greek guerrillas from East German workers and "democratic organizations" in the Soviet zone of Germany.[159] These "gifts" had been offered following a tour of Germany, Austria, and the Soviet satellites by a GDA mission led by General Lambrou, who had been named to head the mission by the Soviet military attaché in Tirana, Colonel Sokolev. The GDA mission was also reported to have made purchases for the guerrillas to be paid for by the Albanian State Bank from a special dollar account established by the Soviet GOSBANK (Gosudarstvennyi Bank) in favor of the Greek guerrillas. Among the supplies delivered under this agreement were a small number of light transport vehicles from Bratislava.

In addition to facilitating the delivery of military supplies to the GDA, the Albanian government made available to the GDA a number of training, medical, and logistical facilities within Albania, as shown on Map 3.[160] For a time the headquarters of the Provisional Government and the GDA General Command were located at Leskovic (Leskoviki). The principal GDA reception and training camps in Albania were located at Koritsa (Korça; Korce), Skodra (Scutari; the modern Shkodër), Souht, and Burrelli with smaller camps at Elbasan, Fieri, Leskovic, Moskhopolis, Nikolitsa, Prens, Rubig, and Shijak (Siaki). Many of the reception and training camps also included facilities for the collection and maintenance of noncombatants, the camps at Skodra and Prens each containing in early 1949 some 3,000–3,500 women, children, and other noncombatants. A

Map 3
GDA Bases in Albania and Entry Routes from Albania into Greece

concentration camp for abducted Greeks was located at Elbasan. GDA medical facilities in Albania included hospitals at Argyrokastron, Elbasan, Grajdani, Koritsa, Leskovic, Lesnica (Lesinitsa), Moskhopolis, Pogradets, Shijak, Sotira, Souht, and Tirana. There were first-aid evacuation centers at Biglitsa (Bilishte), Bozigrad (Bojigrad), Erseka, Kamenik, Kapetitsa, Rakovo, Tsere, and Zagradec. GDA supply centers were located at Argyrokastron, Biglitsa, Bozigrad, Erseka, Kioutentsa, Kokovic, Koritsa, Leskovic, Pogradets, Vernik, and Viglista.

The UNSCOB observers in Epirus and western Macedonia noted that among the most important support provided by the Albanians to the GDA was transport. There were numerous reports of matériel being moved by truck as well as mule from Albania into Greece. UNSCOB observers also reported that

for the guerrillas themselves to have transported shells, mortars, grenades, mines and small arms ammunition in the quantities used during their long approach marches, and in all tactical phases of the battle, would have been impossible . . . [and] . . . that the large consumption of ammunition by the guerrillas was out of proportion to the transport of which they might normally be expected to dispose, especially in mountainous country.[161]

The Greek-Albanian frontier extends for some 190 kilometers through extremely rugged mountain terrain. It is divided into two sections by the northern extension of the Pindus range.[162] The Greek region of Epirus lies to the south of Albania on the western side of the Pindus, and the Greek region of western Macedonia lies to the northeast of Albania, toward the east of the Pindus. The main GDA base area in the Grammos was immediately adjacent to the border along a major portion of its length in the latter section, and the southwestern end of the Vitsi base area touched Albania in the north around Lake Little Prespa. As shown on Map 3, three main motor routes crossed the border from Albania into Greece: two in the south—one from Argyrokastron to Ioannina and the other from Permet to Ioannina—and one in the north from Koritsa to Florina in western Macedonia. A spur left the main Argyrokastron-Ioannina road just north of the border and ran southeast via Kokovic to Pogoniani. GDA forces controlled the Grammos area completely, and major concentrations of guerrillas also operated in the region through which the two southern routes passed. There were few improved roads on the Greek side of the border, but on the Albanian side a good motor road paralleled the border from Koritsa in the north to south of Leskovic, where it joined the main transborder route from Permet to Ioannina. From this important north-south artery, numerous smaller roads and mule paths extended eastward across the border into Greece, making access relatively easy.

UNSCOB teams conducted close observation of the Greek-Albanian border area from early 1948 and identified several important routes used by the GDA to move men and supplies along and across the frontier from Albania into Greece. Supplies unloaded in the villages on the Greek side of the border, such as Laimos, Ayios Germanos, Oxia, Kariai, Krystallopygi, and Katochori, were moved forward by the three GDA transport battalions to brigades or in some cases to battalions.[163] Backed by the motor road from Koritsa to Leskovic along the border, there were five principal routes used by the GDA to enter Greece from Albania.[164] The first ran from Koritsa via Biglitsa to Krystallopygi, Katokhori, and Pishodherion, with a branch road from Biglitsa to Ayios Dhimitrios and Ieropygi. In June 1949 some 285 vehicles were observed moving on the road from Koritsa to Krystallopygi.[165] A second main route ran from Koritsa via Dardha, Bozigrad, and Kioutentsa to Slimnitsa and on to Monopilon, and a newly constructed road also ran from Bozigrad via Qyteze to Vindehova and then across the frontier. In June 1949, 340 vehicles were observed using this new route.[166] Bozigrad appears to have been a major staging area. In March 1949 the GNA 1st Mountain Division intelligence office reported that guerrilla supplies were delivered by truck to Bozigrad every fifteen days for resupply of the GDA 7th Division, and that GDA supply officers were stationed in Bozigrad to control the movement of supplies, in cooperation with Albanian authorities.[167] The third route ran from Koritsa via Cerje and thence between Lake Prespa and Lake Little Prespa to Laimos, then south to Plati, Kariai, and Trigonon, and on south along the spine of the Vitsi, Signiatsikon, Vourinos and the Orliakis massifs, to end at Helikon southwest of Karpenision. Traffic for the guerrillas also moved across Lake Little Prespa by boat to Mikrolimni. After the loss of Mount Grammos this was a most important route, feeding as it did the internal routes to the Olympus-Ossa-Pelion and Pierria GDA base areas. The fourth major route ran from Argyrokastron via Kokovic to Pogoniani and then north to Delvinaki and ending at the Smolika massif; via Sotira to the Tsamanta area; and via Longo and Kokovic to Ayia Marina. The fifth route ran from Leskovic via Barmash to Khionadhes; via Mertzani to Pogonoskos; and via Kline and the Skordili Bridge to Kastaniani. There were also any number of minor routes, including mule paths over the Kazahit, Fushes, and Badra passes and a track over the Kruquit Pass via Slimnitsa to Monopilon.

Some supplies also moved from Albania to the GDA by sea. In 1947 the GDA apparently obtained a few small ships from Albania, and the Albanians were reported to have provided the Greek guerrillas with an old Italian submarine in March 1948.[168] These vessels, crewed by Albanians as well as Greek guerrillas, were used for the movement of supplies from Albanian ports to guerrillas along the Adriatic coast and in the Peloponnesus.

When Yugoslavian support for the Greek rebels faltered in late 1948 and early 1949 as a result of the Tito-Cominform split, Albania became the principal supplier of the GDA. By the summer of 1949 about 90 percent of the aid reaching the Greek guerrillas was being channeled through Albania.[169] Despite Stalin's well-known desire to terminate support by the Soviet satellites to the Greek Communists and the consequent danger to Albania's own political and economic position, the Albanians continued to support the Greek guerrillas right up to August 1949, when it became obvious that the Greek government forces had all but destroyed the GDA and any chance for the success of the Communist insurgency in Greece. On 26 August 1949, General Hoxha announced that all

Greek rebels in Albania would be disarmed and interned. The Albanian Army was incapable of carrying out Hoxha's orders immediately, but an attempt was made to close the border, restrict the movements of GDA elements or concentrate them in camps, and cut off the delivery of supplies.[170]

Bulgaria

From the beginning of the civil war in Greece, the Bulgarians provided the Greek Communist guerrillas with refuge, facilitated transit of the Greek-Bulgarian border, provided arms and other supplies, collected funds, food, and clothing, and offered other assistance. Nonetheless, Bulgarian enthusiasm for supporting the Greek Communists, particularly before the Tito-Cominform split in June 1948, was restrained, and for several reasons.[171] The relationship between Greeks and Bulgarians had been marked by mutual hatred for over a thousand years. The Balkan Wars and the active role played by Bulgaria in the invasion and occupation of Greece during both World War I and World War II had intensified the distrust between the two peoples and their governments. Greco-Bulgarian enmity was further intensified by long-standing Bulgarian claims on Greek territory. Bulgaria desired an outlet on the Aegean Sea, claimed the entirety of western Thrace, and had aspirations to dominate the Slavic separatist movement in Macedonia. Macedonia had been awarded to Greece in the Treaty of London in 1913 following the Balkan Wars, and Bulgaria had lost Thrace to Greece in 1919 following the First World War. In October 1925 Greece had created a free zone at Salonika to provide both Yugoslavia and Bulgaria with an outlet on the Aegean, but that move had satisfied neither the Yugoslavs nor the Bulgarians.

The Communist takeover in Bulgaria occurred later than it did in either Yugoslavia or Albania. The Bulgarian monarchy was rejected by a referendum held in September 1946, and in October a Communist majority was returned in the Bulgarian general elections. In November the Bulgarian Communist leader Georgi Dimitrov assumed control of the Bulgarian government. A nationalist like Tito in Yugoslavia and Hoxha in Albania, Dimitrov despised the right-wing monarchist government in Greece and was therefore favorably disposed to the Greek Communists and willing to support the KKE's armed insurrection, both for ideological reasons and because the Greek Communists might be more amenable to satisfying Bulgarian claims in Thrace and Macedonia.[172]

Even before the Communists came to power in Bulgaria, Bulgaria had hosted and participated in the Petrich meeting in December 1945. Bulgaria also participated in the Bled conference in August 1947. In December 1948, at the Fifth Congress of the Bulgarian Communist Party, the question of increased aid to the Greek guerrillas was raised; the Bulgarian authorities approved a plan to permit the GDA to concentrate forces in an area twenty kilometers north of Momtchilovgrad (Mestanli), where bases for the guerrillas would be established under a group of twenty-one GDA officers to receive arms and ammunition sent from the port of Burgas.[173] The GDA facilities proposed for the Momtchilovgrad area included bases for the GDA 7th and 11th Infantry Brigades and the Mountain Artillery Brigade, a group headquarters, a training center, an evacuation center, and two hospitals.

Although Bulgaria was distant from the major concentration of the GDA in the Grammos and Vitsi in northwestern Greece, where the principal battles of the civil war took place, the Bulgarians provided a variety of support to the Greek Communist guerrillas. Like Yugoslavia and Albania, Bulgaria granted free transit across its borders to the Greek rebels, and GDA forces escaped pursuing Greek government forces by slipping across the border. They maneuvered freely on Bulgarian territory and provided supporting fire from positions in Bulgaria.[174] Armed Greek guerrillas were free to cross the border dividing Bulgaria and Greece at will and without question; unarmed personnel, however, were detained and interrogated by the Bulgarian authorities.[175] The border area itself was sprinkled with logistical facilities of various types—repair shops for weapons, clothing, and shoes; bakeries; and even a veterinary hospital—and the Bulgarian authorities provided the GDA with a variety of equipment and supplies, particularly arms, ammunition, and mines.[176] In mid-1948 the Bulgarian Army also had a detachment of 500 men at Marikostenovo, the duties of whom were reported to be to train and supply the Greek guerrillas.[177] The exact number of Greek guerrillas sheltered, armed, fed, and trained in Bulgaria is not known, but unsubstantiated reports at the time put the total as high as 10,000.[178]

The handling of supplies for the guerrillas was well organized by Bulgarian authorities, and matériel was moved to central depots near the frontier by truck and railroad.[179] One large depot north of Ali Butus was operated by GDA personnel and was organized with separate sections for small arms and small arms ammunition, artillery and artillery ammunition, and rations. From the forward depots the supplies were moved to the frontier under Bulgarian Army control and turned over to the GDA, the main delivery points being at Krasokhori, in the eastern Beles region, in Haidu, and near Sarpidhonia. Until it was overrun by Greek government forces in March 1949, the Angistron-Krasokhori area was a major GDA base, and there was constant communication between Krasokhori and the Bulgarian village of Lehovo just across the border. As UNSCOB reported,

Supplies came by train to Marikostenovo, then by truck to Katuntsi, where there was a large storehouse. From here deliveries were made by night to the guerrillas in Krasokhori by convoys of mules with Bulgarian soldiers in charge. When the guerrillas were firmly in possession of this area, Bulgarian trucks crossed the border into Greece to deliver supplies of arms, ammunition, and food to Angistron.[180]

The Bulgarian government also used private firms to cover the delivery of supplies and equipment to the Greek rebels. In July 1948 the U.S. military attaché in Turkey forwarded a report indicating that the Bulgarian government had sold automobiles to the GDA through an engine repair shop in Sofia operated by one Vasil Kochef Hristoff Mushanoff.[181] The cars had been driven to guerrilla-held areas by Mushanoff's drivers.

In Bulgaria, just as in the other Communist states, both voluntary and involuntary public contributions were taken up to support the Greek guerrillas, the lead being taken by the Bulgarian Red Cross and the *Pomist Organizatsia*.[182] A Bulgarian National Committee for Assistance to the Greek Democratic People was established on 22 December 1947, under the auspices of prominent Bulgarian public figures, including members of the *Sobranje* (Parliament) and Madame Rosa Dimitrova, the wife of the Bulgarian Communist leader. Regional committees were formed; considerable amounts of money, food, and clothing were collected for the GDA; and rallies were held throughout Bulgaria voicing support for the Greek rebels. Bulgarian civil servants and even factory workers were also required to contribute a portion of their salaries to support the Greek rebels. The sale of stamps and coupons was another common technique for raising money for the GDA. One Bulgarian teacher told Greek authorities that he had been required by the inspector of his school district to sell one "Aid to Greek Refugees" coupon worth twenty *levas* to each household in his village, and that if he had been unable to do so, the value of the coupons would have been withheld from his pay.[183]

Sick and wounded Greek guerrillas received medical care in Bulgarian hospitals, and Bulgarian Red Cross ambulance aircraft were used to fly wounded Greek guerrillas from the border regions to hospitals deeper in Bulgaria.[184] The Bulgarian Red Cross was also reported to have donated some four million *levas'* worth of medical and other equipment to the GDA.[185] Recovered guerrillas were returned to the border region by Bulgarian trucks.[186] Berkovitsa was apparently the assembly point for guerrillas being returned to Greece from hospitals in Rumania as well as Bulgaria.[187]

There were numerous GDA training camps, medical facilities, and supply bases in Bulgaria, as shown on Map 4.[188] The largest GDA base in Bulgaria was at Berkovitsa, where at any given time some 300 to 1,000 guerrillas were in training, 800 being the usual complement. The Berkovitsa camp provided reinforcements and supplies for GDA forces in the Haidu, Krasokhori, and Korona areas in particular. Other GDA training camps were located at Doupnitsa, Glavanitsa, Haskovo, Kalyvia Doutra, Katuntsi (Katoundje), Kolibarovo, Malko-Graditse, Mandritsa, Petrich, Pounitza, Slivene, Stara-Zagora, and Turnovo. Rest and transit camps were at Gotsiano, Meden Bouk, Mekrevo, and Voulkovo, and at Byelogradchik there was a camp for noncombatants. GDA hospitals in Bulgaria were located at Asenovgrad, Berkovitsa, Dospat, Glavanitsa, Gorna-Djoumaya, Haskovo, Katuntsi, Kolibarovo, Kostenets, Lehovo, Mandritsa, Marikostenovo, Momtchilovgrad (Mestanli), Nevrokop, Ortakioi (Ivajlovgrad), Oustovo, Petkovo, Petrich, Petrovo, Plovdiv, Satovska, Smolyan, Sofia, and Svilengrad. First-aid evacuation centers were located at Avren, Baroutin, Dospat, Gaitanovo, Gotsevo (Godesevo), Kroumovgrad, Lehovo, Libahovo, Mezek, Pe-

Map 4
GDA Bases in Bulgaria and Entry Routes from Bulgaria into Greece

trovo, Roudozem, and Tchakalarovo. GDA supply centers were located north of Ali Butus and at Baroutin, Berkovitsa, Elhovo, Gaitanovo, Glavanitsa, Ortakioi, Katuntsi, Kolibarovo, Lehovo, Ljoubimets, Mezek, Petrich, Petrovo, Roudozem, Tchamtcha, Tchavbaritsa, Turnovo, and Yanovo.

The Greek-Bulgarian border extends for some 400 kilometers in a generally east-west direction. The western half of the frontier, from the Beles range to the Rhodope range, is mountainous terrain, but the eastern half of the border area is less rugged. Small-scale but widespread Communist guerrilla activity in the border regions caused the Greek government to abandon most of its border posts, and as a consequence most of the Greek-Bulgarian border was easily transited by GDA forces.[189] UNSCOB observers found investigations along the Bulgarian border difficult and were able to collect information only during GNA operations or under heavy escort.[190]

There were four main routes for the movement of men and supplies from Bulgaria to Greece, as shown on Map 4.[191] The first route ran down the Struma Valley from Sofia via Sevtvratch, Marikostenovo, and Koulata to the Angistron-Krasokhori area. The second ran from Roudozem via Rsamadas to the Mount Rhodope area. The third route ran from Kroumovgrad via Auren to the Komotini area. The fourth ran from Ortakioi via Mandritsa to the Evros River area. There were also some indications that supplies were provided to the Greek rebels from Bulgaria by air.[192]

Even after the defeat of the GDA in the Grammos-Vitsi in August 1949 and the consequent collapse of the Communist insurrection, the Bulgarians continued to provide refuge and assistance to Greek Communists, and small groups of Greek Communist guerrillas were reported in Bulgaria well into the 1950s.[193] Only 178 Greek guerrillas were reported to be operating in eastern and central Macedonia and western Thrace in December 1950, but some 2,500 to 3,000 Greek guerrillas were reported to be training in various camps across the border in Bulgaria.[194]

Other Communist States

Although the other satellites of the Soviet Union took their cues from Stalin and generally opposed the Greek Communist insurrection (at least officially), the Greek guerrillas nevertheless received some assistance from Rumania as well as East Germany, Poland, Czechoslovakia, and Hungary. This assistance took the form of hospitalization and medical supplies for wounded guerrillas, training and schools, the collection of money and supplies, and some limited recruiting.[195] Among the supplies received by the GDA from the other Soviet satellite states were such luxuries as coffee and sugar from Czechoslovakia, canned meat from Hungary, and leather jackets from Rumania.[196] The use of facilities in the Soviet satellite states for the training of Greek Communist guerrillas continued well into the 1950s, long after open military insurrection Greece had ceased.[197]

Apart from Albania, Yugoslavia, and Bulgaria, Rumania was the principal

Communist supporter of the KKE/GDA. Greek guerrillas were treated in Rumanian hospitals, Rumanian funds and supplies were collected, and Rumanian citizens were reported to have gone to Yugoslavia and Bulgaria to provide more direct support.[198] A Rumanian National Committee to Aid the Greek People was active in the collection of funds and supplies, and it also coordinated the reception of children evacuated from Greece. UNSCOB reported that after November 1948, numerous sick and wounded Greek guerrillas were treated at Rumanian medical facilities in Bucharest, Brasov, Sinaia, Kasimova, and Moniassa, being returned to Greece via the training camp at Berkovitsa, Bulgaria. Supply dumps were also organized; one in particular, located between Ploesti and Campian, dispatched weapons captured from the Germans by rail to the Greek guerrillas, on a regular basis. The Radio Free Greece transmitter was also relocated from Yugoslavia to a site near Bucharest in 1949. The Rumanians appear to have been especially active in recruiting for the GDA. Greek nationals from Rumania told Greek Army intelligence officers that there was an office in Bucharest for the registration of those who wished to volunteer for service with the GDA, and that a battalion of the Rumanian Army located at Timserva was engaged in the assembly of recruits for the GDA. It was also reported that the Rumanian General Staff had issued orders that forty men from each Rumanian regiment would be detached to form a special contingent to reinforce the GDA.

A delegation of Greek Communists traveled to East Germany in late January 1949, and they were received as "heroes of the struggle for freedom" at a conference of the Socialist Unity Party (SED) in East Berlin.[199] The usual fund and supply drives were conducted in East Germany, and there were reports of East German police and others being recruited, although no East Germans were ever shown to have served with the GDA in the field. In Poland, a Society of the Friends of Greek Democracy raised cash and supplies for the GDA and participated in recruiting activities, as did the Polish Communist youth organization. Czechoslovakia was a principal source for arms purchases by the KKE/GDA. Delegations from the KKE/GDA visited Prague on several occasions to arrange the purchase of weapons and other military supplies; some of these consignments were reported to have been shipped to the guerrillas in the Peloponnesus by submarine. Another purchasing mission is reported to have sought 10,000 automatic weapons and pistols from the famous Skoda works, the weapons to be provided by the Cominform at no cost to the Greek guerrillas. Food, clothing, and medical supplies were collected in Hungary for the Greek guerrillas, Hungarian civil servants had "voluntary" contributions withheld from their pay, and "Aid to Greece" stamps were required for certain official documents, the money supposedly going to the guerrillas.

Western Sources

The degree to which the Greek Communist guerrillas obtained material support from countries other than the Communist states of Eastern Europe and the

Balkans is unclear, but there is no doubt that the KKE/GDA did in fact purchase arms and equipment from commercial firms in the West. In November 1947, for example, the U.S. military attaché in Paris reported on three firms that were accepting orders from KKE representatives: Établissements Jacques Wasser of Paris; J. H. Hilse of Vaduz, Switzerland, and Milan; and Charles English, Ltd., of London.[200] The GDA also appears to have obtained in Italy some of the equipment and supplies it required. In August 1947, the American embassy in Rome reported that the Greek diplomatic representative in Italy had provided information suggesting that the GDA was being supplied from Italy via Albania with new, British-made rifles, machine guns, revolvers, and ammunition.[201] In April 1948 the U.S. naval attaché in Rome reported that many small craft from the Dodecanese Islands were calling at the Italian ports of Brindisi, Bari, and Gallipoli with merchandise for sale on the Italian market, and then loading at night and in secrecy with supplies for the Greek rebels.[202]

The Communist parties in various Western countries also provided some support for the Greek Communist guerrillas, as did the overseas offices of the Federation of Greek Maritime Unions (OENO), the Communist-dominated labor union.[203] For example, a clandestine committee for aid to the guerrillas formed in Belgium collected money and medical supplies and gathered recruits (fewer than a hundred), who were subsequently sent on through France. In 1947 OENO organized an office in Marseilles to collect money and recruits for the GDA, and by late 1948 similar offices were in operation in Buenos Aires, New York, Cardiff, Alexandria, Hamburg, and Genoa. One former OENO leader alleged that the union sent some seven million gold francs to the guerrillas, and there were also reports that OENO carried out undercover missions for the KKE.

The Question of International Volunteers

The possible intervention of an organized Communist international volunteer force remained a preoccupation of both the GDA and the GNF throughout the civil war, although there is no evidence that any serious attempt was made to form such a force.[204] A camp or headquarters for the assembly and training of such a force was apparently established in Toulouse, France, but it never amounted to anything. From time to time the Greek General Staff or Western intelligence agencies reported foreign volunteers serving in the GDA, but such reports usually turned out to be in error. Nachmani notes that some such reports were based on nothing more substantial than unusual clothing or "the fact that they spoke only foreign languages and used foreign expressions, such as that reported by one witness, who heard the *andartes* address their officer as 'comrade captain.'"[205] Even the U.S. embassy in Athens conceded that "foreign nationals occasionally visit guerrilla headquarters south of the frontier, [but] no such persons have been confirmed as fighting with the guerrillas."[206] Although the GNA alleged that the guerrilla operations in Epirus in 1947 and 1948 displayed a level of planning and coordination that the guerrillas could not have achieved by themselves, the UNSCOB observers felt that the guerrilla operations were not "beyond the understanding of any intelligent man who knew the topography of Greece and had been fighting in the mountains." They concluded that "neither the nature of the operations nor the various statements made by the Greek officers, [captured] guerrillas and refugees gave any direct evidence that foreign officers were working with the guerrillas."[207]

Rumors of the imminent arrival in Greece of a well-armed and well-prepared international volunteer army on the model of the International Brigades of the Spanish Civil War served to bolster guerrilla morale—and to diminish morale, when it did not arrive. U.S. military authorities apparently took the rumors seriously and estimated that

international volunteers previously employed under similar circumstances in other countries have been well trained, well equipped and aggressive. It may be assumed that guerrilla volunteers raised to fight in Greece will be experienced soldiers. . . . An increase in volunteer strength to some point between 20,000 and 40,000 would require outside military assistance to prevent the disintegration of the Greek Army and to insure the stability of the present constitutional government in Greece.[208]

There were, of course, Yugoslavian liaison officers as well as occasional Soviet military observers at GDA General Command inside Greece, and both the Greek government and its American ally were convinced that the apparent coordination of the efforts of the various Communist states to aid the Greek Communist rebels would not be possible unless the GDA and the rebellion in Greece was controlled by outside forces.[209] The Greek Communists were, of course, extremely sensitive to such allegations and consistently denied any foreign domination of their movement, as in a letter published in the Communist newspaper, *Rizospastis*, on 22 November 1946:

The HQ of the Democratic Army, Northern Greece, on behalf of all the persecuted people's warriors, who constitute this Army, denies with disgust the lewd calumny that the Democratic Army has relations with or is supplied or directed by foreigners or any foreign country. The chief supplier of arms and ammunition is the British Army of Occupation, through the monarchist bands which they arm; and secondarily the Army and Gendarmerie stores as well as the Gendarmes and soldiers taken prisoner by us.[210]

CONCLUSION

The Greek Communist guerrillas received substantial material support from outside sources, although the external aid received by the GDA was minuscule in comparison to the quantities and types of matériel provided to the Greek Government by Britain, the United States, and other Western nations. The role of the Soviet Union in providing support to the Greek rebels remains ambiguous even after fifty years; Stalin is known to have discouraged aid to the Greek comrades, but there is considerable evidence that much of the matériel channeled to the GDA through its principal supporters—Yugoslavia, Albania, and Bulgaria—and the other Soviet satellite countries may have originated in the Soviet Union and that Soviet military personnel participated in the delivery of it to the Greek rebels. It appears likely that despite his public pronouncements and private instructions to the Yugoslavians and others to terminate their support of the GDA, Stalin nevertheless permitted some limited clandestine support. It is even more likely that the Soviet satellite states—Yugoslavia, Albania, and Bulgaria in particular—were willing to disregard Stalin's orders in pursuit of their own nationalist interests and share with the Greek Communist rebels a portion of the Soviet largess they received.

UNSCOB observers demonstrated conclusively that Yugoslavia, Albania, and Bulgaria not only provided the Greek guerrillas with arms, ammunition, food, and other equipment and supplies, but that they also opened their borders to the guerrillas and permitted the GDA to conduct tactical maneuvers and even to support their operations by fire from positions located inside their territory. Moreover, UNSCOB documented the widespread use of military personnel and government facilities in the three Communist states to assist the Greek insurgents. Diplomatic support and the use of state-controlled media for propaganda purposes, as well as the facilitation of recruitment and the collection of funds, food, clothing, and other supplies for the Greek rebels by quasi-official agencies, were also well documented.

Despite the significant aid provided from beyond the frontiers, the leaders of the KKE/GDA were disappointed that their "socialist comrades" were not more generous, and the inability of the GDA to make good its internal logistical deficits from external sources led ultimately to its defeat and the failure of the rebellion. Had the Greek Communist leaders elected to engage in a sustained guerrilla war rather than form a conventional army, the level of support that their outside supporters were able and willing to provide might have proved sufficient. As it was, the consumption of a large conventional army employing conventional tactics exceeded the types and quantities of logistical support that the friendly neighboring states could or would make available.

In large part, the leaders of the KKE/GDA brought about their own disappointment with outside support. The decision to support the Cominform in its dispute with Tito and the consequent cutoff of Yugoslavian aid and closure of the Yugoslavian border to the GDA in July 1949 is often cited as the turning point in the Greek civil war, as the one event that brought about the defeat of the Communist insurrection in Greece.[211] The loss of Yugoslavian support was indeed a major blow to the GDA, but it must be pointed out that by the spring of 1949, when the decrease of Yugoslavian assistance began to be felt, the Greek national forces had been increased in size, rearmed with American aid, re-energized by General Papagos with the assistance of General Van Fleet and JUSMAPG, and was well on its way to defeating the GDA anyway. By 10 July 1949, when Tito closed his border to the Greek guerrillas and terminated all aid to them, the final, decisive GNF offensive in the Grammos-Vitsi was under way, and for all intents and purposes the issue had already been decided.

NOTES

1. For contemporary U.S. assessments of the political, military, and economic situation in the various Balkan countries see United States Military Attaché–Greece (Capt. Charles M. Conover), Intelligence Report R-571-48 (ID No. 483973), Athens, 3 August 1948, subject: Intelligence Report on Neighboring Countries [in Box 3132, Assistant Chief of Staff, G-2, Intelligence, Numerical Series of Intelligence Document File ("ID Files"), 1944–1955, Record Group 319 (Records of the Army Staff), National Archives II, College Park, MD] [the location of other documents from the "ID Files" will be cited hereafter simply as "in Box *x*, ID Files, RG 319, NA" and on second and subsequent citations such documents will be identified solely by their ID number]; United States Military Attaché–Greece (Col. Harvey H. Smith), Intelligence Report R-28-49 (ID No. 526849), Athens, 20 January 1949, subject: Intelligence Bulletin on Countries Neighboring to Greece Inclosing Greek General Staff Intelligence Bulletin Concerning the States Neighboring Greece ("Information Bulletin on Foreign Situation from 16 July to 30 September 1948," dated 30 September 1948) [in Box 3411, ID Files, RG 319, NA].

2. Amikam Nachmani, *International Intervention in the Greek Civil War: The United Nations Special Committee on the Balkans, 1947–1952* (New York: Praeger, 1990), 3.

3. United States Military Attaché–Greece (Maj. Harold A. Tidmarsh), Intelligence Report R-96-49 (ID No. 538916), Athens, 8 March 1949, subject: Memorandum to UNSCOB from the Greek Government Concerning Aid to Guerrillas, 7 [in Box 3482, ID Files, RG 319, NA].

4. J. C. Murray, "The Anti-Bandit War [Part IV]," *Marine Corps Gazette* 38, no. 4 (April 1954), 60.

5. Frank Smothers, William Hardy McNeill, and Elizabeth Darbishire McNeill, *Report on the Greeks* (New York: Twentieth Century Fund, 1948), 153.

6. On the UN Commission of Investigation and UNSCOB, see the official reports of the two committees (cited below); Nachmani, *International Intervention in the Greek Civil War*; Van Coufoudakis, "The United States, the United Nations, and the Greek Question 1946–1952," in John O. Iatrides, ed., *Greece in the 1940s: A Nation in Crisis* (Hanover, NH: University of New England Press, 1981), 275–97; and Harry N. Howard, *The United Nations and the Problem of Greece*, Department of State Publication 2909, Near Eastern Series 9 (Washington: USGPO [Division of Publications, Office of Public Affairs, Department of State], 1947).

7. The formation and operation of the Commission are described by Howard, who also reproduces the relevant documents, including the Report of the Commission (UN Document S/360, 27 May 1947). According to Nachmani (page 154), the UN Commission of Investigation Concerning Greek Frontier Incidents was, together with the UN Consular Commission on Indonesia, the first instance in which the UN deployed military personnel, even though they acted as observers rather than peacekeepers and operated under the control of their respective national authorities rather than of the United Nations per se.

8. Christopher M. Woodhouse, *The Struggle for Greece, 1941–1949* (London: Hart-Davis, MacGibbon, 1976), 197–98.

9. The central points are contained in Chapter I, Part III: Conclusions, of the Report (UN Document S/360, 27 June 1947), reproduced as Annex 3 in Howard, 52–56.

10. For the text of the proposals, see Howard, 75–77.

11. Nachmani, 155.

12. Ibid., 5 and 37.

13. Ibid., 111.

14. The composition, equipment, and training of the observer teams are discussed by Nachmani, 40–49 passim. The guidance provided to the UNSCOB observers, as well as a general description of the organization of the teams, is recapitulated in United Nations, General Assembly, *Report of the United Nations Special Committee on the Balkans*, General Assembly, Official Records: Fourth Session, Supplement No. 8 (A/935) (Lake Success, NY: United Nations General Assembly, 1949), 21–24 (¶3), and further elucidated in United Nations, General Assembly, *Report of the United Nations Special Committee on the Balkans*, General Assembly, Official Records: Sixth Session, Supplement No. 11 (A/1857) (New York: United Nations General Assembly, 1951), 29–31 (Annex ¶3).

15. Nachmani, 48–49.

16. Ibid., 59.

17. Ibid., 46–48.

18. Lawrence S. Wittner, *American Intervention in Greece, 1943–1949* (New York: Columbia University Press, 1982), 256. See also Lars Baerentzen, "The 'Paidomazoma' and the Queen's Camps," in Lars Baerentzen, John O. Iatrides, and Ole L. Smith, eds., *Studies in the History of the Greek Civil War, 1945–1949* (Copenhagen: Museum Tusculanum Press, 1987), 134.

19. Nachmani, 150.

20. United Nations, General Assembly, *Report of the United Nations Special Committee on the Balkans*, General Assembly, Official Records: Third Session, Supplement No. 8 (A/574) (Lake Success, NY: United Nations General Assembly, 1948), 28 (Chapter IV: Conclusions, ¶188). Insofar as the Communist states simply provided hospitalization and medical treatment of wounded guerrillas, no violation of international law or custom was involved, and the protests of the Greek government and its Western supporters would have received little attention in the international community. However, the sick and wounded guerrillas, restored to health, were assisted in returning to active service in Greece, the outside supporters of the GDA found themselves afoul of international conventions (see ID No. 538916, 11).

21. United Nations, General Assembly, *Supplementary Report of United Nations Special Committee on the Balkans covering the period from 17 June to 10 September 1948*, General Assembly, Official Records: Third Session, Supplement No. 8A (A/644) (Paris: United Nations General Assembly, 1948), 9 (Conclusions, ¶63.III).

22. Woodhouse, 181.

23. Soviet attitudes and actions during the first two rounds of the Greek civil war are summarized in Wittner, 26–27.

24. Dominique Eudes, *The Kapetanios: Partisans and Civil War in Greece, 1943–1949* (New York: Monthly Review Press, 1972), 258.

25. The successive attempts of the KKE leadership to obtain support from the Soviet Union after the meeting of the Second Plenum in February 1946 are described in John

O. Iatrides, "Perceptions of Soviet Involvement in the Greek Civil War, 1945–1949," in Baerentzen, Iatrides, and Smith, eds., 246–48.

26. John O. Iatrides, "Civil War, 1945–1949: National and International Aspects," in Iatrides, ed., 203.

27. Iatrides, "Perceptions of Soviet Involvement," 246.

28. Woodhouse, 230.

29. Iatrides, "Perceptions of Soviet Involvement," 247–48.

30. Wittner, 58–59.

31. Woodhouse, 182.

32. Djilas' account of Stalin's comments are reported in Elizabeth Barker, "Yugoslav Policy towards Greece, 1947–1949," in Baerentzen, Iatrides, and Smith, eds., 272–73; Wittner, 262–63; and Evangelos Averoff-Tossizza, *By Fire and Axe: The Communist Party and the Civil War in Greece, 1944–1949* (New Rochelle, NY: Caratzas Brothers, 1978), 268.

33. Nachmani, 80.

34. Barker, "Yugoslav Policy," 294.

35. Quoted in Woodhouse, 182.

36. Nachmani, 3–4.

37. Quoted in Wittner, 26.

38. Nachmani, 117 and 123.

39. Ibid., 112–14 passim.

40. Wittner, 258–59; Iatrides, "Civil War," 208; Woodhouse, 210–11. Albania was also excluded, but it joined later.

41. Edgar O'Ballance, *The Greek Civil War, 1944–1949* (New York: Praeger, 1966), 150.

42. United States Central Intelligence Agency, *Current Situation in Greece*, ORE 4-50 (Washington: Central Intelligence Agency, 28 February 1950), 9. Both Nachmani (pages 3–4) and Barker ("Yugoslav Policy," 266–67) have noted that Stalin's principal long-term interests in the Balkans involved Rumania, Bulgaria, and access from the Black Sea to the Mediterranean—not Greece.

43. Nachmani, 114.

44. United States Central Intelligence Agency, *Continuing Satellite Aid to the Greek Guerrillas*, ORE 67-48 (Washington: Central Intelligence Agency, 8 October 1948), 1–3; United States Central Intelligence Group, *The Greek Situation*, ORE 6/1 (Washington: Central Intelligence Group, 7 February 1947), 12.

45. Quoted by Iatrides, "Perceptions of Soviet Involvement," 235.

46. Ibid., 237.

47. United States Central Intelligence Agency *Consequences of Certain Courses of Action with Respect to Greece*, ORE 10-48 (Washington: Central Intelligence Agency, 5 April 1948), 5.

48. Wittner, 255.

49. Ibid., 270–71.

50. ORE 67-48, 2.

51. Stephen Merrill, *The Communist Attack on Greece*, Special Report No. 15, 21st Regular Course, U.S. Strategic Intelligence School (Washington: U.S. Strategic Intelligence School, 28 July 1952), 47.

52. United States Military Attaché–Soviet Union (Lt. Col. Peter L. Urban), Intelligence Report R-35-49 (ID No. 536807), Moscow, 3 March 1949, subject: "Russians" in

Greek Guerrilla War, 1 [in Box 3470, RG 319, NA]. The Greek chargé's comments were taken as tending to disprove rumors of Soviet Army officers and men in the front lines in the Greek guerrilla war, although the wounded were alleged to have included aviators and men who had served in the "Vasilovska Partisan Brigade."

53. Averoff-Tossizza, 199.

54. Col. Harvey H. Smith (United States Military Attaché–Greece), "Memorandum of Arrangements, Itinerary and Conversations with House Armed Services and Appropriations Committee," Athens, 19 November 1947, 12 [in Folder 2, William G. Livesay Papers, Archives Branch, United States Army Military History Institute, Carlisle Barracks, PA].

55. United States Naval Attaché–Greece, Intelligence Report GR-37-48 (ID No. 464690), Athens, 12 April 1948, subject: Greece—Naval Section—JUSMAPG Report, ¶1 [in Box 3004, ID Files, RG 319, NA]; United States Naval Attaché–Italy, Intelligence Report R-65-48 (ID No. 465199), Rome, 20 April 1948, subject: Jugoslavia/Greece—Navy—Operations—Movement of Vessels (Delivery of War Materiel to Greek Rebels Organized by Jugoslav Navy Headquarters in Split and Effected by Jugoslav Submarines), 2 [in Box 3007, ID Files, RG 319, NA].

56. Reports of the delivery of supplies by air to the GDA are described in Merrill, 47.

57. Wittner, 163–264 and 275–76.

58. Averoff-Tossizza, 178.

59. The mutual antagonism of Greece and its Slavic neighbors went back to the fourth century A.D. It was exacerbated by Greece's struggle to gain its independence from the Ottoman Empire, the Balkan Wars of 1912–1913, and World War II, in which both Albania and Bulgaria participated with the Axis powers in the invasion and occupation of Greece (see Allison Butler Herrick and others, *Area Handbook for Greece*, DA Pam 550-87 [Washington: USGPO, June 1970], 180).

60. United States Military Attaché–Greece (Col. Harvey H. Smith), Intelligence Report R-188-48 (ID No. 448978), Athens, 16 March 1948, subject: Estimate of the Situation, 32 [in Box 2900, ID Files, RG 319, NA].

61. Nachmani, 126 note 71; Iatrides, "Civil War," 203.

62. Dimitrios George Kousoulas, *Revolution and Defeat: The Story of the Greek Communist Party* (London: Oxford Univ. Press, 1965), 231–32.

63. Averoff-Tossizza, 161–72. Woodhouse (pages 155, 160, and passim) expresses skepticism that the Petrich meeting ever took place: "It seems probable, therefore, that if the meeting at Petrich actually took place in December 1945, it was an occasion at which the KKE bewailed its predicament rather than one at which the Balkan Communists plotted a rebellion in Greece." He also notes that in any event no message from Stalin was received at the meeting.

64. Eudes, 258.

65. UNSCOB Report A/644, 14 (Annex I).

66. Iatrides, "Civil War," 203.

67. Averoff-Tossizza, 199–200.

68. The Bled conference is described in O'Ballance, 150; Averoff-Tossizza, 234–35; United States Army Command and General Staff College, *Internal Defense Operations: A Case History, Greece 1946–49*, USACGSC RB 31-1 (Fort Leavenworth, KS: United States Army Command and General Staff College, 1 November 1967), 132 and 153. O'Ballance (page 150) notes that Soviet officers were also present, and Woodhouse (page

210) asserts that Tito and Dimitrov met at Bled at the same time to sign a preliminary agreement on the long-planned Balkan Federation.

69. *Internal Defense Operations* 153. The "international legion" was supposed to attack Florina in support of the GDA attack on Konitsa in December 1947, but it never materialized—then or ever. The question of international volunteers is discussed in greater detail below.

70. Averoff-Tossizza, 234–35.

71. Ibid., 234.

72. Eudes, 284.

73. Merrill, 35.

74. Nachmani, 115–16; O'Ballance, 124–25; Murray, "The Anti-Bandit War [Part IV]," 53–54.

75. Wittner, 58.

76. Elizabeth Barker, "The Yugoslavs and the Greek Civil War of 1946–1949," in Iatrides, Baerentzen, and Smith, eds., 302.

77. Ibid., 301.

78. Barker, "The Yugoslavs and the Greek Civil War," 301 (citing Vladimir Dedijer, *Novi Prilozi za Biografiju Josipa Broza Tita, Treci Tom* [Belgrade, 1984], 268).

79. Woodhouse, 230–231.

80. O'Ballance, 143.

81. See the successive UNSCOB reports listed in the Selected Bibliography. Two UNSCOB observer groups were deployed along the Greek-Yugoslavian border: Group 2, with headquarters at Kozani and later at Florina, on 22 January 1948; and Group 3, with headquarters at Kilkis, on 6 February 1948 (see UNSCOB Report A/574, 23).

82. UNSCOB Report A/574, 24–25; UNSCOB Report A/935, 14.

83. Cited by Barker, "The Yugoslavs and the Greek Civil War," 302.

84. Ibid.

85. O'Ballance, 158 note 1. According to O'Ballance, the price of this heavy artillery was GDA acquiescence to Yugoslavian territorial claims in Macedonia.

86. UNSCOB Report A/574, 17.

87. Ibid.

88. Merrill, 39. Like most Communist "volunteer" recruitments, those who did not volunteer were accused of lacking "true devotion to democratic principles."

89. UNSCOB Report A/574, 24; UNSCOB Report A/644, 7–8.

90. UNSCOB Report A/574, 18. At some point before 10 July 1949, the guerrilla Radio Free Greece was moved from Yugoslavia to a site near Bucharest, Rumania (see UNSCOB Report A/935, 13).

91. Merrill, 39.

92. UNSCOB Report A/935, 14.

93. Merrill, 39; Kousoulas, 177.

94. The development of the Boulkes camp is described in Eudes, 250–52.

95. United States Military Attaché–Greece (Lt. Col. Allen C. Miller II), Intelligence Report R-426-46 (ID No. 329005), Athens, 27 November 1946, subject: Influence of Foreign Powers in Formenting [*sic*!] the Internal Disorders of Greece, 2 [in Box 2166, ID Files, RG 319, NA]. The grant included twelve farm tractors, 160 horses, and 1,000 oxen; the tract was occupied by fifteen Serbian families, who remained to work the land.

96. Kousoulas, 237.

97. United States Military Attaché–Greece (Maj. Harold A. Tidmarsh), Intelligence

Report R-110-49 (ID No. 542941), Athens, 22 March 1949, subject: Organization of the Bandit Forces and Tactics Employed by the Bandits, 3 [copy in file "Geog. L Greece 370.64." General Reference Branch, U.S. Army Center of Military History, Washington, DC].

98. Quoted by Woodhouse, 191.

99. Merrill, 37. For example, the "Encyclopedia Department" was responsible for military training.

100. ID No. 542941, 12; Woodhouse, 191.

101. Eudes, 251.

102. ID No. 329005, 2; Eudes, 288–90.

103. United States Military Attaché–Greece (Lt. Col. Allen C. Miller II), Intelligence Report R-451-46 (ID No. 329029), Athens, 3 December 1946, subject: Influence of Foreign Powers in Fomenting the Internal Disorders of Greece, 1–2 [in Box 2166, ID Files, RG 319, NA].

104. ID No. 329005, 1–4.

105. Merrill, 38. The training mission was emphasized after the March 1946 visit of Zachariades, who criticized the lack of sufficient attention to military training at the camp.

106. UNSCOB Report A/644, 7; ID No. 542941, 3; ID No. 329023, 2; ID No. 526849, 18.

107. The locations of GDA facilities in Yugoslavia are given in ID No. 538916, ¶II; ID No. 526849, 18; Merrill, Annex I to Appendix I, 1; and Woodhouse, 142.

108. Murray, "The Anti-Bandit War [Part IV]," 60. Murray notes that although the Grammos was supplied almost entirely from Albania, the matériel for the Greek guerrillas did not necessarily originate in Albania, and that before January 1949 the bulk of the supplies entering the Vitsi came from Yugoslavia.

109. The routes from Yugoslavia into Greece are described in UNSCOB Report A/935, 13–14; UNSCOB Report A/644, 8; and ID No. 538916, 10.

110. ID No. 465199, 2; Merrill, 40.

111. Wittner, 58–59.

112. Barker, "Yugoslav Policy," 270.

113. Woodhouse, 230.

114. Quoted by Barker in "Yugoslav Policy," 275.

115. The Tito-Stalin split is summarized in Eudes, 324–25.

116. The pertinent factors are described in ORE 67-48, 3; Murray, "The Anti-Bandit War [Part III]," *Marine Corps Gazette* 38, no. 3 (March 1954), 52; and ID No. 483973, 13–14.

117. Averoff-Tossizza, 278.

118. Regarding the Western offers, see Wittner, 269 and 272–74; Barker, "Yugoslav Policy," 268; and United States Central Intelligence Agency, *The Yugoslav Dilemma*, ORE 16-49 (Washington: Central Intelligence Agency, 10 February 1949).

119. Barker, "The Yugoslavs and the Greek Civil War," 300. Barker puts the Yugoslav decision in November or December 1948, but the defeat of the GDA at Konitsa in December 1947 no doubt began the process of reevaluation (see Averoff-Tossizza, 278).

120. Joze Pirjevec, "The Tito-Stalin Split and the End of the Civil War in Greece," in Iatrides, Baerentzen, and Smith, eds., 316.

121. Merrill, 59; Averoff-Tossizza, 277.

122. Woodhouse, 230.

123. Wittner, 266; United States Military Attaché–Greece (Col. Harvey H. Smith),

Intelligence Report R-130-49 (ID No. 548336), Athens, 11 April 1949, subject: Interrogation of Guerrilla (Ex-GNA) Lt. Z. G. ASTRIHADES, 6 [in Box 3539, ID Files, RG 319, NA].

124. Barker, "Yugoslav Policy," 282–83.

125. UNSCOB Report A/935, 13.

126. Robert W. Selton, "Communist Errors in the Anti-Bandit War," *Military Review* 45, no. 9 (September 1965), 73.

127. United States Military Attaché–Greece (Col. Harvey H. Smith), Intelligence Report R-133-49 (ID No. 548337), Athens, 11 April 1949, subject: Interrogation of Surrendered Guerilla Captain Paragiotis MARGARITOPOULOS (17 March 1949), 4 [in Box 3539, ID Files, RG 319, NA].

128. UNSCOB Report A/935, 13.

129. Ibid., 14.

130. Merrill, 60.

131. Ibid.

132. Ibid.

133. Barker, "Yugoslav Policy," 293.

134. Quoted by Averoff-Tossizza, 279. Tito did not, however, suspend his aid to the Slavo-Macedonian guerrillas of NOF. For example, the medical treatment of sick and wounded Slavo-Macedonian guerrillas continued even after the closure of the Yugoslavian border (see Merrill, 59).

135. Woodhouse, 273.

136. Selton, 76; Murray, "The Anti-Bandit War [Part I]," *Marine Corps Gazette* 38, no. 1 (January 1954), 19.

137. O'Ballance, 195.

138. Merrill, 43.

139. United States Central Intelligence Agency, *Current Situation in Albania*, ORE 71-49 (Washington: Central Intelligence Agency, 15 December 1949), 11.

140. ORE 4-50, 9; Wittner, 279–80; O'Ballance, 199.

141. Capt. Charles T. Katsainos, Memorandum for Record, Washington, 7 October 1949, subject: Greek Deputy Chief of Staff's Interview with U.S. Army General Staff Director of Intelligence, Maj. Gen. Irwin, 3 October 1949, 1 [in file "210.681 Greece to 335.11 Greece {1 January 1949 through 1950}," Box 157 {"000.244 Greece to 560. Greece"}, Assistant Chief of Staff, G-2, Project Decimal Files, 1949–1950, RG 319, NA].

142. United States Military Attaché–Greece (Maj. Paul E. Andrepont), Intelligence Report R-227-48 (ID No. 450800), Athens, 24 March 1948, subject: Albanian Aid to Greek Guerrillas, 2–3 [in Box 2912, ID Files, RG 319, NA]; ID No. 483973, 24–26. See also the successive UNSCOB reports cited in the Selected Bibliography. Two UNSCOB observer groups were assigned to the Greek-Albanian border region: Group 1, based at Ioannina, covered the Epirus section; and Group 2, based at Kozani and later at Florina, covered western Macedonia (see UNSCOB Report A/574, 22).

143. United States Military Attaché–Greece (Maj. Harold A. Tidmarsh), Intelligence Report R-407-47 (ID No. 410405), Athens, 12 October 1947, subject: Greek-Albanian Frontier Incidents, 1 and 5 [in Box 2651, ID Files, RG 319, NA].

144. UNSCOB Report A/935, 9.

145. UNSCOB Report A/574, 23.

146. ID No. 526848, 6; UNSCOB Report A/935, 9.

147. For examples, see Merrill, 45–46; UNSCOB Report A/574, 22; UNSCOB Report A/644, 6–7; UNSCOB Report A/935, 9.

148. UNSCOB Report A/644, 7.

149. UNSCOB Report A/574, 23.

150. Ibid., 17–18.

151. O'Ballance 149 note 2; UNSCOB Report A/935, 9. The Democratic Army Radio (Radio Free Greece) later relocated to Yugoslavia.

152. UNSCOB Report A/935, 11.

153. ID No. 526848, 4–5; Nachmani, 60.

154. UNSCOB Report A/935, 10.

155. United States Military Attaché–Greece (Maj. Paul E. Andrepont), Intelligence Report R-405-47 (ID No. 410407), Athens, 21 October 1947, subject: Albanian Aid to Greek Guerrillas—Evacuation and Care of Wounded Guerrillas in Albania, 1–4 [in Box 2651, ID Files, RG 319, NA]. Slimnitsa was a small village on the Greek-Albanian border that was frequently reported as a collection point for wounded guerrillas. Apostolidis also reported the existence of a GDA hospital in the Grammos, consisting of ten barracks and under the direction of Dr. Sakellariou (the Director of the GDA Medical Service). For a similar example, see United States Military Attaché–Greece (Maj. Paul E. Andrepont), Intelligence Report R-404-47 (ID No. 410408), Athens, 21 October 1947, subject: Albanian Aid to Greek Guerrillas—Evacuation of Wounded Guerrilla into Albania [in Box 2651, ID Files, RG 319, NA].

156. For Soviet deliveries to Albania see ORE 71-49, 8–11. The Albanian Army was itself in particularly poor condition—uniforms of different colors, worn-out shoes, and insufficient rations (see United States Military Attaché–Greece [Col. Harvey H. Smith], Intelligence Report R-27-49 [ID No. 526848], Athens, 20 January 1949, subject: Situation Relative Abducted and Refugee Greeks in ALBANIA, 6 [in Box 3411, ID Files, RG 319, NA]).

157. ORE 71-49, 6–7.

158. United States Military Attaché–Greece (Maj. Harold A. Tidmarsh), Intelligence Report R-154-49 (ID No. 554333), Athens, 27 April 1949, subject: COMINFORM Assistance to the Greek Bandits, 1–3 [in Box 3573, ID Files, RG 319, NA]. Major Tidmarsh's assessment of the article was that "the factual type information contained in this article should be treated with great reserve. . . . [T]o-date [there has been] no firm evidence that supplies have been dropped to guerrillas in Greece."

159. Ibid., 3.

160. For the location of GDA facilities in Albania see Report A/574, 23; UNSCOB Report A/935, 10; ID No. 538916, ¶III; ID No. 450800, 2–3; Merrill, Annex I to Appendix I, 2; and Woodhouse, 142.

161. UNSCOB Report A/574, 23.

162. The Greek-Albanian border region and its transportation infrastructure is described in UNSCOB Report A/574, 21–22.

163. United States Military Attaché–Greece [Col. Harvey H. Smith], Intelligence Report R-666-48 (ID No. 507127), Athens, 13 November 1948, subject: Preliminary Interrogation Report of Captured Bandit, Major REPA, Assistant Intelligence Officer, MARKOS' HQ, 6 [in Box 3286, ID Files, RG 319, NA].

164. The routes from Albania to Greece are described in UNSCOB Report A/644, 6; UNSCOB Report A/935, 9 note 112; ID No. 450800, 3; ID No. 483973, 28; and ID No. 538916, 7–9.

165. United States Military Attaché–Greece (Capt. C. R. Meltesen), Intelligence Report R-298-49 (ID No. 589129), Athens, 8 August 1949, subject: Guerrilla Order of Battle—Strength, Organization and Disposition, 4 [in Box 3781, ID Files, RG 319, NA].

166. Ibid.

167. HQ, JUSMAPG, JUSMAPG Operations Report No. 56 (020001–082400 March 1949), Athens, 11 March 1949, Annex 2 (Intelligence Report for period 020001–082400 March 1949, dated 9 March 1949), 5 [Item 8, Case 8, Book II, Section I-B, file "091 Greece," Box 541, Plans and Operations Division Decimal File, 1949–February 1950, RG 319, NA].

168. O'Ballance, 163; Merrill, 46.

169. ORE 71-49, 11.

170. O'Ballance, 200.

171. The reasons are outlined in *Area Handbook*, 180–81; Nachmani, 115–16; and Merrill, 41–42.

172. O'Ballance, 125.

173. Merrill, 42.

174. Various incidents are described in UNSCOB Report A/574, 26; UNSCOB Report A/644, 8–9; and UNSCOB Report A/935, 11–12. UNSCOB Observer teams 3, 4, and 6 covered the Bulgarian frontier (see UNSCOB Report A/574, 17).

175. Nachmani, 61.

176. Ibid. See also the successive UNSCOB reports in the Selected Bibliography.

177. ID No. 483973, 37.

178. Col. Francis J. Graling (Assistant Executive for Foreign Liaison, Military Intelligence Division, U.S. War Department General Staff), Memorandum for Record, Washington, 14 April 1947, subject: [Conversation with Greek Military Attaché, Col. Solon Grikas, on 14 April 1947] [in file "350.05 Greece," Box 225 ("000.1 Greece to 686. Greenland"), Assistant Chief of Staff, G-2, Project Decimal Files, 1946–1948, RG 319, NA]. The Greek military attaché in Washington, Colonel Solon Grikas, claimed that the 10,000 guerrillas were being assembled in Bulgaria to strike at Xanthe, thereby dividing western Thrace. Of course, no such attack took place.

179. The system by which the Bulgarians supplied the GDA is outlined in UNSCOB Report A/935, 12.

180. UNSCOB Report A/935, 12.

181. United States Military Attaché–Turkey (Maj. M. S. Tyler, Jr.), Intelligence Report R-490-48 (ID No. 481663), Ankara, 19 July 1948, subject: Automobiles Being Sold to Greek Guerrillas by Bulgarians, 2 [in Box 3119, ID Files, RG 319, NA].

182. The organization of fund-raising for the GDA in Bulgaria is described in UNSCOB Report A/574, 15–16; UNSCOB Report A/935, 11; and Merrill, 42.

183. Nachmani, 61.

184. Merrill, 42.

185. UNSCOB Report A/574, 16.

186. UNSCOB Report A/574, 27; UNSCOB Report A/644, 9.

187. UNSCOB Report A/935, 12 and 14; ID No. 483973, 46.

188. The location and nature of GDA facilities in Bulgaria are described in UNSCOB Report A/574, 12 and 27; ID No. 526849, 43; ID No. 538916, ¶III; ID No. 483973, 33; Merrill, Annex I to Appendix I, 1–2; Woodhouse, 142; and Letter, Military Attaché, Royal Greek Embassy Washington (Lt. Col. N. Paparrodou) to Foreign Liaison Officer, Headquarters, Department of the Army, Washington, 18 April 1949, subject: Information

on Rebel Activity, Enclosure [in file "370.6-560. Greece," Box 157 ("000.244 Greece to 560. Greece"), Assistant Chief of Staff, G-2, Project Decimal Files, 1949–1950, RG 319, NA]. Over 2,000 Greek guerrillas were reported at Berkovitsa in March 1949.

189. UNSCOB Report A/574, 25.

190. UNSCOB Report A/644, 8.

191. ID No. 538916, 10–11.

192. United States Military Attaché–Turkey (Maj. M. S. Tyler, Jr., USAF), Intelligence Report R-491-48 (ID No. 481662), Adana, 19 July 1948, subject: Supply of Greek Guerrillas by Bulgaria, 2 [in Box 3119, ID Files, RG 319, NA].

193. United States Army Attaché–Greece (Maj. C. E. Roberts), Intelligence Report R-108-51 (ID No. 762359), Athens, 8 February 1951, subject: Monthly [December 1950] Information on the Internal Situation "C" Corps, 1.

194. ID No. 762359, 6.

195. Merrill, 49.

196. JUSMAPG Operations Report No. 56, Enclosure 1 to Annex 2, 4.

197. See UNSCOB Report A/1857, 16–18 and passim.

198. Rumanian support of the GDA is discussed in UNSCOB Report A/935, 14; ID No. 483973, 46; and Merrill, 50.

199. The support for the GDA provided by East Germany, Poland, Czechoslovakia, and Hungary is described in Merrill, 49–50.

200. United States Military Attaché–France (Maj. John S. Wood, Jr.), Intelligence Report R-802-47 (ID No. 413873), Paris, 13 November 1947, subject: Foreign Firms Supplying Greek Revolutionaries and Situation in Greece [in Box 2669, ID Files, RG 319, NA].

201. Intelligence Requirement Document (Control No. E-777), Chief, Intelligence Group, Intelligence Division, U.S. War Department General Staff (Col. R. F. Innis) to Military Attaché–Greece, Washington, 18 September 1947, subject: Guerrillas in Greek Frontier Region Receiving British-Made Arms [in file "370.64 Greece," Box 225 ("000.1 Greece to 686. Greenland"), Assistant Chief of Staff, G-2, Project Decimal Files, 1946–1948, RG 319, NA].

202. United States Naval Attaché–Italy, Intelligence Report R-68-48 (ID No. 465039), Rome, 20 April 1948, subject: ITALY/GREECE—Commerce, Shipping—Movements of Foreign Commerce Vessels [in Box 3006, ID Files, RG 319, NA].

203. The support provided by OENO is discussed in Merrill, 50.

204. On the question of international volunteers for the GDA see United States Army General Staff, Deputy Director of Intelligence (Brig. Gen. Walter E. Todd), Memorandum for the Chief of Staff, Washington, 24 July 1947, subject: Intelligence Division Special Briefing (Estimate of Effect of the Participation of "International Volunteers" in Greece) [in file "370.2 Greece," Box 225, Assistant Chief of Staff, G-2, Project Decimal File, RG 319, NA]; O'Ballance, 134; Nachmani, 12; and Wittner, 257–58.

205. Nachmani, 60–61.

206. Quoted from a cablegram, dated 27 August 1948, in Merrill, 37.

207. Quoted by Nachmani, 77.

208. Deputy Director of Intelligence, Memorandum for the Chief of Staff, 24 July 1947, ¶¶ 2 and 4.

209. Merrill, 37; O'Ballance, 131.

210. United States Military Attaché–Greece (Lt. Col. Allen C. Miller II), Intelligence Report R-453-46 (ID No. 329018), Athens, 3 December 1946, subject: Proclamation by

"the Democratic Army of Northern Greece" [in Box 2166, ID Files, RG 319, NA]. The letter was dated "Somewhere in Northern Greece, 19 November 1946," and was signed by Ypsilantis and Lassanis for the HQ, Democratic Army, Northern Greece.

211. Murray ("The Anti-Bandit War [Part IV]," 60), for example, cites the withdrawal of Yugoslavian logistical support as "the proximate cause of the guerrilla collapse." See also William Hardy McNeill, *Greece: American Aid in Action, 1947–1956* (New York: Twentieth Century Fund, 1957), 42.

7

The Greek Democratic Army: Strategy, Tactics, and Operations

The fateful political decision of the Greek Communist Party (KKE) leadership in early 1947 to convert a successful guerrilla force into a conventional army employing conventional tactics imposed a heavy logistical burden, one that the Greek Democratic Army (GDA), constrained by a lack of manpower, expertise, and reliable sources of supply, could not meet. Political as well as logistical considerations determined the development of GDA strategy and tactics throughout the "Third Round," and the actual conduct and outcome of military operations between February 1945 and August 1949 clearly portray the impact of the decision to adopt a conventional organization and operational doctrine rather than to retain a less demanding and more flexible guerrilla force.

Until well after the decision of the Politburo in February 1947 to begin the conversion of the GDA to a conventional force, the operational initiative lay with the GDA, but as the process of conversion ran on, and most particularly after the relief of Markos Vafiades as commander of the GDA in February 1949, the initiative shifted to the Greek national forces (GNF). Harried by Communist guerrilla attacks and lacking both experience and aggressive leadership, the GNF were hard pressed initially to prevent the extension of Communist control over most of Greece. By early 1948, however, American military aid, both material and advisory, had begun to have the desired effect. The leadership of the Greek National Army (GNA) was improved by the dismissal of ineffective commanders, and small victories over the marauding Communist guerrillas brought an improvement in morale and increased the effectiveness of government forces in the field. At the same time, the GDA, transformed from an effective guerrilla force into a less than effective conventional army, began to experience the predictable disadvantages of a military organization requiring much heavier logistical support and forced by its doctrine to confront an ever-improving enemy on unequal terms. The failure of the GDA to take Konitsa in December 1947 and its expulsion from its Grammos stronghold in the summer of 1948 clearly revealed the weaknesses of the GDA as a conventional force and the growing strength of the government forces. Once the Greek Communist Party leader, Nikos Zachariades, had disposed of his principal rival, Markos Vafiades, and the GDA was wholly committed to conventional operations, the tide quickly turned in favor of the government forces. The success of the GDA counteroffensives in late 1948 and early 1949 would, in retrospect, be seen as only an "Indian summer" preceding a long, dark winter leading to the decisive defeat of the Communist military forces and the end of the "Third Round" of the Greek civil war in August 1949.

STRATEGY

In July 1946, Markos Vafiades assumed command of the Communist forces in the mountains and began to organize them into a coordinated guerrilla army. Soon after the establishment of the GDA General Command in October 1946, Markos' strategy became clear.[1] First, the GDA established and secured its bases in the mountains and its lines of communications and sources of supply within Greece. Then widespread raids were initiated to obtain recruits, food, and other supplies and to eliminate government personnel and sympathizers. Gradually, the frequency, size, and complexity of these operations expanded, and they compelled the government forces to abandon the smaller villages and concentrate in the towns. The GDA then attempted to isolate the government garrisons, by disrupting and destroying their lines of communications, thereby forcing the complete abandonment of large areas, which then fell under GDA control and administration.

Until mid-1947, the strategy of the GDA remained essentially one of classic guerrilla action, directed not only against the government's military forces but against the Greek economy and the morale of the Greek people as well. Evasion, rather than defense or offense, was its chief characteristic. Raids, ambushes, and acts of sabotage and terrorism, followed by dispersal of the guerrilla forces to avoid decisive contact with government forces, were the usual methods employed. Once the decision was taken to establish a Provisional Democratic Government and to protect its territory with a conventionally organized army, the strategy of the GDA shifted. After February 1947 the principal goal of GDA strategy was to protect and enlarge the territory on Greece's northern borders under Communist control and to secure the GDA's lines of communications across the borders to its sources of support in Albania, Yugoslavia, and Bulgaria. To that end the GDA sought to drive government forces and right-wing bands south of a line from Mount Grammos on the Albanian border to Mount Olympus on the Aegean Sea. However, Markos was compelled to expand his operations into south-central Greece and the Peloponnesus, both to mask the fact that the isolation of Macedonia was his principal objective and to evade the charge that the GDA was controlled by Yugoslavia or intended to sever Macedonia from Greece.[2] Moreover, the Parnon and Taygetos Mountains of the southern Peloponnesus were the home territory of Grivas' X Organization, perhaps the most dangerous opponent of the Communists.[3] Operations outside northern Greece also spread thin the resources of the GNA and thereby facilitated the crucial operations in the north; at the same time they produced a wider base for recruiting and the collection of resources, and they demonstrated to the government and outside observers that the rebellion was spread throughout the country, not confined to the northern border area.[4] Nevertheless, the major operations in 1946 and early 1947 were in the north, and no major battles were fought in southern Greece until after February 1947.

The decision to establish the Provisional Democratic Government carried with it, as Markos had feared, a need to carve out and defend a territory in which the Provisional Democratic Government might establish its writ and thus its legitimacy. Accordingly, the political leadership of the KKE exerted increasing pressure upon Markos and the GDA to take and hold a town of suitable size for use as the capital of "Free Greece." Operations to that end led the GDA to undertake a series of "seize and hold" operations that were unsuccessful and exposed it to the full weight of the GNA's growing conventional firepower. Markos correctly assessed such operations as a threat to the survival of the GDA, but Zachariades and his supporters refused to acknowledge that the GDA was doomed to failure in such operations, instead preferring to blame any shortcomings on "traitors."

On 2 December 1947, Zachariades briefed the KKE Politburo on his plan for carrying out the decisions of the Third Plenum. In addition to imposing the requirement to seize and hold a number of larger towns, Zachariades also directed the GDA to form a strategic reserve of 15,000 men in the Grammos before March 1948.[5] Markos argued against the proposal to concentrate in the Grammos, on the ground that it would require a reduction in forces and operations in other areas, thereby reducing opportunities for recruitment and allowing the GNF to concentrate its forces more effectively, but in the end he was forced to concede to Zachariades' unrealistic proposals. As Dominique Eudes has written,

It was not just that the prodigious revolutionary lesson of ELAS had borne no fruit; the Central Committee had thrown away all the urban support it could have provided for the Democratic Army and was now settling in a more abstract attitude than ever. With the dogged, mournful zeal of Stalinist theorists, the Central Committee was preparing to let its "human engineers" loose on the Democratic Army. Zachariadis had failed to wield either "legality" or the partisan struggle at the appropriate moment; his visions of urban insurrection, of establishing soviets in the army, had withered away in the Athens police files. It only remained for him to mutilate the Democratic Army and apply the strategy used by the Red Army in the plains of the Don to Greek mountain conditions, before the drama could end; before another defeat could pay for the omnipotence of orthodoxy.[6]

The basic GDA strategy of territorial expansion and defense of established base areas in the north, combined with offensive action elsewhere to disrupt and divert the GNF, was initially quite successful, the more so because the GNF counterstrategy was seriously flawed. Throughout most of 1947 the government strategy combined "static defense" of selected areas with "time-limited offensives" to clear the guerrillas from certain areas.[7] The strategy of static defense required enormous manpower and left many areas unprotected from the depredations of the guerrillas, while the conduct of "time-limited offensives" dissipated what little offensive capability the GNF had, in fact it favored the GDA guerrillas, who simply evaded the government sweeps and returned to the target area once the GNF had withdrawn. The choice of the time and place for decisive engagements was thus left almost entirely in the hands of the rebels. It was not until after the arrival in February 1948 of Lt. Gen. James A. Van Fleet to head the Joint United States Military Advisory and Planning Group–Greece (JUSMAPG) that the GNF adopted a more effective strategy, one that would ultimately bring about a decisive defeat of the Communists. Under the direction of General Van Fleet and Gen. Alexander Papagos, the GNF discarded the strategy of "static defense" and "time-limited offensives" and replaced it with a strategy of "staggered offense," designed to extend control progressively over selected areas of the country, beginning generally in the south and moving toward the north.[8] The KKE/GDA underground infrastructure was rooted out, GDA formations were pursued relentlessly night and day, GDA base areas were overrun and destroyed, GDA lines of communications were permanently interdicted, and the GDA was deprived of support by the removal of the entire populations of areas adjacent to its strongholds. By the end of 1948, the futility of the GDA strategy and the effectiveness of the government approach were clear to all but the most purblind Communist ideologues.

TACTICS

"Hit and run" guerrilla tactics employing surprise, shock, and mobility were the hallmark of the GDA from February 1945 well into 1947. Eventually, the combination of several guerrilla units for a given operation became more common, operations became larger and objectives more ambitious, although the guerrillas continued to refuse to engage superior forces and usually dispersed as soon as government reinforcements appeared.[9] Whenever possible, hard-pressed GDA units slipped over the borders to safety in Albania, Yugoslavia, or Bulgaria. In defensive situations the guerrillas made excellent use of terrain, employed effective camouflage and deception techniques, and were adept at exfiltration and evasion.

The hundreds of Communist guerrilla attacks between February 1945 and February 1947 generally followed a set pattern.[10] An isolated and relatively small target (a village or government outpost) was attacked unexpectedly and simultaneously from several directions, the garrison was overrun, and any defenders who survived the initial attack were executed, along with prominent progovernment civilians. Food, weapons, and other supplies were then carried off, and the guerrillas disappeared before any Government relief force could arrive. These tactics proved excellent and were improved as time went on.

By mid-1947, the tactics of the GDA were beginning to evolve from typical guerrilla operations (raids, ambushes, sabotage, and terrorism) toward more conventional techniques employing units of battalion size and higher, and GDA formations were able to retain cohesion under attack and deliver sustained attacks on positions held by the GNF. Already in October 1947, Maj. Gen. Stephen J. Chamberlin, U.S. Army, reported that "guerrilla organization and tactics now tend to approximate formal standards, whereas previously the tactics were to disperse, reassemble and retire across the border and re-enter elsewhere."[11] In his post–civil war writings, Markos deplored the haste with which the GDA had been converted from guerrilla to a conventional army, remarking that the GNA "successfully adjusted to its [the GDA's] tactics." Actually, as Woodhouse points out, "It would have been more accurate to say that the Democratic Army made the more serious error of adjusting to its enemy's tactics."[12]

Indeed, the adoption of conventional tactics placed the GDA at an ever-increasing disadvantage, as GDA light infantry forces confronted the Greek National Army, which, with the aid of American weapons and training, was evolving into a balanced combined-arms team, with significant air and artillery support.[13] Nevertheless, the new GDA tactics were successful for some time. The relatively mobile GDA bases in the mountains were protected by the difficult terrain and an outer ring of GDA units, which forced the government troops to deploy and slow down before encountering the well-prepared inner defenses. Whenever the GNF pressed home its attacks, the GDA held for a limited time and then withdrew, eluding the advancing government forces.[14] Elsewhere, GDA units of battalion size or larger continued to carry out raids on important towns and government facilities, holding them for extended periods and collecting whatever resources they might contain. If the government forces rushing to the relief could not be contained by ambushes, the GDA would once more melt away into the nearby mountains having achieved its purposes. The success of such GDA offensive operations depended on good intelligence and surprise, but once the GNF "staggered offensive" strategy began to take hold, the government forces were able to deny intelligence to the GDA, while improving their own ability to avoid surprise.[15]

OPERATIONS, FEBRUARY 1945–FEBRUARY 1947

The victory of the monarchist Populist Party in the Greek general election of 31 March 1946 led to a significant increase in offensive actions on the part of the Communist-led guerrillas. In fact, the first major guerrilla attack came against the village of Litochoron, on the slopes of Mount Olympus, on the very eve of the election, 30–31 March 1946. Thirty-three men, reputedly led by the well-known *kapetanios* Ypsilantis, assaulted the Gendarmerie post in the village and killed twelve gendarmes before withdrawing. Many of the Communist-led guerrilla bands throughout Greece took the attack on Litochoron as the signal for a general uprising, although in retrospect the action has been assessed as only a warning to the Greek national government, carried out on the orders of Zachariades as an exception to the established KKE policy of political rather than armed struggle.[16]

After Litochoron, the frequency and intensity of GDA attacks increased. The fragile Greek economic infrastructure was further compromised by guerrilla attacks and sabotage against highways, railroads, telephone and telegraph lines, power plants, irrigation facilities, and factories. In some areas, movement of government forces and civilian traffic could be achieved only by armed convoys and then only one or two days per week; by September the GDA forces were able to control most road traffic between Macedonia and Thessaly, by issuing their own passes.[17] For some time the guerrillas directed their attacks on civilians and the Gendarmerie while avoiding direct confrontation with the Greek National Army (GNA), which had become operational with three infantry and four mountain divisions in May 1946. In first week of July 1946, that policy was abandoned, and a GNA company at Pondokerasia was attacked; it lost sixteen soldiers killed and thirty who went over to the guerrillas.[18]

By June 1946 the situation for the government had become serious, provoking a determined effort to root out the guerrillas and their supporters. On 8 June the Greek minister of public order, Napoleon Zervas, the former leader of the right-wing EDES guerrilla army, was forced to admit publicly that the situation in Macedonia was out of hand, and on 18 June the Greek parliament passed a number of more restrictive security measures.[19] However, the National Guard and Gendarmerie were no longer able to contain the more aggressive guerrilla bands, and in the summer of 1946 the GNA assumed control of operations against the Communists. Under Zervas' direction, government forces in July and August 1946 detained over 10,000 suspected KKE "terrorists," many of whom were executed.[20]

During the late summer and early fall of 1946, the GNA carried out a series of clearing operations—JAVELIN in the Grammos (10 August–10 September) and WHIRLWIND in Roumeli (19 September–12 October), followed by sweeps around Mount Pelion in October and Mount Ossa in November—to restore government control in the mountains. However, the guerrillas easily evaded the government troops, and as a result of the failure the Chief of the General Staff, General Ventiris, was replaced by General Giantizis.[21] The plebiscite on the restoration of the monarchy was held on 1 September 1946, and some 60 percent of the voters approved the return of the king. Guerrilla operations again intensified after the plebiscite and the return of King George II to Greece on 27 September 1947, and all but the pretense of a political rather than military solution was dropped by the KKE.[22] On 24 September, Communist-led guerrillas commanded by Lassanis mounted a serious attack on Deskati, a large village at the foot of Mount Hassia in Thessaly, and in early October the GDA undertook its first major attack on an important urban area. Four hundred guerrillas under *kapetanios* Ypsilantis, acting with the support of the local population, seized the town of Naousa, annihilated its National Guard defenders, captured a considerable quantity of arms and other supplies, and disappeared before government relief forces arrived.[23]

By the time the GDA General Command was established in October 1946, the Communist-led guerrilla bands were well established in their mountain hideouts and quite capable of evading the sporadic and halfhearted Government clearing operations. As winter approached, Markos stepped up the tempo of operations, determined to establish GDA control in northern Greece before the winter snows restricted operations.[24] In the first half of November 1946, GDA forces mounted over forty attacks in the regions of Verroia and Katerini alone, including an attack by 600 guerrillas on the Katerini Gendarmerie station.[25] At 0400 hours on the morning of 13 November, the GDA made a strong attack on a GNA company stationed in the village of Skra, on the Yugoslavian border, inflicting heavy military and civilian casualties. Contrary to the previous pattern, the guerrillas held the village for over twenty-four hours; government forces were able to recapture it only at 1400 hours on 14 November. The attack on Skra was significant in that it precipitated the Greek government's appeal to the United Nations to investigate the outside aid being received by the guerrillas.[26] By mid-November the GDA controlled most of northern Greece from Mount Olympus to the borders, and the government acknowledged that it could no longer control large sections of the country.[27]

The GDA remained particularly active in Macedonia, Thessaly, and northwestern Greece throughout the winter of 1946–47; the harassed government forces, most of which were tied down in static defensive positions, completely lost the initiative and watched as additional areas fell to the Communists.[28] The officers of the GNA, the National Guard, and the Gendarmerie strove to maintain discipline and morale while keeping a nervous eye on their own troops, whose loyalty was often suspect, and enduring the frustration of seeing the GDA guerrillas cross the border to safety in Albania or Yugoslavia whenever they were closely pursued. Markos' forces took over a hundred villages in Thessaly and Macedonia alone, and eventually most of the northwestern corner of Greece, including the Grammos and Vitsi mountains and the area along the borders with Albania and Yugoslavia, fell under GDA control.

OPERATIONS, FEBRUARY 1947–FEBRUARY 1949

With the reorganization of the GDA into a conventional army came an intensification of GDA operations involving even larger formations, even more ambitious objectives, and the aim of extending the territorial control of the GDA and Provisional Government. During the first half of 1947 the government forces, inadequately manned, undertrained, poorly led, poorly equipped, and limited by their own defensive mentality, failed to cope with the increased guerrilla aggressiveness.[29] The GNF campaign plan for 1947 was to attack first in central Greece and then move northward gradually to eliminate the guerrillas from the Pindus, Khasia, and Agrapha mountains and seal the northern borders against them. Beginning with Operation TERMINUS in Roumeli on 9 April 1947, the series of operations was bedeviled by bad weather, poor timing and coordination, and timid movements. Forced to garrison contested areas, the GNA expended its manpower in penny packets, leaving fewer troops for offensive operations. The guerrillas escaped the GNF traps. The failure of the government offensives can be attributed in large part to the growing tactical skill of Markos and the officers of the GDA, which for the first time began to operate as a regular rather than a guerrilla force.[30] The 1947 spring and early summer offensives achieved little, and government morale dropped.

King George II died on 1 April 1947, and it was hoped that his successor, King Paul I, could unify the government and people to oppose the Communists. By the summer of 1947, however, the authority of the Greek government was largely confined to the area around Athens, the islands, the larger towns, and— intermittently—the principal lines of communications, while the GDA controlled the border areas, most of northern Greece, and a large part of the Peloponnesus. The growing strength of the GDA was underlined by the shootdown of a Royal Hellenic Air Force (RHAF) Spitfire on 22 May 1947 by GDA antiaircraft artillery.[31] The gloomy situation was reflected by Maj. Gen. William G. Livesay, then commander of JUSMAPG, who wrote to Gen. Omar Bradley, the U.S. Army Chief of Staff, "There is evidence that the bandits' activity has been stepped up and foreign aid to the bandits is becoming increasingly effective. . . . [T]here is little likelihood of the bandits being brought under control before July 1948."[32] The newly formed U.S. Central Intelligence Agency characterized the situation as "a deteriorating stalemate . . . paralyzing national recovery."[33]

GDA operations during the summer of 1947 were increasingly focused on major towns, particularly Konitsa, Kastoria, Florina, and Grevena in western Macedonia, Kilkis north of Salonika, and Alexandroupolis in western Thrace. Although the GDA commanders displayed inexperience in handling large formations and in coordinating their attacks, they pressed the government forces hard, and the Communists gained control of large areas.[34]

The operations in western Macedonia, directed by Markos personally, were aimed at securing a capital for the proposed Greek Communist provisional government. On 28 May 1947 some 650 GDA guerrillas launched an attack on Florina but were repulsed by the 500-man government garrison with the aid of the RHAF. The attack was renewed on 1 June, but the GDA was again repulsed, although the garrison remained cut off for the rest of the summer. The town of Konitsa, eight miles from the Albanian border in northwestern Greece, was considered an excellent location for the proposed Communist capital. On 13 July 1947 the largest GDA force yet assembled for a single operation (some 2,500 men in forty units) advanced in three columns against Konitsa from the Albanian border. GNA forces were swept aside, and the town was surrounded, but for three days the GDA attacked the town without success. After some delay, the government defenders were reinforced by air and by a strong ground column. Unable to maintain the cohesion of his forces, Markos was compelled to break off the attack, and the GDA dispersed. The failure to take Konitsa was due not only to the spirited GNA defense but to hesitation, poor coordination, poor communications, inadequate training in assaulting fortified positions, and inexperience on the part of the GDA forces. Subsequent GDA attacks on Kastoria, Grevena, and Alexandroupolis were also unsuccessful, but the GDA gained valuable experience, and the confidence of the GNF was severely tested. During the fall of 1947, the GDA aggressively pursued a campaign of large-scale "hit-and-run" guerrilla raids, which achieved considerable success.[35] Among the largest raids were those on the village of Deskati, near Mount Khasia in Thessaly, and on the town of Naousa in October. Government garrisons were withdrawn, and Communist control was extended over most of northern Greece, from the Grammos mountains to the Aliakmon Valley.

Despite the GDA successes, during the fall and winter of 1947 the GNF situation improved substantially. The high command was reorganized; a 50,000-man National Defense Corps (*Ethnophroura*) was created to relieve the GNA of its static defense responsibilities; American supplies and equipment began to arrive in quantity; and American tactical advisors joined GNA units.[36] Nevertheless, the morale of government troops ebbed, and the assessments of Western observers remained glum. In August and September 1947 the U.S. State Department began contingency planning for actions in case of a Communist victory, and as late as January 1948, George C. Marshall, the secretary of state, expressed concern about the deteriorating conditions in Greece and the need to bolster the Greek government.[37] Reviewing the operations of the GNF up to 1 October 1947, Lieutenant Colonel Fitzgerald, of the British Military Mission in Greece noted that the

initial operations had been highly successful and succeeding ones less so. There are a number of factors which now limit the success of any operation which is undertaken. These are: lack of sufficient troops for each operation, political interference in the allocating of regular Army units to static defense, and efficient guerrilla intelligence, which thus far has pre-determined imminent areas of government operation and, finally a deterioration in morale due to the extended nature of campaigning in Greece.[38]

The Battle of Konitsa, December 1947

The announcement of the formation of the Provisional Democratic Government of Free Greece on 25 December 1947 was accompanied by a determined major attack by the GDA to seize the northwestern town of Konitsa as its capital.[39] Fourteen GDA battalions (over 2,500 guerrillas), led by Markos, moved south from the Grammos on the night of 24–25 December and, aided by diversionary attacks elsewhere in Thessaly and Epirus, seized control of the approaches to Konitsa, which was defended by a GNA garrison of some 900 men. Amply supplied with men, rations, and ammunition from a forward logistical base in the village of Argyrokastron, just over the border in Albania, Markos employed all of his available artillery and mortars—two batteries of 75 mm mountain guns, three or four 105 mm howitzers, and a variety of mortars—to support a number of unsuccessful attacks on the town from different directions. Delayed by heavy rains, the GNA relief forces moving from Grevena and Ioannina did not appear until 30 December. Abandoning the usual guerrilla tactic of withdrawing before the arrival of superior relief forces, the GDA chose to stand and fight. However, the GNA forces, newly equipped with American weapons and supported by both air and artillery, soon drove the Communist troops from the high ground around the town. After suffering heavy casualties, the GDA began to withdraw on the night of 31 December–1 January. By 7 January 1948 the GNA had cleared the immediate area, although fighting continued until 15 January in the surrounding region. The Greek General Staff later estimated that the GDA had committed 4,000–4,500 men to the battle and suffered 1,169 casualties (400 killed, 746 wounded, and 23 captured), while the GNA had suffered 363 casualties (71 killed, 237 wounded, and 55 missing).[40]

The battle of Konitsa was the largest and most sustained Communist offensive up to that time, and it was a serious defeat for the GDA. The dangers of Zachariades' concept of confronting the GNF in conventional operations were made manifest, and Markos' fears were shown to have a basis in reality, although he continued to be overruled in the councils of the KKE/GDA. As Kousoulas has noted,

The Greek Army, far from being on the verge of disintegration, was growing steadily and rapidly in both strength and experience. The Battle of Konitsa showed that a guerrilla army, acting prematurely as a conventional force, loses most of its tactical advantages when it exposes itself to the superior power of its opponents.[41]

The tide was beginning to turn, but despite its setback at Konitsa in December 1947–January 1948, the GDA continued to hold the initiative until the middle of 1948. However, the successful defense of Konitsa and sporadic victories during the winter, such as the near annihilation of a GDA force on Mount Peira in March 1948, encouraged the government and JUSMAPG to believe that an offensive in the spring of 1948 might deal the GDA a decisive blow, leading to clearing operations and an end to the civil war in the summer.[42] As American advice and equipment began to make themselves felt in the spring and early summer of 1948, the operational initiative began to shift to the GNF.

During the first three months of 1948, the Communist and government forces clashed sporadically in several areas without significant result. The GDA mounted two operations designed primarily for psychological effect. On 5 February a 100-man GDA unit took and held for a short time the village of Pyli on Mount Parnis near Athens, and on 10 February 500 GDA troops converged on Salonika and shelled it, without mounting a ground assault.[43] In February and again in March the GNA attempted to clear the so-called "Mourgana salient" near the Albanian border in Epirus, but neither Operation PERGAMOS (28 February–6 March) nor Operation FALCON (30 March–5 April) produced any substantial result other than heavy government casualties and a further lowering of morale.[44] Indeed, during Operation PERGAMOS a company of the Democratic Youth Battalion overran an entire GNA battalion on the night of 4 March, the first time the GDA had succeeded in a direct confrontation with the GNA.[45]

The real turning point came with the arrival on 24 February 1948 of Lt. Gen. James A. Van Fleet to assume command of JUSMAPG. A vigorous and aggressive field commander, Van Fleet did not hesitate to tell his Greek counterparts what had to be done to defeat the Communists, and they responded to his direction, the more so since he controlled the delivery of war matériel necessary to the enlargement and improvement of the GNF.[46] Woodhouse opines—with more than a hint of British "sour grapes"—that

the improvements introduced by the Joint US Military Advisory and Planning Group (JUSMAPG) were not in the end decisive, because their fruits came too late. It was the Greek high command itself which eventually, at the eleventh hour, achieved its own regeneration; and the new tactics which came near to complete success in 1948 were devised by Greek initiative, with no more than moral support from JUSMAPG.[47]

However, most observers, including many Greeks, attribute the renewal of the Greek government forces and the victory over the Communists in major part to Van Fleet, his American advisory teams, and the flood of American arms and equipment. Working with the better and more aggressive Greek commanders, Van Fleet and JUSMAPG devised the plan for government operations in 1948. It called for an offensive in four phases: (1) to clear the Roumeli region in order to ensure GNF lines of communications between Athens and Salonika; (2) to attack the GDA bases in the Grammos area by early June 1948; (3) to conduct commando operations to clear the Peloponnesus; and (4) to prepare and conduct a winter campaign in the Vitsi area to eliminate the GDA.[48]

Operation DAWN

Spurred on by General Van Fleet's call to "Get out and fight!" the GNF initiated its 1948 campaign by launching Operation DAWN on 15 April 1948.[49] Designed to clear the Communists from Roumeli, Operation DAWN was the first major operation undertaken by the GNF under the new strategy of "staggered offense," with no announced time limit and aggressive, sustained pursuit of the rebels. Some 20,000 men of the I Army Corps (later redesignated A Corps) were involved, reinforced to twenty-seven infantry battalions, sixteen National Guard battalions, six Gendarmerie battalions, two mountain commando (LOK) battalions, forty-eight artillery pieces, and a regiment of armored cars. They moved quickly to establish three concentric lines surrounding some 2,000 GDA guerrillas in the Roumeli region.[50] While two commando groups blocked the mountain passes to the north and the Royal Hellenic Navy in the Gulf of Corinth covered the operation to the south, the GNA 1st, 9th, and 10th Divisions, supported by two commando groups, attacked from the north, east, and west to clear the 4,500-square-kilometer area. Forty days were required to comb the difficult terrain, but when the operation ended on 26 May, it had dealt a serious blow to the GDA. Many of the GDA guerrillas had been able to escape to the north or hide in Roumeli itself, but the GDA underground organization had been broken up, large quantities of supplies had been captured, and the guerrillas had suffered over 2,000 casualties (610 killed, 310 wounded, and 995 *aftoamyna* personnel captured).[51] For the time being, the Roumeli was cleared of organized GDA units, and government communications between Athens and Salonika were reestablished. As Dominique Eudes has noted, "Operation Dawn marked a turning-point in the war . . . the trial of strength between the West's tanks and Zachariadis' orthodox principles. Anglo-Saxon empiricism had adapted itself to the terrain much more thoroughly than the Central Committee's dogma."[52]

Operation DAWN was followed by similar, but smaller, attacks on GDA forces in the Othrys and Agrapha Mountains; neither resulted in a decisive engagement with the guerrillas. During the late spring, the government forces conducted a series of small operations, each of which crept closer to the GDA stronghold in the Grammos, the defenses of which the GDA reinforced to some 6,000 troops by late May 1948.[53] In May the GNA 2d Division began to move into position in western Macedonia to surround the Grammos region. All indicators pointed toward the coming of a major engagement in the area of the Metsovon Pass in the Pindus Mountains and a stubborn defense by the GDA of the Grammos refuge.

Operation CROWN

The major government operation for 1948 was launched on 20 June 1948 and continued in two stages until 21 August. The objective of Operation CROWN (or SUMMIT), was to clear out the main GDA stronghold in the Grammos Mountains.[54] The area of operations took the form of a trapezoid, with three sides of about a hundred kilometers each and a fourth side of some fifty kilometers bordering on Albania to the north. The entire area was extremely rugged, with steep ridges of 1,500–2,500 meters, covered with rocks or dense forests and totally without roads, on the Greek side. An old road, somewhat improved by the Italians during the 1940–1941 campaign, ran along the short face of the area on the Albanian side of the border. The area was an ideal stronghold, in that it was isolated from the rest of Greece but could be supplied from Albania. The GDA defenses, directed from the village of Aetomilitsa and consisting of two lines of fortifications each several kilometers in depth, were strong and well manned. The outer defense ring blocked the passes leading through deep ravines to the interior of the region; the inner ring, protecting the core area, included numerous well-camouflaged machine gun bunkers constructed of logs.

Within the Grammos stronghold, some 11,400–12,500 GDA combatants led by Markos faced some 50,000–70,000 government troops of the B Corps, initially commanded by Lt. Gen. P. Kalogeropoulos, and the A Corps, under Lt. Gen. Thrasyboulos Tsakalotas. The initial GNA deployment consisted of a total of five divisions (some 40,000 men) supported by air, artillery, and a full complement of logistical units, with an additional 7,500 GNA and 4,500 National Guard troops to protect the government lines of communications in Epirus. The GNA plan called for a three-phase operation: (1) to clear areas near the main GDA base; (2) to attack and occupy positions along the GDA outer defense belt; and (3) to cut the lines of communications between the Grammos and GDA support bases in Albania, followed by a general assault from all directions against the GDA inner defenses. The main attack was entrusted to Kalogeropoulos' B Corps, while Tsakalotas' A Corps was assigned the mission of protecting the lines of communication and dealing with the GDA units in Epirus.

Markos knew of the GNA plans. Consequently, he reinforced his two lines of defense and kept some 3,000 men, under the experienced Yiannoulis, in Epirus to interdict GNA supply lines once the battle began. The initial government attacks proceeded slowly, hampered by the well-prepared and tenaciously held GDA defenses among the rocky peaks as well as by poor leadership, a lack of aggressiveness, inadequate communications, poor coordination, and the diversion of GNA troops to protect lines of communication against the effective attacks of Yiannoulis' guerrillas. Temporarily halted, the GNA paused to reorganize and revise its plan of attack. The offensive resumed on 28 June, but despite determined attacks by government forces well supported by tactical airpower, a stalemate ensued as both sides attempted to reinforce their positions.

The government offensive resumed on 15 July, and in very heavy fighting between 26 July and 1 August the key GDA position on 6,000-foot Mount Kleftis overlooking Konitsa and controlling access to the Grammos was finally taken by the GNA. At General Van Fleet's insistence, Lieutenant General Kalogeropoulos was replaced as commander of B Corps by the vigorous Lt. Gen. Stylianos Kitrilakis, and the equally aggressive Lieutenant General Tsakalotas moved northwest with the bulk of the government forces in hand to take a more prominent part in the main battle. The GDA finally abandoned the heights of Golio, Kardari, and Steno on 7 August, thereby uncovering the GDA inner defense line. On 17 August the heights of Kamenik were taken. After two months of fighting, the remaining 9,000 GDA guerrillas found themselves cornered at the top of Mount Grammos by some 90,000 government troops, who paused on 19 August to reorganize for the final assault.

Facing overwhelming numbers of government troops, Markos ordered a general withdrawal on 18 August. On the night of 20 August his forces broke through the GNA troops blocking the small gap at the northern end of the Grammos near Slimnitsa, and by 22 August some 1,500 of the GDA defenders had slipped over the border into Albania with all of their artillery and some 3,000 wounded, while the bulk—some 6,000–8,000 guerrillas—moved off directly into the alternate GDA stronghold in the Vitsi region—a move anticipated by the B Corps commander, Lieutenant General Kitrilakis, who was, however, unable to prevent it. Operation CROWN officially ended on 21 August 1948. The GNA left one division in the Grammos to deter any return by GDA guerrillas, and a reinforced GNA division moved to attack the GDA positions in the Mourgana area. In two months of hard fighting the government forces had lost some 7,000 casualties and the GDA nearly 10,000, including 2,000 captured or surrendered.[55]

In Operation CROWN, for the first time in the war, the GNA was heavily supported by RHAF aircraft, including two squadrons of Spitfire fighter-bombers based at Ioannina and Kozani, respectively.[56] The RHAF aircraft, employing strafing attacks, rockets, fragmentation bombs, and—for the first time on 20 June—napalm, wreaked serious damage on GDA installations and troops. The RHAF flew 3,474 sorties during Operation CROWN, a daily average of 53.6, reaching a peak during the month of August, when 1,570 sorties were flown. GDA antiaircraft fire hit twenty-three Spitfires, including one that was shot down in flames, with the loss of its pilot.

Operation CROWN has been characterized as "the largest, the most difficult, the longest, and the most deadly battle of the entire war."[57] The GDA's stubborn defense of the Grammos stronghold against overwhelming government forces and its subsequent escape through Albania to the Vitsi were viewed by Zachariades as a sign of the strength and vitality of the GDA and of its conventional organization and tactics. The failures to hold the various positions on the peaks of the Grammos were attributed to tactical ineptness or even treason; several GDA commanders were unjustly tried and executed, including Brigadier Yiannoulis, who was charged with having yielded the key height of Mount Kamenik, which had been viewed by some as the key to the Grammos stronghold.[58] On the other hand, Markos, who had conducted a brilliant if unsuccessful positional defense, correctly interpreted the results of Operation CROWN as a serious defeat for the GDA and an indicator of troubles to come.[59]

From the government point of view, the successful campaign in the Grammos did not bring about any fundamental change in the situation. Despite its growing size and material advantages, and despite its steady improvements in leadership, morale, and aggressiveness, the GNF continued to find that superior numbers and firepower did not bring the hoped-for degree of success against the GDA. The ability of the GDA to take refuge in nearby Albania, Yugoslavia, and Bulgaria was particularly galling, and like many of their GDA counterparts, several GNA commanders were accused of a lack of aggressive leadership.[60] The escape of the GDA from the GNA operation in the Grammos, its stand in the Vitsi, and its eventual reoccupation of the Grammos were viewed by the Greek government and its American ally as collectively "a bitter disappointment."[61]

The Vitsi Campaign, Fall 1948

The Communist forces that escaped from the Grammos through Albania began to reemerge on 25 August in the Vitsi, where they joined their comrades who had proceeded directly to the Vitsi and the GDA forces already established there. Having been forced to abandon their headquarters at Aetomilitsa, the Provisional Democratic Government and the GDA General Command reestablished themselves in the village of Pyxos, near Lake Prespa, and began to reassemble and reorganize their forces. Like the Grammos, the Vitsi was well fortified, and the number of GDA defenders quickly rose to over 12,500.[62] On 29 August, one week after the end of Operation CROWN, the GNA launched a strong attack against the Vitsi position, but the government troops were tired, and the GDA troops defended their base tenaciously.[63] The strong defense, poor weather, and a lack of aggressive leadership retarded the GNA advance. Even so, the government forces were within two kilometers of cutting the GDA line of communications into Albania when on 5 September a determined GDA counterattack drove them back to their original positions. The GNA managed to recover some ground, but on 20 September Markos launched eight battalions supported by thirty field guns against the flank of the GNA forces facing the Vitsi. However, the GDA was also exhausted, and the counterattack soon ran out of steam. Meanwhile, between 6 and 16 September the GNA had also attacked the 1,500 GDA guerrillas remaining in the Mourgana salient on the Albanian border, but the results were inconclusive. Both sides were then forced to pause and catch their breath.

GDA Counterattacks, Fall–Winter 1948

The GDA had weathered the government offensive in the Grammos and Vitsi in the summer of 1948, but it had suffered its first serious losses.[64] During late September and early October, Markos reorganized his forces—now numbering some seventy-five to eighty battalions—and prepared them for operations to recover the lost territory in northwestern Greece. Having repulsed a GNA commando attack on Mount Vitsi on 18 October, the GDA surged forward against the tired government troops and regained most of the territory lost during the summer before being forced to halt due to exhaustion, casualties, loss of good leaders, and logistical shortages.[65] Meanwhile, the GDA had reoccupied the Grammos by infiltrating through the two GNA divisions guarding the area, and by late 1948 three GDA brigades had reestablished the guerrilla stronghold there.[66] With major operations out of the question for the time being, the GDA concentrated on sabotage and classic small-scale guerrilla attacks. On 29 October the government was forced to extend martial law over the entire country.[67]

During the last two months of 1948 and into January 1949, GDA attacks on major towns throughout Greece increased significantly; many of the places attacked, such as Siatista in Macedonia and Voulgareli, the birthplace of Napoleon Zervas in Epirus, were held for one or two days.[68] The last operation, under Markos' direction, was yet another attack on Grevena, in the Metsovo region, at the beginning of November 1948. The GDA force, 400 men strong, took the town, stripped its arsenal, and recruited a hundred men before departing unscathed.[69] Not all the GDA attacks were successful. On 10–11 November, a GDA unit took the height of Bikovik overlooking the town of Kastoria, but the position was retaken three days later by a determined GNA counterattack that has been characterized as "the National Army's El Alamein, redeeming the Tobruk which they had suffered in Vitsi."[70] On 1 December, 183 of a force of a thousand GDA guerrillas were annihilated by "a deluge of napalm" on the outskirts of Serres.[71]

Determined to take his revenge for the unsuccessful attack on Konitsa in December 1947, Zachariades initiated a series of bloody attacks on towns in December 1948 that killed large numbers of civilians and severely damaged government morale. The most serious of these attacks was carried out by some 6,000 GDA troops against the town of Karditsa, on the plain of Thessaly, a town then swollen to a population of 50,000 by refugees from other areas and defended by a reinforced GNA battalion (55 officers and 860 men).[72] Four GDA infantry brigades, a cavalry brigade, a three-gun mountain battery, and a section of the GDA Officers' School, all commanded by Kostas Karageorgis, blocked the approach routes, snapped up the government outposts, and struck the town on the night of 11–12 December. Karageorgis' troops seized the town and held it until early on 13 December, being dislodged only after an eighteen-hour battle. In the process the guerrillas lost some 600 men and women and inflicted some 200 casualties on the garrison. They also killed thirty-seven civilians, wounded another 105, and abducted 980, over a third of whom were women. The railway station, two flour mills, and forty houses were set afire, and the hospital was sacked. The raid on Karditsa represented, as Woodhouse has written, "a compromise between the doctrines of Markos and those of Zakhariadis . . . a guerrilla operation under a divisional command: the order of battle was that of Zakhariadis, the tactics those of Markos."[73] It also demonstrated the threat that the GDA continued to pose to the government's ability to control its larger towns.

On 21–22 December, three GDA brigades attacked the important towns of Edessa and Naousa on the road from Salonika to Florina.[74] The assault on Edessa failed, but Naousa was taken and held for three days; the guerrillas departed on 26 December with sixty new recruits, food, and a large quantity of medical supplies looted from the hospital. The same three GDA brigades retook Naousa, then defended by a 900-man GNA garrison, on 11–12 January 1949 and held it for another three days. The GDA attackers again escaped in good order on the night of 14–15 January with large quantities of supplies and over 600 recruits, their tracks being covered by a blizzard. The GDA brigades lost 177 killed and seventy captured or surrendered during the battles for the two towns.

Meanwhile, the GDA forces that had attacked Karditsa on 11–12 December moved south through the Pindus Mountains and reached the area of Karpenision, an important town on the road from Larissa to Agrinion, on 5 January.[75] On the night of 19–20 January, the force of more than 3,000 Communist fighters, led by two of the best GDA brigade commanders, Diamantis and Yiotis, attacked the town, and by 21 January they had overwhelmed its 1,400 defenders. The town was pillaged and partly burned, and the GDA brigades held it for eighteen days until 8–9 February, when they were forced to withdraw by superior GNA forces led by General Tsakalotas. No other town was held for so long during the entire civil war. The GDA abducted 500 hostages and conscripted some 1,300 men before fleeing, their withdrawal once again being conveniently covered by a snowstorm. Credit for the victory went to Zachariades' supporter, Major General Vlantas, but the attack on Karpenision was the last major offensive that the GDA would be able to mount in central Greece.[76]

Operation PIGEON

While the more or less conventional operations of 1947 and 1948 unfolded on the mainland, the GDA continued to employ guerrilla tactics with considerable success in the Peloponnesus. Small bands of thirty to a hundred guerrillas suffused the area, attacking at times and places of their choosing and withdrawing before being decisively engaged by the government forces. By late 1948 there were some 4,000 GDA combatants active in the Peloponnesus.[77]

Having already suppressed the right-wing terrorists of Grivas' X organization in the southern Peloponnesus, the Greek government undertook to eliminate the Communist menace on the peninsula. Operation PIGEON began on 19 December 1948 with a force of some 11,000 men, including the entire GNA 9th Division and several mountain commando (LOK) units, under the direction of the commander of A Corps, Lieutenant General Tsakalotas.[78] The operation was to proceed in two phases: (1) a main effort to clear the northern part of the peninsula supported by a secondary effort to neutralize the guerrillas in the south; and (2) a thorough sweep from north to south to clear out the guerrillas.

The execution of Operation PIGEON was nearly flawless. The Greek navy secured the coasts of the Peloponnesus, particularly along the Gulf of Corinth in the north, to prevent reinforcement or resupply of the GDA forces and to prevent their escape by sea. One of General Tsakalotas' first measures, taken without consultation with his superiors on the night of 28–29 December, was to arrest some 4,000 suspected members of the *aftoamyna*. Many of them were quickly deported to detention camps on the islands, thereby depriving the guerrilla combatants of their intelligence and logistical infrastructure. General Tsakalotas' bold stroke against the GDA infrastructure in the Peloponnesus was a major factor in the decisive results of his campaign, the second phase of which began on 3 January with aggressive clearing operations. Proceeding in a methodical manner, Tsakalotas' forces hunted down the guerrillas, few of whom escaped the net. The strongest GDA brigade in the Peloponnesus was destroyed at Ayios Vasileios on 22 January, and by 25 March 1949 the Greek General Staff estimated that no more than 250 GDA guerrillas remained in the Peloponnesus. In seven weeks the GDA lost 679 killed, 1,601 captured, and 628 surrendered.[79] In addition, the *aftoamyna* apparatus in the Peloponnesus was completely destroyed. Having attained his objectives, General Tsakalotas left the mopping-up to mobile Gendarmerie detachments and groups of armed peasants under regular army officers.

OPERATIONS, FEBRUARY–AUGUST 1949

The dismissal of Markos Vafiades as commander in chief of the Communist forces in January 1949 and the assumption of direct command by Nikos Zachariades completed the conversion of the GDA from a reasonably effective guerrilla army to a weak and increasingly ineffective conventional force. Zachariades' strategic policy of sustained attacks against well-defended urban areas, along with a static defense of the Grammos and Vitsi, concentrated the lightly armed GDA and exposed it to the devastating effects of the GNF's superior numbers, massive artillery, and aerial firepower. Foiled at Florina in February 1949, the GDA lost the operational initiative and began a short but precipitous drop to its final defeat by government forces in the Grammos and Vitsi in the summer of 1949.

The Battle of Florina, 12–15 February 1949

The Fifth Plenum, meeting at the end of January 1949, adopted a six-point military plan for 1949. Entirely unrealistic, this plan called for the GDA to (1) continue its attacks on urban areas throughout the country; (2) continue to enlarge the amount of territory in northern Greece under KKE/GDA control; (3) continue to harass the GNF in Thessaly and Roumeli; (4) continue pressure on Salonika; (5) create a new front in the Peloponnesus; and (6) create a third front by a mass uprising in the cities and countryside.[80]

Eager to achieve a spectacular victory and thus prove his military skill as well as the correctness of his decision to relieve Markos as commander of the GDA, Zachariades committed the GDA to a major attack on the town of Florina on 12 February 1949 with the ultimate objective of advancing swiftly to take Salonika and all of northern Greece.[81] Advancing down the Pisoderi Gorge from their base some twenty-five miles away in Albania, 4,000 troops of the GDA 10th and 11th Divisions, reinforced by additional combat and support units and commanded by George Gousias, opened the attack at 0330 hours on 12 February with an artillery barrage of some 1,500 shells. The 10th Division, which consisted of the 14th and 103d Brigades, two saboteur companies, one antitank company, one antiaircraft artillery platoon, and one anti–armored car artillery troop, made the supporting attack. The 11th Division made the main attack; it consisted of the 18th and 107th Brigades, two saboteur companies, one antitank company, one antiaircraft artillery platoon, one anti–armored car artillery troop, a battalion from the Kaimaktsalan Headquarters, two cavalry squadrons, three and a half mountain artillery troops, one transport battalion plus one truck company, and one stretcher-bearer battalion. The leading brigade of the 11th Division entered the southern part of the town at dawn, while the other 11th Division brigade seized the surrounding heights and blocked the approach routes. Winter weather slowed the approach of government relief forces, but the GNA division garrisoning the town, commanded by General Nicholas Papadopoulos (known as "Grandfather" because of his luxuriant mustaches), was well supported by the RHAF, which fired rockets and dropped bombs and napalm on the advancing guerrillas. The assault was stopped, and by 1900 hours the GNA forces had the situation in hand and had inflicted heavy casualties on their attackers. The GDA attacks petered out over the next two days as government reinforcements arrived to drive the guerrillas out of Florina and the surrounding mountains. By 15 February the GDA forces were beginning to disintegrate, and the guerrillas retreated in panic back up the Pisoderi Gorge, leaving behind a good deal of new arms and other equipment.

GDA casualties in the battle of Florina were heavy. In all, 799 guerrillas were killed, about 1,500 were wounded, and 350 were captured or surrendered.[82] GDA casualties included one brigade commander killed and over 400 frostbite casualties in one brigade alone. One GDA unit (425th Battalion, 18th Brigade, 11th Division) lost 25 percent of its strength in the first three hours of the attack.[83] In addition, the GDA lost four 81 mm and one 60 mm mortars, eighteen machine guns, ninety Bren guns, 120 submachine guns, 405 rifles, 441 antitank rockets, 126 mines, 460 81 mm mortar rounds, 200 60 mm mortar rounds, 103,000 Bren gun rounds, 210 hand grenades, 133 prepared charges, 160 "Molotov cocktails," and twenty mules.[84] Government casualties amounted to forty-four killed, 220 wounded, and thirty-five missing in action.[85]

The first battle directed by Zachariades thus ended in a serious defeat rather than the hoped-for spectacular victory. It did not, however, appear to shake Zachariades' confidence in his own skills or in the correctness of his organizational and tactical doctrines. Instead, speaking to key GDA leaders on 5–6 March, he blamed the GDA defeat on faulty leadership, inadequate supervision by senior commanders, inadequate staff ability at brigade and division level, poor preparation for administration and communications, a low standard of execution, failure of reserves to intervene at the proper time, and "unacceptable revival of guerrilla type warfare."[86] Ignoring the obvious defects of his own doctrine, the inability of the GDA to endure prolonged fighting against superior forces, and the constant government artillery and air bombardment, he stated,

Basically the plan was sound. . . . [W]e lost the battle of Florina on account of inadequacy in war technique and lack of leadership all along the line. Our men did their job. The main objectives were captured, but the leadership lacked an active and decisive intervention right at the moment it was necessary in order to continue the success. The battle of Florina showed that, as far as staff and operational ability is concerned, we have not learned to fight with skill, and this evil can and must be eliminated by using the experience of Florina as well as that of our entire Army, [however] positive or negative this experience might be.[87]

From the government point of view, the battle of Florina was a great success. For the first time in the civil war, the GNF had a clear-cut victory and had seized the initiative from the GDA. In the first flush of victory JUSMAPG reported that the

operation at Florina is first major engagement between Guerrilla and GNA forces since announcement of relief of Markos as Guerrilla leader. Crushing defeat to Guerrilla forces at Florina may weaken prestige of new Guerrilla High Command to such extent as to create lack of confidence throughout Guerrilla elements in Greece. Every effort being made to have GNA take advantage this opportunity by aggressive action in all sectors particularly in Vitsi. . . . Political repercussions within and without Greece may be great.[88]

According to General Van Fleet,

The defeat of the guerrilla forces at Florina was the first successful operation against bandit attacks on large villages. While many tactical errors were made, I consider the operation very successful, first, because plans had been drawn for the defense of Florina, secondly, orders when issued were obeyed, third, the training paid off, fourth, morale of the GNA and the Greek civilians was improved, and last but not least, about 1,000 bandits were eliminated.[89]

Florina was the last major GDA attack on a large defended town and, with few exceptions, the last GDA offensive outside the stronghold in the Grammos and Vitsi. However, despite the growing difficulties of recruiting and of assembling sufficient troops for a sustained offensive, Zachariades continued to urge the faltering GDA forward. To augment his declining forces, Zachariades was forced to shut down the eight GDA training centers in the mountains. The men and women from these centers were formed into "old style" guerrilla units, and the officer cadets were used to reinforce the Grammos.[90] On 19 March the GDA launched an abortive attack on Arta, but the guerrillas were forced to retreat toward the southeast, into Agrapha.[91] On 1–2 April a large GDA force moving in from Albania and supported by artillery attacked GNA forces at Alevitza, near Mount Grammos, the main attack being supported by secondary attacks on the GNA rear by GDA forces also from Albania.[92] On 5 May two GDA brigades took the small village of Neo Petritsi, in eastern Macedonia, and held it for twenty-four hours; on 15 May a 700-man GDA brigade took the village of Metaxades and held it for three days; and on 20 June a GDA brigade seized a GNA frontier post on the Bulgarian frontier in the Beles Mountains, but the guerrillas were forced out the following day.[93] In May and June the GDA also conducted diversionary attacks between Florina and Amynataion to relieve pressure on the Vitsi stronghold.[94] These attacks achieved nothing of permanence and served only to sacrifice GDA fighters uselessly. Indeed, casualties on both sides were heavy during the first four months of 1949. Between 20 January and 20 April, the GNF lost 4,332 officers and men, but the GDA losses were much heavier—on the order of 14,237, of which 6,225 had been killed, 8,011 combatants had been captured or surrendered, and 1,559 *aftoamyna* personnel had been taken into custody.[95]

The 1949 Government Campaign Plan

After Florina the initiative passed to the GNA, which henceforth could dictate the times and places of operations. In late March 1949, General Van Fleet developed a campaign plan for 1949. Van Fleet's plan was to use the 50,000-man National Defense Corps to free the GNA from its static defense obligations, contain the GDA in northern Greece with minimum forces, and conduct mobile operations with the bulk of the 147,000-man GNA to: (1) clear the Peloponnesus; (2) clear central Greece; (3) attack and clear the GDA strongholds in the Grammos and Vitsi; and (4) mop up the remaining Communist guerrillas throughout Greece.[96] Tactically, the four phases of the campaign would be conducted by first rounding up all suspected *aftoamyna* personnel and other Communist sympathizers in the area of operations; advancing on a broad front and in depth; acting vigorously with mobile forces; and pursuing the Communists day and night.[97] The destruction of the *aftoamyna* was a very important first step to dealing with the main GDA forces, in that it would deprive them of intelligence, recruiting, and logistical support.[98] The British Military Mission strongly opposed Van Fleet's plan, citing the urgent necessity to first cut the GDA's supply lines with the neighboring Communist states, but in the end Van Fleet was able to persuade General Papagos and the Greek General Staff, and the campaign plan, chistened Operation ROCKET was adopted.[99]

Operation ROCKET, 25 April–31 July 1949

By the end of April 1949, the first phase of the Government's 1949 campaign plan—the clearance of the Peloponnesus (Operation PIGEON)—had been completed, and on 25 April the GNF launched Operation ROCKET to clear the GDA from central Greece.[100] The GNA A Corps, commanded by the aggressive Lieutenant General Tsakalotas and consisting of nearly 50,000 men well supported by artillery, armor, and airpower, first blocked the mountain passes leading into northern Greece and then on 5 May launched its main attack. Facing the government onslaught were some 12,000 GDA combatants under the general command of Kostas Koliyannis, who had replaced Karageorgis as commander of the Echelon General Headquarters, Southern Greece.

Koliyannis' forces included the remnants of the GDA 1st and 2d Divisions, commanded by Yiotis and Diamantis respectively, a cavalry brigade, and area

236 The Withered Vine

forces. Yiotis and Diamantis, two of the GDA's best field commanders, recognized the danger and recommended that the GDA forces break up into small, 80 to 120-man groups and try to avoid contact with the advancing government troops. The government forces also formed small groups to hunt down the guerrillas relentlessly, and the operation devolved into a series of skirmishes spread over three months. On 21 June Diamantis was killed, and the GDA defense began to disintegrate. By the end of July Tsakalotas' forces had driven the remaining GDA guerrillas north of the Aliakmon River; central Greece, Thessaly, and the southern Pindus Mountains were clear. GDA casualties as a result of Operation ROCKET were 1,059 killed, 2,558 captured, and 1,021 surrendered.[101] Among the dead were the commander of the GDA 2d Division (Diamantis), three brigadiers, nine lieutenant colonels, eighteen battalion commanders, forty company commanders, and fifty-one other officers, plus four doctors.[102] Koliyannis, Yiotis, and a small group of 250 to 300 guerrillas managed to escape the trap and made their way with great hardship to the Grammos. The surviving guerrillas in Central Greece were scattered and incapable of organized operations.

Operations ARIS and AJAX

Constant pressure by government forces in the second quarter of 1949 kept the Communist forces constantly on the move; by the end of June the GDA was unable to operate freely and was being contained effectively in the northern border areas. Consequently, the number and frequency of GDA offensive actions declined significantly between March and July 1949. The total number of incidents in June 1949 was 159, thirty-nine less than in May and forty-eight less than in March.[103] At the same time, the remaining GDA units were being compressed back into the Grammos-Vitsi stronghold. In early April 1949 some 65 percent of the GDA was disposed on the northern borders; three months later, much of southern and central Greece had been cleared by government forces, and 90 percent of the GDA combatants were on the northern borders, about 12,000 of them in the Grammos and Vitsi.[104]

To prepare for the main operation in the Vitsi and Grammos, the GNF conducted a number of smaller operations to clear critical areas on the periphery of the rebel stronghold. Between 5 and 12 May 1949, the GNA C Corps conducted Operation ARIS to bring the GDA forces in the Angistron-Krasokhori area to battle and destroy them.[105] Although the number of Communist guerrillas killed and captured was small (226 killed and ninety-eight captured or surrendered), the operation was successful and took a very important GDA base area. A considerable amount of arms, ammunition, and other supplies were captured by the GNA. In Operation AJAX on 4–8 July 1949, C Corps successfully attacked the GDA forces in the Kaimaktsalan Mountains east of the Monastir Gap to relieve guerrilla pressure on Edessa and Ardhea, destroy the guerrilla base, and interdict the guerrilla lines of communications through the Kaimaktsalan from the Vitsi to Tzenapaikon.[106] Some 125 guerrillas were killed, sixty-three were captured, and forty-one surrendered, and the GNA took a huge quantity of supplies and equipment (estimated at over 1,000 mule loads).[107] The GDA survivors moved over the border into Yugoslavia, where they were disarmed. Operation AJAX was particularly important in that it physically separated the GDA forces in the Beles Mountains on the Bulgarian border from the main body in the Grammos and Vitsi and thus created a number of command and control and logistical problems for the GDA, while leaving the government forces free to concentrate on reducing the Grammos-Vitsi stronghold.[108]

Operation TORCH, August 1949

The GNA plan for Operation TORCH, the major thrust to drive the GDA from its bases in the Grammos and Vitsi mountains on the Albanian-Yugoslav border, envisioned a diversionary attack on the Grammos (TORCH A) followed by the main assault on GDA forces in the Vitsi (TORCH B) and a subsequent thrust to clear the Grammos (TORCH C).[109] Six GNA divisions of A Corps, commanded by Lieutenant General Tsakalotas, and B Corps, commanded by Lieutenant General Maniadakis, reinforced by mountain commandos, artillery, armor, and air power, were assembled for the main operation. The 1,200 GDA guerrillas remaining in the so-called Beles Pocket to the east of the Vitsi along the Bulgarian border were to be dealt with in a separate operation carried out by C Corps, commanded by Lt. Gen. T. Grigoropoulos and consisting of two divisions and two independent infantry brigades (see Map 5).

Facing the government forces were some 7,500–8,000 GDA combatants in the Vitsi and another 5,000 in the Grammos, all of whom had been ordered to defend their bases "without any thought of withdrawal."[110] Apparently, Zachariades and his senior commanders hoped to hold out until winter weather forced the government forces to end their operations; then they would conduct a counteroffensive to defeat the GNA, take the urban areas, and enlarge the territory of Free Greece. Zachariades and his adherents were nothing if not optimists. The rank and file of the GDA shared that optimism, and their morale remained strong despite the odds against them.

The diversionary attack in the Grammos (TORCH A) began on 5 August and lasted a week, but it made little progress. However, several key positions were taken, and the GDA lines of communications into Albania were threatened. Attacks continued in the Grammos as phase two of the operation (TORCH B) got under way. By 10 August the GNA A Corps under Lieutenant General Tsakalotas was able to turn toward the heavily fortified, 375-square-mile Vitsi. The fighting in the Vitsi was terrible, as the GDA defenders—supported directly for forty-eight hours at one point by Albanian troops—defended their base bravely and fiercely. On 14 August the GDA forces counterattacked from the Grammos toward Konitsa but were driven back with heavy losses. On 16 August the remnants of six GDA brigades withdrew from the Vitsi. Some 4,000 guer-

Map 5
Operation TORCH, August 1949

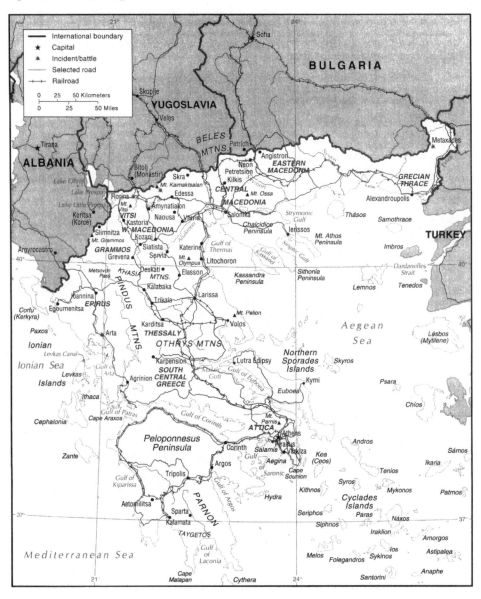

rillas managed to reach the Grammos through Albania to await the final government onslaught. Another thousand fled into Yugoslavia, where they were disarmed and interned. The Provisional Government abandoned its capital at Pyxos and took refuge in Albania.

GDA casualties during TORCH B included 997 killed, 509 captured, and 133 surrendered, as well as twenty Albanian soldiers killed and seven captured.[111] The GDA 14th, 105th, and Officer School Brigades lost 50 percent of their strength, and only the 103d Brigade was able to withdraw into Albania with most of its personnel and equipment intact. As might be expected, no member of the KKE Politburo, the Supreme War Council, or the GDA high command was among the dead. The GDA also lost forty-three artillery pieces, 115 mortars, one 75 mm antitank gun, two antiaircraft guns, twenty-five antiaircraft machine guns, ninety-six heavy machine guns, 300 light machine guns, 142 rocket launchers, and 3,392 rifles, plus 1,650 mines and well over 7,500 artillery shells. Government forces lost 229 killed, 116 wounded, and three missing.

Having cleared the Vitsi, the government forces paused to reorganize and prepare the final assault. On 19 August the GNA C Corps launched a supporting attack against the remaining GDA forces in the Beles Mountains on the Bulgarian border. The guerrillas held for four days under a devastating ground and air attack before the one thousand survivors retreated over the Bulgarian border, aided in their crossing by Bulgarian troops, who had also fired on GNA forces from Bulgaria.[112]

The final assault on the 220-square-mile Grammos region began on the night of 24–25 August, supported by several heavily armed Curtiss divebombers newly arrived from the United States.[113] The GDA defenders numbered 7,000–8,000 combatants in three understrength divisions (nine brigades) plus the remnants of the five brigades that had escaped from the Vitsi. The government forces available to General Ventiris, the overall GNA commander, included five divisions (fifteen brigades) reinforced by four regiments of mountain infantry, five regiments of field artillery, three medium artillery batteries, five mountain artillery batteries, a battery of antitank guns, and a regiment plus two squadrons of armor.[114] Outnumbering the GDA forces ten to one, the GNA advanced steadily, taking many of the key GDA positions on the first day. Indeed, the battle was decided on 25 August. The GDA position on Mount Grammos itself fell on 27 August, and the following day the GNA sealed off the two main passes into Albania—Starias and Baroukas. The GDA defenders hung on for three more days before yielding the last strongpoint, Mount Kamenik, on the morning of 30 August. The fighting ceased at 1000 hours on 30 August, and some 8,000 GDA fighters fled over the border into Albania, where they were subsequently disarmed by Albanian forces. In this final phase of Operation TORCH the GDA suffered some 1,694 casualties (847 killed, 741 captured, and 106 surrendered), while government forces lost 221 killed, 1,309 wounded, and seven missing.[115] Enormous amounts of GDA arms and equipment were captured, including twelve artillery pieces, eleven 120 mm mortars, 125 heavy mortars, thirty-five light mortars, sixteen antiaircraft guns, two antiaircraft machine guns, seven antitank guns, eighty-five heavy machine guns, 489 light machine guns, fifty-eight miscellaneous automatic weapons, and 2,206 rifles.[116] The Grammos had become the tomb of the GDA rather than of "monarcho-fascism," as the KKE Politburo had so confidently predicted.[117]

Operation TORCH was successful in every respect, destroying the "impregnable" GDA fortress in the Grammos and Vitsi and driving the remaining GDA forces into exile in Albania. Zachariades' ideologically motivated decision to stand and conduct a conventional static defense of his bases in the Grammos and Vitsi had produced the disaster predicted by Markos Vafiades long before. In twenty-one days of heavy fighting the Communist forces lost 1,919 killed and 1,586 prisoners along with fifty-seven artillery pieces, 216 heavy mortars, 102 light mortars, twenty-one antitank guns, 142 rocket launchers, nineteen antiaircraft guns, 227 heavy machine guns, 416 light machine guns, more than 6,000 rifles, and enormous amounts of ammunition, food, and other supplies.[118] Government casualties during Operation TORCH included 472 killed, 2,568 wounded, and 14 missing.[119]

CONCLUSION

With the successful conclusion of Operation TORCH on 31 August 1949, the victorious government forces were redeployed to seal the borders and to clear the remaining scattered guerrilla bands from the interior. On 26 August, just as the final battle in the Grammos began, Radio Tirana announced that the Communist leader of Albania, Enver Hoxha, had ordered that any Greek guerrillas entering Albania would be disarmed and detained.[120] Fearing an invasion by the Greek national forces, Hoxha also halted all firing from Albania in support of the GDA. Bulgaria soon followed suit, at least publicly, and on 1 October the Soviet Union rejoined the UN Commission on the Balkans and issued appeals for reconciliation.[121] Even so, Zachariades and his supporters continued to hold out hope for a resumption of the fight. Bulgaria remained friendly; Rumania promised assistance. With some 8,000–8,500 personnel in Albania, 5,000 in Yugoslavia, 3,000–3,500 in Bulgaria, and some 1,000 still at large, although scattered and demoralized, in Greece itself, the GDA remained in existence.[122] However, the Sixth Plenum of the Central Committee of the Greek Communist Party met on 9 October 1949, and the decision to discontinue temporarily the armed struggle was taken, perhaps at Stalin's insistence.[123] On 16 October, Radio Free Greece announced,

The Greek Provisional Government is ceasing hostilities to prevent the total destruction of Greece. The Democratic Army has not laid its weapons aside, but has suspended its operations for the time being. This should not be taken to mean that the Greeks are giving up the struggle for the rights of the people. The Anglo-American Imperialists and their monarcho-fascist agents would be mistaken if they assumed that the struggle was over and that the Democratic Army had ceased to exist.[124]

Despite Zachariades' threat of continued armed action, the Greek government and its American ally were confident of their victory.[125] On 7 November 1949 the Intelligence Division of the U.S. Army General Staff issued an estimate of the situation in Greece that declared, "The Greek Government is now able to control the present situation and will probably be able to cope with any likely guerrilla threat in the foreseeable future, and [is] also on a course to relieve the economic strain of maintaining large military forces to the detriment of national recovery."[126] The same month, President Harry Truman announced to Congress the victory in Greece. The Greek civil war was over.

NOTES

1. The development of GDA strategy is outlined in Christopher M. Woodhouse, *The Struggle for Greece, 1941–1949* (London: Hart-Davis, MacGibbon, 1976), 179; Edgar O'Ballance, *The Greek Civil War, 1944–1949* (New York: Praeger, 1966), 143; J. C. Murray, "The Anti-Bandit War [Part I]," *Marine Corps Gazette* 38, no. 1 (January 1954), 16–17; Amikam Nachmani, *International Intervention in the Greek Civil War: The United Nations Special Committee on the Balkans, 1947–1952* (New York: Praeger, 1990), 11–12; and United States Military Attaché–Greece (Maj. H. A. Tidmarsh), Intelligence Report R-698-48 (ID No. 515268), Athens, 10 December 1948, subject: Review of GNA Operations during the Summer of 1948, 5 [in Box 3341, Assistant Chief of Staff, G-2, Intelligence, Numerical Series of Intelligence Document File ("ID Files"), 1944–1955, Record Group 319 (Records of the Army Staff), National Archives II, College Park, MD. The location of similar documents from the "ID Files" will be cited hereafter simply as "in Box *x*, ID Files, RG 319, NA," and on second and subsequent citations such documents will be identified solely by their ID number.

2. United States Central Intelligence Group, *The Greek Situation*, ORE 6/1 (Washington: Central Intelligence Group, 7 February 1947), 12.

3. Dominique Eudes, *The Kapetanios: Partisans and Civil War in Greece, 1943–1949* (New York: Monthly Review Press, 1972), 177.

4. Woodhouse, 231–32; J. C. Murray, "The Anti-Bandit War [Part IV]," *Marine Corps Gazette* 38, no. 4 (April 1954), 54–55; O'Ballance, 130; Nachmani, 12.

5. Eudes, 304–305.

6. Ibid., 303.

7. Dimitrios G. Kousoulas, *Revolution and Defeat: The Story of the Greek Communist Party* (London: Oxford University Press, 1965), 241–42.

8. Ibid., 258–59. General Van Fleet arrived in Greece on 24 February 1948. General Papagos, the hero of the World War II Albanian campaign, was reappointed as commander in chief of the government forces on 21 January 1949, but he had played an active role in the development of GNF strategy for some time before that date.

9. For a detailed description of GDA tactics, see United States Military Attaché–Greece (Maj. E. A. Tidmarsh), Intelligence Report R-110-49 (ID No. 542941), Athens, 22 March 1949, subject: Organization of the Bandit Forces and Tactics Employed by

the Bandits, 14–20 [in File "GEOG. L. Greece 370.64 (Guerrillas)," General Reference Branch, US Army Center of Military History, Washington, DC], and E. E. Zacharakis, "Lessons Learned from the Anti-Guerrilla War in Greece (1946–1949)," *Revue Militaire Générale* 7 (July 1960).

10. The pattern is described in Evangelos Averoff-Tossizza, *By Fire and Axe: The Communist Party and the Civil War in Greece, 1944–1949* (New Rochelle, NY: Caratzas Brothers, 1978), 173 and 176, and M. A. Campbell, E. W. Downs, and L. V. Schuetta, *The Employment of Airpower in the Greek Guerrilla War, 1947–1949*, Project No. AU-411-62-ASI (Maxwell Air Force Base, AL: Concepts Division, Aerospace Studies Institute, United States Air University, December 1964), 4–5 [cited hereafter as *Employment of Airpower*].

11. Extract-Summary of the Report of Maj. Gen. Stephen J. Chamberlin to U.S. Army Chief of Staff, 20 October 1947, Summary ¶1, 1 [in file "GEOG. L. GREECE 370.02 (Civil War)," General Reference Branch, United States Army Center of Military History, Washington, DC] [cited hereafter as Chamberlin Report].

12. Woodhouse, 212. The only real adjustment made by the GNA was the creation in early 1947 of the mountain commando units (LOK), which achieved some success in harassing the guerrillas but were unable to carry out sustained offensive operations (see Woodhouse, 212–13).

13. J. C. Murray, "The Anti-Bandit War [Part II]," *Marine Corps Gazette* 38, no. 2 (February 1954), 52.

14. O'Ballance, 177–78.

15. Ibid., 178.

16. Woodhouse, 169–70; Eudes, 262.

17. Theodossios Papathanasiades, "The Bandits' Last Stand in Greece," *Military Review* 30, no. 11 (February 1951), 22; Woodhouse, 184.

18. Nachmani, 10–11; Woodhouse, 179.

19. Stephen Merrill, *The Communist Attack on Greece*, Special Report No. 15, 21st Regular Course, U.S. Strategic Intelligence School (Washington: U.S. Strategic Intelligence School, 28 July 1952), 25.

20. O'Ballance, 148; Woodhouse, 209.

21. Woodhouse, 185 and 209.

22. ORE 6/1, 4.

23. Eudes, 273; Averoff-Tossizza, 173. The rebels had besieged Naousa earlier, on 6–8 August 1946, without suffering significant losses (see Woodhouse, 184).

24. O'Ballance, 128.

25. United States Military Attaché–Greece (Lt. Col. Allen C. Miller II), Intelligence Report R-461-46 (ID No. 329020), Athens, 4 December 1946, subject: Monthly Estimate of the Situation (November 1946), 5–6 [in Box 2166, ID Files, RG 319, NA].

26. Ibid., 3.

27. Merrill, 26–27; O'Ballance, 128–29.

28. O'Ballance, 133–35.

29. Ibid., 161. The authorized strength of the GNA was increased to 120,000 in March 1947 and to 130,000 plus 20,000 recruits in October of that year (see Draft Memorandum for Record, [Athens], 6 October 1947, subject: Conversation—Greek Minister of War Mr. Stratos with Major General Chamberlin—6 October 1947, 1 [in file "091.41-092.–Greece, 1 January 1946–31 December 1948," Box 225, Assistant Chief of Staff G-2 Project Decimal Files, 1946–1948, RG 319, NA]). Although after February

1947 the Communist military forces were evolving toward a conventional army employing conventional tactics, the use of the term "guerrillas" to denominate the Communist regular forces will be retained herein as a matter of convenience and to distinguish them more clearly from the regular forces of the GNA.

30. Woodhouse, 207.

31. Ibid., 206. Eventually, the RHAF would lose fifty-four aircraft to GDA gunners plus another 495 aircraft damaged.

32. Notes by Maj. Gen. William G. Livesay for Gen. Omar N. Bradley, Athens, 10 September 1948 [*sic!* should be 1947], subject: Review of the Military Situation in Greece, 1–2 [in Folder 2, William G. Livesay Papers, Archives Branch, United States Army Military History Institute, Carlisle Barracks, PA].

33. United States Central Intelligence Agency, *The Current Situation in Greece*, ORE 51 (Washington: Central Intelligence Agency, 20 October 1947), 4–5.

34. Operations in the summer of 1947 are described by O'Ballance, 145–47; Eudes, 294–95; and Woodhouse, 207.

35. O'Ballance, 126 and 156–57.

36. United States Central Intelligence Agency, *Current Situation in Greece*, ORE 28-48, (Washington: Central Intelligence Agency, 17 November 1948), 3–4.

37. Wittner, 232.

38. Quoted in Lt. Col. Theodore J. Conway (JUSMAPG), Memorandum for Record, Athens, 1 October 1947, subject: Conference Held at British Military Mission (Greece), 1 October 1947, ¶5 [in file "091.41-092.–Greece, 1 January 1946–31 December 1948," Box 225 ("000.1 Greece to 686. Greenland"), Assistant Chief of Staff, G-2, Project Decimal File, 1946–1948, RG 319, NA].

39. The battle for Konitsa is described in O'Ballance, 160–62; Eudes, 308–309; and United States Military Attaché–Greece (Maj. Harold A. Tidmarsh), Intelligence Report R-42-48 (ID no. 432477), Athens, 21 January 1948, subject: Battle of Konitsa [in Box 2786, ID Files, RG 319, NA].

40. ID No. 432477, 6.

41. Kousoulas, 249–50.

42. O'Ballance, 162. A GDA winter recruiting expedition led by Paleologos ended in disaster on the heights of Mount Peira on 11–12 March 1948, when the survivors of a long march in terrible weather were surrounded by GNA forces and all but annihilated. Paleologos started out with 1,500 men and recruited another 1,000, but he returned to his base with only 1,200, the remaining 1,300 having succumbed, four-fifths of them to starvation and the cold (see Eudes, 311–12).

43. Averoff-Tossizza, 256–57.

44. Ibid., 257–58.

45. Ibid., 257.

46. Floyd A. Spencer, *War and Postwar Greece: An Analysis Based on Greek Writings* (Washington: European Affairs Division, Library of Congress, 1952), 114–15; Frank J. Abbott, *The Greek Civil War, 1947–1949: Lessons for the Operational Artist in Foreign Internal Defense*, School of Advanced Military Studies thesis (Fort Leavenworth, KS: School of Advanced Military Studies, U.S. Army Command and General Staff College, May 1994), 18–19.

47. Woodhouse, 238.

48. Abbott, 18–19.

49. Operation DAWN is described by Kousoulas, 255 and 257; Abbott, 19–21;

Averoff-Tossizza, 258–60; Eudes, 320; Woodhouse, 239–40; Merrill, 63–64; and ID No. 515268.

50. Averoff-Tossizza (page 258) put the number of GDA personnel in the region at 3,800 fighters and an additional 2,000 self-defense (*aftoamyna*) auxiliaries.

51. Averoff-Tossizza, 260. The Greek General Staff estimated that about 800 guer-rillas escaped, many of them during a GDA preemptive attack on the B Commando Group lines on the night of 14–15 April at the very beginning of the operation. See Maj. Gen. A. R. Bolling (Deputy Director of Intelligence, Office of the Assistant Chief of Staff, G-2 Intelligence, U.S. Army General Staff), Memorandum for the Chief of Staff, Washington, 20 April 1948, subject: Intelligence Division Special Briefing—Greek Army Spring Offensive Begins (in file "381. Greece," Box 225 ["000.1 Greece to 686. Green-land"], Assistant Chief of Staff G-2 Project Decimal File, 1946–1948, RG 319, NA).

52. Eudes, 320.

53. Col. Carter W. MacGruder (Deputy Director of Intelligence, Office of the As-sistant Chief of Staff, G-2 Intelligence, U.S. Army General Staff), Memorandum for the Chief of Staff, Washington, 21 May 1948, subject: Intelligence Division Daily Briefing—Current Developments in the Greek Military Situation (in file "350.09 Greece," Box 225 ["000.1 Greece to 686. Greenland"], Assistant Chief of Staff G-2 Project Decimal File, 1946–1948, RG 319, NA).

54. Operation CROWN is described by Abbott, 21–23; Kousoulas, 254 and 260; O'Ballance, 170–73; Woodhouse, 240–43; Eudes, 326–28; and Averoff-Tossizza 280–86.

55. O'Ballance (page 173) gives the GNA losses for the eight-week battle as 801 killed, about 5,000 wounded, and 31 missing, and GDA casualties as 3,128 killed, 589 captured, and 603 surrendered.

56. *Employment of Airpower*, 43–45 and 52.

57. Averoff-Tossizza, 280.

58. United States Military Attaché–Greece (Col. Harvey H. Smith), Intelligence Re-port R-666-48 (ID No. 507127), Athens, 13 November 1948, subject: Preliminary Inter-rogation Report of Captured Bandit, Major REPA, Assistant Intelligence Officer, MARKOS' HQ, 7 [in Box 3286, ID Files, RG 319, NA].

59. Kousoulas, 260.

60. Abbott, 25.

61. Wittner, 244.

62. O'Ballance, 174.

63. The fighting in the Vitsi is described by Wittner, 243; Murray, "The Anti-Bandit War [Part I]," 18; Abbott, 23–26; O'Ballance, 173–74; and Eudes, 333.

64. Wittner, 245.

65. Averoff-Tossizza, 300–301; O'Ballance, 176.

66. Abbott, 27.

67. O'Ballance, 176.

68. Averoff-Tossizza, 311; Eudes, 339.

69. Eudes, 304.

70. Woodhouse, 246.

71. Eudes, 339. O'Ballance (page 184) put the GDA losses at 389, of whom 183 were killed.

72. The attack on Karditsa is described by Woodhouse, 256–57; Averoff-Tossizza, 309–10; Eudes, 339–40; O'Ballance, 183; and Kousoulas, 261–62.

73. Woodhouse, 257.

74. The Edessa and Naousa operations are described by Kousoulas, 261–62; Eudes, 339–40; Averoff-Tossizza, 310; and O'Ballance, 184.

75. The attack on Karpenision is described by Averoff-Tossizza, 325–27; Woodhouse, 260–61; Kousoulas, 262; and Eudes, 340.

76. Averoff-Tossizza, 325; Woodhouse, 261.

77. Abbott, 30.

78. Operation PIGEON is described by Abbott, 30–34; Kousoulas, 266; O'Ballance, 188; Eudes, 340; Merrill, 63; and Averoff-Tossizza, 311–12.

79. Woodhouse, 261.

80. Ibid., 263.

81. The Battle of Florina is described by O'Ballance, 189–90; Averoff-Tossizza, 327–28; and Letter, Lt. Gen. James A. Van Fleet (Director, JUSMAPG) to Maj. Gen. R. T. Maddocks (Chief, Plans and Operations Division, Headquarters, Department of the Army), Athens, 22 March 1949, subject: Guerrilla Attack on Florina, 12 February 1949, Summary 1 [in file "319.—Reports—Florina Operation 1949," Box 55 ("1949: 311.–319.1"), Joint United States Aid Group–Greece General Decimal Correspondence File, RG 334 (Records of Interservice Agencies), NA].

82. Letter, Van Fleet to Maddocks, 22 March 1949, Summary 1.

83. United States Military Attaché–Greece (Col. Harvey H. Smith), Intelligence Report R-130-49 (ID No. 548336), Athens, 11 April 1949, subject: Interrogation of Guerrilla (Ex-GNA) Lt. Z. G. ASTRIHADES, 6 [in Box 3539, ID Files, RG 319, NA].

84. Letter, Van Fleet to Maddocks, 22 March 1949, Summary Tab A (HQ JUSMAPG Detachment B, [Col. Jesse L. Gibney], Situation Report, Kozani, 21 February 1949, subject: SITREP—110001 to 142400 February 1949, SITREP—150001 to 172400 February 1949, and Special Operations Report—Florina Operation), ¶8.

85. Ibid., Summary 1.

86. United States Military Attaché–Greece (Col. Harvey H. Smith), Intelligence Report R-273-49 (ID No. 576384) Athens, 13 July 1949, subject: Guerrilla Strategical and Tactical Problems, 1948, 10–11 [in Box 3707, ID Files, RG 319, NA].

87. Ibid., 11.

88. Chief, United States Army Group–Greece, to Chief, Plans and Operations Division, Headquarters, Department of the Army, Message No. L-2694, Athens, 15 February 1949, 1–2 [Item 7, Case 4, Section I-A, Book I, File "091. Greece (Incoming Messages)," Box 541, Plans and Operations Division Decimal Files, 1949, RG 319, NA].

89. Letter, Van Fleet to Maddocks, 22 March 1949, 1. The GNA victory was due in large part to good intelligence work (see Woodhouse, 262).

90. Averoff-Tossizza, 338.

91. Woodhouse, 269.

92. Letter, Lt. Col. N. Paparrodou (Military Attaché, Royal Greek Embassy, Washington), to Foreign Liaison Officer, Headquarters, Department of the Army, Washington, 22 April 1949, subject: Albania's Support to Communist Guerrillas, with two enclosures (Information Sheet, dated 22 April 1949, "Rebels Attack of April 1–2, 1949, on Mt. GRAMMOS," and Information Sheet from letter dated Washington, 5 April 1949, on same subject) [in file "370.6-560.," Box 157 ("000.244 Greece to 560. Greece"), Assistant Chief of Staff, G-2, Intelligence, Project Decimal File, 1949–1950, RG 319, NA].

93. O'Ballance, 194.

94. Woodhouse, 269.

95. Averoff-Tossizza, 334.

96. *Employment of Airpower*, 30; Papathanasiades, 23.

97. Papathanasiades, 23.

98. O'Ballance, 192–93.

99. Abbott, 34. The overall campaign between April and September 1949 was known as Operation ROCKET, but the same code name was also used for the second phase of the campaign—the operation to clear central Greece, conducted between 25 April and 31 July 1949.

100. Operation ROCKET is described by Abbott, 35; Averoff-Tossizza, 336–38; and O'Ballance, 193–94.

101. Averoff-Tossizza, 338.

102. Ibid.

103. Col. George S. Smith (Chief, Intelligence Group, Intelligence Division, Headquarters, Department of the Army), to Chief, Plans and Operations Division (ATTN: LTC Sievers), Headquarters, Department of the Army, Disposition Form, Washington, 17 August 1949, subject: Greek Guerrilla Situation and Greek Army Operations, Tab A ("Greek Guerrilla Situation as of 30 June 1949," dated 17 August 1949), 2 [in file "370.60-560. Greece, 1 January 1949 thru 1950," Box 157 ("000.224 Greece to 560. Greece"), Assistant Chief of Staff, G-2, Intelligence, Project Decimal File, 1949–1950, RG 319, NA].

104. Ibid., 1.

105. Operation ARIS is described in the report of Col. Temple G. Holland (Chief, JUSMAPG Detachment, Headquarters, C Corps) to Lt. Gen. James A. Van Fleet (Director, JUSMAPG), Salonika, 13 May 1949, subject: Special Operations Report, Operation "ARIS," 5–12 May 1949 [in file "319.1—"C" Corps Monthly Reports," Box 55 ("1949: 311.–319.1"), Joint United States Aid Group–General Decimal Correspondence File, RG 334, NA].

106. Operation AJAX is described in the report of Maj. Albert L. Pence (Acting Chief, JUSMAPG Detachment, Headquarters, XI Division) to Lt. Gen. James A. Van Fleet (Director, JUSMAPG), Nea Khalkidon, 15 July 1949, subject: Special Operations Report, Operation "AJAX," 4–8 July 1949 [in file "319.1-"C" Corps Monthly Reports," Box 55 ("1949: 311.–319.1"), Joint United States Aid Group–Greece General Decimal Correspondence File, RG 334, NA]. See also O'Ballance, 195–97.

107. Ibid. O'Ballance (page 196) and others give the GDA casualties in the Kaimaktsalan as 400 killed.

108. O'Ballance, 195–96; Eudes, 352.

109. Operation TORCH is described by Eudes, 352–54; Abbott, 35–37; Averoff-Tossizza, 339–49; Murray, "The Anti-Bandit War [Part I]," 18; *Employment of Airpower*, 31–33; O'Ballance, 195–99; and Woodhouse, 280–83.

110. Averoff-Tossizza, 340.

111. Both GDA and government losses during TORCH B are discussed in *Employment of Airpower*, 64–65, and Papathanasiades, 26. O'Ballance (pages 197–98) notes that the Albanians killed and captured had aided the GDA individually, and that there is no reliable evidence that Albanian forces were committed to the battle officially.

112. O'Ballance, 148.

113. The Curtiss SB2C-5 Helldiver Navy dive-bomber was capable of carrying two tons of bombs as well as rockets, cannon, and machine guns. The U.S. Navy had rushed fifty-one of the planes to Greece by aircraft carrier and placed them at the disposal of

the RHAF (see *Employment of Airpower*, 49 and 53; Averoff-Tossizza, 345–46). They played an important role in the final phase of Operation TORCH.

114. Woodhouse, 280–81.

115. Col. R. W. Mayo (Europe and Middle East Branch, Plans and Operations Division, U.S. Army General Staff), Director's Notes, Washington, 8 September 1949, subject: Operation TORCH [Item 40, Case 4, Book I, Section I-A, Box 541 ("091 Greece"), Plans & Operations Division Decimal File, 1949–February 1950, RG 319, NA].

116. Ibid.

117. Woodhouse (page 283) quotes a resolution of the Politburo issued on 20 August declaring, "Our watch-word is: Grammos will be the tomb of monarcho-fascism."

118. Kousoulas, 270 note 21.

119. Ibid.

120. Eudes, 354.

121. Ibid.

122. O'Ballance, 202; Averoff-Tossizza, 352. As late as the end of February 1950, American intelligence agencies still estimated that about 1,000 Communist guerrillas held out in Greece, scattered in small, ineffective bands along the Bulgarian border, in the Grammos and Vitsi, and elsewhere. Actually, by then the KKE had abandoned the attempt to seize power by force and had reverted to a policy of exploiting economic and political weaknesses of the Greek government (see United States Central Intelligence Agency, *Current Situation in Greece* [ORE 4-50; Washington: Central Intelligence Agency, 28 February 1950], 3).

123. Averoff-Tossizza, 352–53. O'Ballance (page 201) notes that the decision was forced by Stalin, who may have entertained some idea of using the GDA against Tito or of forcing the repatriation of its members to Greece, where they could resume the political struggle.

124. Quoted by Eudes, 354.

125. Merrill, 67.

126. Chief, Intelligence Division, Headquarters, Department of the Army, to Chief, Plans and Operations Division, Headquarters, Department of the Army, Disposition Form, Washington, 7 November 1949, subject: Capabilities of the Greek Guerrillas and the Greek Armed Forces, Enclosure (Estimate, Project No. 5226: "Capabilities of the Greek Guerrillas and the Greek Armed Forces"), 1–4 [in file "091.112–200.6 Greece (1 January 1949–31 December 1950)," Box 157 ("000.244 Greece to 560. Greece"), Assistant Chief of Staff, G-2, Intelligence, Project Decimal File, 1949–1950, RG 319, NA].

Logistics and the Failure of the Insurrection in Greece

With the successful conclusion of Operation TORCH on 31 August 1949, the victorious Greek government forces were redeployed to seal the borders and clear the remaining scattered guerrilla bands from the interior. On 26 August, just as the final battle in the Grammos began, the Albanian leader, Enver Hoxha, had announced that any Greek guerrillas entering Albania would be disarmed and detained, and the Bulgarians had soon followed suit, at least publicly. Nevertheless, many of the defeated Communist guerrillas slipped over the borders to take refuge in the neighboring Communist states. The Greek Democratic Army (GDA) remained in existence, and the guerrillas who had escaped the climactic battle in the Grammos-Vitsi in the summer of 1949 were reassembled and continued to train in Albania, Bulgaria, Hungary, Poland, and the Soviet Union. Western intelligence sources estimated their strength as late as November 1949 at some 2,000 armed guerrillas remaining in Greece and another 12,000 combat-ready cadres located in the nearby Communist states.[1] As time went on the number of GDA cadres under arms declined, and many former guerrillas were given work in the satellite states and settled down to a near-normal existence. In July 1952 fewer than 100 Communist guerrillas were reported active in Greece, most of them located along the Bulgarian border.[2]

The surviving leaders of the Provisional Democratic Government, the Greek Communist Party (KKE), and the Greek Democratic Army (GDA) also dispersed to the Communist satellite states. Zachariades, Roussos, and Partsalides were reported in Prague, Kokkalis and Ioannides in Bucharest, and others, including Bartziotas and Vlantas, in Albania.[3] From their various places of exile they reorganized the KKE into three branches, the most prominent of which came to be called the "official KKE," or the "KKE of the exterior." The two smaller branches operated clandestinely within Greece, but the "official KKE" continued to govern itself through a Central Committee and Politburo, to hold periodic congresses, and to engage in propaganda, although its members were scattered throughout the Soviet bloc, with even a sizable contingent in Tashkent, Uzbekistan.[4] The exile group continued to be dominated by Zachariades and his clique; it continued to declare its approval of Zachariades' actions and its solidarity with the Soviet Union.

At the Third Party Congress in October 1950, the dissenters—Markos Vafiades, Kostas Karageorgis, and Dimitrios Partsalides—were formally dismissed from the party leadership, and George Siantos, the former General Secretary of the KKE, was condemned posthumously as a British agent and enemy of the working class.[5] Although dismissed from his positions as prime minister of the Provisional Democratic Government and commander of the GDA in January 1949, Markos was not formally read out of the party until the Third Congress. Reports of his illness and death were "premature" he was held in house arrest for some time in Tirana, Albania, and then transferred to Moscow. Following the death of Stalin in 1953, Markos was rehabilitated by the Sixth Party Congress of the KKE, but he soon antagonized the party leaders and in 1955 he was expelled once again. The KKE leaders prevailed upon Soviet authorities to exile Markos to the town of Mensa in the Urals. He remained there, working as a watchmaker and isolated from the other Greek political refugees, until March 1983, when he returned to Athens under the terms of a political amnesty declared by Greek prime minister Andreas Papandreou.[6]

Kostas Karageorgis reportedly died in detention in the basement of Zachariades' private house some time before 1956, but Dimitrios Partsalides survived to become the leader of the KKE upon the purge of Nikos Zachariades in 1957.

In the aftermath of their decisive defeat, Zachariades and his supporters continued to hold out hope for a resumption of the fight. That hope faded slowly among the exiled leaders of the KKE/GDA, and it disappeared only with the purge of Zachariades and his followers in the period 1955–1957, the aging of the onetime guerrillas, the improvement of economic conditions in Greece, and the continued vigilance of the Greek security forces.[7] Despite its avowed intention to resume the struggle whenever it became possible to do so, the KKE in fact reverted to the old attempt to gain its goals through political action rather than armed insurrection. Infiltration, propaganda, subversion, and the use of surrogate political agents became again the principal methods of the Greek Communists. In the Greek elections of 1950, the EDA—a Communist surrogate party—won 10 percent of the popular vote and ten seats in the parliament.[8] After 1950 the Communists, in various disguises, continued to garner about 15 percent of the popular vote in Greece, demonstrating the continued vitality of the political ideals that had motivated the insurrection.[9]

The Sixth Plenum of the Central Committee of the Greek Communist Party decided on 9 October 1949 to discontinue temporarily the armed struggle, but it warned that "the Anglo-American Imperialists and their monarcho-fascist agents would be mistaken if they assumed that the struggle was over and that the Democratic Army had ceased to exist."[10] Indeed, although publicly confident in their victory, the Greek government and the Western powers continued to fear a resumption of active guerrilla warfare in Greece for some time, being "almost sure that the Democratic Army was merely seeking a breathing space in which to recover to fight again another day, as it had done so often before."[11] The possibility of such a revival was considered to depend entirely on whether or not the Soviet Union desired to resume the battle. As U.S. Army intelligence officers stated in November 1949,

The ability of the guerrillas to reestablish themselves in Greece will depend in large part on the Soviet decision regarding future plans for a guerrilla effort in Greece. The status and activity, if any, of the Greek guerrillas in coming months undoubtedly will reflect the nature of the Soviet decision. If the guerrillas were to be reorganized, re-equipped, and regrouped with Communist assistance and logistical support on a scale similar to that which obtained when over 20,000 guerrillas were actively engaged in Greece, the present guerrilla force in Albania and Bulgaria could reinfiltrate several organized units into Greece and attempt to resume a relatively large scale campaign against the Greek Army. On the other hand, the available current information indicates that little or no effort is being made to revitalize the guerrilla organization.[12]

The Soviet Union demonstrated no overt desire to resume the armed insurrection in Greece, but the Greek government's concern with infiltration, subversion, espionage, and even the resumption of armed conflict was not totally unwarranted. In 1950–1951 at least two major underground rings of Communist agents were uncovered in Athens and Salonika, fully equipped with arms, radio transmitters, and printing presses. Also, small Communist bands—fewer than a hundred men in all—continued to mount occasional attacks on remote villages or even as close to Athens as Mount Parnassos.[13]

Whatever desires to continue to promote the Communist insurrection in Greece the leaders of the Communist satellites states may still have harbored after the defeat of the GDA were all but expunged by the Stalinist purge that took place in the last half of 1949.[14] Intent on eliminating "Titoism" among his Balkan stooges, Stalin eliminated about one-fourth of the members of the Eastern European Communist parties. Traicho Kostov, the General Secretary of the Bulgarian Communist Party, was expelled from the party in March and executed for treason in December; Stalin's chief henchman in Bulgaria, Georgi Dimitrov, traveled to Moscow in June 1949 and died there, presumably from natural causes. The Albanian deputy prime minister, Gen. Koci Xoxe, was convicted of "Titoism" in June 1949 and executed the same month, thereby no doubt impressing upon Enver Hoxha the wisdom of suspending support to the Greek rebels and returning to a pure Stalinist line.

Despite the fears of the Greek government and its Western allies, however, the armed Communist insurrection in Greece in fact ended with the defeat of the Greek Democratic Army in the Grammos and Vitsi in August 1949. The only serious threats to the stability and prosperity of Greece that remained after that time were those that had existed at the start of the Communist rebellion:

economic chaos, political instability, social injustice, and the intense divisions among the Greek people themselves.

THE COSTS OF THE WAR

In August 1949 the Greek government and its Western allies had emerged victorious over the Communist insurgents, but at what cost? Like most wars, the 1945–1949 civil war in Greece was the occasion of tremendous loss of life and the destruction of property. Out of a total population of about 7.5 million, some 158,000 Greeks on both sides lost their lives, one million were made homeless, and 28,000 children were abducted.[15] Estimates of total Greek Democratic Army casualties during the war range between 50,395 and 83,925, with the most likely figures being those provided by Angeliki Laiou: 24,235 killed, 9,871 captured, 16,289 surrendered, and uncounted thousands of wounded.[16] During the "Third Round," the Greek national forces lost 16,753 killed, 40,398 wounded, and 4,788 missing.[17] Civilian casualties included 4,288 persons executed by the guerrillas, including 165 clergymen, and 931 killed by mines.[18] At the peak in 1949 there were some 684,300 refugees (nearly one-tenth of the Greek population) and perhaps two to two and a half million people on public welfare.[19]

The Greek General Staff estimated that the destruction caused by the Communist guerrillas between June 1946 and December 1949 included 46,626 houses completely or partly destroyed and another 100,000 abandoned houses damaged; 15,139 agricultural buildings destroyed; fifty churches destroyed; 139 schools completely or partly destroyed; 439 railroad and 476 highway bridges destroyed; eighty railroad stations burned; 137 kilometers of road damaged; and 860 civilian and 918 military vehicles destroyed or damaged.[20] In addition, the Greek General Staff listed 2,269 major incidents of sabotage against transportation and communications lines; 3,030 attacks and harassments against villages; 7,690 villages and towns looted; 5,570 attacks, ambushes, and harassments against government military units; and well over 51,000 mines planted by the guerrillas, of which 3,640 exploded. The Greek ministry of coordination estimated the economic losses of the civil war period (June 1946–December 1949) at 3,685,900,000,000 drachmae (at 15,000 drachmae to the dollar).[21] By category, the losses were (in billions of drachmae):

Buildings	1,284.0
Agriculture	821.2
Stock breeding	714.7
Personal property	286.3
Forestry	231.8
Food and commercial stocks	165.0

Public utilities and services	50.2
Industry	32.3
Road nets	31.7
Railroads	30.9
Communications	29.5
Vehicles	8.3

Moreover, the devastation of the civil war of 1945–1949 came atop—and greatly exceeded—the death and destruction of the five years of war and occupation by foreign powers that had preceded it. When the entire period 1940–1949 is considered, over 2,000 villages and approximately one-fourth of all the buildings in Greece were damaged or destroyed, the cultivated area declined by over 25 percent, industry came to a standstill, exports virtually ceased, imports were reduced to one-tenth of prewar levels, and one-third of the population was forced onto public aid.[22]

THE CAUSES OF DEFEAT

Historians who have studied the Greek civil war of 1945–1949 have cited a number of reasons for the military defeat of the Greek Democratic Army and the consequent failure of the Communist insurrection.[23] Although each historian advances his own list of causes, all are agreed that the defeat of the GDA stemmed from multiple factors rather than any one cause. The principal factors that contributed to the failure of the Communist insurgency in Greece were four in number. Three of these causative factors were beyond the control of the leaders of the KKE/GDA: the dramatic improvement in strength, morale, and effectiveness of the Greek national forces after 1947 as a result of American economic and military aid; the limited internal resources of Greece, both inherently and as a result of World War II; and the decision of Stalin to withhold support for the Greek guerrillas. The fourth factor was much more important: the triumph of Nikos Zachariades and his clique in the internal conflict within the Greek Communist Party and the consequent adoption of four fatal policy decisions that sealed the fate of the GDA by depriving it of essential resources. Logistical considerations played a major role in all of these factors, so much so that if one were forced to select a single explanation for the defeat of the GDA it would have to be *inadequate logistics.*

The Development of the Greek National Forces

The "Second Round" of the Greek civil war was decided by armed British intervention in December 1944–January 1945; the "Third Round" was decided by American economic and military aid. Small, poorly trained and equipped, inexperienced, and lacking competent, aggressive leadership, the GNF were unable to prevent the extension of Communist control over most of Greece during 1945–1947. By early 1948, however, American economic and military aid had begun to have the desired effect, and in 1948 and early 1949 the GNF underwent a phenomenal transformation. From an ill-equipped and ill-disciplined collection of disparate elements led by complacent and often inept commanders, the GNF was transformed by early 1949 into a well-equipped, well-disciplined, well-trained, aggressive combined-arms team fully capable of dealing in time with any internal military threat and most of the likely external ones as well. At the end of March 1949, on the eve of the GNF's final decisive campaign against the GDA, the Greek government had 244,211 men under arms plus another 509,500 trained reserves.[24] The Greek National Army (GNA) of 147,000 men boasted five fully equipped and fully trained mountain infantry divisions, three field infantry divisions, three independent brigades, and four commando groups, backed by a full range of administrative and logistical services and a National Defense Corps of 50,000 men in ninety-six battalion-sized units. The GNA was also supported by a 25,000-man Gendarmerie; the 15,170-man Royal Hellenic Navy (RHN), with two destroyers, twelve destroyer escorts, and six submarines; and the Royal Hellenic Air Force (RHAF), of 7,041 officers and men with 282 aircraft in three fighter squadrons, one reconnaissance squadron, and one transport squadron. These forces were well supplied with modern weapons, including artillery and aircraft, excellent communications, a full range of logistical services including motor transport, and copious quantities of food, fuel, ammunition, and other supplies.

The transformation of the GNF was made possible by the application of the enormous fiscal resources and determination of the United States. While the exact amount of outside economic and military assistance provided to the Greek Communist guerrillas is unknown, there can be little doubt that whatever its dimensions, it was dwarfed by the aid provided to the Greek national government by the United States and other Western nations. Delivery of supplies to the GNF from the United States began in August 1947, and during the following five months some 74,000 tons of military equipment arrived.[25] By the end of 1949 the United States had provided some $353.6 million worth of military aid to Greece, including hundreds of aircraft and ships; 4,130 mortars and artillery pieces; 159,922 small arms; 89,438 bombs and rockets; 7.7 million artillery and mortar shells; and 455 million rounds of small arms ammunition.[26] In all, between 30 June 1947 and 1 July 1950 the United States poured into Greece some $760.7 million in economic aid and another $476.8 million in military aid, a total of $1,237.5 million.[27]

In some ways, the military expertise provided by the United States to the GNF was even more significant to the final outcome of the struggle against the Communist insurgents than was the material aid. American advisors contributed the technical and administrative skills needed to distribute and employ the new military equipment effectively and efficiently, and they infused their Greek counterparts with the aggressiveness and determination essential to victory. The director of the Joint United States Military Advisory and Planning Group–Greece (JUSMAPG), Lt. Gen. James A. Van Fleet, and his subordinates were not bashful in their efforts to purge the GNF of lackadaisical and inept commanders or to urge a more aggressive strategy on their Greek counterparts. The reappointment of Gen. Alexander Papagos as commander in chief of the GNF in early 1949 was the turning point. American assistance provided the wherewithal; Papagos provided the moral direction that led to the dismissal of ineffective commanders, increased aggressiveness, and a new determination to pursue and defeat the Communist guerrillas. Improvements in leadership, equipment, and training soon led to small victories over the marauding guerrillas, which brought further improvements in morale and increased effectiveness in the field.

The comparison with the Greek Democratic Army is stark indeed. Western intelligence estimates from the early days of the "Third Round" posited that some 700,000 adults, or about 10 percent of the entire Greek population, considered themselves leftists, and that 150,000 to 200,000 of these were prepared to take some sort of active role in antigovernment activities.[28] But at its peak in April 1948, the GDA counted only about 26,210 active fighters inside Greece plus another 20,000 reserves (including recruits in training) in the neighboring countries and about 50,000 active auxiliaries in the *aftoamyna*.[29] In March 1949 the combatant strength of the GDA was only 21,810, and by July 1949 it had fallen to 17,635, of which nearly 90 percent were fighting for their lives in the Grammos-Vitsi stronghold in northwestern Greece. In contrast to the well-supplied GNF, in 1949 the nine small divisions, twenty-five double companies, and eighteen independent companies of the GDA disposed only sixty field guns, thirty-one antiaircraft guns, forty-one antitank guns, and twelve heavy mortars.[30] There were no aircraft or combatant naval vessels, communications and transport equipment was inadequate; and food, clothing, ammunition, repair parts, and other supplies were chronically in short supply. Shortages of ammunition, particularly artillery shells, directly restricted tactical operations, and the comparative lack of motor transport limited both tactical and logistical mobility, as well as siphoning off considerable manpower and other resources to care for the large number of animals required.

Greece's Limited Internal Resources

The sea in which the Greek Communist guerrillas swam was not a rich one. Even in the best of times, Greece was a poor country. Agricultural production was comparatively low, even in the fertile valleys and plains, and industrial output was limited in both range and quantity. Moreover, the transportation infrastructure was not well developed, and geography made the distribution of people and goods difficult. The devastation of the economy by the World War II occupation and resistance reduced the internal resources of Greece to such a degree that even a small guerrilla army was hard pressed to obtain its most basic needs—food, clothing, and medical supplies—locally, either by purchase or forced requisition. Once existing caches were depleted, arms, ammunition, and other military supplies could be obtained only by capture from the government forces or from outside supporters. The difficult terrain and severe climate of the principal area of operations in the barren and sparsely populated mountains of northwestern Greece increased guerrilla requirements for food, forage, clothing, and fuel and at the same time impeded the collection and distribution of supplies.

Given the lack of internal resources, as the Greek Democratic Army increased in size and transformed itself into a more or less conventional army, it was forced to rely increasingly on its friendly Communist neighbors not only for heavy artillery, antiaircraft guns, antitank guns, communications equipment, and mines, but also for food, clothing, medical supplies, small arms, and ammunition. Regardless of its limited scope, outside support could not substitute for direct access to adequate internal resources. Outside suppliers could be fickle, the delivery of essential supplies could be irregular or untimely, and the movement of matériel to where it was needed was always difficult.

Stalin's Failure to Support the Communist Insurgency in Greece

Although the Greek government and its American ally were convinced that the Communist insurgency in Greece was inspired and supported by the Soviet Union, the available evidence suggests that Soviet support for the Greek guerrillas was equivocal at best. Indeed, it appears that Stalin, unwilling to risk a direct confrontation with the Western powers in what to him appeared a peripheral region, provided little or no direct economic or military aid to the KKE/GDA. Despite Stalin's repeated warnings that the Greek insurgency should be terminated, many of the Soviet satellite states—particularly Albania, Yugoslavia, and Bulgaria—acted on the basis of their own national interests to support the Greek guerrillas. However, their support was tempered by their own dependence on the Soviet Union for economic support and military aid.

Throughout the "Third Round," the leaders as well as the rank and file of the KKE and GDA waited in vain for the military assistance of the Soviet Union. What they received was ambiguous pro forma diplomatic and propaganda support rather than massive infusions of money, arms, and ammunition. Without such direct aid—or at least Soviet encouragement of the satellite states to provide it—the Greek rebels had little hope for a successful outcome in their struggle. If there was ever a monolithic, worldwide Communist conspiracy directed from Moscow and aimed at the overthrow of democratic states by force of arms, it certainly did not apply to Greece.

The Four Fatal Decisions

The Greek civil war of 1945–1949 is a striking object lesson in what happens to an armed revolutionary movement when it is divided against itself on such basic matters as foreign policy and the organization and employment of its military capabilities. Throughout 1945–1949 the Greek Communist Party was in crisis—split into competing factions, each with its own idea of the course to be followed. The main split within the KKE pitted the ideologue General Secretary of the KKE, Nikos Zachariades, and his Stalinist, "internationalist" adherents against the more pragmatic, nationalist commander of the GDA, Markos Vafiades, and his supporters. The division between the two groups was most obvious with respect to the organization and employment of the GDA, but their differences also extended to important matters of foreign policy. The outcome of the conflict between Zachariades and Markos—which had personal as well as political overtones—was not preordained, but at each successive stage Zachariades was able to impose his will and his concepts on the KKE and GDA in the face of strenuous objections from Markos. In the end Zachariades' triumph was complete, and in January 1949 Markos was dismissed as prime minister of the Provisional Democratic Government of Free Greece and as commander of the GDA, and his followers were subsequently purged from the leadership of both the party and the army.

The internal divisions within the KKE profoundly affected all aspects of the development of the Greek Communist military forces—organization, strategy, tactics, and logistics. The dominance of Zachariades and his clique led to four important decisions with far-reaching negative effects on the GDA. First, Zachariades declined to mobilize the Communist cadres in the towns and cities at the beginning of the rebellion in 1946, when their resources in manpower and matériel might have had a decisive impact on a weak and faltering Greek government. Second, Zachariades' strict Stalinist policies alienated popular support for the Communist cause among ordinary Greeks, and what little popular support remained was all but destroyed by his decision to support the concept of an independent Macedonia under Bulgarian domination. Third, the declaration of KKE support for the Cominform in its conflict with Tito offended the GDA's principal external supporter and persuaded Tito to abandon his logistical support of the GDA and close his borders to the Greek guerrillas. Finally, Zachariades' ill-considered and ill-timed decision to convert a successful guerrilla army to a conventional army on the Soviet pattern and to adopt a strategy of positional warfare placed on the fragile GDA logistical system demands that it could not meet and that contributed directly to its failure.

The principal fault of Zachariades' four major policy decisions lay in the fact that they were based on ideological considerations rather than on a careful and accurate assessment of the actual political-military situation and the vital interests of the Greek Communists. The quality of Zachariades' decisions was also adversely affected by his own shortcomings as the leader of the party. Zachariades, who had spent the important World War II resistance period in jail or in the Dachau concentration camp, lacked military experience at both the tactical and strategic level and was also out of touch with the political, economic, and social conditions in his native land. Unable to see—or perhaps just unwilling to honor—the genuine interests and aspirations of the Greek people, Zachariades preferred to let his ideological convictions and slavish adherence to the interests of the Soviet Union and international Communism dictate his policies. The results were reduced internal and external support for the GDA and fatally premature transition to the third, final, and theoretically decisive stage of insurgency.

Arguably, Markos Vafiades was better equipped to make the key political and military decisions affecting the KKE and GDA. He possessed considerable political and military experience from his time as a leader in ELAS, and he was closely attuned to the temper of the Greek people, the limits of external support, and the nature of modern warfare. Whether or not Markos' alternate strategy of a prolonged guerrilla war on the classic pattern would ultimately have produced success is problematic, but he almost certainly would have avoided the traps into which Zachariades jumped headlong.

The Failure to Mobilize the Towns

Zachariades' first fateful decision was his refusal to heed Markos' repeated pleas in 1946 for the mobilization of the KKE in the town and cities. Instead, he preferred to conserve the manpower and material resources of the urban KKE cadres for some future urban uprising of the proletariat, in the classic Marxist-Leninist mode. Apart from scattered and largely ineffective acts of sabotage and terrorism, the ideologically prescribed urban revolt never took place, and it was not until March of 1948 that Zachariades consented to issue a call for the mobilization of the urban cadres. By then the critical moment had passed, and in any event the call went largely unanswered. Thus, the GDA was deprived of vitally important manpower and logistical resources when they would have been most effective in the effort to overthrow a weak Greek government.

Greece was scarcely a proletarian society ripe for a worker's revolt. In fact, Greek workers—a small group in any event—and even the KKE cadres in the urban centers of Greece were largely indifferent to the struggle of the Communist guerrillas in the mountains. Zachariades' refusal to order their mobilization at the critical moment when the GDA and the GNF were "evenly matched in their weakness rather than their strength" spared the government forces long enough for American aid to alter the equation irrevocably.[31] Even as late as the fall of 1947 the GDA had the GNA on the ropes; Markos' guerrillas dominated 80 percent of the country from their mountain redoubts, and the government forces were largely restricted to the towns and major routes of communications. The situation changed dramatically in the course of 1948, as U.S. aid transformed the GNA into a well-equipped, aggressive force with good morale. Consequently, the GNF was able to destroy the guerrilla intelligence and logistics infrastructure in the towns as well as in the countryside, and the considerable resources of the urban KKE were never brought into play.

The Alienation of Popular Support

Public support of the Communist cause was never strong or widespread, and what little support there was was dissipated by Zachariades' orthodox Communist approach to party discipline and the use of executions, forced recruitment, confiscatory taxation, and other stringent methods to force support for the KKE/GDA. The classic Soviet-style discipline and use of terror to intimidate and coerce the civilian population were entirely counterproductive when applied to a people as proud and independent-minded as the Greeks. In essence, Zachariades ignored the first rule of insurgent warfare: win and retain the hearts and minds of the majority of the population. As O'Ballance has pointed out,

Whereas considerate treatment might have gained many converts, the harshness of the Communist yoke over both foe and potential friend alike caused a swing away from Communism by the uncommitted. Many of the peasant class, with no fixed political convictions, who had found themselves in Communist-dominated territory had been sickened and revolted by what they had seen and experienced.[32]

Moreover, many Greeks who supported the KKE/GDA in the early days of the civil war hoped for national independence, territorial integrity, economic and political stability, and social justice as well as protection from the depredations of the monarchist government and the right-wing bands that it tolerated. Once the "internationalist" and Stalinist nature of the KKE program put forth by Zachariades became clear, support for the party and the armed insurrection evaporated. Zachariades' ideological focus on the urban workers and corresponding disdain for the revolutionary potential of the large mass of peasants and petit bourgeois further reduced the numbers of those who might have supported the Communist cause. Even experienced and capable military personnel, essential to the success of the GDA, were turned away in favor of party hacks with little or no military expertise but willing to follow the party line rigidly.

In any event, the state of the Greek economy in general made support of the guerrillas by the populace unreliable. As has been noted,

Because of widespread economic chaos and social disorganization, the population lacked the physical, moral and emotional resources to aid the insurgency even if they had wished to do so. The hardships of 7 years of war and famine had left most Greek peasants apathetic toward armed conflict of any kind. In many cases the peasants refused to cooperate with either the Greek National Army and security forces, or the rebel Greek Democratic Army.[33]

What little popular support remained to the KKE/GDA once Zachariades' program was known was all but wiped out by his decision to support the formation of an independent Slavic Macedonia under Bulgarian hegemony as proposed by the Cominform, a policy that the KKE had abandoned in the 1930s and that most Greeks viewed as little short of treason. Even in practical terms, advocating the abandonment of 1.5 million Greeks to gain the support of only 80,000 Macedonians was not a good bargain. Once again, Zachariades' ideological purity was sustained at great cost to the rebel fighters.

The Alienation of Tito and the Loss of Yugoslavian Support

The second principle of insurgent warfare is to gain and maintain continuous external logistical support. Even though the Soviet Union declined to aid the Greek guerrillas directly, the Communist regimes on the borders of Greece—Albania, Yugoslavia, and Bulgaria—provided their Greek comrades with money, food, clothing, arms, ammunition, and other supplies as well as advice, refuge, medical care, and also secure assembly, training, and storage facilities. The other Soviet satellite nations also provided aid to the Greek guerrillas in lesser amounts, and the rebels even found Western suppliers willing to sell them war matériel. The amount of supplies and other support provided by the Communist countries on the borders of Greece was substantial, but the Communist states bordering Greece acted in their own interests. Moreover, the amounts and types of support they were willing and able to provide were limited by the natural weaknesses of their economies, by the need for resources to repair the effects of five years of world war and occupation, and by the inherent difficulties in the continuous and expeditious delivery of significant quantities of war matériel. In the end, foreign assistance to the GDA remained inadequate to its needs. In any event, it could not have altered the balance of forces once U.S. support for the Greek government began in 1947.

Yugoslavia was the most generous supplier of the Greek Communist guerrillas. The expulsion of Yugoslavia from the Cominform in June 1948 and the subsequent heightening of tensions between Yugoslavia and the Soviet Union caused Tito to conserve his military resources for possible use in defense of the homeland. Nevertheless, the Yugoslavians continued to support the Greek Communist guerrillas for more than a year, and they ceased to do so only when the KKE under Zachariades' guidance declared publicly in favor of the Cominform and accused Tito of collusion with the Greek national government and of other "crimes." Unwilling to tolerate such calumny, Tito suspended all Yugoslavian support for the rebels, and on 10 July 1949 he closed the Yugoslavian borders to them. The loss of Yugoslavian support was a major blow to the GDA; the resulting logistical deficit could not be made up by Albania and Bulgaria, both of which continued to support the GDA, but more cautiously, lest they should incur the enmity of Stalin and the Cominform and suffer the fate of Yugoslavia. Only in the late summer of 1949, when it became clear that the GDA was about to be defeated by the Greek national forces, did Albania and Bulgaria withdraw their support.

Zachariades' decision to support the Cominform in its dispute with Tito and the consequent loss of Yugoslavian aid are often cited as the turning point in the Greek civil war and as the two events that brought about the defeat of the Communist insurrection in Greece.[34] But it should be borne in mind that by 10 July 1949, when Tito closed his border to the Greek guerrillas and terminated all aid, the final decisive battle in the Grammos-Vitsi was under way, and the issue had already been decided.

The Premature Transition to Conventional Warfare

The beginning of the penultimate phase of the Greek civil war was marked by the decision of the KKE leadership to abandon guerrilla organization and strategy and to create a conventional army, with which to fight a positional war against the numerically superior and steadily improving Greek national forces. This decision, formally announced at the Third Plenum of the KKE Central Committee in September 1947 but actually taken by the KKE Politburo in February of that year, was promoted by Zachariades and his supporters among the party ideologues but was strenuously opposed by Markos and his adherents as premature and unwise. In the event, the decision proved disastrous, in large part because it placed upon the fragile logistical system of the GDA a burden that it could not sustain. Thus, the ill-timed and ill-advised decision to transition to conventional organization and positional warfare led directly to the defeat of the GDA in the summer of 1949 and the end of the Communist attempt to seize political power in Greece by force.

In part, the decision in favor of a conventional army and conventional tactics was predicated on Zachariades' perception of the need to seize and defend a well-defined, KKE-administered "state," with a fixed capital, in the hope of political recognition and overt support by the Soviet Union and other Communist states. Equally important were his desire to restructure the decentralized guerrilla forces so as to facilitate greater centralized control and party discipline, and his admiration for the Red Army as a model. The important military questions involved, particularly the logistical requirements of a conventional force and the correlation of forces, Zachariades either did not understand or chose to ignore in favor of a decision based solely on ideological and political grounds.

Most successful post–World War II nationalist insurgencies—both Communist and non-Communist—have demonstrated a classic pattern of development. This pattern, followed in China, Indochina, Algeria, and elsewhere, has consisted of three stages, which have been called "guerrilla warfare," "protracted (or mobile) warfare," and "positional warfare" (or "the general counteroffensive phase"). In its classic form, the first phase, essentially clandestine and defensive, has involved the establishment of a viable military force and a supporting infrastructure, with overt military action limited to defensive actions and small-scale ambushes, raids, and acts of terrorism. In the second phase, rebel forces have initiated more substantial direct action to harass and demoralize the enemy while continuing to build up their own military strength. Offensive military action during the second phase has included larger ambushes and raids as well as coordinated attacks on enemy facilities and lines of communications, and limited campaigns to secure resources and influence popular opinion. In the third and final phase the rebel forces, having been organized and equipped as a conventional army, have passed over to a sustained full-scale offensive campaign to eliminate enemy military and political organs or force their withdrawal from the field. The classic examples of the successful application of this three stage process are Mao Tse-tung's victory in China and the defeat of the French by the Viet Minh in Indochina.[35]

The most critical decision that insurgent leaders must make is when to pass from the second to the third stage. For the transition to be successful, the enemy's strength and morale, both military and civilian, must have been thoroughly sapped, and the guerrilla forces must be prepared in all respects to organize, man, arm, support, and control a large conventional army. As Kousoulas has noted,

In the end, to consummate its plans, a guerrilla force must pass from the subconventional to the conventional stage, replacing hit-and-run tactics with conventional military operations aiming at lasting territorial gains. . . . Once this transition takes place, the guerrillas lose the tactical advantage . . . and are forced to face their opponent on equal terms. In fact, the guerrilla army is placed at a serious disadvantage because, as a rule, it is inferior in numerical strength, supplies, and ammunition.[36]

The Viet Minh insurgency in Indochina and the nationalist revolt in Algeria from 1954 to 1962 provide excellent examples of how important the timing of this decision is. The Viet Minh offensives in the Red River Valley in 1949 illustrate the dangers of attempting to make the transition before the conditions are ripe, and the events of 1953–1954 culminating in the decisive defeat of the French at Dien Bien Phu demonstrate what happens when the decision is made at the proper time. The 1954–1962 revolt in Algeria presents a slightly different case. The rebels of the Algerian National Liberation Front (ALN) thoroughly mixed the various phases and attempted to proceed too rapidly from one phase to the next. By 1957 the ALN forces inside Algeria were well into the second stage and felt sufficiently strong to proceed to the third stage. However, the completion of the Morice Line by the French effectively cut them off from their sources of men and matériel in Tunisia and Morocco, and they were severely mangled by the French Challe offensives in 1959–1960. The rebels who survived were forced to revert to the second, or mobile warfare, stage, and the conventional ALN forces in Tunisia and Morocco, equipped and trained for the all-out third-phase offensive, were prevented from being brought into action at all.[37]

The Communist insurgency in Greece depicts a classic case of attempting to make the transition before the conditions are right and is thus closer to the Algerian than to the Viet Minh model. Zachariades insisted on making the transition from the second to the third stage well before the GDA itself was prepared logistically for the transition and before the enemy's morale and will to fight had been sufficiently sapped. Indeed, the classic requisites for the second to third stage transition were exactly reversed—GDA morale and support among the populace were already falling and the strength and morale of the GNF were increasing when the decision was made, in early 1947. As Kousoulas has pointed out,

Their most basic error was the decision to start a guerrilla operation and then pass into the conventional stage at a time when the Greek Government, supported by American aid and with the great majority of the people united around the national leadership, was getting stronger and more stable every day.[38]

In order to be successful, a guerrilla army must transform itself at some point into a conventional army able to meet the enemy on equal terms and to seize and hold ground. The timing of the transition is critical, and once the decision has been made it is seldom possible to revert to the earlier phase of protracted guerrilla warfare and go on to ultimate success. The Viet Minh were able to accomplish just that, but their opponent was far weaker than that faced by the Greek Communist guerrillas. The Algerian nationalists achieved their goals in the end, but through political rather than military means. The Communist insurgents in Greece were neither as strong as the Viet Minh nor as clever as the Algerians, and Zachariades' insistence on an early transition to the third stage was thus a major factor in their defeat. As Woodhouse has noted, "Markos was right in believing that the timing had been wrongly chosen in 1947–8, but Zakhariadis was right in maintaining that, once made, the choice was irreversible in 1948–9."[39]

THE LOGISTICAL IMPACT OF THE CONVERSION TO A CONVENTIONAL ARMY

The transition from the second stage of mobile guerrilla warfare to the final stage of conventional positional warfare is necessary and must come in time. In and of itself, the transformation of a guerrilla army into a conventional army is not necessarily a bad thing, but if the changes in organization, strategy, and tactics are to be successful, the necessary preconditions must be in place, and the insurgent leaders must carefully weigh both the existing correlation of forces and the potential consequences of the proposed transition. Zachariades failed to assess correctly either the situation or the impact of his decisions; the result was the defeat of the GDA and the collapse of the Communist insurgency in Greece.

The state of the GDA's logistics was marginal at best, even during the period of successful guerrilla warfare. The requirements of the Greek guerrillas were substantial, but the internal resources available to satisfy those requirements were limited, and the dependability of outside support was uncertain. In addition, the distribution of arms, ammunition, and other war matériel received from outside sources was difficult and time-consuming due to the harsh climate, rugged terrain, and lack of transport infrastructure, as well as the increasingly effective government interdiction efforts. These problems were compounded by the fact that the organic GDA logistical organization was small and generally inexperienced. The clandestine *aftoamyna* organization on which the GDA relied for the collection, storage, and distribution of supplies and the provision of transport and other services proved vulnerable once the Greek government forces began to act aggressively against it. Thus, even at the peak of its development and effectiveness in late 1948, the inadequacies of the GDA logistical system limited sustained Communist offensive and defensive operations to areas near the border, which could be supplied easily from bases in Albania, Yugoslavia, or Bulgaria.

Even without an all-out transition to the conventional warfare stage, successful guerrilla forces tend to grow in size and eventually become unable to sustain themselves solely by local resources. The assembly of large combat units operating far afield thus requires the establishment of elaborate supply and transport networks and the continuous resupply of food and other essentials, often from external sources. Larger, less mobile guerrilla formations are more vulnerable to enemy action, as are their training camps, supply dumps, hospitals and other semifixed facilities as well as their lines of communications. At the same time, they become less able to sustain the spontaneous, incessant, and ubiquitous pinpricks that do so much to sap the strength and morale of the enemy. For a conventional army these handicaps are multiplied many times.

The decision of the leadership of the KKE/GDA to proceed with the conversion of the GDA to a much larger conventional army posed two essential problems: how to recruit the necessary men and how to supply them. Manpower and logistics were the two salient weaknesses of the Greek Democratic Army. The attempt to create a conventional army imposed upon the GDA requirements for both combat and logistical personnel that it could not meet. As Nachmani has written,

Holding territory and manning field positions increased the demands on the GDA's manpower. Establishing a regular army required growing numbers of administrative auxiliaries and noncombatants for repair-shops, printing works, military police, the military legal system, medical personnel, officers for liaison with the civilian population, and so on. The heavy casualties inflicted on the GDA, the additional demands of conventional warfare, and the Greek government's intentional evacuation of hundreds of thousands of people from areas susceptible to falling into Communist hands all deprived the guerrillas of crucial manpower.[40]

The comparative lack of logistical support personnel that gives a guerrilla army its advantage in tactical mobility and flexibility is a source of great weakness in a conventional army, which must have a steady flow of food, fuel, arms, ammunition, and other supplies as well as a complete range of services—maintenance, medical, and administrative. Thus, the GDA's chronic lack of trained logistical personnel and staff officers, as well as its lack of logistical resources, became a serious fault once the process of conversion to a conventional force began. The newly formed conventional formations found their mobility limited and their staying power severely restricted by the lack of an adequate system to supply the fighting elements and by the inadequacies of their communications system, on which the logistical as well as the command and control systems of the GDA relied.[41]

At best, the GDA appears to have been capable of supporting an armed force of only about 25,000 men engaged in sustained large-scale guerrilla operations; contemporary U.S. intelligence analysts estimated that even at the 25,000-man level, the scope and effectiveness of guerrilla operations in the long term would be limited by the lack of air and heavy artillery support, and by inadequate communications, supply, and transport.[42] Markos estimated that 50,000–60,000 men would be required for a conventional army capable of meeting the GNF head on. Not only would that force be twice the size of the sustainable guerrilla army, it would also require significantly increased amounts of food, clothing, medical supplies, arms, ammunition, fuel, and other supplies as well as large, secure training bases and logistical facilities, which would have to be manned by personnel with experience and technical skills generally unavailable to the GDA.[43] Larger units and more intense and widespread operations would also require additional transport and improved communications.

Thus, the much larger, conventionally organized force proposed by Zachariades significantly increased the number of men and animals to be supported and broadened the types of support required, to include additional kinds of supplies and a higher level of technical skills. The accompanying strategy of positional defense also involved a greater expenditure of ammunition, particularly heavy artillery. Larger, conventionally organized units were less able to sustain themselves off the countryside, which in any event was so devoid of resources as to constitute in many of the mountainous areas of Greece a desert. The conversion to a conventional army also placed a strain on the limited transport resources available to the GDA. More mules and porters were required, lines of communications had to be expanded, and in some cases roads and bridges had to be constructed in order to accommodate the motor transport necessary for the movement of heavy weapons and large quantities of ammunition. Already depleted by the aggressive action of the GNF, the *aftoamyna* was hard pressed to establish and operate the multiple lines of communications required for a large conventional army.

In the end, the Greek Communist forces were simply unable to obtain and distribute the food, arms, ammunition, and other supplies required by a large conventionally organized military force engaged in almost continuous heavy action, either from internal resources or with the assistance of outside supporters. The inability of the GDA to generate sufficient logistical resources to pursue successfully the strategy adopted had predictable results. Inadequate logistical support limited the size of the GDA, limited its mobility (both tactical and logistical), and limited its firepower and endurance in combat. These would not have been fatal flaws except for the fact that the Greek government forces simultaneously improved by virtue of U.S. aid. Whether or not the GDA could have sustained a smaller guerrilla army, as Markos Vafiades argued, and prolonged the civil war long enough for the Greek government to flag and seek a negotiated settlement is problematic.

So long as the GDA continued as a guerrilla army—even up to the fall of 1948—there was hope that the war could be prolonged to a negotiated settlement, but once the fatal decision was made to create a conventional army, to fight positional battles against a constantly improving GNA that had the advantage in firepower, the fate of the GDA was sealed.[44] It has even been suggested that while Markos was aware that a conventional army would require both increased manpower resources and a greatly expanded logistical structure, neither of which it could manage, Zachariades also understood these factors yet elected to create a conventional army and use it for prolonged attacks on towns and the sustained defense of GDA positions out of some perverse desire to satisfy Stalin's wish that the Greek insurrection be terminated. In short, one not-implausible theory is that the rebellion was betrayed by its political head in favor of a foreign master.[45]

CONCLUSION

The Greek civil war of 1945–1949 must be seen in the context of the Cold War, the actions and fate of both sides being determined largely by considerations of international power relationships in the post–World War II years. Stalin declined to provide direct assistance to the Communist rebels in Greece because he feared a direct confrontation with the United States and Great Britain. Yugoslavia, Albania, and Bulgaria supported the GDA as a means of asserting their independence from the Soviet Union, to achieve long-standing national goals, and to create a buffer to protect them against the perceived threat of Western intervention. The United States provided aid to the Greek national government as a means of limiting Soviet expansion in the postwar period, while at the same time it supported the deployment of United Nations observers in the hope of avoiding the necessity for a full-scale military intervention that might have brought U.S. and Soviet troops into a direct confrontation, leading to a wider and more devastating war.

As the first major confrontation of the Cold War, the Greek civil war was a testing ground for the tactics and techniques of insurgent-counterinsurgent warfare, which would mark military affairs for the ensuing four decades. The Soviet Union grew in confidence and learned from the situation in Greece that Communist insurgencies and "wars of national liberation" could be cheap and relatively safe means of engaging the West in a long-term struggle of attrition leading to the achievement of Soviet global goals. Having declined to participate actively in the testing of the prototype, the Soviet Union rushed the new model into full production around the globe—in Africa, the Caribbean, South America, and Asia. From the perspective of the United States, the American intervention in Greece set the pattern for the use of U.S. military forces for nearly half a century, by establishing four important trends: (1) the provision of large-scale military assistance to a foreign government in peacetime; (2) the use of U.S. military personnel as advisors to indigenous forces in the conduct of active military operations; (3) the development of counterguerrilla tactics as a paramount requisite of the Cold War; and (4) involvement in military hostilities without the commitment of maximum U.S. resources.[46]

The Greek civil war also established the pattern for fifty years of international cooperation in peacekeeping. The deployment of the United Nations Commission of Investigation Concerning Greek Frontier Incidents (December 1946–September 1947) was one of the first two instances in which the UN deployed military personnel, even though they acted as observers rather than peacekeepers and operated under the control of their respective national authorities rather than of the United Nations per se.[47] The Commission of Investigation and its successor, the United Nations Special Committee on the Balkans (UNSCOB) (October 1947–December 1951), were the prototypes for UN observer and peacekeeping forces subsequently deployed in the Sinai, the Gaza Strip, the Congo, West Irian, Cyprus, the Golan Heights, Lebanon, and elsewhere. As such, they established the principles and methods for all future UN interventions and displayed all of the problems faced by observer and peacekeeping forces since that time.[48]

For Greece, the civil war of 1945–1949 settled none of the divisive issues that had stymied national unity and development since the turn of the century. The Greek Communists failed to achieve their goals of national unity, economic security, and social justice—laudable in themselves—because Zachariades and his clique, intent on imposing their vision of a Soviet-style conventional army and a strategy of positional warfare, were isolated from the people, ignorant of the nature of modern war and even of the depleted state of the resources of their own society, and blind to the faults of Marxism-Leninism and international Communism. Internally divided, the Communist leaders did not speak or act as one. Their opponents could do no better. The military triumph of the Right was only temporary, and Greece soon fell back into its old pattern of political conflict between Left and Right, between monarchists and republicans, between "haves" and "have-nots." Political instability, retarded economic and social development, and incipient internecine warfare continued to be the characteristics of Greek national life. The right-wing monarchist victors of 1949 were soon supplanted by the politicians of the moderate Left, who in turn were forced to deliver up power to the reactionary colonels of the 1960s. They in turn yielded to a revivified Left in the 1970s. All the while, ordinary Greeks suffered from the uncertainty of their situation and enjoyed little of the remarkable economic and social progress experienced elsewhere in Europe during the period. Their motto—as well as the epitaph for the Greek Democratic Army—can be found in the words of the Greek national anthem, Solomos' "Ode to Liberty,"

If hatreds divide them,
They do not deserve to be free.[49]

NOTES

1. Lawrence S. Wittner, *American Intervention in Greece, 1943–1949* (New York: Columbia Univ. Press, 1982), 280.
2. Stephen Merrill, *The Communist Attack on Greece*, Special Report No. 15, 21st Regular Course (Washington: U.S. Strategic Intelligence School, 28 July 1952), 69.
3. Ibid., 68.
4. Evangelos Averoff-Tossizza, *By Fire and Axe: The Communist Party and the Civil War in Greece, 1944–1949* (New Rochelle, NY: Caratzas Brothers, 1978), 366–67.
5. Ibid., 367.
6. Markos Vafiades' fate following the defeat of the GDA in August 1949 is summarized in "Interview with General Markos Vafiades, former Leader of ELAS, by the Greek Trotskyist paper *Socialist Change*, 1983," found on the Internet at http://werple. net.au/~deller/bs/1983mv.htm. The fate of Karageorgis and Partsalides is noted in Averoff-Tossizza, 367.
7. Averoff-Tossizza, 354.
8. Merrill, 76.
9. Allison Butler Herrick and others, *Area Handbook for Greece*, DA Pam 550-87 (Washington: USGPO, June 1970), 6 [cited hereafter as *Area Handbook*].
10. Quoted by Dominique Eudes, *The Kapetanios: Partisans and Civil War in Greece, 1943–1949* (New York and London: Monthly Review Press, 1972), 354.
11. Edgar O'Ballance, *The Greek Civil War, 1944–1949* (New York: Praeger, 1966), 202.
12. Chief, Intelligence Division, Headquarters, Department of the Army, to Chief, Plans and Operations Division, Headquarters, Department of the Army, Disposition Form, Washington, 7 November 1949, subject: Capabilities of the Greek Guerrillas and the Greek Armed Forces, Enclosure (Estimate, Project No. 5226: "Capabilities of the Greek Guerrillas and the Greek Armed Forces"), 2 [in file "091.112–200.6 Greece (1 January 1949–31 December 1950)," Box 157 ("000.244 Greece to 560. Greece"), Assistant Chief of Staff, G-2, Intelligence, Project Decimal File, 1949–1950, Record Group 319 (Records of the Army Staff), National Archives II, College Park, MD].
13. Floyd A. Spencer (Preparer), *War and Postwar Greece: An Analysis Based on Greek Writings* (Washington: European Affairs Division, Library of Congress, 1952), 120; Amikam Nachmani, *International Intervention in the Greek Civil War: The United Nations Special Committee on the Balkans, 1947–1952* (New York: Praeger, 1990), 137.
14. The purges are described in Wittner, 279.
15. Eudes, 354; Nachmani, 23; Wittner, 283.
16. Angeliki E. Laiou, "Population Movements in the Greek Countryside during the Civil War," in John O. Iatrides, Lars Baerentzen, and Ole L. Smith, eds., *Studies in the History of the Greek Civil War, 1945–1949* (Copenhagen: Museum Tusculanum Press, 1987), 55–58 (Table I). As might be expected the official American estimate (cited by John Iatrides, "Civil War, 1945–1949—National and International Aspects," in John O. Iatrides, ed., *Greece in the 1940s: A Nation in Crisis* [Hanover, NH: Univ. of New England Press, 1981], 390 note 79) was somewhat higher: 38,421 killed, 23,960 captured, and 21,544 surrendered. The Greek government estimated the total number of casualties suffered by the GDA between June 1945 and March 1949 at 70,027, of which 28,992 were killed, 13,105 captured, and 27,931 surrendered (see O'Ballance, 192). Averoff-

Tossizza (page 355) puts the number at over 36,839 killed, 20,128 made prisoner, and 21,258 deserted.

17. Dimitrios G. Kousoulas, *Revolution and Defeat: The Story of the Greek Communist Party* (London: Oxford University Press, 1965), 270 note 21. The official Greek government figures given by Merrill (Appendix V, 1) include only 14,890 officers and men killed, 32,450 officers and men wounded, and 3,800 men missing. Averoff-Tossizza (page 355) puts government casualties at 12,777 officers and men killed and 37,732 officers and men wounded, plus another 1,579 killed and 2,329 wounded in the Gendarmerie.

18. Greek General Staff, Intelligence Directorate, Study (Ref. No. F8206/95/2-12-50) [Athens, 12 February 1950], subject: Guerrilla Warfare: The Organization and Employment of Irregulars, 53 [cited hereafter as "Guerrilla Warfare"]. The number does not include those killed in the fighting or by the GNF or those who died of famine or disease associated with the war.

19. Christopher M. Woodhouse, *The Struggle for Greece, 1941–1949* (London: Hart-Davis, MacGibbon, 1976), 266.

20. "Guerrilla Warfare," 52–53. The same data is included in Merrill, Appendix V, 1–2.

21. Ibid., 55. Actual damage was believed to exceed the amounts indicated, which in any event do not account for the loss of value caused by the interruption of commerce, industry, and agriculture or the greater costs associated with increased military expenditures.

22. *Area Handbook*, 195–96.

23. For opinions on the causes of the GDA's defeat see Averoff-Tossizza, 357–66; O'Ballance, 210–13; Iatrides, "Civil War," 216–19; and J. C. Murray, "The Anti-Bandit War [Part V]," *Marine Corps Gazette* 38, no. 5 (May 1954), 58.

24. United States Army General Staff, Assistant Chief of Staff, G-2, Intelligence, three fact sheets (15 March 1949, 29 March 1949, and undated), Washington, 29 March 1949, subject: Brief Intelligence Estimate on Countries Involved in Military Aid Program (Project 4861) [in Box 2904 (Projects 4346–5791), Assistant Chief of Staff, G-2, Intelligence, Administrative Division, Document Library Branch, Serial Sets of Printed Intelligence Reports (Publication ["P"] Files), 1929–1951, RG 319, NA]. By 31 July 1949 the Greek national ground forces had increased to 235,632 men, including 24,958 in the Gendarmerie and 7,477 civil police, a navy of 13,584 men, and an air force of 7,484 men, for a total of 256,700 men under arms (see United States Central Intelligence Agency, *Current Situation in Greece* [ORE 4-50; Washington: Central Intelligence Agency, 28 February 1950], 4).

25. O'Ballance, 153.

26. Wittner, 253.

27. William Hardy McNeill, *Greece: American Aid in Action, 1947–1956* (New York: Twentieth Century Fund, 1957), 229 (Appendix 1). The sums represent funds appropriated by Congress.

28. Iatrides, "Civil War," 197.

29. Iatrides, "Civil War," 213; Robert W. Selton, "Communist Errors in the Anti-Bandit War," *Military Review* 45, no. 9 (September 1965), 71.

30. Woodhouse, 257.

31. Ibid., 188.

32. O'Ballance, 111.

33. United States Army Command and General Staff College, *Internal Defense Operations: A Case History, Greece 1946–49*, USACGSC RB 31-1 (Fort Leavenworth, KS: United States Army Command and General Staff College, 1 November 1967), 126.

34. J. C. Murray, "The Anti-Bandit War [Part IV]," *Marine Corps Gazette* 38, no. 4 (April 1954), 60; McNeill, 42.

35. For a theoretical analysis of the two events see Mao Tse-tung's *On Protracted War* (in Mao Tse-tung, *Selected Works*, 3 volumes, translated from the Chinese [New York: International Publishers, 1954–1955]), and Truong Chinh, *La Resistance vaincra* (Hanoi: Éditions en Langues Étrangères, 1962), published in English as *Primer for Revolt* (New York: Praeger, 1963).

36. Kousoulas, 243–44 note 9.

37. France, Ministère de la Défense Nationale et des Forces Armées, *Counter Guerrilla Operations for Maintaining Order in French North Africa (Opérations de contre guerilla dans le cadre du maintien de l'ordre en A. F. N.)*, Manual T. T. A. 123, translated and edited by Office of the Assistant Chief of Staff for Intelligence, Headquarters, Department of the Army (Washington: Headquarters, Department of the Army, Office of the Assistant Chief of Staff for Intelligence, 24 August 1956), 13.

38. Kousoulas, 249–50.

39. Woodhouse, 276.

40. Nachmani, 21.

41. J. C. Murray, "The Anti-Bandit War [Part II]," *Marine Corps Gazette* 38, no. 2 (February 1954), 51; Murray, "The Anti-Bandit War [Part IV]," 58; Iatrides, "Civil War," 211.

42. Iatrides "Civil War," 213.

43. Moreover, the creation of a conventional army had the unforeseen effect of reducing the number of capable officers in the combat units, as the best and most experienced officers had to be reassigned to manage the expanding combat service support system (see O'Ballance, 182).

44. O'Ballance, 216.

45. Eudes passim.

46. Robert W. Selton, "The Cradle of U.S. Cold War Strategy," *Military Review* 46, no. 8 (August 1966), 48.

47. Nachmani, 154.

48. Ibid., 155.

49. Quoted in John O. Iatrides, *Revolt in Athens: The Greek Communist "Second Round," 1944–1945* (Princeton, NJ: Princeton University Press, 1972), 61.

Appendices

Appendix A
Greek Democratic Army Order of Battle

The Greek Democratic Army (GDA) was in a state of constant organizational change throughout the Greek civil war of 1945–1949. Moreover, units were frequently transferred from one region to another to meet strategic and tactical requirements. There was considerable cross-attachment, and units were frequently reassigned permanently from one major headquarters to another. The commanders changed over time as individuals became casualties, were dismissed, or rose in rank and responsibility. The strength of individual units also varied according to the casualties taken and the success of recruiting efforts. No comprehensive order of battle generated by the GDA general command appears to have survived, and the GDA order of battle must be reconstructed from often inaccurate and incomplete Greek government and U.S. intelligence estimates. For all of these reasons, it is difficult to present a completely accurate picture of the GDA order of battle at any given time. However, the following depiction of the GDA order of battle on 30 June 1949, the eve of its destruction, should provide some rough idea of the structure of the GDA as it evolved in the last year of the war.

The GDA order of battle presented here has been compiled from a number of sources, the most important of which are Greek General Staff, Intelligence Directorate, Staff Study, Ref. No. F8206/95/2-12-50, Athens, 12 February 1950, subject: Guerrilla Warfare: The Organization and Employment of Irregulars; and United States Military Attaché–Greece (Capt. C. R. Meltesen), Intelligence Report R-298-49 (ID No. 589129), Athens, 8 August 1949, subject: Guerrilla Order of Battle—Strength, Organization and Disposition [in Box 3781, Assistant Chief of Staff, G-2, Intelligence, Numerical Series of Intelligence Document File ("ID Files"), 1944–1955, Record Group 319 (Records of the Army Staff), National Archives II, College Park, MD].

Table A.1
GDA Order of Battle as of 30 June 1949

Units	Cmdr	Location	No. of Men	Comments
GDA GENERAL COMMAND	Goussias	Vronderion	250	
24th Infantry Brigade	Nemertsikas	Kaimaktsalan	650	Remnants
Cavalry Battalion	Thanasis	Kaimaktsalan		
107th Infantry Brigade	Velissaris	Grammos	750	At times subordinate to 11th Inf Div
538th Infantry Battalion	Midis	Grammos		
539th Infantry Battalion	Soumidis	Grammos		
588th Infantry Battalion	Stefanos	Grammos		
108th Infantry Brigade	Zara	Grammos	600	Zara KIA 24 Jul 49
648th Infantry Battalion	Montas	Grammos		
585th Infantry Battalion	Skotidas	Grammos		
725th Infantry Battalion	Zois	Grammos		
159th Infantry Brigade	Petritis	Pogoniani		Remnants
Officers School Brigade		Vitsi	300	
Independent Infantry Battalion	Anapodos	Euboea	150	
Saboteur Brigade	Vratsianos	Oreikas-Vourinos-Sniatsikon		Scattered remnants
Artillery Complement		Vitsi-Grammos		9 btrys in early 1949
3rd Battery		Vitsi-Grammos		
5th Battery		Vitsi-Grammos		
9th Battery		Vitsi-Grammos		
25th Battery		Vitsi-Grammos		
34th Battery		Vitsi-Grammos		
40th Battery		Vitsi-Grammos		
60th Battery		Vitsi-Grammos		
65th Battery		Vitsi-Grammos		
67th Battery		Vitsi-Grammos		
Cavalry Brigade	Gatsoras	Ossa		As of 25 Aug 49
Cavalry Battalion	Tzimas	Ossa-Pilion	90	
Engineer Battalion		Grammos	80	
Engineer Battalion	Andaras	Vitsi		
Signal Battalion		Vitsi-Grammos	280	
315th Static Battalion	Papagianko-poulos	Vitsi		
Static Battalion		Vitsi		
Unidentified Battalion		Samos	180	
88th Area Unit	Gouras	Parnassos	80	Double Company
Stretcher Bearer Battalion		Vitsi?		
Stretcher Bearer Battalion		Grammos?		
Transport Battalion		Vitsi		
Transport Battalion		Vitsi		
Transport Battalion		Grammos		
711th Duty Company		Kaimaktsalan		Double Company
712th Duty Company		Kaimaktsalan		Double Company
713th Duty Company		Siniatsikon		Double Company
Duty Company	Tzavelas	Siniatsikon		Double Company
Duty Company	Mavroudis	Pierria-Olympus	150	Double Company

Table A.1 (continued)

Units	Cmdr	Location	No. of Men	Comments
1ST INFANTRY DIVISION	Viotis?	Orthris-Xinias-Agrafa		Remnants; subordinate to GHQ So. Greece; included 77th Inf Bde and Cavalry Bde in early 1949
123th Infantry Brigade	Ferreos	Grammos and Olympus area	290	Operating as combined bde wth 192nd Inf Bde elements
138th Infantry Brigade		Agrafa		Scattered remnants
192nd Infantry Brigade	Bandekos	Grammos-Othris-Xinias		Scattered remnants operating as combined bde with 123rd Inf Bde; Bandekos captured 2 Aug 49
2ND INFANTRY DIVISION		Vardhousia		Remnants; subordinate to GHQ So. Greece
126th Infantry Brigade				Remnants only
144th Infantry Brigade				Remnants only
172nd Infantry Brigade				Remnants only
3RD INFANTRY DIVISION	Giouzelis	Peloponnesus		Destroyed in Opn PIGEON; included 22nd and 55th Inf Bdes in early 1949
6TH INFANTRY DIVISION	Petris	West Beles	1,600	Subordinate to GHQ Eastern Macedonia-Western Thrace
20th Infantry Brigade	Fivos	Beles	350	
Duty Company	Kolokotronis	Beles		Double Company
Duty Company	Akritas	Beles		Double Company
132nd Infantry Brigade	Diplarakos	Beles	550	
Duty Company	Garefis	Beles		Double Company
Duty Company	Ananias	Beles		Double Company
Labor Duty Co.		Beles		Double Company
650th Infantry Battalion	Stathis	Beles		Rear area unit
Thanasis Cavalry Unit		Beles		
677th Duty Company	Stefanidis	Beles		Double Company
7TH INFANTRY DIVISION	Khimaros	Haidou	700	Subordinate to GHQ Eastern Macedonia-Western Thrace
350th Infantry Battalion	Mesinezis	NW Haidou		
560th Infantry Battalion	Ghitis	NW Haidou		

Table A.1 (continued)

Units	Cmdr	Location	No. of Men	Comments
8TH INFANTRY DIVISION	Fokas	Grammos	1,020	Directly subordinate to GDA Gen Cmd
75th Infantry Brigade	Lambros	Grammos		
Infantry Battalion	Sidiropoulos	Grammos		
Infantry Battalion	Anaratiades	Grammos		
Infantry Battalion	Kanitsis	Grammos		
Static Battalion	Parapanos	Grammos		
9TH INFANTRY DIVISION	Palaiologos	Grammos	820	Directly subordinate to GDA Gen Cmd
16th Infantry Brigade	Papa-dimitriou	Grammos		Papadimitriou KIA 7 Aug 49
Infantry Battalion	Xanthos	Grammos		
Infantry Battalion	Melas	Grammos		
10TH INFANTRY DIVISION	Skotidas	Vitsi	1,330	Skotidas KIA 11 Aug 49; replaced by Tomboulithas; directly subordinate to GDA Gen Cmd
14th Infantry Brigade	Sofianos	Vitsi	910	
580th Infantry Battalion	Ermis	Vitsi		
589th Infantry Battalion	Dalianis	Vitsi		
601st Infantry Battalion	Grivas	Vitsi		
105th Infantry Brigade	Lasanis	Vitsi	420	
551st Infantry Battalion		Vitsi	150	
552nd Infantry Battalion	Kaplanis	Vitsi		
553rd Infantry Battalion		Vitsi		
11TH INFANTRY DIVISION	Vainas	Vitsi	1,670	Directly subordinate to GDA Gen Cmd
18th Infantry Brigade	Prikos	Vitsi	800	
425th Infantry Battalion	Argiris	Vitsi		
426th Infantry Battalion	Petsos	Vitsi		
427th Infantry Battalion	Tsolakis	Vitsi		
102nd Infantry Brigade		Vitsi		
Infantry Battalion		Vitsi		
Infantry Battalion	Lesits	Vitsi		
Infantry Battalion	Golinatas	Vitsi		
103rd Infantry Brigade	Akhilieas	Vitsi	870	
Infantry Battalion	Adakos	Vitsi		
Infantry Battalion	Takis	Vitsi		
Infantry Battalion	Papas	Vitsi		
15TH INFANTRY DIVISION		Grammos?		Unconfirmed; probably directly subbordinate to GDA Gen Cmd

Appendix B
Organizational Diagrams—GDA Units

In February 1947 the Politburo of the Greek Communist Party (KKE) made the decision, subsequently confirmed by the Third Plenum of the Central Committee of the KKE in September 1947, to proceed with the reorganization of the Greek Democratic Army (GDA) along the lines of a conventional force. The transformation of the GDA was still only partially completed when the GDA was overwhelmed by Greek national forces in the Grammos and Vitsi in August 1949. Before the final, decisive defeat, the GDA General Command prepared a series of standard tables of organization and equipment (TOEs) for various types of tactical units. Although the reorganization was never completed and the tactical units of the GDA never attained the levels of manpower and weapons authorized by the TOEs, the organizational diagrams included in this appendix are useful as indicators of the planned development of the GDA and of the aspirations of its leaders.

The principal sources for the following organizational diagrams are United States Military Attaché–Greece (Maj. Harold A. Tidmarsh), Intelligence Report R-110-49 (ID No. 542941), Athens, 22 March 1949, subject: Organization of the Bandit Forces and Tactics Employed by the Bandits, Enclosures 2–6, and Greek General Staff, Intelligence Directorate, Study (Ref. No. F8206/95/2-12-50) [Athens, 12 February 1950], subject: Guerrilla Warfare–The Organization and Employment of Irregulars, ¶125 and Charts C–F [both in file "GEOG. L. Greece 370.64 (Guerrillas)," General Reference Branch, United States Army Center of Military History, Washington, DC].

Figure B.1
Greek Democratic Army Infantry Brigade

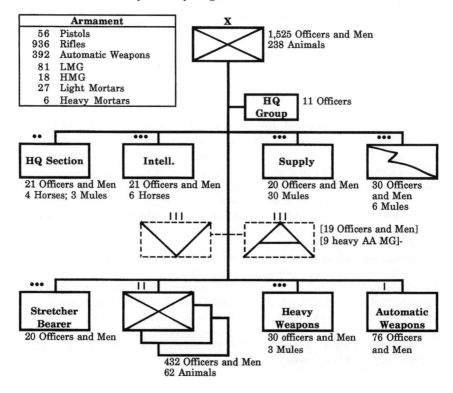

Armament	
56	Pistols
936	Rifles
392	Automatic Weapons
81	LMG
18	HMG
27	Light Mortars
6	Heavy Mortars

X
1,525 Officers and Men
238 Animals

HQ Group — 11 Officers

HQ Section
21 Officers and Men
4 Horses; 3 Mules

Intell.
21 Officers and Men
6 Horses

Supply
20 Officers and Men
30 Mules

30 Officers
and Men
6 Mules

[19 Officers and Men]
[9 heavy AA MG]-

Stretcher
Bearer
20 Officers and Men

432 Officers and Men
62 Animals

Heavy
Weapons
30 officers and Men
3 Mules

Automatic
Weapons
76 Officers
and Men

Figure B.2
Greek Democratic Army Light Infantry Brigade

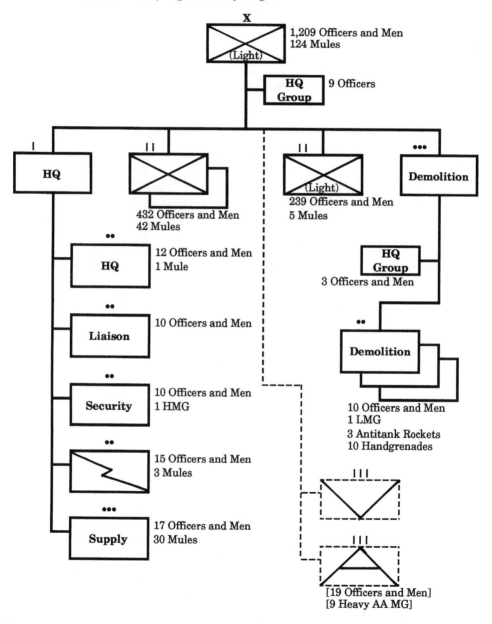

Figure B.3
Greek Democratic Army Infantry Battalion

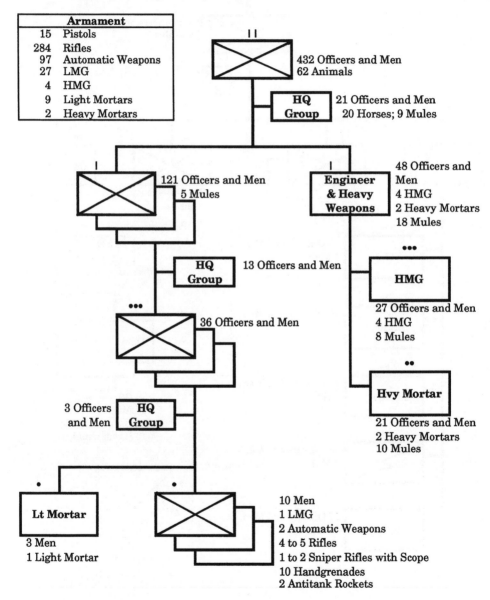

Armament	
15	Pistols
284	Rifles
97	Automatic Weapons
27	LMG
4	HMG
9	Light Mortars
2	Heavy Mortars

II

432 Officers and Men
62 Animals

HQ Group — 21 Officers and Men
20 Horses; 9 Mules

121 Officers and Men
5 Mules

Engineer & Heavy Weapons — 48 Officers and Men
4 HMG
2 Heavy Mortars
18 Mules

HQ Group — 13 Officers and Men

HMG — 27 Officers and Men
4 HMG
8 Mules

36 Officers and Men

3 Officers and Men — HQ Group

Hvy Mortar — 21 Officers and Men
2 Heavy Mortars
10 Mules

Lt Mortar
3 Men
1 Light Mortar

10 Men
1 LMG
2 Automatic Weapons
4 to 5 Rifles
1 to 2 Sniper Rifles with Scope
10 Handgrenades
2 Antitank Rockets

Figure B.4
Greek Democratic Army Light Infantry Battalion

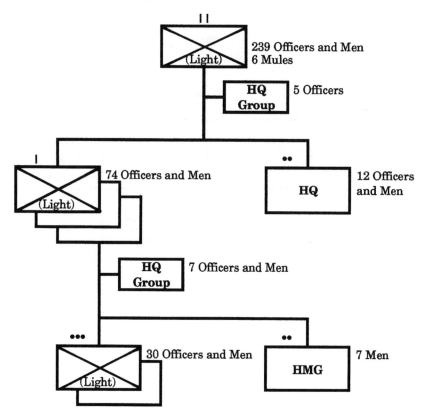

239 Officers and Men
6 Mules

5 Officers

74 Officers and Men

12 Officers and Men

7 Officers and Men

30 Officers and Men

7 Men

Figure B.5
Greek Democratic Army Artillery Troop

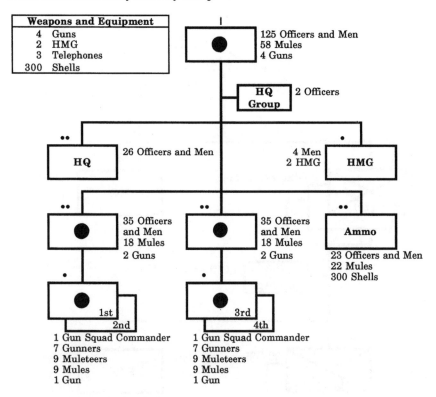

NB: Two troops constituted a battery.

Figure B.6
Greek Democratic Army Independent Artillery Section

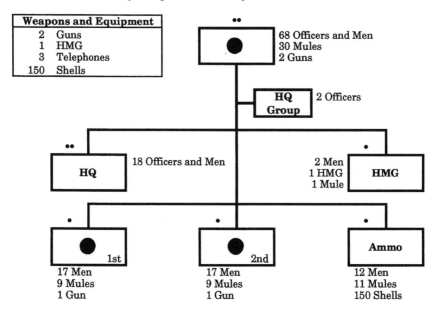

Weapons and Equipment	
2	Guns
1	HMG
3	Telephones
150	Shells

68 Officers and Men
30 Mules
2 Guns

HQ Group — 2 Officers

HQ — 18 Officers and Men

HMG — 2 Men, 1 HMG, 1 Mule

1st — 17 Men, 9 Mules, 1 Gun

2nd — 17 Men, 9 Mules, 1 Gun

Ammo — 12 Men, 11 Mules, 150 Shells

Appendix C
Common Map Symbols

TYPE OF UNIT

Infantry		Armored Cavalry
Armor		Antiaircraft Artillery
Artillery		Antitank
Cavalry		Airborne/Parachute
Commando (Cdo)		Gendarmerie (G)
Engineer		Transportation
Signal		Ordnance
Quartermaster		Medical Service

Appendix C (continued)

SIZE OF UNIT

• □	Squad
•• □	Section
••• □	Platoon
I □	Company/Battery
II □	Battalion/Squadron

III □	Regiment
X □	Brigade
XX □	Division
XXX □	Corps
□	Command Post

Glossary

AA	Antiaircraft
AAA	Antiaircraft artillery
AAA	*Arkhigeion Apeleftherotikou Agonos* (Liberation Struggle Command)
AAMG	Antiaircraft machine gun
ADM	Admiral
AFB	Air Force Base
aftoamyna	GDA clandestine auxiliary organization responsible for recruitment, tax collection, intelligence, and logistics
AKE	Greek Agrarian Party
AMAG	American Mission for Aid to Greece
AMFOGE	Allied Mission for Observing Greek Elections
AMM	Allied Military Mission
andarte	A Greek guerrilla
AT	Antitank
Bde	Brigade
BMM	British Military Mission
Bn	Battalion
Br	British
Brig. Gen.	Brigadier General
ca.	circa (approximately)
Capt.	Captain
Cdr.	Commander
Chams	An Albanian tribe, some members of which resided in northern Epirus

CIA	Central Intelligence Agency (U.S.)
CIG	Central Intelligence Group (U.S.)
Co	Company
Col.	Colonel
Cominform	Communist Information Bureau
Comintern	(Third) Communist International
Cpl.	Corporal
DAG	*See* GDA
Dakota	U.S. C-47 (DC-3) cargo aircraft
DAS	*See* GDA
Dept	Department
DES	*See* GDA
Div	Division
drachma	Greek currency unit (15,000 *drachmae* = $1.00 U.S. in 1945–1949)
EAM	*Ethnikon Apeleftherotikon Metopon* (National Liberation Front)
ECA	Economic Co-operation Administration
EDES	*Ellenikos Demokratikos Ethnikos Syndesmos* (Greek Democratic National League)
EEE	Greek Fascist Party
EKKA	*Ethniki kai Koinoniki Apeleftherosis* (National and Social Liberation)
ELAN	*Ethnikon Laïkon Apeleftherotikon Nautikon* (National People's Liberation Navy)
ELAS	*Ethnikos Laikos Apeleftherotikos Stratos* (National People's Liberation Army)
ELASite	A member of ELAS
ELD	*Enosis Laïkos Demokratias* (Union of Popular Democracy)
EOA	National Organization of Officers
EOEA	*Ethniki Organosis Ellinikon Andarton* (Greek Nationalist Guerrilla Units) (*see* EDES)
EP	*Ethniki Politophylaki* (National Civil Guard)
EPON	*Eniaia Panellinios Organosis Neolaias* (National All-Greek Organization of Youth; Greek Communist youth movement)
ERGAS	*Ergatikos Antifasistikos Syndesmos* (Worker's Antifascist League; Greek Communist-dominated labor organization)
ERP	European Recovery Program
ES	"Greek Army"
ETA	*Epimeletis tou Andarte* (taxation and supply organization of ELAS)
1st Lt.	First Lieutenant
FM	Field Marshal

GA	General Assembly (United Nations)
GB	Great Britain
GDA	Greek Democratic Army (*Demokratikos Stratos Ellados*)
Gen.	General
GHQ	General Headquarters
GNA	Greek National Army
GNF	Greek national forces
GR	Greece
Grk	Greek
Helldiver	U.S. dive-bomber
HMG	Heavy machine gun
HQ	Headquarters
hvy	Heavy
IDEA	*Ieros Desmos Ellinon Axiomatikon* (Sacred Band of Greek Officers)
ILO	International Labor Organization
ipefthiros	"The Responsible," chief EAM local official (mayor)
JUSMAPG	Joint U.S. Military Advisory and Planning Group–Greece
kapetanios	"Captain"; Greek guerrilla leader; sometimes used in referring to GDA political commissars
KEN	Seamen's Partisan Committee
kg	Kilogram (2.2046 pounds)
KGAKAMT	*Klimakion Genikou Arkhigeiou Kentrikis kai Anatolikis Makedonias kai Thrakis* (Echelon of General Headquarters for Central and Eastern Macedonia and Thrace)
KGANE	*Klimakion Genikou Arkhigeiou Notiou Ellados* (Echelon of General Headquarters for Southern Greece)
KKE	*Kommounistikon Komma Ellados* (Communist Party of Greece)
kleftes	Bandits (of the traditional heroic type)
KM	Kilometer (0.6214 miles)
KOEN	Communist Organization of Greek Macedonia
KOSSA	Communist Organization of the Army and Security Corps
liaison unit	*See yiafaka*
LK	*Laïkon Komma*: Greek Popular Party (principal royalist party led by Metaxas)
LMG	Light machine gun
LOK	*Lokhoi Oreinon Katadromeon* (Companies of Mountain Rangers; GNA commandos)
lt	Light
Lt.	Lieutenant

Lt. Col.	Lieutenant Colonel
Lt. Gen.	Lieutenant General
MAD	*Monades Aposmasmaton Dioxeos* (Units of Pursuit Detachments; GNA mobile militia organization)
Maj.	Major
Maj. Gen.	Major General
MAY	*Monades Asphaleias Ypaithrou* (Units for the Defense of the Countryside; GNA militia organization, static)
mdm	Medium
metric ton	2,204.62 pounds
mm	Millimeters
NA	National Archives (U.S.)
NOF	*Narodni Osvoboditelni Front* (Slav-Macedonian National Liberation Front)
OB	Observation Base
OENA	Slav-Macedonian Organization
OENO	Federation of Greek Maritime Unions (Communist dominated)
OG	Observation Group
oka	A Greek unit of volume/weight; roughly equal to one kilogram
OPLA	*Omades Prostasias Laikou Agonos* (Organization for the Protection of the People's Struggle; KKE secret security and terror apparatus)
OSS	Office of Strategic Services (U.S.)
oz	Ounce(s)
£	Pound sterling; ca. 1943, £1 = ca. 5 gold sovereigns = approx. $20 U.S.
panzerfaust	German hand-held antitank rocket
PAO	*Panellinios Apeleftherotiki Organosis* (Panhellenic Liberation Organization)
PDEG	Democratic Women's Organization of Greece (Communist dominated)
PDGFG	Provisional Democratic Government of Free Greece
PEAN	Patriotic Group of Fighting Youth
PEEA	*Politiki Epitropi Ethnikis Apeleftherosis* (Political Committee of National Liberation)
PFC	Private First Class
PK	*Phileleftheron Komma*; Greek Liberal Party (conservative republican party of Venizelos)
Plat	Platoon
plenum	Full meeting of Communist Party Central Committee

POC	Peace Observation Commission (Greece)
POL	Petroleum, oils, and lubricants
Pvt.	Private
RAF	Royal Air Force (British)
Regt	Regiment
Republican Army	*See* GDA
RG	Record Group
RHAF	Royal Hellenic Air Force
RHN	Royal Hellenic Navy
RN	Royal Navy (British)
2d Lt.	Second Lieutenant
SC	Security Council (United Nations)
Sect	Section
Sgt.	Sergeant
SMG	Submachine gun
SNOF	*Slavomakedonski Narodnoosloboditelniot Front* (Slavo-Macedonian National Liberation Front; later reorganized as NOF)
Sobranje	Bulgarian Parliament
SOE	Special Operations Executive (British)
Spitfire	British fighter aircraft
Sqd	Squad
Sqdn	Squadron
ST	Short ton (2,000 pounds)
Thessalonike	Salonika
UNRRA	United Nations Relief and Rehabilitation Administration
UNSCOB	United Nations Special Committee on the Balkans
USA	United States Army
USACMH	United States Army Center of Military History
USAF	United States Air Force
USAMHI	United States Army Military History Institute
USMC	United States Marine Corps
USN	United States Navy
USSR	Union of Soviet Socialist Republics
WO	Warrant Officer
X	An extreme right-wing Greek organization led by Col. George Grivas

yafka   Russian term for a secret, secure meeting place or "safe house"; name given to KKE cells responsible for intelligence gathering, recruitment, and supply

yiafaka   GDA liaison unit responsible for intelligence, recruitment, taxation, and logistics in one of twenty-five sectors; sometimes used to refer to the entire KKE/GDA clandestine auxiliary force (the *aftoamyna*)

YTO   GDA Security Service (internal police)

Selected Bibliography

PRIMARY MATERIALS

Carlisle Barracks, Pennsylvania, United States Army Military History Institute Archives

James A. Van Fleet Papers. 1 small box. Correspondence, biographical material, background material for oral history, and interview questions, ca. 1940–1960. Van Fleet was Director, Joint United States Military Planning and Advisory Group–Greece, 1948–1950.

Stirling Loop Larabee Papers. 1 small box. Biographical data, writings, and official and personal correspondence with, *inter alia*, George S. Patton, Billy Mitchell, Constantine Ventiris, and Ambassador McVeagh, ca. 1910–1950. Larabee was the U.S. military attaché in Greece.

William G. Livesay Papers. 1 small box. Official correspondence and reports, historical studies, diaries, notes, and clippings, 1947–1948. Livesay was first director, and later deputy director under Lt. Gen. Van Fleet, of the Joint United States Military Planning and Advisory Group–Greece. Materials include Livesay's diary for the period 13 June–4 November 1947 (typescript, 47 pages) and a variety of documents, 1947–1948, including notes, maps, figures on equipment and supplies required, background material on the Greek Civil War, and lists of the personnel of the Greek General Staff and the British headquarters in Greece.

Carlisle Barracks, Pennsylvania, United States Army Military History Institute Library

Joint United States Military Aid Program to Greece, Reports and Records Section. *JUSMAPG—Brief History, 1 January 1948 to 31 December 1949*. Mimeo [Athens]: Reports and Records Section, Joint United States Military, 3 February 1950. 26 pages. Includes organization charts, statistics, and strength/location data on Communist rebels in Greece.

Miscellaneous documents pertaining to the Joint United States Military Advisory Group–Greece. (MHI MAAG-T9-MDAP).

United States Joint Military Aid Group–Greece. "Material Programmed, Received and Required under Approved Mutual Defense Assistance Programs." Athens: JUSMAGG, n.d. (MHI MAGG-C8-MDAP-CS-MP).

College Park, Maryland, United States National Archives II

The following Record Groups and file groupings were consulted. Individual documents are cited in full in the text.

Record Group 319: Records of the Army Staff

Assistant Chief of Staff, G-2, Intelligence. Numerical Series of Intelligence Documents File ["ID" Files], June 1944–1951.
———. Plans and Operations Division, Decimal File, 1949–February 1950.
———. Project Decimal Files, 1946–1948.
———. Project Decimal Files, 1949–1950.
———. Serial Sets of Printed Intelligence Reports (Publication ["P"] Files), 1929–1951.
Assistant Chief of Staff, G-3, Plans and Operations Division, Decimal File, 1946–1948.

Record Group 334: Records of Interservice Agencies

Joint United States Aid Group, Greece, United States Army Section Group, Adjutant General Section, Central Files Unit. General Decimal Correspondence File, 1947–1954.
———. Publications File (Orders, Bulletins, Memoranda, and Other Administrative Directives Pertaining to the Army's Participation in the Military Aid to Greece Program), 1947–1954.

Washington, DC, United States Army Center of Military History, General Reference Branch

Draft Studies

Gardner, Hugh H. Civil War in Greece, 1945–1949 (Incomplete Draft). Washington: Office of the Chief of Military History, Department of the Army, n.d. Pagination varies.
———. Guerrilla and Counterguerrilla Warfare in Greece, 1941–1945 (Draft). Washington: Office of the Chief of Military History, Department of the Army, 1962. 234 pages.
Hermes, Walter G. Survey of the Development of the Role of the U.S. Military Advisor (Draft). Washington: Office of the Chief of Military History, Department of the Army, n.d. 95 pages.

File GEOG. L. GREECE 370.02 (Civil War)

Extract-Summary of Report of Maj. Gen. S. J. Chamberlin to [U.S.] Army Chief of Staff, 20 October 1947. 6 pages.
Letter, Lt. Gen. James A. Van Fleet (Director, JUSMAPG) to General Alexander Papagos

(CINC, Greek Armed Forces), Athens, 26 January 1949, subject: "Command Failures in GNA." 1 page plus enclosure (Letter, Brig. Gen. Reuben E. Jenkins [Assistant Director, JUSMAPG] to Lt. Gen. T. Kitrilakis [Deputy Chief of Staff, Greek General Staff], 26 January 1949, subject: Failures of GNA at Karditsa, Naousa, and Karpenision. 3 pages).

File GEOG. L. GREECE 370.64 (Guerrillas)

Greek General Staff, Intelligence Directorate. Study (Ref. No. F8206/95/2-12-50), Athens, [12 February 1950], subject: Guerrilla Warfare—The Organization and Employment of Irregulars. 60 pages.
United States Military Attaché–Greece (Maj. Harold A. Tidmarsh). Intelligence Report R-110-49 (ID No. 542941), Athens, 22 March 1949, subject: Organization of the Bandit Forces and Tactics Employed by the Bandits. 20 pages and 6 enclosures.

PUBLISHED OFFICIAL DOCUMENTS

United Nations

United Nations General Assembly. *Report of the United Nations Special Committee on the Balkans.* General Assembly, Official Records: Third Session, Supplement No. 8 (A/574). Lake Success, NY: United Nations General Assembly, 1948. 36 pages.
———. *Report of the United Nations Special Committee on the Balkans.* General Assembly, Official Records: Fourth Session, Supplement No. 8 A/935. Lake Success, NY: United Nations General Assembly, 1949. 25 pages.
———. *Report of the United Nations Special Committee on the Balkans.* General Assembly, Official Records: Fifth Session, Supplement No. 11 A/1307. Lake Success, NY: United Nations General Assembly, 1950. 33 pages.
———. *Report of the United Nations Special Committee on the Balkans.* General Assembly, Official Records: Sixth Session, Supplement No. 11 A/1857. New York: United Nations General Assembly, 1951. 32 pages.
———. *Supplementary Report of United Nations Special Committee on the Balkans Covering the Period from 17 June to 10 September 1948.* General Assembly, Official Records: Third Session, Supplement No. 8A A/644. Paris: United Nations General Assembly, 1948. 17 pages.

United States Central Intelligence Agency

United States Central Intelligence Agency. *Consequences of Certain Courses of Action with Respect to Greece.* (ORE 10-48). Washington: Central Intelligence Agency, 5 April 1948. 12 pages.
———. *Continuing Satellite Aid to the Greek Guerrillas.* (ORE 67-48). Washington: Central Intelligence Agency, 8 October 1948. 4 pages.
———. *Current Situation in Albania.* (ORE 71-49). Washington: Central Intelligence Agency, 15 December 1949. 13 pages.
———. *The Current Situation in Greece.* (ORE-51). Washington: Central Intelligence Agency, 20 October 1947. 5 pages.

————. *Current Situation in Greece.* (ORE 28-48). Washington: Central Intelligence Agency, 17 November 1948. 9 pages and map.

————. *Current Situation in Greece.* (ORE 4-50). Washington: Central Intelligence Agency, 28 February 1950. 12 pages and map.

————. *Estimate of the Yugoslav Regime's Ability to Resist Soviet Pressure during 1949.* (ORE 44-49). Washington: Central Intelligence Agency, 20 June 1949. 12 pages.

United States Central Intelligence Agency. *Evaluation of Soviet-Yugoslav Relations (1950).* (ORE 8-50). Washington: Central Intelligence Agency, 11 May 1950. 8 pages.

————. *Possible Consequences of Communist Control of Greece in the Absence of US Counteraction.* (ORE-69). Washington: Central Intelligence Agency, 9 February 1948. 9 pages.

————. *The Yugoslav Dilemma.* (ORE 16-49). Washington: Central Intelligence Agency, 10 February 1949. 3 pages.

United States Central Intelligence Group. *The Greek Situation.* (ORE 6/1). Washington: Central Intelligence Group, 7 February 1947. 16 pages.

United States Department of State

Howard, Harry N. *The United Nations and the Problem of Greece.* Department of State Publication 2909, Near Eastern Series 9. Washington: USGPO (Division of Publications, Office of Public Affairs, Department of State), 1947. 97 pages. Consists of three articles and ten annexes. The articles, which appeared originally in the *Department of State Bulletin,* were written by Harry N. Howard, who was Chief, Near East Branch, Division of Research for Near East and Africa, and who served as an adviser on the U.S. Delegation to the United Nations Commission of Investigation Concerning Greek Frontier Incidents. Many of its documents are reproduced here.

United States Department of State. *Report of the Allied Mission to Observe the Greek Elections.* Department of State Publication No. 2522. Washington: USGPO, 1946.

United States Office of Strategic Services

United States, Office of Strategic Services, Research and Analysis Branch. *The Present Balance of Political Forces in Greece.* Research and Analysis No. 2862. Washington: Research and Analysis Branch, Office of Strategic Services, 27 February 1945. 32 pages.

United States Senate

United States Senate, Committee on Foreign Relations. *Legislative Origins of the Truman Doctrine Hearings held in Executive Session before the Committee on Foreign Relations, United States Senate, 80th Congress, 1st Session, on S.938: A Bill to Provide for Assistance to Greece and Turkey.* Historical Series. Washington: USGPO, 1973. 224 pages.

SECONDARY WORKS

Abbott, Frank J. *The Greek Civil War, 1947–1949: Lessons for the Operational Artist in Foreign Internal Defense.* School of Advanced Military Studies Thesis. Fort Leavenworth, KS: School of Advanced Military Studies, USACGSC, May 1994. 55 pages. Case study of U.S. government efforts to help Greece defeat its Communist insurgency, 1946–1949.

The American University, Counterinsurgency Information Analysis Center, Special Operations Research Office. *Peak Organized Strength of Guerrilla and Government Forces in Algeria, Nagaland, Ireland, Indochina, South Vietnam, Malaya, Philippines, and Greece.* Washington, DC: Special Operations Research Office, Counterinsurgency Information Analysis Center, American University, n.d. [ca. 1965].

Averoff-Tossizza, Evangelos. *By Fire and Axe: The Communist Party and the Civil War in Greece, 1944–1949.* New Rochelle, NY: Caratzas Brothers, 1978. 438 pages. By a former defense minister of the Greek national government.

Baerentzen, Lars. "The 'Paidomazoma' and the Queen's Camps," In Lars Baerentzen, John O. Iatrides, and Ole L. Smith, eds., *Studies in the History of the Greek Civil War, 1945–1949.* Copenhagen: Museum Tusculanum Press, 1987, 127–57.

Baerentzen, Lars, John O. Iatrides, and Ole L. Smith, eds., *Studies in the History of the Greek Civil War, 1945–1949.* Copenhagen: Museum Tusculanum Press, 1987. 325 pages.

Balcos, Anastase. "Guerrilla Warfare," *Military Review* 37, no. 12 (March 1958), 49–54.

Barker, Elizabeth. "Yugoslav Policy towards Greece, 1947–1949." In Lars Baerentzen, John O. Iatrides, and Ole L. Smith, eds., *Studies in the History of the Greek Civil War, 1945–1949.* Copenhagen: Museum Tusculanum Press, 1987, 263–95.

———. "The Yugoslavs and the Greek Civil War of 1946–1949." In Lars Baerentzen, John O. Iatrides, and Ole L. Smith, eds., *Studies in the History of the Greek Civil War, 1945–1949.* Copenhagen: Museum Tusculanum Press, 1987, 298–308.

Campbell, M. A., E. W. Downs, and L. V. Schuetta. *The Employment of Airpower in the Greek Guerrilla War, 1947–1949.* Project No. AU-411-62-ASI. Maxwell Air Force Base, AL: Concepts Division, Aerospace Studies Institute, United States Air University, December 1964. 74 pages.

Coufoudakis, Van. "The United States, the United Nations, and the Greek Question, 1946–1952." In John O. Iatrides, ed., *Greece in the 1940s: A Nation in Crisis.* Hanover, NH: Univ. of New England Press, 1981.

Curtin, Edwin P. "American Advisory Group Aids Greece in War on Guerrillas," *Armored Cavalry Journal* 58, no. 1 (January–February 1949), 8–11 and 34–35.

Dear, I.C.B., General ed. *The Oxford Companion to World War II.* Oxford: Oxford University Press, 1995. 1,343 pages.

Eudes, Dominique. *The Kapetanios: Partisans and Civil War in Greece, 1943–1949.* New York: Monthly Review Press, 1972. 381 pages. Interesting Leftist account; pro-*kapetanios* and anti-Stalinist.

France, Ministère de la Défense Nationale et des Forces Armées. *Counter Guerrilla Operations for Maintaining Order in French North Africa* (original title: *Opérations de contre guerilla dans le cadre du maintien de l'ordre en A.F.N.*). *Manual T.T.A. 123.* Translated and edited by Office of the Assistant Chief of Staff for Intelligence, Headquarters, Department of the Army. Washington, DC: Headquarters, Department of the Army, Office of the Assistant Chief of Staff for Intelligence, 24 August 1956. 84 pages.

Great Britain, Royal Navy, Naval Intelligence Division. *Greece*. B.R. 516: Geographical Handbook Series. 3 volumes. [London]: Naval Intelligence Division, Royal Navy, 1944. Provides excellent details of ports, roads, etc., of pre–World War II Greece.

Herrick, Allison Butler, and others. *Area Handbook for Greece*. DA Pam 550-87. Washington, DC: USGPO, June 1970. 355 pages.

Hondros, John L. "The Greek Resistance, 1941–1944: A Reevaluation." In John O. Iatrides, ed., *Greece in the 1940s: A Nation in Crisis*. Hanover, NH: University of New England Press, 1981, 37–47.

Iatrides, John O. "Civil War, 1945–1949: National and International Aspects." In John O. Iatrides, ed., *Greece in the 1940s: A Nation in Crisis*. Hanover, NH: University of New England Press, 1981, 195–219.

———. "Perceptions of Soviet Involvement in the Greek Civil War 1945–1949." In Lars Baerentzen, John O. Iatrides, and Ole L. Smith, eds., *Studies in the History of the Greek Civil War, 1945–1949*. Copenhagen: Museum Tusculanum Press, 1987, 225–48.

———. *Revolt in Athens: The Greek Communist "Second Round," 1944–1945*. Princeton, NJ: Princeton University Press, 1972. 340 pages. Foreword by William Hardy McNeill.

Iatrides, John O., ed. *Greece in the 1940s: A Nation in Crisis*. Hanover, NH: University of New England Press, 1981. 444 pages.

Kousoulas, Dimitrios G. *The Price of Freedom: Greece in World Affairs, 1939–1953*. Syracuse, NY: Syracuse University Press, 1953. 210 pages.

———. *Revolution and Defeat: The Story of the Greek Communist Party*. London: Oxford University Press, 1965. 306 pages. Kousoulas was a participant in the events described.

Laiou, Angeliki E. "Population Movements in the Greek Countryside during the Civil War." In Lars Baerentzen, John O. Iatrides, and Ole L. Smith, eds., *Studies in the History of the Greek Civil War. 1945–1949*. Copenhagen: Museum Tusculanum Press, 1987, 55–103.

Langer, William L., ed. *An Encyclopedia of World History*. 5th edition revised and updated. Boston: Houghton Mifflin, 1972.

Legg, Keith. "Musical Chairs in Athens: Analyzing Political Instability 1946–1952." In Lars Baerentzen, John O. Iatrides, and Ole L. Smith, eds., *Studies in the History of the Greek Civil War, 1945–1949*. Copenhagen: Museum Tusculanum Press, 1987, 2–24.

Loomis, Frederick H. "Report from Greece," *Military Review* 30, no. 1 (April 1950), 3–9.

McNeill, William Hardy. *Greece: American Aid in Action, 1947–1956*. New York: Twentieth Century Fund, 1957. 240 pages.

———. *The Greek Dilemma—War and Aftermath*. Philadelphia: J. B. Lippincott, 1947. 291 pages.

Mavrogordatos, George T. "The 1946 Election and Plebiscite—Prelude to Civil War." In John O. Iatrides, ed., *Greece in the 1940s: A Nation in Crisis*. Hanover, NH: University of New England Press, 1981, 181–94.

Merrill, Stephen. *The Communist Attack on Greece*, Special Report No. 15, 21st Regular Course, U.S. Strategic Intelligence School. Washington, DC: U.S. Strategic Intelligence School, 28 July 1952. 84 pages and 7 appendices.

Murray, J. C. "The Anti-Bandit War [Parts I–V]," *Marine Corps Gazette* 38, no. 1 (January 1954), 14–23; 38, no. 2 (February 1954), 50–59; 38, no. 3 (March 1954), 48–57; 38, no. 4 (April 1954), 52–60; 38, no. 5 (May 1954), 52–58.

Nachmani, Amikam. *International Intervention in the Greek Civil War: The United Nations Special Committee on the Balkans, 1947–1952*. New York: Praeger, 1990. 196 pages.

O'Ballance, Edgar. *The Greek Civil War, 1944–1949*. New York: Praeger, 1966. 237 pages.

Papastratis, Procopis. "The Purge of the Greek Civil Service on the Eve of the Civil War." In Lars Baerentzen, John O. Iatrides, and Ole L. Smith, eds., *Studies in the History of the Greek Civil War, 1945–1949*. Copenhagen: Museum Tusculanum Press, 1987, 41–54.

Papathanasiades, Theodossios. "The Bandits' Last Stand in Greece," *Military Review* 30, no. 11 (February 1951), 22–31.

Pirjevec, Joze. "The Tito-Stalin Split and the End of the Civil War in Greece." In Lars Baerentzen, John O. Iatrides, and Ole L. Smith, eds., *Studies in the History of the Greek Civil War, 1945–1949*. Copenhagen: Museum Tusculanum Press, 1987, 309–16.

Richter, Heinz. "The Second Plenum of the Central Committee of the KKE and the Decision for Civil War: A Reappraisal." In Lars Baerentzen, John O. Iatrides, and Ole L. Smith, eds., *Studies in the History of the Greek Civil War, 1945–1949*. Copenhagen: Museum Tusculanum Press, 1987, 179–87.

———. "The Varkiza Agreement and the Origins of the Civil War." In John O. Iatrides, ed., *Greece in the 1940s: A Nation in Crisis*. Hanover, NH: University of New England Press, 1981 pages 167–80.

Roubatis, Yiannis P. *Tangled Webs: The U.S. in Greece, 1947–1967*. New York: Pella, 1987. 228 pages.

Sarafis, Stefanos. *Greek Resistance Army: The Story of ELAS*. London: Birch Books, 1951. 324 pages. Personal account by the wartime commander of ELAS; covers up to the Varkiza Agreement of February 1945.

Selton, Robert W. "Communist Errors in the Anti-Bandit War," *Military Review* 45, no. 9 (September 1965), 66–77.

———. "The Cradle of US Cold War Strategy," *Military Review* 46, no. 8 (August 1966), 47–55.

Shrader, Charles R. *Communist Logistics in the Korean War*. Westport, CT: Greenwood Press, 1995. 278 pages.

Smith, Ole L. "Self-Defense and Communist Policy, 1945–1947." In Lars Baerentzen, John O. Iatrides, and Ole L. Smith, eds., *Studies in the History of the Greek Civil War, 1945–1949*. Copenhagen: Museum Tusculanum Press, 1987, 159–77.

Smothers, Frank, William Hardy McNeill, and Elizabeth Darbishire McNeill. *Report on the Greeks*. New York: Twentieth Century Fund, 1948.

Spencer, Floyd A. (preparer). *War and Postwar Greece: An Analysis Based on Greek Writings*. Washington: European Affairs Division, Library of Congress, 1952. 175 pages. An annotated bibliographical essay.

Truong Chinh. *La Resistance vaincra*. Hanoi: Éditions en Langues Étrangères, 1962. Published in English as *Primer for Revolt*. New York: Praeger, 1963.

United States Army Command and General Staff College. *Internal Defense Operations: A Case History, Greece 1946–49*. USACGSC RB 31-1. Fort Leavenworth, KS:

United States Army Command and General Staff College, 1 November 1967. 176 pages. Consists of previously published articles and other materials.

Wainhouse, Edward R. "Guerrilla War in Greece, 1946–49: A Case Study," *Military Review* 37, no. 3 (June 1957), 17–25.

Wittner, Lawrence S. *American Intervention in Greece, 1943–1949*. New York: Columbia University Press, 1982. 445 pages.

Woodhouse, Christopher M. *The Struggle for Greece, 1941–1949*. London: Hart-Davis, MacGibbon, 1976. 324 pages. Woodhouse was the deputy chief of the British Military Mission in Greece during World War II.

Xydis, Stephen G. *The Economy and Finances of Greece under Occupation*. New York: Greek Government Office of Information, n.d. [post–World War II]. 48 pages.

Zacharakis, E. E. "Lessons Learned from the Anti-Guerrilla War in Greece (1946–1949)," *Revue Militaire Générale* 7 (July 1960), 179–202.

Zachariades, Nikos. *For a Lasting Peace! For a People's Democracy!* Bucharest: 15 November 1948.

Index

X (right-wing organization), 31, 56 n.157, 217, 231; role in death of Aris Velouchiotis, 56 n.158. *See also* Grivas, Lt. Col. George

AAA. *See Arkhigeion Apeleftherikon Agonos*

Advisors, American, with GNF, 223, 254–55

Aetomilitsa, 6, 226; PDGFG and GDA headquarters at abandoned, 229

aftoamyna (KKE self-defense organization): decline in effectiveness, 119; impact of forced relocations on, 125; logistical responsibilities, 118–21; organization and functions, 61–62, 80, 92, 116, 148, 226; in the Peloponnesus, 120, 231; strength, 61, 114–15, 118, 255; as target of 1949 GNF campaign plan, 235

Air drop zones (GDA), Bulgarian map of, 147

Air force (GDA), proposed, 146

Albania: disputes with Greek government, 9, 186–87; reasons for supporting GDA, 186–87; recruitment for GDA in, 188; services provided to GDA by Albanian peasants, 188–89; Soviet shipments to, 171, 189; supply of GDA by sea from, 145–46; support for GDA, 160, 172–83, 186–94

Albanian Army, 194; poor condition of, 210 n.156; soldiers killed and captured in Operation TORCH B, 239

Albanian State Bank, purchases for GDA paid from, 190

Alevitza, GDA attack on GNA forces at (April 1949), 234

Alexander (king of Greece), 11

Alexandria (Egypt), as base for surviving Greek forces after 1941, 16

Alexandroupolis, 222

Alexis, *Kapetanios* (head of YTO at Boulkes), 179

Algerian National Liberation Front, 262–63

Ali Butus (Bulgaria), GDA depot at, 195

Aliakmon River, 6, 236

Allied Military Mission (AMM), 34–35

Allied Mission for Observing the Greek Elections (AMFOGE), 46

Ammunition (GDA), 135–36; artillery, 137; basic loads prescribed by GDA General Command, 135; requirements, 135–36, 156 n.149; scarcity of, 133. *See also* Arms (GDA); Arms and ammunition (ELAS)

andartes, 22, 48

andartisses, 110

Andon, Tsaous, 31–32, 40

Angistron-Krasokhori area, GNA operations in, 236

strength, 30–31, 51 n.59. *See also* Zervas, Col. Napoleon

Ethnikos Laïkos Apeleftherotikos Stratos (ELAS): breakup of, 44; contact with Albanian Communist guerrillas under Hoxha, 37; discipline in, 26–27; drives Gotchev's SNOF guerrillas over border into Yugoslavia, 37; eliminates or absorbs other guerrilla groups, 34–35; evolution toward a conventional force, 27; food and clothing, 28–29; formation by EAM, 23; heavy weapons battalion, 26; inclusion of commissioned officers of prewar Greek Army, 49 n.24; logistical arrangements, 27–30; medical personnel and treatment, 50 n.44; military defeat by British, 42; military effectiveness, 27; offensive in Athens-Piraeus area (December 1944–January 1945), 39–43; reorganization, 26, 35; request to support Tito's partisans rejected by British, 37; reserve elements, 26, 40; strength, 23, 37; surrender of weapons under the Varkiza Agreement, 43–44; training, 26; withdrawal from Athens-Piraeus battle (January 1945), 42; women in, 26

Ethnikos Laïkos Apeleftherotikos Stratos (ELAS) Central Command, 25, 36, 50 n.27, 53 n.93

Ethnikos Laïkos Apeleftherotikos Stratos (ELAS) Central Committee, 40, 42

Ethnikos Laïkos Apeleftherotikos Stratos (ELAS) General Headquarters, 24, 36, 37, 50n.27

Ethnikos Laïkos Apeleftherotikos Stratos (ELAS) units, 25–26, Cavalry Brigade, 40; 1st Athens Army Corps, 40; 1st Thessaly Division, 27, 41; 2d Attica Brigade, 26; 2d Attica Division, 40; 3d Peloponnesus Division, 40; 5th Attica-Euboea Brigade, 28; 6th Division, 26; 8th Epirus Division, 35, 41; 9th Macedonian Division, 41; 10th Division, 26, 74 n.32; 11th Macedonian Division, 26; 13th Roumeli (Central Greece) Division, 26, 40, 41; 16th Thessaly Division, 26, 28, 35

Evacuation, medical. *See* Medical services (GDA)

Evacuation, of children: by Greek Government, 126–27; by KKE/GDA, 126

Evacuation, of civilians, forced, Greek Government policy of, 125–26

Exchange of minority populations (Greek/Turkish), 8–10

Facilities, logistical and training (GDA): in Albania, 190–92; in Bulgaria, 196–98; in Yugoslavia, 178–80. *See also* Base areas (GDA)

Failure, to resolve basic issues in Greek political, social, and economic life, 267

Famine, in Greece during Axis occupation, 17

Federation of Greek Maritime Unions (OENO), 60, 200

First-Aid stations (GDA). *See* Medical services (GDA)

"First Round" of Greek civil war, 34–36

Florence, Protocol of (1913), 18 n.2

Florina, 2, 6, 15; battle of (February 1949), 232–35; GDA attack on (May and June 1947), 222

Forage, 27; GDA requirements for, 128–29

Force 133 (Br), 53 n.113

Forests, destruction of Greek in World War II period, 55 n.149

Frederika (queen of Greece), 126–127

Fuel, GDA requirements for, 131

GDA. *See* Greek Democratic Army

Gendarmerie (Greek National), 220, 221, 225, 232

General Labor Confederation, dominated by KKE, 13

George I (king of the Hellenes), 10–11

George II (king of Greece), 11, 12, 14, 16, 19 n.24, 220, 222

Germany (East), support for GDA, 190, 199

GNA. *See* Greek National Army

GNF. *See* Greek national forces

Gold: contribution to inflation in postwar Greece, 47; provided by British to Greek resistance groups, 33, 52 n.75

About the Author

CHARLES R. SHRADER is an independent historian and consultant who currently serves as the Executive Director of the Society for Military History. A Vietnam veteran, he retired from the United States Army in 1987 as a Lieutenant Colonel. He taught history at West Point, the U.S. Army Command and General Staff College, and the Army War College. He also served at the NATO Defense College. His other books include *U.S. Military Logistics, 1607–1991: A Research Guide* (Greenwood Press, 1992), *Communist Logistics in the Korean War* (Greenwood Press, 1995), and *The First Helicopter War: Logistics and Mobility in Algeria, 1954–1962* (Praeger, 1999).